Stepping Stones
to Christianity

Stepping Stones *to* Christianity

Reflections on Intelligent Design,
Natural Theology, and the Historical Jesus

PETER S. WILLIAMS

WIPF & STOCK · Eugene, Oregon

STEPPING STONES TO CHRISTIANITY
Reflections on Intelligent Design, Natural Theology, and the Historical Jesus

Copyright © 2025 Peter S. Williams. All rights reserved. Except for brief quotations in critical publications or reviews, no part of this book may be reproduced in any manner without prior written permission from the publisher. Write: Permissions, Wipf and Stock Publishers, 199 W. 8th Ave., Suite 3, Eugene, OR 97401.

Wipf & Stock
An Imprint of Wipf and Stock Publishers
199 W. 8th Ave., Suite 3
Eugene, OR 97401

www.wipfandstock.com

PAPERBACK ISBN: 979-8-3852-4474-4
HARDCOVER ISBN: 979-8-3852-4475-1
EBOOK ISBN: 979-8-3852-4476-8

VERSION NUMBER 101025

Creative Commons Attribution License (4.0). Image from *OpenStax Biology*, https://openstax.org/books/biology/pages/3-4-proteins. OpenStax Copyright Holders: Rice University. Publishers: OpenStax. Latest Version: 10.53. First Publication Date: Aug 22, 2012. Latest Revision: May 27, 2016. No changes were made (apart from putting the image into greyscale). My use of this image does not suggest the licensor endorses me, my use of the image or the views expressed in this book.

Scripture quotations marked (CEV) are from the Contemporary English Version Copyright © 1991, 1992, 1995 by American Bible Society. Used by Permission.

Scripture quotations marked (ESV) are taken from The ESV® Bible (The Holy Bible, English Standard Version®), © 2001 by Crossway, a publishing ministry of Good News Publishers. Used by permission. All rights reserved.

This book is dedicated to
Børge Elliot Bentsen

> "The truth that I'd be looking for
> is one that contains goodness and beauty
> as a kind of integral part of it."
>
> —Jonathan Rowson,
> Perspectiva, "What Is Metamodernism
> and Why Does It Matter?"

Contents

Author's Preface | ix

Chapter One
Reflections on Intelligent Design | 1

Chapter Two
Reflections on Natural Theology | 61

Chapter Three
Reflections on the Historical Jesus | 110

Recommended Resources | 199
Resources for Chapter 1 | 200
Resources for Chapter 2 | 211
Resources for Chapter 3 | 219

Bibliography | 235

Author's Preface

Is CONSCIOUS, RATIONAL, PERSONAL agency a fundamental reality, or even *the* fundamental reality? If so, is this fundamental agency something we can identify as "God"? If so, is this "God" the deity of any specific religious tradition? To seek answers to these questions is to embark upon a highly significant philosophical quest.

Philosophy aims at the wise pursuit and dissemination of true answers to significant questions through the practice of intellectual virtues. In other words, philosophy is matter of thinking and arguing in a wise way about important things.[1]

People should care about the wise pursuit and dissemination of true answers to the interrelated questions of God's existence and nature, because, as American philosopher Mortimer J. Adler affirmed: "More consequences for thought and action follow the affirmation or denial of God than from answering any other basic question."[2]

Every fully functioning human being has a "way of life" (i.e., a spirituality) that aims to integrate their "head" (including the worldview *assumptions* they have about reality), their "heart" (including the *attitudes* they have towards what they assume to be true of reality) and their "hands" (that is, the *actions* that grow from the pairing of their "head" with their "heart"). Since the God question concerns the nature of fundamental reality, it is directly connected to questions about the nature, meaning and purpose of the cosmos in general, and of human life in particular. Consequently, the God question is of deeply practical significance, affecting all of human life and culture.

---

1. See Baehr, *Deep in Thought*; Copan, *Little Book for New Philosophers*; Cowan and Spiegel, *Love of Wisdom*; Geisler and Feinberg, *Introduction to Philosophy*; King, *Excellent Mind*; O'Hear, *Philosophy*; Sinnott-Armstrong, *Think Again*; Williams, *Faithful Guide to Philosophy*; Wood, *Epistemology*.

2. Adler, *Great Books of the Western World*, 561.

Doing philosophy is like being a traveller in search of stepping stones (i.e., arguments) they can use to get from one bank of a river (what they presently know) to the other (what they do not presently know, but can come to know). The aim of this book is to provide an introduction to some of the intellectual "stepping stones" that can be used to rationally cross over from the land of non-belief in the existence of the Christian God to the land of belief.

The chapters of this book are revised and expanded versions of material originally written to introduce three volumes of my "Essays on..." book series.[3] The relevant volumes respectively focused upon Intelligent Design Theory, Natural Theology, and the Quest for the Historical Jesus. I hope that uniting all three topics in one volume will equip readers to enter into the philosophical quest for the nature of fundamental reality, and into the question of how we should live our lives in relation to that reality, especially by wrestling with Jesus's question "who do you say that I am?" (Mark 8:29, ESV.)

The order in which the chapters of this volume are presented is deliberate. As the skeptical Enlightenment philosopher David Hume pointed out, to make a case for design in nature (a case introduced in Chapter 1) is not the same thing as making a case for monotheism. According to Hume, someone who follows an evidentially motivated hypothesis of design "is able perhaps to assert . . . that the universe, sometime, arose from something like design: but beyond that position . . . cannot ascertain one single circumstance . . ."[4]

Hume's basic insight here is accepted by "intelligent design theory," a scientific theory "which uses the methods of historical sciences to infer that many features of nature are best explained by an intelligent cause rather than an (apparently) undirected cause . . ."[5] As philosopher Francis J. Beckwith explains, according to intelligent design theory,

> intelligent agency, as an aspect of scientific theory making, has more explanatory power in accounting for the specified, and sometimes irreducible complexity of some physical systems, including biological entities, and/or the existence of the universe as a whole, than the blind forces of . . . matter.[6]

---

3. See Williams, *Behold the Man*; *An Informed Cosmos*; *A Universe From Someone* and *Apologetics in 3D*.
4. Hume, *Dialogues Concerning Natural Religion*, Part V.
5. Luskin, "Intelligent Design as Fuel for Scientific Discovery" (YouTube video).
6. Beckwith, *Law, Darwinism, and Public Education*, xiii.

Proponents of intelligent design theory (along with many of its opponents), believe the theory can legitimately be called a "scientific" theory; but this is a secondary issue, because arguments can be sound without being scientific (just as they can be scientific without being sound). Either way, Hume highlights the philosophical distance between the hypothesis of "design" and the hypothesis of "designed by God" - let alone "designed by the God of a particular religion." To cross Hume's gap requires a philosophically robust intellectual stepping stone (or set thereof), and is a philosophical exercise in "natural theology."

Natural theology is the philosophical discipline that addresses the question of whether or not there are good arguments for the belief that God exists, where a good argument would be a set of premises that are jointly more plausibly true than false, and from which a conclusion follows with logical validity that adds something to the case for God's existence.

Of course, natural theology does not simply, or even necessarily, build upon the case for design. Rather, it subsumes the case for design into a wider metaphysical discourse about the nature of fundamental reality. In other words, while readers who see some merit in intelligent design theory might be open to viewing it as a gateway into natural theology, any readers who remain unpersuaded should nevertheless press ahead into Chapter 2's discussion of arguments for the belief that God exists.

After a brief period in the academic wilderness during the twentieth century, natural theology is today a thriving philosophical discipline. As philosopher William Lane Craig explains,

> Back in the 1940s and '50s, many philosophers believed that talk about God, since it is not verifiable by the five senses, is meaningless ... This verificationism finally collapsed, in part because philosophers realized that verificationism itself could not be verified! The collapse of verificationism was the most important philosophical event of the 20th century. Its downfall meant that philosophers were free once again to tackle traditional problems of philosophy that verificationism had suppressed. Accompanying this resurgence of interest in traditional philosophical questions came something altogether unanticipated: a renaissance of Christian philosophy.[7]

Craig goes on to note that this renaissance

> has been accompanied by a resurgence of interest in natural theology . . . . all of the traditional arguments for God's existence,

---

7. Craig, "God Is Not Dead Yet."

not to mention creative new arguments, find articulate defenders today.[8]

Indeed, as fellow philosopher James Brent observes: "Natural theology today is practiced with a degree of diversity and confidence unprecedented since the late Middle Ages."[9]

I think there is a broad array of defensible arguments for God that are best seen as mutually-reinforcing strands in a cumulative case, where different arguments bring different (perhaps overlapping) pieces of information to the table with respect to our understanding of God's nature.

In general, the arguments of natural theology try to rationally motivate recognition of a relationship between some particular aspect of the cosmos on the one hand and God on the other hand, where each relationship tells us something about God's nature (so there's a close relationship between "natural theology" and the exploration of God's nature in "philosophical theology").

Two additional points about natural theology. First, what Oxford University philosopher Richard Swinburne calls a "ramified natural theology" (that is, an "expanded natural theology") highlights the fact that the "Christian evidences" traditionally considered within the theological discipline of Christian apologetics (e.g., historically grounded arguments concerning Jesus's Divine self-understanding, his fulfilment of Old Testament prophecies, or his bodily resurrection from the dead), don't merely build upon the philosophical case for God with reasons to believe in a specifically Christian God, but can also work as part and parcel of the cumulative philosophical case for God.[10] Consequently, while the "Quest for the historical Jesus" is inevitably shaped by the worldviews of the researchers who conduct it, this quest can in turn shape the worldview of the investigator. Hence, whilst Chapter 3's introduction to this quest is framed by a discussion of contemporary worldviews, and can be seen as building upon the topics covered in Chapters 1 and/or 2, it can also be seen as part of a "ramified" natural theology that encompasses all three chapters.

Second, as atheist philosopher Thomas Nagel reminds us: "Philosophy has to proceed comparatively."[11] On the one hand, this means the case for Christian theism must be balanced against the case for every alternative worldview. On the other hand, this means the case for Christian theism is

8. Craig, "God Is Not Dead Yet."
9. Brent, "Natural Theology."
10. See Menuge and Taliaferro. "Introduction to a Special Issue"; Menuge, "Ramified Personalized Natural Theology: A Third Way?"; Holder, *Ramified Natural Theology*.
11. Nagel, *Mind and Cosmos*, 127.

reinforced by whatever negative case can be made against those alternative worldviews. As we'll see, I think there are good reasons, quite besides the positive arguments of a "ramified natural theology," to be skeptical about the viability of competing worldviews, such as naturalism and pantheism.

I'd like to note my thanks to the following:

- Dr. Andrew Ter Ern Loke, for a useful conversation on the "dynamical parameters" objection to cosmic fine-tuning at the 2025 European Leadership Forum in Poland.

- For their informal peer-review of material behind Chapter 1 (i.e., the material originally published in my book *An Informed Cosmos*): Dr. Michael J. Behe (professor of biochemistry at Lehigh University), Dr. Neil Broom (emeritus professor of chemical and materials engineering at the University of Auckland), David W. Swift MSc, and Dr. Steinar Thorvaldsen (professor of information science at the Arctic University of Norway).

- For personal correspondence relating to material in Chapter 1: Dr. Douglas Axe (Maxwell professor of molecular biology at Biola University), Dr. Ola Hössjer (professor of mathematical statistics at Stockholm University), Dr. Brian Miller (research coordinator for the Center for Science and Culture at Discovery Institute), Dr. Paul Nelson (senior fellow of the Discovery Institute and adjunct professor in the Master of Arts Program in Science & Religion at Biola University) and David W. Swift MSc.

- Professor Lydia McGrew, for her detailed feedback on, and valuable correspondence about, drafts of what became Chapter 3 of this book.

- Everyone at Wipf and Stock.

- My church and church small-group, for their encouragement and prayers.

- My patrons, whose support allowed my work in philosophy and apologetics to continue after my part-time job with NLA University College ended due to funding constraints.

- My friends at NLA University College (www.nla.no/en/), alongside whom I now serve as an "Adjunct Professor in Communication and Worldviews."

- Last but not least, thanks go to my parents for their constant love and support.

Peter S. Williams (MA, MPhil, PGCert) – September 2025

Chapter One

Reflections on Intelligent Design

This whole reductive programme - this mindless materialism,
this belief in something called "matter" as the answer to all questions
- is not really science at all. It is, and always has been,
just an image, a myth, a vision, an enormous act of faith.
—Mary Midgley, *What is Philosophy For?*, 90.

In science, the only thing that counts is the evidence,
and the logic of the argument itself.
—Neil deGrasse Tyson, *Cosmos*.

WE LIVE IN AN information age. The reader may have downloaded this book from a cloud onto their tablet (a statement that would cause past generations some confusion). If so, what they downloaded was *information*. To be more precise, it was "complex specified information" or "specified complexity," terms that refer "to events that have high probabilistic complexity [i.e., that are very unlikely] but whose identifying patterns have low descriptive complexity."[1] The natural and rationally warranted inference from this

---

1. Dembski, "Success of Mathematics," para. 81. See also Williams, "Specified Complexity" (YouTube playlist); Mind Matters, "Run the Gambit of Complexity" (Podcast); Dembski, "Specification"; Meyer, "Yes, Intelligent Design Is Detectable"; Montañez,

specific type of information is to the conclusion that it is the product of "intelligent design" (that is, of genuine rather than merely apparent design). As the influential American philosopher William Lane Craig observes:

> in a poker game any deal of cards is equally and highly improbable, but if you find that every time a certain player deals he gets all four aces, you can bet this is not the result of chance but of design.[2]

To give another illustration, imagine you are watching someone drawing Scrabble tiles out from a bag, sight unseen. On the one hand, a long string of random letters would be *complex* (i.e., unlikely), but it wouldn't exhibit *specified* complexity. That is, it wouldn't conform to an independently given, "simple, easily described"[3] pattern (such as "a grammatical sentence"). On the other hand, a short string of letters could easily turn out to be *specified*—like "this" (which is "a word")—but it wouldn't be *complex* enough to outstrip the ability of the available probabilistic resources to plausibly explain this conformity. Neither complexity without specificity, nor specificity without complexity signals intelligent design. However, if you observed an event like that portrayed in Douglas Adams's *The Hitchhikers Guide to the Galaxy*, where Arthur Dent gets a sequence of Scrabble tiles spelling out the sentence "What do you get when you multiply six by nine,"[4] you'd naturally and quite rightly infer design.

Even if you couldn't work out how the "trick" had been pulled off, you'd be sure there was a "trick" involved and that this contingent arrangement of Scrabble tiles had somehow been informed by some intelligence or other. Arthur's sequence of tiles is specified, because (aside from the missing question mark) it conforms to the independently given rules of English spelling and grammar. It is also a sufficiently complex arrangement of contingent parts to make it unreasonable to attribute this conformity to chance. Indeed, this combination of specificity with sufficient complexity warrants an inference to intelligent design, because in our experience "the creation of new information [i.e., complex specified information] is habitually associated with conscious and rational activity."[5]

"Unified Model"; Williams "Design Inference from Specified Complexity"; Cicero, *Nat. d.* 215; Dembski and Ewert, *Design Inference*; Dembski and Wells, *Design of Life*, chap. 7.

    2. Craig, "Fine Tuned Universe," para. 2.
    3. Dembski, "Specification," 15.
    4. See Adams, "Hitch-Hiker's Guide."
    5. Quastler, *Emergence of Biological Organization*, 16.

THE INFORMATION REVOLUTION

To the discomfort of anyone invested in the ancient Greek belief that the natural world can ultimately be explained without remainder in terms of the blind, intelligence-free interplay of physical "Chance and Necessity,"[6] since the middle of the twentieth century science has uncovered a rising tide of counter-evidence.

Cosmic (and Local) Fine Tuning

Starting with astrophysicist Fred Hoyle's 1953 prediction of a "finely tuned" resonance state in the carbon-12 atomic nucleus (later verified and known as "the Hoyle state"), scientists have reached a consensus recognizing that the existence of complex material states, up to and including organic life, and especially "embodied conscious agents (ECAs)"[7] with the opportunity to "develop scientific technology and discover the universe,"[8] depends upon a staggering degree of cosmic "fine tuning." In the words of Nobel laureate in physics Arno Penzias, we live in "a universe . . . delicately balanced to provide exactly the conditions required to support life."[9] As cosmologist Stephen Hawking (1942–2018) ruminated with co-author Leonard Mlodinow, for life to exist, "the initial state of the universe had to be set up in a very special and highly improbable way."[10] (Life on Earth also relies upon, or benefits from, various contingent "local" conditions concerning properties of our galaxy, solar system, planet, moon and sun that are, at the very least, atypical.[11])

Over and above the finely tuned nature of natural laws as such, there are two fundamental aspects to cosmic fine-tuning:

---

6. See Monod, *Chance and Necessity*.

7. Holder, *Ramified Natural Theology*, 56.

8. Collins, "Anthropic Fine-Tuning: Three Approaches," 173–91. See also Collins, "Argument from Physical Constants: The Fine-Tuning for Discoverability"; Denton, *Miracle of Man*; Gonzalez and Richards, *Privileged Planet*, chap. 10.

9. Penzias quoted in Margenau and Varghese, *Cosmos, Bios, Theos*, 83. On the Big Bang and its implications, see Meyer, *Return of the God Hypothesis*.

10. Hawking and Mlodinow, *Grand Design*, 130.

11. See Williams, "Rare Earth Hypothesis" (YouTube playlist); ID the Future, "Problem of Earth Privilege" (Podcast); ID the Future, "Privileged Place for Life and Discovery" (Podcast); Denton, *Miracle of Man*; Denton, *Nature's Destiny*; Gonzalez, "Local Fine-Tuning"; Gonzalez and Richards, *Privileged Planet*; Eberlin, *Foresight*, chap. 2; Waltham, *Lucky Planet*; Ward and Brownlee, *Rare Earth*.

> When the laws of nature are expressed as mathematical equations, you find appearing in them certain ... unchanging quantities, like the force of gravity, the electromagnetic force, and the subatomic weak force. These unchanging quantities are called constants. The values of these constants are not determined by the laws of nature... Depending on the values of those constants, universes governed by the same laws of nature will look very different... In addition to the constants, there are ... initial conditions on which the laws of nature operate ... An example would be the amount of thermodynamic disorder (or entropy) in the early universe ... Now what scientists have been surprised to discover is that these constants and quantities must fall into an extraordinarily narrow range of values if the universe is to be life-permitting.[12]

To give just a few examples:

> The force of gravity is so finely tuned that an alteration in its value by even one part out of 10^{50} would have prevented a life-permitting universe. Similarly, a change in the value of the so-called cosmological constant, which drives the acceleration of the universe's expansion, by as little as one part in 10^{120} would have rendered the universe life-prohibiting ... the odds of the universe's initial low entropy condition's existing by chance is on the order of one chance out of $10^{10(123)}$ ... [13]

There are also various crucial ratios between constants (such as "the ratio of the nuclear strong force to the electromagnetic force" or "the ratio of the electromagnetic force constant to the gravitational force constant"[14]).

Multiplying together the odds of the relevant laws, constants,[15] and initial conditions *all* falling by chance within the specification provided by the narrow, life-permitting range of values, gives an improbability that's beyond astronomical! Physicist Lee Smolin "has calculated that the odds of life-compatible numbers coming up by chance is 1 in 10^{229}."[16] *Prima*

---

12. Craig, *Does God Exist?*, 44–45.
13. Craig, *Does God Exist?*, 45.
14. Latham, "Fine-Tuned Universe," para. 9–10.
15. Roger Trigg reports the estimate "that there are 30 constants in basic physics and modern cosmology that must be fine-tuned for the emergence of life." Trigg, *Does Science Undermine Faith?*, 25.
16. Goff, "Our Improbable Existence," para. 1.

facie, cosmic fine-tuning is an example of specified complexity that's best explained by intelligent design.[17]

Dawkins's Complexity Objection to Cosmic Design

Faced with the design inference from cosmic fine-tuning, Richard Dawkins attempts to argue (in venues such as his best-selling book *The God Delusion*) that any intelligence one might infer from the fine-tuning data must themselves exhibit the very same type of design-indicating complexity (i.e., "specified complexity"), and should consequently be dismissed as an unparsimonious hypothesis.

However, in the competition between hypotheses, explanatory adequacy trumps parsimony. One only has to ask whether inferring the existence of an author to explain of one of Dawkins's own books makes an explanatory advance compared to the "no author" hypothesis! Clearly, the hypothesis of an author does constitute an explanatory advance over the "no author" hypothesis, even though it appeals to an entity that itself stands in need of explanation. As William Lane Craig observes:

> In order to recognize an explanation as the best, you don't need to have an explanation of the explanation. This is an elementary point in the philosophy of science.... in order to recognize that intelligent design is the best explanation of the appearance of design in the universe, you don't need to be able to explain the designer. Whether the designer has an explanation can simply be left an open question for future inquiry.[18]

---

17. See FOCLOnline, "Can We Believe in God in an Age of Science? The Big Bang & Cosmic 'Fine Tuning'" (YouTube video); FOCLOnline, "Can We Believe in God in an Age of Science? Cosmology and God" (YouTube video); Williams, "Christian Worldview and Science in Apologetic Perspective: Cosmos" (Podcast); "Cosmic Fine Tuning: Design or Multiverse?" (Podcast); "Introduction to An Informed Cosmos" (Podcast); and *Outgrowing God?*, chap. 9. See also Williams, "Cosmic Fine Tuning" (YouTube playlist); Mind Matters, "Universe Is so Fine Tuned" (Podcast); Barnes, "Fine-Tuning in the Context of Bayesian Theory Testing"; Collins, "Argument from Physical Constants"; "Exploration of the Fine-Tuning of the Universe"; "Teleological Argument: An Exploration"; and "Teleological Argument"; Díaz-Pachón et al., "Is it Possible to Know Cosmological Fine-Tuning?"; Díaz-Pachón et al., "Is Cosmological Tuning Fine or Coarse?"; Gordon, "Balloons on a String"; Holder, *God, the Multiverse, and Everything*; Holder, *Big Bang, Big God*; Løkhammer, "Fine-Tuning Argument"; Lewis and Barnes, *Fortunate Universe*; Meyer, *Return of the God Hypothesis*; Moreland and Craig, *Philosophical Foundations* (2nd edition), 493–500.

18. Craig, "Richard Dawkins on Arguments for God", 27.

Moreover, Dawkins fails to give any reason for thinking that all possible candidates for the source of fine-tuning would necessarily be "complex" *in the relevant sense* (i.e., exhibiting specified complexity), which would require them to be *a contingent arrangement of separable parts*. The argument that Dawkins gives in this context confuses "complexity of function" with "complexity of structure," and begs the question against the possibility of a designer with a necessarily existent essential nature.[19] By definition, a necessarily existent nature cannot be "complex" (i.e., unlikely) in the relevant, design-indicating sense of exhibiting specified complexity, since it lacks contingency.

Alternative Hypotheses

Rebuttals of the design inference from cosmic fine-tuning normally focus upon trying to show that although the cosmos is indeed specified, by virtue of its life-permitting configuration, it is not sufficiently complex (i.e., unlikely) to justify making a design inference. Note that these objections implicitly endorse the premise that specified complexity is a reliable indicator of intelligent design.

Recent research has added to evidence suggesting that the hypothetical "dark energy" many cosmologists posit to account for the accelerating expansion of the universe may not be a "constant" force after all, but may have weakened over time, inasmuch as there appears to be an observed decline in the rate at which the expansion of the universe has accelerated over time.[20] This might encourage the suggestion that various "constants" that appear fine-tuned for the sort of complexity required by life could actually be "dynamical" parameters that would naturally reach life-permitting value-ranges at some point in their existence. Does this hypothesis rebut the cosmic fine-tuning argument?

In the first place, this "dynamical parameters" objection doesn't address either the finely tuned nature of natural laws as such, or of the "initial

---

19. See FOCLOnline, "Can We Believe in God in an Age of Science? The Big Bang & Cosmic 'Fine Tuning'" (YouTube video); FOCLOnline, "Can We Believe in God in an Age of Science? Cosmology and God" (YouTube video); Brierley and Byrom, "Goldilocks Universe" (Podcast); Williams, "Christian Worldview and Science in Apologetic Perspective: Cosmos" (Podcast); "Cosmic Fine Tuning: Design or Multiverse?" (Podcast); "Introduction to An Informed Cosmos" (Podcast); and "Veritas 2022: Outgrowing God?" (Podcast); Craig, "Richard Dawkins on Arguments for God."

20. See Clery, "Mystery Force Behind the Universe's Accelerating Expansion"; Tonkin, "Dark Energy 'Doesn't Exist.'"

conditions on which the laws of nature operate."[21] Therefore, this rebuttal exhibits inadequate explanatory scope.

In the second place, even if dark energy is a genuine "dynamical parameter," it doesn't follow that other cosmological "constants" are therefore dynamical. Occam's razor favours the simpler hypothesis of constant parameters in the absence of specific evidence to the contrary.

In the third place, if we hypothesize that multiple cosmic "constants" are in fact "dynamical," it seems that the coordination of these parameters so they will jointly hit upon the requisite life-permitting combination of values—both at the same time and for a sufficient length of time—is an outcome that exhibits at least as much fine-tuning as the fine-tuning of the "constants" they hypothetically replace. Indeed, such a coordination of dynamical parameters would seem to require *more* fine-tuning.[22]

The leading objection to the design inference from cosmic fine-tuning is the hypothesis that "our universe is just one universe in a *multiverse*."[23] This is like the cards player who keeps getting quad aces whenever they deal saying we should forego any suspicion they are cheating because *there might be lots of other card games going on*, which would increase the odds of *someone* getting this result.

Note that adding the "selection effect" of a gunslinger who will shoot everyone at the table dead if our suspected cheater is about to reveal any hand besides quad aces (so that our suspect having quad aces is a precondition of our observing his hand) does nothing to alleviate our suspicion, because it does nothing to explain *why* our suspect is so conspicuously beating the apparent odds.

To return to our Scrabble illustration, the multiverse response to the argument from cosmic fine-tuning is like saying that Arthur Dent's Scrabble-tile question doesn't indicate design because *if* Scrabble letters "were thrown together into some receptacle"[24] before being randomly taken out one at a time *enough times, then* the same result could in theory be produced without design. Somehow making the emergence of "a grammatical sentence" a precondition of our observing the tiles wouldn't help explain the emergence of this precondition.

Clearly, in the absence of independent evidence for the existence of enough card games, or enough Scrabble letters being drawn for long enough, the "many chances" hypothesis is *ad hoc* and the "design" hypothesis remains

---

21. Craig, *Does God Exist?*, 44–45.
22. Thanks to Dr Andrew Ter Ern Loke for a conversation on this point.
23. Dawkins, *Outgrowing God*, 269.
24. Cicero, *Nat. d.* 2.15.

preferable. Likewise, even granting that *if* a large enough multiverse existed *then* it would produce the fine-tuning of our universe by chance, in the absence of independent evidence for the existence of enough differently tuned universes, the design hypothesis remains preferable. However, in the words of astrophysicist Adam Frank, "There is no empirically grounded scientific reason to believe there is such a thing as a Multiverse of parallel realities."[25]

In fact, the multiverse hypothesis is in general *disconfirmed* by "the amount of order found in this universe," because "Our universe is far more special than we would expect it to be, even if it were merely a random member of the subset of universes compatible with our existence."[26]

Atheist cosmologist Roger Penrose highlights the overly special nature of our universe by asking us to:

> consider how ridiculously cheaper (in the sense of improbabilities) it would be simply to produce, by mere random collisions of particles, the entire solar system with all its life ready-made, or even just a few conscious brains. So the problem is: why did we not come about *this* way, rather than from an absurdly less probable 1.4×10^{10} tedious years of evolution? It seems to me that this conundrum simply points to the incorrectness of the bubble-universe idea.[27]

Theoretical astrophysicist and cosmologist Luke Barnes comments that "If only very special multiverses avoid this problem, then the multiverse itself is fine-tuned."[28] And, of course, an objection to the design inference from cosmic fine-tuning that postulates the existence of a "very special" (i.e., finely tuned) multiverse is self-defeating. Indeed, as philosopher of science Stephen C. Meyer points out,

> In order to explain the origin of the fine tuning in our universe, both inflationary cosmology and string theory (and versions of the multiverse that combine them) posit universe-generating mechanisms that themselves require prior unexplained fine tuning.[29]

---

25. Frank, "There Is No Empirical Evidence," para. 3.
26. Holder, *God, the Multiverse, and Everything*, 158.
27. Penrose, *Fashion, Faith and Fantasy*, 327–28.
28. Barnes, "Good God!," para. 40.
29. Meyer, *Return of the God Hypothesis*, 339.

Moreover, Meyer argues that "not only does the universe-generating mechanism in inflationary cosmology require prior unexplained fine tuning. It actually requires more fine-tuning than it was proposed to explain."[30]

Biological Fine-Tuning

Pure reductionism will not work, precisely because it does not analyse the kind of complexity organisms display.

—MARY MIDGELY[31]

British chemist and molecular biologist Leslie Orgel, a pioneer in the study of the origins of life, observed that: "Living organisms are distinguished by their specified complexity. Crystals such as granite fail to qualify as living because they lack complexity; mixtures of random polymers fail to qualify because they lack specificity."[32] In the words of cosmologist and origin-of-life researcher Paul Davies: "Living organisms are mysterious not for their complexity per se, but for their tightly specified complexity."[33]

Francis Crick and James Watson announced their discovery of the double helical structure of DNA in 1953 (see Fig. 1).

---

30. Meyer, *Return of the God Hypothesis*, 340.
31. Midgely, *What Is Philosophy For?*, 26.
32. Orgel, *Origins of Life*, 189.
33. Davies, *Fifth Miracle*, 112.

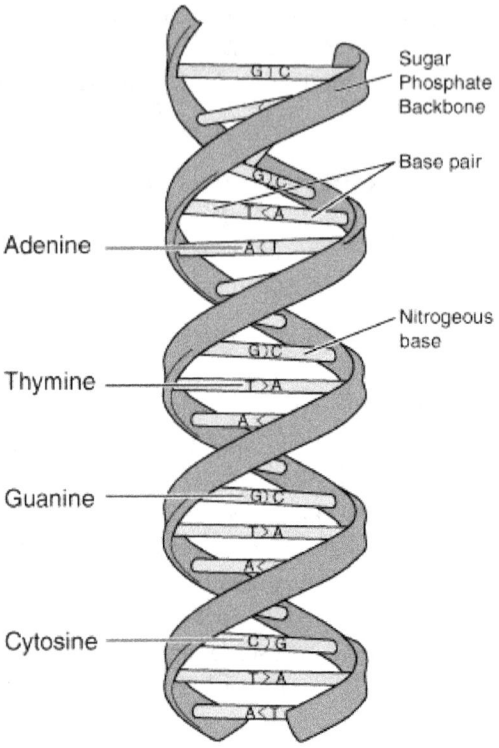

Fig. 1. Key structural features of the DNA double helix.[34]

In 1958, Crick theorized that "the sequence specificity of amino acids in proteins derives from a prior specificity of arrangement in the nucleotide bases on the DNA molecule,"[35] which "functioned just like alphabetic letters in an English text or binary digits in software or a machine code."[36] Experiments in the 1960s established that the sequential arrangement of amino-acids in proteins is indeed derived (via messenger RNA) from information encoded within the nucleotide rungs of the DNA ladder (see Fig. 2).[37]

---

34. https://en.wikipedia.org/wiki/Molecular_Structure_of_Nucleic_Acids:_A_Structure_for_Deoxyribose_Nucleic_Acid#/media/File:DNA-structure-and-bases.png.
35. Meyer, *Signature in the Cell*, 101.
36. Meyer, *Signature in the Cell*, 100.
37. See Williams, "Protein Synthesis." (YouTube playlist.)

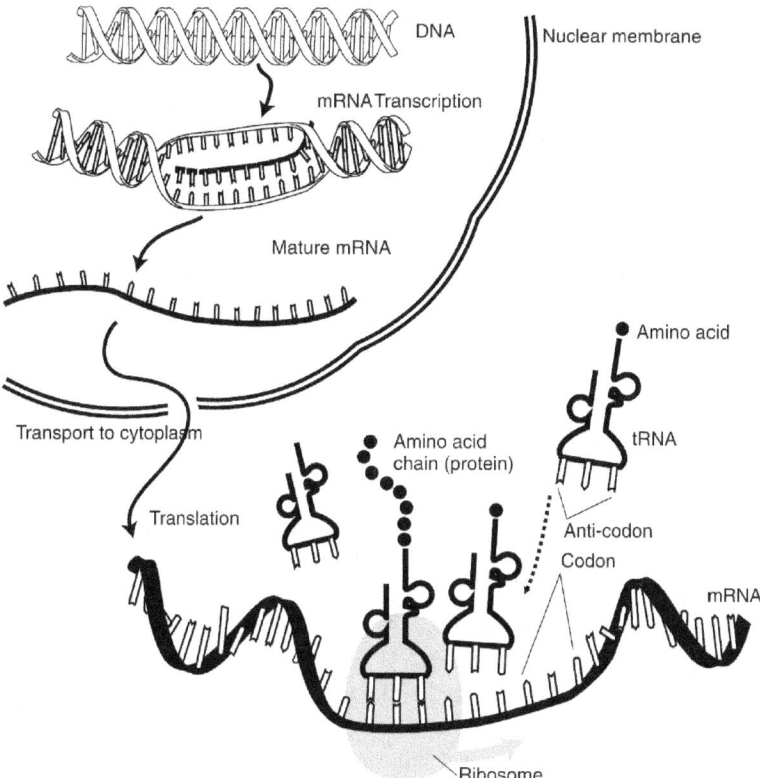

Fig. 2. Protein synthesis.[38]

Hence Richard Dawkins's striking observation that

> at the bottom of my garden is a large willow tree, and it is pumping downy seeds into the air [containing] DNA whose coded characters spell out specific instructions for building willow trees. . . . It is raining instructions out there; it's raining programs. . . . That is not a metaphor, it is the plain truth.[39]

That said, we now know that things are rather more complex than biochemist Jean Brachet's simple mantra that "DNA makes RNA makes protein."[40] Instead, "DNA is becoming known as a more of a team member in a society of biomolecules. In some ways, it is more a patient than a doctor.

---

38. http://media.opencurriculum.org/articles_manual/ck12_biology/protein-synthesis/6.png. See Williams, "Protein Synthesis." (YouTube playlist.)
39. Dawkins, "Genes Aren't Us," 105.
40. See Cobb, "60 Years Ago," 4.

It gets operated on by numerous machines that alter its message."[41] As Meyer reports,

> Biologists still affirm that DNA contains specified information, but they have discovered that the information for building a given protein is not always (or even usually) located in just one place along the DNA molecule. They have also discovered that depending upon how the cell processes the information stored in DNA, a single gene may contribute to the production of thousands of proteins and other gene products.... The cell also uses genetic information to produce critical RNA molecules that do not undergo translation, but instead direct the processing of other genetic information. Further, during the translation process, additional processes edit the chains of amino acids produced before they fold into their final functional forms. Equally revolutionary is the discovery that biological information beyond (not resident in) DNA plays a critical role in the development of organisms.... As molecular biology and genomics have revealed new features of the cell's information storage and processing system, they have inspired a new conception of the gene—one in which the gene is no longer understood as a singular, linear, and localized entity on a DNA strand, but rather one in which the gene is understood as a distributive set of data files available for retrieval and context-dependent expression by a complex information-processing system.[42]

In sum, as American physicist and information theorist Hubert P. Yockey (1916–2016) explains:

> Information, transcription, translation, code, redundancy, synonymous, messenger, editing, and proofreading are all appropriate terms in biology. They take their meaning from information theory (Shannon, 1948) and are not synonyms, metaphors, or analogies.[43]

---

41. Evolution News, "Surprises in Cell Codes," para. 4.

42. Meyer, *Signature in the Cell*, 459, 460. See Evolution News, "Octopus Genetic Editing"; Evolution News, "Alternative Splicing"; Luskin, "As Predicted by Intelligent Design."

43. Yockey, *Information Theory*, quoted by Wedgwood, *DNA*, 229.

Life Transcending Physics and Chemistry

Starting with Hungarian-British scientist and philosopher Michael Polanyi's landmark 1967 paper "Life Transcending Physics and Chemistry,"[44] the recognition that information lies at the heart of biology has formed the basis for increasingly sophisticated arguments against reductive explanations of life framed in terms of blind physical chance and/or necessity.[45] As William B. Collier, senior professor of physical chemistry at Oral Roberts University, explains:

> The specific structure of DNA was figured out by James Watson and Francis Crick in 1953 at Cambridge University. It took another 10 to 15 years to understand how that information was coded into the DNA strand and then translated and transported to the ribosomes to produce new protein machines. By the mid 1960's Polanyi realized that this information was independent of the DNA strand, and that in fact it had to be. The DNA code could be recorded on paper, magnetic tape, computer hard drives, or books like any other kind of specified information.... This information was extrinsic and independent of the medium that carried it and completely unexplainable by any known chemical or physical phenomena, implying that the living cell could never be *reduced* or explained by natural laws.[46]

In the words of Neil Broom (emeritus professor of chemical and materials engineering at the University of Auckland):

> The sequence making up a particular DNA strand is not dependent on any preferred bonding between the individual bases. Each base is the molecular equivalent of the dot or dash in the Morse code and can be arranged in any linear combination without breaking the rules of chemical bonding.... The structure of DNA therefore contrasts with ordinary chemical molecules or crystals, whose structures reflect the most stable arrangement of their constituent atoms ... on this basis alone life is inexplicable in terms of the lower-level laws of physics and

---

44. Polanyi, "Life Transcending Physics and Chemistry," 54–69.

45. See the Evolutionary Informatics Lab at https://evoinfo.org/; Bracht, "Natural Selection as an Algorithm"; Meyer, "DNA by Design"; Meyer, "DNA and the Origin"; Miller, "Evolutionary Informatics"; Sewell, "Entropy and Evolution"; Trevors and Abel, "Three Subsets of Sequence Complexity"; Voie, "Biological Function"; Meyer, *Signature in the Cell*; Thaxton et al., *Mystery of Life's Origin: The Continuing Controversy*.

46. Collier, *From Darwin to Eden*, 120.

chemistry. Some other, higher level of control that transcends the purely material laws is required.[47]

Indeed, according to John C. Lennox, emeritus fellow in mathematics and the philosophy of science at Green Templeton College, Oxford: "results from theoretical computer science point towards the existence of something like a law of conservation of information that would preclude biogenesis by unguided processes."[48]

On the one hand, while the "laws" of physical necessity can *transmit* complex specified information, they can't *create* it. What physical necessity creates is the sort of simple, repetitive order seen in a crystal. As Hurbert P. Yockey and Dean L. Overman explain,

> a law of nature is a very short algorithm.... Life requires much more information than contained in these laws. The genetic information contained in even the smallest living organism is much larger than the information contained in the laws of physics and chemistry.[49]

Hence Lennox argues,

> just as no algorithm is likely to exist to produce the works of Shakespeare ... so also DNA, as a string, would seem to be essentially incompressible and, therefore, not at all likely to be the product of a short algorithm.[50]

On the other hand, specified contingency can be rationally attributed to "chance" *if and only if it isn't too complex* (i.e., unlikely). As Dawkins recognizes, "We can accept a certain amount of luck in our explanations, but not too much."[51] The poker player who keeps getting quad aces whenever they deal can't reasonably undermine our suspicion by appealing to luck. Likewise, the specified information exhibited by life is sufficiently complex to justify an inference to design.[52]

---

47. Broom, *How Blind Is the Watchmaker?*, 54.
48. Lennox, *Cosmic Chemistry*, 206. See Miller, "Evolutionary Informatics."
49. Yockey and Overman. "Information, Algorithms."
50. Lennox, *Cosmic Chemistry*, 199.
51. Dawkins, *Blind Watchmaker*, 139.
52. Miller, "Unraveling the Myth"; Meyer, "Origin of Biological Information"; Meyer, *Darwin's Doubt*; Meyer, *Signature in the Cell*.

An Experience-Based Inference

Life is a matter of interdependent and hierarchically nested complex specified information, and it depends upon an information-rich "cosmic" backdrop.[53] The inference from all this "finely tuned" information to the conclusion of design is just as valid as the inference from this book to design. This is not an argument from analogy.[54] Nor is it an "argument from ignorance" (there's no "author of the gaps" fallacy being committed here). As atheist philosopher Jeffery Jay Lowder acknowledges, "the arguments for intelligent design . . . are NOT god of the gaps arguments."[55] Rather, the argument from specified complexity to intelligent design is a standard inference to the best explanation. As Meyer observes, "Our experience-based knowledge of information-flow confirms that systems with large amounts of specified complexity . . . invariably originate from an intelligent source."[56]

THE EVOLUTION OF A THEISTIC EVOLUTIONIST

I was the child of Christian parents who fell in love at teacher training college in Portsmouth, England. My father began his career in 1971, teaching general science at a secondary modern school. A year later, my mother began her career as a biology teacher (first at secondary and then junior school levels). After my birth in 1974, my father obtained a bachelor's degree in biological sciences (including oceanography and geology) from The Open University (1975–79).[57] Later, he taught A-level physics and general science at a comprehensive school. He would take students on geology field-trips to see the Cretaceous and Eocene era coastline of Whitecliff Bay on the nearby Isle of Wight, with its vertical, fossil-bearing strata (see Fig. 3).[58]

---

53. See Thorvaldsen and Hössjer, "Using Statistical Methods." See also Luskin, "Repentant Biology Journal."

54. While it is commonly reported that William Paley's theistic argument from design offers an analogy between life and a watch, this is not the case. Rather, Paley draws attention to certain identical properties of watches and of life from which he argues that design can be inferred. See Williams, *Faithful Guide to Philosophy*, chap. 6.

55. Lowder, quoted by McLatchie, "Atheist Philosopher Explains."

56. Meyer, "Origin of Biological Information."

57. In the 2000s, my mother took a year-long course in cell biology with The Open University.

58. See Wikipedia, "Whitecliff Bay and Bembridge Ledges." The Isle of Wight is the best place in Europe to find dinosaur fossils. See Palaeo Pictures, "Giant Dinosaur"; University of Southampton, "Two New Species."

Fig. 3: One of my Father's photographs of Whitecliff Bay on the Isle of Wight.

In other words, I was raised in a household at ease with belief in the creator God of the Bible *and* the orthodox scientific account of origins. This account included Big Bang cosmology, an Earth about 4.5 billion years old, and a dazzling array of life-forms (including humans) that evolved from a common ancestor by a process described in my parent's copy of J. Bronowski's *The Ascent of Man* as "the evolution of complexity by statistical processes . . . evolution by natural selection."[59] This book, which was tied in to Dr. Bronowki's land-mark 1973 BBC/Time-Life Films documentary series, was published in the year he died and I was born (i.e., 1974).[60] As a young child, I had a knitted teddy-bear called "Dr. Bronowski."

As I understood the situation in my teens, believing that this natural history was *intended, initiated and sustained in existence by God* wasn't part and parcel of any "scientific" theory as such (that is, *qua* "science"). However, neither did any scientific theory as such (*qua* "science") *deny* such a divine framing of reality. In fact, even if one suspected on philosophical and/or theological grounds that God had *guided* the evolutionary process, this wasn't something the scientific theory of evolution would contradict (as long as one didn't think that positing or inferring such guidance was a "scientific" move). After all, as British philosopher Keith Ward observed whilst defending his own theistic understanding of evolution, "as far as physics is concerned, it is quite possible for God to influence the outcome of physical events, within certain limits, in ways undetectable by us."[61] Hence, although

---

59. Bronowski, *Ascent of Man*, 317.
60. See "Ascent of Man."
61. Ward, *God, Chance & Necessity*, 81.

secular scientists were free to interpret science through the philosophical lens of their naturalistic/materialistic worldview, it was entirely legitimate to interpret science through the philosophical lens of a theistic worldview.

According to Bronowski, "The theory of evolution is no longer a battleground."[62] This was an overstatement, even in the 1970s. I soon became aware that "young-earth creationists" took a different view of natural history, rejecting—among other things—Darwin's extrapolation from observed microevolution (which they acknowledged) to unobserved macroevolution. Convinced I should give this minority report a fair hearing, I read some "young earth" literature. However, I found the "young earth" interpretation of Scripture unconvincing, and I found little in their scientific arguments that seemed to me to be at all persuasive.[63]

My parents had a bookcase that introduced me to the worlds of science and philosophy. I developed a taste for popular science books by authors such as Paul Davies, Richard Dawkins, Sally Ferguson, John Gribbin, Stephen Hawking, John Houghton, Donald Mackay, John Polkinghorne, and Russell Stannard. But I always payed attention to how the philosophical worldview of the authors interacted with their scientific theorizing. Thus, as I left home and discovered the joys of philosophy at the Universities of Cardiff, Sheffield, and finally East Anglia (in Norwich), I thought of myself as a well-informed "theistic evolutionist."

Unshackling Science from Methodological Naturalism

It is important that students bring a certain ragamuffin, barefoot irreverence to their studies; they are not here to worship what is known but to question it.

—J. Bronowski[64]

As philosophers J. P. Moreland and William Lane Craig explain, "The central aspect of [intelligent design] theory is the idea that the designedness

62. Bronowski, *Ascent of Man*, 313.

63. See Williams, "Young Earth Creationism" (YouTube playlist); Barnes, "Why I'm No Longer"; Garvey, "Does it Follow?"; Hayers, "Narrative Form of Genesis 1"; Hill, "Noachian Flood"; Kofoed, "Approaching Genesis and Science"; LeFebre, *The Liturgy of Creation*; LeFebre, "Reading Genesis 1"; Jones, "Origins of Young Earth Creationism"; Keathley, "Confessions of a Disappointed Young-Earther"; Marston, "Understanding the Biblical Creation Passages"; Collins, *Reading Genesis Well*; *Genesis 1–4*; and *Science and Faith*; Daryl, *Reading Genesis 1–2*; Hill et al., *Grand Canyon*; Moreland and Reynolds, *Three Views on Creation*; Stump, *Four Views on Creation*; Young, *Bible Rocks and Time*.

64. Bronowski, *Ascent of Man*, 360.

of some things that are designed can be identified as such in scientifically acceptable ways."[65] In this broad sense, intelligent design is the science of detecting design. Strictly speaking, then, we should distinguish between "intelligent design" (ID) as a *general* science of design detection on the one hand, and "intelligent design theory" as the application of ID to historical sciences of *origins* on the other hand. That is, the theoretical apparatus of "intelligent design" (of design detection) underlies but is distinct from its application in what we might call "the theory of intelligent origins." As mathematician and philosopher William A. Dembski argues:

> Many special sciences already fall under intelligent design, including archaeology, cryptography, forensics, and SETI (the Search for Extraterrestrial Intelligence). Intelligent design is thus already part of science. Moreover, it employs well-defined methods for detecting intelligence. These methods together with their application constitute the theory of intelligent design. The question, therefore, is not whether intelligent design constitutes a genuine scientific theory but whether, as a scientific theory, it properly applies to [questions of cosmic and biological origins].[66]

During my philosophical studies, I became interested in questions about what it means to call this or that activity "science," and whether it is appropriate to make design inferences within "science." Bearing in mind that there is no universally accepted formal definition of science, I would define science as:

- a fallible, first-order discipline wherein humans seek to use epistemically virtuous methods to understand, explain and/or predict as much as they can about physical or social realities, especially by paying attention to how empirical experience can confirm or undermine such truth-claims.

The above definition does not include the directive articulated in the 1998 US National Academy of Sciences assertion that "The statements of science must invoke only natural things and processes."[67] The technical name for this directive is "methodological naturalism," because it is supposed to limit the sort of things we are free to talk about in "science" without making the philosophical claim that reality is *metaphysically* naturalistic.

---

65. Moreland and Craig, *Philosophical Foundations*, 356.
66. Dembski, "On the Scientific Status," para. 4.
67. *Teaching about Evolution*, 2.

The advocates of methodological naturalism typically exclude appeals to design from the natural sciences whilst allowing them in both social[68] and applied sciences. No one takes issue with design hypotheses in archaeology, cryptography, forensic engineering, forensic science, or the search for extraterrestrial intelligence. Yet, if we bear methodological naturalism in mind, this rather broad design-permitting exception actually requires the metaphysical assumptions that a) any design mentioned in the social and applied sciences will be explicable in naturalistic terms, and that b) any design that might be mentioned within the natural sciences will not be explicable in naturalistic terms. There are good reasons for thinking the first of these assumptions is false.[69] Be that as it may, the point I want to press here is that, without these *metaphysical* assumptions, the design-permitting exception for applied and social sciences is guilty of inconsistency. In other words, a "methodological naturalism" that selectively excludes design from the natural sciences whilst allowing it in the social and applied sciences can only avoid inconsistency *by presupposing metaphysical naturalism*.

In contrast to such inconsistent methodological naturalism (IMN), there are two consistent versions of a genuinely "methodological" naturalism.[70] On the one hand, "Hard-Line Methodological Naturalism" (HMN) excludes "intelligent design" from *any* "science." Of course, HMN exiles from "science" social and applied sciences that everyone wants to call sciences. On the other hand, "Soft Methodological Naturalism" (SMN) allows "intelligent design" into social, applied, *and* natural "science," as long as metaphysical questions about the source of design are left to the disciplines of philosophy and/or theology.

A typical commitment to design-excluding "methodological naturalism" finds expression in biologist Scott Todd's statement that "Even if all the data point to an intelligent designer, such an hypothesis is excluded from science because it is not naturalistic."[71] Now, as Thomas Nagel observes, "a purely semantic classification of a hypothesis or its denial as belonging or not to science is of limited interest to someone who wants to know whether the hypothesis is true or false."[72] However, dogmatically insisting that design hypotheses be excluded from science (even if only from "natural science") leads to a marginalization of science that favors the elevation of

---

68. Natural sciences, which study the physical world, are typically contrasted with social sciences, which study "the manner in which people behave and influence the world around us." UK Research and Innovation, "What Is Social Science."

69. See Menuge, *Agents Under Fire*; Williams, *Faithful Guide to Philosophy*, part III.

70. A proposal I first made in Williams, "Reviewing the Reviewers."

71. Todd, "View from Kansas," 423.

72. Nagel, "Public Education and Intelligent Design," 195.

an alternative discipline with definitional boundaries permitting critical assessment of design hypotheses. The traditional label of "natural philosophy" would suit such a discipline nicely.[73] Still, we may as well tweak the design-excluding definition of "science" whilst retaining the term, for "a rose / By any other name would smell as sweet."[74]

It seems to me that "design" should no more be *excluded a priori* from the natural sciences than it should be *assumed a priori*. At the 137th Annual Meeting of the US National Academy of Sciences (held in Washington, DC in 2000), the President of the Academy, biochemist Bruce Alberts, said that "Science is basically the search of truth,"[75] and that "a system that does not permit the search for truth cannot be a scientific system."[76] This vision of science as a search for truth is clearly at odds with the methodological naturalism that leads science writer John Farrell to declare "It is the job of scientists to find out how apparent design in nature can be explained by natural processes. The best explanation right now is Darwinian evolution."[77] With Alberts, I'd prefer the job of scientists be to find out how apparent design in nature should be explained *truthfully*. The *scientific* question is surely this: *what explains apparent design in nature?* Since methodological naturalism, in either its "inconsistent" or "hard" forms, prevents scientists from simply pursuing a true answer to this question, it is patently "a system that does not permit the search for truth."[78] It follows that a so-called "science" shackled to the "inconsistent" or "hard" forms of methodological naturalism "cannot be a scientific system."[79]

As philosophers Garry DeWeese and J. P. Moreland report, "The inadequacy of methodological naturalism [is now] widely acknowledged by philosophers of science, even among those who are atheists."[80] For example, atheist philosopher of science Bradley Monton argues that

> If science really is permanently committed to methodological naturalism, it follows that the aim of science is not generating true theories. Instead, the aim of science would be something

---

73. Indeed, I think natural science just *is* natural philosophy that's learnt the relevance of empirical observation and experimentation (a lesson bequeathed to the natural philosophy of classical antiquity by Christian theology).

74. Shakespeare, *Romeo and Juliet*, 2.2.

75. Alberts, "Science and Human Needs," para. 2.

76. Alberts, "Science and Human Needs," para. 2.

77. Klinghoffer, "In the Matter," para. 10.

78. Alberts, "Science and Human Needs," para. 2.

79. Alberts, "Science and Human Needs," para. 2.

80. DeWeese and Moreland, *Philosophy Made Slightly Less Difficult*, 146.

like: generating the best theories that can be formulated subject to the restriction that the theories are naturalistic . . . science is better off without being shackled by methodological naturalism.[81]

Likewise, theoretical physicist Sean Carroll warns that

methodological naturalism, while deployed with the best of intentions by supporters of science, amounts to assuming part of the answer ahead of time. If finding truth is our goal, that is just about the biggest mistake we can make.[82]

The Grand Evolutionary Story

In every academic field there is a certain consensus about the truth of the field in which you operate and you work within the framework. It's considered to be incredibly threatening and almost heresy to question a paradigm.

—JEFFREY WOOLF[83]

Having concluded that the intelligent design movement had its philosophy of science right, I became open to asking what else it might be right about, if anything. At this juncture, it is important to realize that the orthodox scientific account of origins—the official creation story of Western culture that one might call "The Grand Evolutionary Story"—can be broken down into a number of distinct claims.[84] It is not a monolithic construct that must be accepted or rejected wholesale. Thus:

- **The Big Bang Theory** says the cosmos has a finite past and that it expanded from an extremely hot, dense and finely tuned state some 13.8 billion years ago.[85]

81. Monton, "Is Intelligent Design Science?," 2, 9–10.

82. Carroll, *Big Picture*, quoted in Evolution News, "Intelligent Design and Methodological Naturalism," para. 2.

83. Jeffrey Woolf (historian and Professor of Talmud at Bar-Ilan University), quoted by Sokol, "Orthodoxy Can Withstand."

84. See FOCLOnline, "Can We Believe in God in an Age of Science? Darwinism" (YouTube video); Williams, "Christian Worldview and Science in Apologetic Perspective: Bios (a)." (Podcast.)

85. See Hossenfelder, "Is the Cosmic Microwave Background a Huge Mistake?"; Cooper, "James Webb Space Telescope"; Kinney and Stein, "Cyclic Cosmology and Geodesic Completeness"; Koberlein, "JWST Fails to Disprove the Big Bang"; Miller, "Science Journal Reaffirms"; "Paul Steinhardt's Cyclical Cosmology Fails"; and "Another

- **The Ancient Earth Thesis** says the earth is around 4.54 billion years old (± 0.05 **billion years**).[86]
- **The Progress Thesis** says that living things have exhibited increased complexity over time, so that "the history of life show's a general progression from the simplest type of prokaryote single-celled organism to birds and mammals."[87]
- **The Common Ancestry Thesis** says that contemporary organisms are the modified descendants of (on average simpler) ancestral organisms. Most contemporary evolutionary theorists hold that the evolutionary lineages of the three domains of life (i.e., bacteria, archaea, and eukaryotes) all trace back to a "last universal common ancestor" (i.e., "Luca").

It is worth noting that

> the progression found in the natural [fossil] record is not what Darwin predicted given the mechanism he proposed to explain descent with modification (nor is it what his theory seems to require). Darwinism predicts a record of slow, random, gradual change. The geological record presents changes in life forms occurring in leaps and jumps (geologically speaking).[88]

As paleontologist Stephen Jay Gould observed:

> The absence of fossil evidence for intermediary stages between major transitions in organic design, indeed our inability, even in our imagination, to construct functional intermediates in many cases, has been a persistent and nagging problem for gradualistic accounts of evolution.[89]

Evolutionary biologist Edmund R. R. Moody and computational biologist Sandra Álvarez-Carretero report that, while some studies "push back Luca's age close to the birth of Earth," others "think this is impossible because of the time it would take to establish the genetic code and DNA

Attempt by an Esteemed Cosmologist to Avoid a Cosmic Beginning"; Orf, "Scientist Thinks the Universe Bounced"; Siegel, "Ask Ethan"; Sutter, "Is the Universe Inside a Black Hole?"; Copan and Craig, *Kalam Cosmological Argument, Vol. 2*; Meyer, *Return of the God Hypothesis*.

86. See Hill, *Grand Canyon*; Young, *Bible Rocks and Time*.

87. Charlesworth and Charlesworth, *Evolution*, 131.

88. Keathley and Rooker, *40 Questions about Creation*, 327–28. See Williams, "Fossil Record" (YouTube playlist); Bechly, "Fossil Friday"; Bechly and Meyer, "Fossil Record"; Klinghoffer, *Debating Darwin's Doubt*; Meyer, "Cambrian Explosion"; Meyer, "Origin of Biological Information"; Meyer, *Darwin's Doubt*.

89. Gould, "Is a New and General Theory?," 127.

replication machinery."[90] In the 1990s Luca was standardly dated "between about 3.8 and 3.2 billion years ago."[91] However, recent research has pushed this date back, thereby placing an additional strain on naturalistic accounts of evolution.

For example, a 2024 peer-reviewed paper by Moody and colleagues estimated that "Luca roamed the Earth around 4.2 billion years ago."[92] Moreover, Moody et al concluded

> that LUCA had a genome of at least 2.5 [megabases] ... encoding around 2,600 proteins, comparable to modern prokaryotes. Our results suggest LUCA ... possessed an early immune system. Although LUCA is sometimes perceived as living in isolation, we infer LUCA to have been part of an established ecological system.[93]

As the co-authors observe:

> How evolution proceeded from the origin of life to early communities at the time of LUCA remains an open question, but the inferred age of LUCA ... compared with the origin of the Earth and Moon suggests that the process required a surprisingly short interval of geologic time.[94]

Of course, its one thing to argue that "the genetic code, protein translation, and life itself must have evolved ... almost right after the Earth was formed,"[95]—within a time-frame of "100 million years or less"[96]—and quite another thing to just assume that all this evolved by "blind" natural processes, before concluding, on this question-begging basis, that such a surprising amount of apparently "impossible"[97] naturalistic evolution must be easy after all![98]

90. Moody and Álvarez-Carretero, "Scientists Reveal How They Identified the Ancestor," para. 6.

91. Encyclopedia Britannica, "Last Universal Common Ancestor."

92. Moody and Álvarez-Carretero, "Scientists Reveal How They Identified the Ancestor," para. 23.

93. Moody et al., "Nature of the Last Universal Common Ancestor," Abstract.

94. Moody et al., "Nature of the Last Universal Common Ancestor," Conclusions.

95. Moody and Álvarez-Carretero, "Scientists Reveal How They Identified the Ancestor," para. 23. See also Bell et al., "Potentially Biogenic Carbon Preserved."

96. Aaron Goldman quoted by Patel, "Meet the Surprisingly Complex Ancestor."

97. Moody and Álvarez-Carretero, "Scientists Reveal How They Identified the Ancestor," para. 6.

98. See Luskin, "Study Finds Life's Origin"; Luskin, "'That Is a Lot of Evolution.'" See also Hunter, "False Science: A Claim to Simulate Protein Evolution."

- While Darwin himself allowed in the final paragraph of the final edition of *The Origin of Species* that life had been "originally breathed by the Creator into a few forms or into one,"[99] **The Universal Common Ancestry Thesis** holds that "all living things are descended from one original primordial organism."[100] According to the thesis of universal common ancestry, there is a single "tree of life" (see Fig. 4).

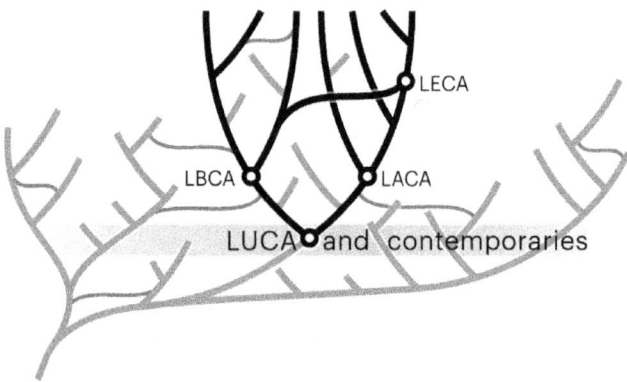

Fig. 4: The Tree of Life.[101] Description: "Branches on the tree of life that have left sampled descendants today are coloured black, those that have left no sampled descendants are in grey. As the common ancestor of extant cellular life, LUCA is the oldest node that can be reconstructed using phylogenetic methods. It would have shared the early Earth with other lineages . . . that have left no descendants among sampled cellular life today. However, these lineages may have left a trace in modern organisms by transferring genes into the sampled tree of life [by horizontal gene transfer] . . ."[102]

- According to the philosophical **Blind Watchmaker Thesis**, "descent with modification" (that is, "evolution" in the sense described by the common ancestry and universal ancestry theses) is wholly explained by "natural processes requiring no divine guidance or non-material orienting force."[103] As philosopher of science Michael Ruse affirms, "organisms came from other forms . . . by a process or processes that

---

99. Darwin, *The Origin of Species*. 6th ed., 429.

100. West, "Debating Common Ancestry," para. 3. See Wikipedia, "First Universal Common Ancestor."

101. "Reconstruction of LUCA."

102. Moody et al., "Nature of the Last Universal Common Ancestor."

103. Johnson, "Religion of the Blind Watchmaker."

are entirely natural, that is to say, governed by and only by unguided natural regularities or laws."[104]

- The combination of common ancestry and/or universal common ancestry with the blind watchmaker thesis, against the backdrop of the Ancient Earth and the Progress theses, constitutes the (broadly speaking) philosophically "Darwinian" theory of "descent with modification through natural selection." As such, **Darwinism** is the thesis that descent with modification exhibits a general progression in complexity over time that can and must be fully explained by a blind, stochastic interplay between what Nobel Prize–winning biochemist and atheist Jacques Monod (1910–76) called "Chance and Necessity."[105]

- **The Modern Evolutionary Synthesis** combines a "Darwinian" theory of biological evolution (usually including universal common ancestry) with the science of genetics to produce the "Neo-Darwinian" theory that "descent with modification" is explained by a process of "blind" genetic "mutation and selection—and perhaps other similarly undirected mechanisms [e.g., genetic drift]..."[106]

However, to quote from a recent paper in the journal *Progress in Biophysics & Molecular Biology*, there has been "limited progress to the modern synthesis [because] selection based on survival of the fittest is insufficient for other than microevolution."[107] As Indiana University biologist Armin Moczek remarks,

> The first eye, the first wing, the first placenta.... Explaining these is the foundational motivation of evolutionary biology. And yet, we still do not have a good answer. This classic idea of gradual change, one happy accident at a time, has so far fallen flat.[108]

Consequently, there has emerged an ongoing debate between adherents of the Modern Evolutionary Synthesis and advocates of an Extended Evolutionary Synthesis.[109] In the words of biologist Peter A. Corning,

104. Ruse, *Darwinism and Its Discontents*, 25.
105. Monod, *Chance and Necessity*.
106. Meyer, "Origin of Biological Information." On "genetic drift" see Amoeba Sisters, "Genetic Drift" (YouTube video); Meyer, *Darwin's Doubt*, 325.
107. Brown and Hullender, "Neo-Darwinism Must Mutate."
108. Moczek, as quoted by Buriani, "Do We Need a New Theory?"
109. See Buriani, "Do We Need a New Theory?"; Dierker, "Why One-Third of Biologists"; Zimmer, "Biologists Who Want to Overhaul"; The Royal Society, "New Trends in Evolutionary Biology"; Shedinger, *Mystery of Evolutionary Mechanisms*.

Many theorists in recent years have been calling for evolutionary biology to move beyond the Modern Synthesis—the paradigm that has long provided the theoretical backbone for the discipline. Terms like "postmodern synthesis," "integrative synthesis," and "extended evolutionary synthesis" have been invoked by various critics in connection with the many recent developments that pose deep challenges—even contradictions—to the traditional model and underscore the need for an update, or a makeover.[110]

According to Professor Kevin Laland and colleagues, writing in *Nature*, the Modern Synthesis has a

> "gene-centric" focus [that] fails to capture the full gamut of processes that direct evolution. Missing pieces include how physical development influences the generation of variation (developmental bias); how the environment directly shapes organisms' traits (plasticity); how organisms modify environments (niche construction); and how organisms transmit more than genes across generations (extra-genetic inheritance).[111]

As Meyer explains,

> developing embryos require *epi*genetic information in the form of specifically arranged (a) membrane targets and patterns, (b) cytoskeletal arrays, (c) ion channels, and (d) sugar molecules on the exterior of cells (the sugar code) . . . much of this epigenetic information resides in the structure of the maternal egg and is inherited directly from membrane to membrane independently of DNA. This three-dimensional structural information interacts with other information-rich molecules and systems of molecules to ensure the proper development of an animal.[112]

This means that "Gene products provide necessary, but not sufficient, conditions for the development of three-dimensional structure within cells, organs, and body plans."[113] Consequently, "natural selection acting on genetic variation and mutations alone cannot produce the new forms that arise in the history of life."[114]

---

110. Corning, "Beyond the Modern Synthesis."

111. Laland et al., "Does Evolutionary Theory Need a Rethink?"

112. Meyer, *Darwin's Doubt*, 365. See Wells, "Not in the Genes"; Woodward and Gills, *Mysterious Epigenome*.

113. Meyer, *Darwin's Doubt*, 284.

114. Meyer, *Darwin's Doubt*, 284.

In his opening talk at the 2016 Royal Society Extended Evolutionary Synthesis meeting, Professor Gerd B. Müller stated,

> The [Modern] Synthesis theory is a theory that is focused on variation in populations, and on its genetic underpinnings ... and ... it explains very well ... genetic variation in evolving populations ... the gradual variation of phenotypic characters, explains adaption of characters, and explains some of [the] genetic features of speciation. However, what it does *not* explain are all these complex levels of evolution ... such as the origin of these body plans ... the standard theory is focused on characters that exist *already* and their variation across populations, but not on how they originate ... and all the non-genetic factors of evolution that are involved, are not addressed.[115]

Likewise, according to philosopher and biologist Massimo Pigliucci: "The Modern Synthesis doesn't cut it because it's got the conceptual tools to tell us how quantitative variation[s] evolve, but not how qualitatively new traits arise."[116] In the words of biologist Scott Gilbert, "The modern synthesis is remarkably good at modeling the survival of the fittest, but not good at modeling the arrival of the fittest."[117]

Defenders of the Modern Synthesis say they "do not think that these processes [of epigenetic inheritance, etc.] deserve such special attention as to merit a new name such as 'extended evolutionary synthesis,'"[118] because they are "'add-ons' to the basic processes that produce evolutionary change. None of these additions is essential for evolution, but they can alter the process under certain circumstances."[119]

However, while none of the additions made by advocates of an extended synthesis are "essential for evolution" *per se*, the epigenetic information discussed by Müller and Meyer is essential *for macroevolution*. As Scott Gilbert, John Opitz, and Rudolf Raff jointly observe,

> Starting in the 1970s, many biologists began questioning [Neo-Darwinism's] adequacy in explaining evolution. Genetics might be adequate for explaining microevolution, but

---

115. Müller, "Extended Evolutionary Synthesis."

116. Massimo Pigliucci, NSF Workshop on the Origin of Novel Features at Indiana University on October 6–8, 2006.

117. Gilbert, quoted by Whitfield, "Biological Theory: Postmodern Evolution?," 282.

118. Wray et al., "Does Evolutionary Theory Need a Rethink?"

119. Wray et al., "Does Evolutionary Theory Need a Rethink?" See also Grant, "Should Evolutionary Theory Evolve?"

microevolutionary changes in gene frequency were not seen as able to turn a reptile into a mammal or to convert a fish into an amphibian. Microevolution looks at adaptations that concern the survival of the fittest, not the arrival of the fittest.[120]

The discovery of epigenetic information renders what Paul Davies calls a "purist [i.e., gene-centric] version of [Neo-]Darwinian"[121]—one postulating that "Major evolutionary changes largely reflect changes of the same type as more minor events, accumulated over longer time periods"[122]—as dead as the proverbial Dodo. In other words, it is *in principle* impossible to explain the origination of new animal phyla simply by extrapolating the micro-evolutionary effects of genetic mutation and natural selection over long periods of time.

This doesn't mean that a less gene-centric Extended Evolutionary Synthesis that still assumes the blind watchmaker thesis can necessarily rectify the explanatory deficits of The Modern Synthesis. Indeed, it's interesting to note atheist philosopher Jerry Fodor (1935–2017) and cognitive scientist Massimo Piatelli-Palmarini affirming both that "Darwin's theory of natural selection is fatally flawed" *and* that "As far as we can make out, nobody knows exactly how phenotypes [different types of organism] evolve."[123] Likewise, paleoanthropologist and neuroscientist David Edelman comments that "there are a critical number of scientists from a variety of disciplines who believe we're still at a loss in terms of an explanation for the evolution of phyla. There's a lot of frustration."[124] As Meyer explains,

> These newer post-neo-Darwinian theories of evolution—self-organization, evolutionary developmental biology, neo-Lamarkian epigenetic inheritance, neutral theory, natural genetic engineering, and others—... invariably either... do not explain the origin of necessary genetic and ontogenic information or they simply presuppose unexplained, preexisting sources of such information.[125]

While the Extended Evolutionary Synthesis expands the blind watchmaker's toolkit, whatever non-question-begging, information-poor "tools" you give a "watchmaker" that's "blind" in the philosophically Darwinian

---

120. Gilbert et al., "Resynthesizing Evolutionary and Developmental Biology," 361.

121. Davies, *Demon in the Machine*, 130.

122. Charlesworth and Charlesworth, *Evolution*, 5.

123. Fodor and Piatelli-Palmarini, *What Darwin Got Wrong*, xvi, 153.

124. Mazur, *Royal Society*, 136.

125. Meyer, *Return of the God Hypothesis*, 209. See also Woodward and Gills, *Mysterious Epigenome*, 146.

sense, its use of those "tools" (and thus what it can accomplish through them) is limited by the fact that it operates without intentionality or foresight.[126]

Despite their differences, for both the "Modern" and "Extended" Evolutionary Syntheses: "the overall picture of evolution is still one of variations [gene-centric or not] filtered by natural selection."[127] Indeed, biochemist Michael Behe argues that the Extended Evolutionary Synthesis still leaves "the heavy lifting to orthodox neo-Darwinism, either explicitly or implicitly," since

> At best evo-devo and other EES ideas kick in only after life has achieved an enormous degree of sophistication . . . Thus neo-Darwinism is still the keystone of modern evolutionary thought . . . each of the proffered alternatives points to one or a few classes of phenomena that it has a reasonable shot of accounting for, at least in part. But none of them have the resources to explain the basic, functional, sophisticated molecular machinery of life. In fact, none even try to do so.[128]

In the words of science writer Stephen Buranyi,

> There are certain core evolutionary principles that no scientist seriously questions. Everyone agrees that natural selection plays a role, as does mutation and random chance. But how exactly these processes interact—and whether other forces might also be at work—has become the subject of bitter dispute. "If we cannot explain things with the tools we have right now," the Yale University biologist Gunter Wagner told me, "we must find new ways of explaining."[129]

That being said, the "modern" and "extended" neo-Darwinian syntheses share a Darwinian commitment to explaining descent with modification in terms that avoid genuine purpose or design,[130] and thus to providing explanations framed in terms of "an unguided, unplanned process."[131] On this philosophical view, as noted paleontologist George Gaylord Simpson famously asserted, "Man is the result of a purposeless and natural process

---

126. See Behe, "Michael Behe Takes on."
127. Bishop, "Extended Synthesis (Reviewing 'Darwin's Doubt')."
128. Behe, *Darwin Devolves*, 137, 251.
129. Buriani, "Do We Need a New Theory?"
130. See Eberlin, "Game of Thrones"; Gauger, "Teleonomy and Evolution."
131. Letter from Nobel Laureates to Kansas State Board of Education, September 9, 2005.

that did not have him in mind."[132] However, this *philosophical* commitment cannot avoid the *scientific*, evidential question of whether or not "an unguided physical process can account for the emergence of all biological complexity and diversity."[133]

Finally, The Grand Evolutionary Story is crucially completed by:

- **The Naturalistic Origins Thesis**, which holds that life arose from non-living matter by virtue of "an unguided, unplanned"[134] physical process of prebiotic "chemical evolution." As noted above, recent research indicates that life "must have evolved . . . almost right after the Earth was formed,"[135] within a time-frame of only "100 million years or less."[136]

Note that it is clearly possible, in most cases, to doubt this or that part of "The Grand Evolutionary Story" without doubting the whole story.[137] Darwin himself argued for common ancestry whilst being agnostic about universal common ancestry. Then again, Jerry Fodor points out that common ancestry "could be true even if the adaptationism [i.e., evolution by natural selection] isn't."[138]

Moreover, note that the first few theses in The Grand Evolutionary Story stand on far stronger ground than the last few. To quote philosopher Alvin Plantinga:

> There is excellent evidence for an ancient earth. . . . There is . . . good evidence in the fossil record for the Progress Thesis, the

---

132. Simpson, *Meaning of Evolution*, 345.

133. Dembski, "Introduction: The Myths Of Darwinism," xx. On the hypothesis that certain biological processes require a present tense input from some sort of "immaterial genome," see Williams, "'Immaterial Genome' Hypothesis" (YouTube playlist); Garte, "Reasonable Ineffectiveness of Mathematics in the Biological Sciences"; Levin, "Ingressing Minds"; Miller, *Plato's Revenge*"; Miller, "Math Behind the Immaterial Genome"; Witt, "Eavesdropping in the Platonic Academy"; Zmirak, "Sternberg's Immaterial Genome"; Klinghoffer, *Plato's Revenge*. Note that the concept of Platonic "forms" invoked in many of these discussions either is not being, or at least need not be, invoked in a strict philosophical sense (see Zmirak, "Sternberg's Immaterial Genome"). For a critique of Platonism, see Craig, *God Over All*.

134. Letter from Nobel Laureates to Kansas State Board of Education.

135. Moody and Álvarez-Carretero, "Scientists Reveal How They Identified the Ancestor."

136. Aaron Goldman quoted by Patel, "Meet the Surprisingly Complex Ancestor."

137. The exceptions being that the Common Ancestry thesis is entailed by the Universal Common Ancestry thesis, and that the Blind Watchmaker account of biological evolution requires the Ancient Earth thesis.

138. Fodor, "Why Pigs Don't Have Wings."

claim that there were bacteria before fish, fish before reptiles, reptiles before mammals, and mice before men . . . the Naturalistic Origins Thesis . . . seems to me to be for the most part mere arrogant bluster; given our present state of knowledge, I believe it is vastly less probable . . . than is its denial.[139]

Philosophers Michael J. Murray and Michael Rea concur that "evidence for an ancient earth seems quite strong, while the evidence for the naturalistic origin of life is, in fact, virtually non-existent."[140]

Eminent Expressions of Doubt

Although criticizing any element of The Grand Evolutionary Story makes one culturally heterodox—and the more far-ranging one's critique the more heterodox one becomes—it is true to say that what was once a trickle of dissatisfaction with this narrative has become a rather more prevalent cultural stream.[141] Nor is such dissent the preserve of theists.[142] Indeed, in the words of philosopher Michel Ruse, "we have today a vocal anti-Darwinian party, consisting somewhat surprisingly not only of the evangelical Christians of the American South but of some of today's most eminent atheist philosophers."[143]

For example, "one of the most important philosophers of recent times"[144] was Mary Midgley (1919–2018), a senior lecturer in philosophy at Newcastle University. Midgely observed that while "our current belief in our evolutionary origin calls for matter to take over the burden of creation . . . the physical difficulties facing this enterprise seem bad enough."[145] She called attention to the problem of explaining the supposedly unplanned *arrival* as well as the naturally selected *survival* of the biologically fit:

---

139. Plantinga, "When Faith and Reason Clash."

140. Murray and Rea, *Introduction to the Philosophy of Religion*, 211.

141. See Sewell, "Scientific Establishment"; Thorvaldsen and Hössjer, "Using Statistical Methods." See also Luskin, "Repentant Biology Journal."

142. The following critiques come from a variety of worldview perspectives: Gelernter, "Giving Up Darwin"; Bandea, *God of the Details*; Berlinski, *Deniable Darwin & Other Essays*; Dembski, *Uncommon Dissent*; Denton, *Evolution: A Theory in Crisis*; Flew with Varghese, *There Is a God*; Fanu, *Why Us?*; Fodor and Piatelli-Palmarini, *What Darwin Got Wrong*; Houston, *Natural God*; Midgley, *Are You an Illusion?*; Nagel, *Mind & Cosmos*; Thomas, *Taking Leave of Darwin*.

143. Ruse, "Darwinism as Religion."

144. Dyer, "Mary Midgley," para. 2.

145. Midgley, *Are You an Illusion?*, 14–15.

> The idea of natural selection, which ... is usually called in to account for this vast creative surge, is already looking increasingly inadequate to explain evolution. ... Natural selection is only a filter and filters do not provide the taste of the coffee that pours through them. Similarly, the range of evolutionary alternatives between which selection takes place has to be there already in matter. How it comes to be present there is the real mystery about creation.[146]

Midgely also noted the existence of "increasing difficulties about matters like the origin of life."[147]

While John Dupré, a philosopher of biology at the University of Exeter, recognizes that "Differential survival is an important process,"[148] he records being "increasingly inclined to think [that] we overestimate the abilities of natural selection to shape organisms in new ways."[149] Dupré states, "What's clear to me is that we do not have a good understanding of evolutionary novelty and evolutionary change."[150]

American philosopher Thomas Nagel argues that

> the reductive account of life ... faces problems of probability that I believe are not taken seriously enough, both with respect to the evolution of life forms through accidental mutation and natural selection and with respect to the formation from dead matter of physical systems capable of such evolution. The more we learn about the intricacy of the genetic code and its control of the chemical processes of life, the harder those problems seem.[151]

Not that such dissent is the preserve of philosophers. Günter Theißen, who holds the chair of genetics at Friedrich Schiller University of Jena, says that although we know a lot about how organisms adapt to their environment,

> much less is known about the mechanisms behind the origin of evolutionary novelties, a process that is arguably different from adaptation. Despite Darwin's undeniable merits, explaining how the enormous complexity and diversity of living beings on

---

146. Midgley, *Are You an Illusion?*, 16.
147. Midgley, *Are You an Illusion?*, 12.
148. Dupré in Mazur, *Royal Society*, 57.
149. Dupré in Mazur, *Royal Society*, 57–58.
150. Dupré in Mazur, *Royal Society*, 63.
151. Nagel, *Mind & Cosmos*, 9.

our planet originated remains one of the greatest challenges of biology.[152]

Likewise, Peter Corning, of the Institute for the Study of Complex Systems, writes that "Darwin's theory does not provide an explanation for the rise of biological complexity. . ."[153] As paleobiologist Graham Budd muses, "When the public thinks about evolution, they think about the origin of wings and the invasion of the land . . . [b]ut these are things that evolutionary theory has told us little about."[154]

Ducking the Question

> Evolutionary theory . . . certainly seems to be the most reasonable position, once one has taken a naturalistic position.
>
> —MICHAEL RUSE[155]

Richard Dawkins famously describes biology as "the study of complicated things that give the appearance of having been designed for a purpose."[156] As philosopher Robert C. Koons argues,

> The inference from complex, interdependent functionality to intelligent design is the natural, default position. Darwinian biologists and their pupils overlook that fact at their own cognitive peril.[157]

In other words, the belief that life is the product of design is warranted by the *prima facie* appearance that it is the product of design, in the absence of sufficient reason for doubt. Dawkins concedes this burden of proof in his definition of biology, but he invokes the "modern synthesis" theory of descent via "blind" genetic variation and natural selection as a theory able to shoulder that burden.

The question here is not whether neo-Darwinian evolution can explain descent with modification *per se*. It can. Rather, the question is whether it can *plausibly* account for descent with *enough* modification to cover all the

---

152. Theißen, "Saltational Evolution."
153. Corning, quoted by Witt, "Another Call for a 'New Synthesis.'"
154. Whitfield, "Biological Theory," quoting Graham Budd.
155. Ruse, "Nonliteralist Antievolution."
156. Dawkins, *Blind Watchmaker*, 1.
157. Koons, "Check Is in the Mail," 9–10.

biological facts. As Koons points out, giving a positive answer to this question requires a serious analysis of the relevant probabilistic factors:

> Hypothetical Darwinian pathways leading to actual adaptive forms [must be] described in sufficient detail and with sufficient understanding of the underlying genetic and developmental processes that it seems virtually certain that these pathways represent genuine possibilities. These pathways must be possible, not only in the sense of involving no violation of physical or chemical laws, but also in the sense that every step in the path can be assigned an estimated probability that is sufficiently high for the joint probability of the entire pathway to be consistent with a reasonable belief that such a thing might really have happened.[158]

Darwin insisted that "natural selection can act only by taking advantage of slight successive variations; she can never take a leap, but must advance by the shortest and slowest steps."[159] Likewise, Dawkins argues that

> the larger the leap through genetic space, the lower the probability that the resulting change will be viable, let alone an improvement. [Hence] evolution must in general be a crawl through genetic space, not a series of leaps.[160]

Faced with the challenge of showing that such a "crawl through genetic space" is plausible, Dawkins ducks the question. To quote Nobel Prize–winning physicist Brian Josephson,

> In books such as *The Blind Watchmaker*, a crucial part of the argument concerns whether there exists a continuous path, leading from the origins of life to man, each step of which is both favoured by natural selection, and small enough to have happened by chance. It appears to be presented as a matter of logical necessity that such a path exists, but actually there is no such logical necessity; rather, commonly made assumptions in evolution require the existence of such a path.[161]

Dawkins famously likens the process of evolution to the process of climbing a mountain in his book *Climbing Mount Improbable* (1996).[162] Mount Improbable presents organisms with a sheer cliff of statistical

---

158. Koons, "Check Is in the Mail," 9–10.
159. Darwin, *Origin of Species* (1st ed.), 149.
160. Dawkins, "Darwin Triumphant," 86.
161. Josephson, "Letter to the Editor."
162. See Dawkins, *Climbing Mount Improbable*; Meyer, "Stephen Meyer Critiques."

improbability (complexity), a cliff so imposing that that it can't be conquered in single "leap." Evolving the specified complexity of "The first eye, the first wing, the first placenta,"[163] clearly isn't the sort of thing that a "blind watchmaker" can plausibly accomplish in a single leap, or even in a handful of uncoordinated leaps. (Indeed, no matter what tools you give it, a "blind watchmaker" operating without intentionality or foresight can't readily "turn a reptile into a mammal or convert a fish into an amphibian."[164]) However, Dawkins follows Darwin in assuring us that around the backside of Mount Improbable there exists a contiguous series of individually and jointly attainable, naturally selectable steps that lead all the way up to whatever functionally specified summit we may be trying to explain. At the same time, Dawkins freely admits that we have no idea *what* specific series of steps any organism took up Mount Improbable. As biochemist Franklin M. Harold wrote, "we must concede that there are presently no detailed Darwinian accounts of the evolution of any biochemical or cellular system, only a variety of wishful speculations."[165] Nevertheless, Dawkins declares that

> however daunting the sheer cliffs that the adaptive mountain first presents, graded ramps [i.e., evolutionary pathways composed of a contiguous series of individually and jointly attainable steps] can be found the other side and the peak eventually scaled.[166]

Thus, Dawkins assures us, "Darwin tells us exactly how nature's trick is done: cumulative natural selection."[167]

How does Dawkins square the claim that "graded ramps can be found" up Mount Improbable with the admission that we don't know of any? His answer is a matter of armchair philosophy: "Without stirring from our chair, we can see that it must be so, because nothing except gradual accumulation could, in principle, do the job."[168] That is, of course, *the job of explaining life without intelligent design*! Dawkins simply *assumes* that "graded ramps" up Mount Improbable exist in order to fill the explanatory gap created by the philosophical exclusion of design from natural science. In the words of atheist philosopher Daniel Dennett:

---

163. Armin Moczek, as quoted by Buriani, "Do We Need a New Theory?"
164. Gilbert et al., "Resynthesizing Evolutionary and Developmental Biology," 361.
165. Harold, *Way of the Cell*, 205.
166. Dawkins, *Devil's Chaplain*, 211–12.
167. Richard Dawkins Foundation for Reason & Science, "Richard Dawkins 2016 Reason Rally Speech," 2:23–28 (YouTube video).
168. Dawkins, *Devil's Chaplain*, 212.

> This is a purely theory-driven explanation, argued a-priori from the assumption that natural selection tells the true story—some true story or other—about every curious feature of the biosphere ... it assumes that Darwinism is basically on the right track.[169]

In *Outgrowing God* (2020), Dawkins notes that "Since our ancestors were fish crawling out of the sea, three million centuries have gone by. That's an awful lot of time—a huge opportunity for change—step by step down the generations."[170] Yet he never tries to quantify how much change one can reasonably expect, "step by step down the generations." As biophysicist Lee Spetner complains,

> When one deals with events having small probabilities and many trials, one ... should not just stand gaping at the long time available for trials, ignore the small probability, and conclude that anything can happen in such a long time. One has to calculate.[171]

Without a principled way to distinguish between what a Darwinian process of variation and natural selection can and can't plausibly accomplish in the available timeframe, all Dawkins has to offer is a vague just-so story that begs the question against the proper burden of proof.

Begging of the question against design is built into orthodox scientific accounts of origins—to both "Modern" and "Extended" Evolutionary theories alike—via the philosophical declaration that "scientific" study of the physical world is beholden to (a suitably interpreted version of) "methodological naturalism." Thus Franklin Harold affirms that "We should reject, as a matter of principle, the substitution of intelligent design for the dialogue of chance and necessity."[172] But why restrict scientist's academic freedom in this way when it promotes the tortuous "logic" that we know the appearance of design in nature must be misleading because "Nature does the job all by itself,"[173] and we know that "Nature does the job all by itself" *because we aren't allowed to consider design* as a potential explanation for the appearance of design in biology?!

Reading *The Origin of Species*, I saw that Darwin made a similar burden-of-proof shifting move:

---

169. Dennett, "Leibnizian Paradigm," 49.
170. Dawkins, *Outgrowing God*, 179.
171. Spetner, *Not by Chance*, 1.
172. Harold, *Way of the Cell*, 205.
173. Dawkins, *Outgrowing God*, 179.

> If then we have under nature variability and a powerful agent [i.e., natural selection] always ready to act and select, why should we doubt that variations in any way useful to beings ... would be preserved, accumulated, and inherited? ... What limit can be put to this power, acting during long ages ... favouring the good and rejecting the bad? I can see no limit to this power, in slowly and beautifully adapting each form.[174]

Darwin thus awarded the presumption of truth to his extrapolation from small-scale microevolution to large-scale macroevolution, shifting between saying that he *saw* no limit to what evolution by natural selection could achieve to saying that we should assume there *was* no limit, until shown otherwise. In this way, Darwin made a question-begging "argument from ignorance."[175] Moreover, Darwin asserted that an explanation framed in terms of divine design was "not a scientific explanation."[176] That is, Darwin propped up his theory by appealing to an inconsistent form of methodological naturalism that conflated divine design with design *per se*. In sum, Darwin's theory of evolution, and its likeminded descendants, arose from a clutch of philosophical errors.

By contrast with the likes of Darwin and Dawkins, I discovered that intelligent design theorists rejected *a priori* arguments in favor of grappling with the detailed probabilistic questions orthodox science so often avoided. It is the advance of scientific knowledge since *The Origin of Species* was published that means we are now in a position to demonstrate that philosophically Darwinian theories of descent with modification fall short of explaining all the relevant data.

The Limits of Evolution

> Suspicion towards Neo-Darwinism [is] justified by statistical considerations.
>
> —Jørn Dyerberg, Professor Emeritus in Human Nutrition at the University of Copenhagen.[177]

The existence of biological information is not only the key problem for the origin of life (abiogenesis),[178] but for explaining such biological realities as

---

174. Darwin, *Origin of Species* (1st ed.), 353.
175. See All Grey Matters, "'Argument from Ignorance' Fallacy."
176. Darwin, *Origin of Species* (6th ed.), 383.
177. Pultz, "Our Danish Correspondent."
178. See Meyer, *Signature in the Cell*.

the origin of novel protein folds,[179] the origin of molecular machines,[180] and the origin of new cell-types and body-plans[181] over the course of natural history.

Michael J. Behe summarizes some of the problems facing evolution's putative "blind watchmaker":

> Mutation supplies the variation upon which natural selection acts, but the greatest amount of that variation comes from damaging or outright breaking previously working genes. In the case of an already functioning complex systems, natural selection shapes it more and more tightly to its current role, making it less and less adaptable to other complex roles. . . . The need for multiple coordinated mutations [multiplies] the troubles for Darwinism [and] irreducible complexity effectively prohibits the development of intricate molecular machinery by mutation and selection.[182]

With respect to the first of these problems, Behe explains that

> evolution proceeds mainly by damaging or breaking genes, which, counterintuitively, sometimes helps survival. In other words, the mechanism . . . promotes the rapid loss of genetic information. Laboratory experiments, field research, and theoretical studies all forcefully indicate that, as a result, random mutation and natural selection make evolution self-limiting.[183]

---

179. See Discovery Institute, "Biologist Douglas Axe"; Zentrum für BioKomplexität & NaturTeleologie, "Thermodynamic Analysis"; Axe, "Extreme Functional Sensitivity"; Axe, "Estimating the Prevalence"; Axe, "Case Against a Darwinian Origin"; Axe and Gauger, "Model and Laboratory Demonstrations"; Behe, "Waiting Longer for Two Mutations"; Gauger and Axe, "Evolutionary Accessibility"; Reeves et al., "Enzyme Families."

180. See Williams, "Irreducible Complexity" (YouTube playlist); Behe, "Darwinism Gone Wild"; Behe, "Irreducible Complexity"; Behe, "'Resurrected' Flagella"; Dembski, "Irreducible Complexity Revisited"; Dembski, "Still Spinning Just Fine"; Evolution News, "Three Flagellum Updates"; Luskin, "Why the Type III Secretory System"; Luskin, "Study Challenges Evolutionary Relationship"; Behe, *Darwin's Black Box* (2nd ed.); "Appendix: Clarifying Perspective"; and "Appendix C"; Miller, "Advances in Biology"; Dembski, *No Free Lunch*; Dembski and Wells, *Design of Life*; Eberlin, *Foresight*, 77–82; Miller, "Engineering Principles," 206–9.

181. See Meyer, "Origin of Biological Information"; Meyer, *Darwin's Doubt*; Klinghoffer, *Debating Darwin's Doubt*.

182. Behe, *Darwin Devolves*, 246–47. See Discovery Science, "Secrets of the Cell" (YouTube Video).

183. Behe, *Darwin Devolves*. See also Behe, "Experimental Evolution"; Evolution News, "Darwin Devolves, Again."

REFLECTIONS ON INTELLIGENT DESIGN 39

Casey Luskin elucidates one particularly impressive aspect of the informational complexity science has discovered in the DNA of higher genomes:[184]

> Try writing a sentence which has two different meanings: One meaning is gained when you start with one letter of the first word, and then an entirely different meaning is understood when you start reading with the second letter of the first word. Such a sentence would be most impressive, but what if such "sentences" existed in our DNA? ... A [2007] article in *Public Library of Science* discussed how dual-coding genes—genes which overlap and code for multiple proteins when read through different reading frames—are "hallmarks of fascinating biology" and "nearly impossible by chance" to the extent that evolutionary biologists have held "skepticism surrounding" their very existence. Now it seems they do exist.[185]

Genes with "alternate reading frames" (ARFs) are so tightly specified that it seems almost impossible to improve (i.e., evolve) one of the "sentences" therein by making a random alteration without simultaneously spoiling the meaning of the alternate sentences. As Professor John C. Stanford argues,

> The problem of ubiquitous, genome-wide poly-constrained DNA seems absolutely overwhelming for evolutionary theory. Changing *anything* seems to potentially change *everything*! The poly-constrained nature of DNA serves as strong evidence that higher genomes cannot evolve via mutation/selection—except on a trivial level.[186]

As outlined in the abstract of a paper by Montañez et al.,

> There is growing evidence that much of the DNA in higher genomes is poly-functional, with the same nucleotide contributing to more than one type of code.... We show that: a) the probability of beneficial mutation is inversely related to the degree that a sequence is already optimized for a given code; b) the probability of beneficial mutation drastically diminishes as the number of overlapping codes increases. The growing evidence for a high degree of optimization in biological systems, and the growing evidence for multiple levels of poly-functionality within DNA,

---

184. See Coppedge, "Genetics."
185. Luskin, "Dual Coding Genes." See also Chung et al., "First Look at ARFome."
186. Stanford, *Genetic Entropy*, 133.

both suggest that mutations that are unambiguously beneficial must be especially rare.[187]

Meyer comments:

> one gene or region of the genome, in concert with extragenomic codes and machinery, can produce many thousands of different RNA messages and proteins ... as a result of the overlapping genetic messages and different modes of information processing, the specified information stored in DNA is now recognized to be orders of magnitude greater than was initially thought in the immediate wake of the molecular biological revolution.[188]

About 2 percent of the human genome codes for the assembly of amino acids into proteins. Brian and Deborah Charlesworth affirm that:

> Given the correct sequence of amino acids, the protein chain folds up into the shape of the working protein. The complex three-dimensional structure of a protein is completely determined by the sequence of amino acids in its constituent chain or chains; in turn, this sequence is completely determined by the sequence of chemical units of the DNA ... of the gene that produces the protein.[189]

Yet no physical forces determine the complex and specific sequence of chemical units in the genes that code for the production of proteins. Moreover, the forces between amino acids that fold proteins are very weak, so the need to have enough force to hold a protein in its folded and thus functional state requires proteins to have a minimum chain-size of several dozen links.[190] Now, as evolutionary biologist David S. Goodsell reports:

> only a small fraction of the possible combinations of amino acids will fold spontaneously into a stable structure. If you make a protein with a random sequence of amino acids, chances are that it will only form a gooey tangle when placed in water.[191]

---

187. Montañez et al., "Multiple Overlapping Genetic Codes." See also Luskin, "*BioEssays* Editor: '"Junk" DNA.'"
188. Meyer, *Signature in the Cell*, 462.
189. Charlesworth and Charlesworth, *Evolution*, 26.
190. See Axe, "Case Against a Darwinian Origin"; Axe, "Don't Be Intimidated"; Evolution News, "Collective Motion."
191. Goodsell, *Machinery of Life* (2nd ed.), 17, 19.

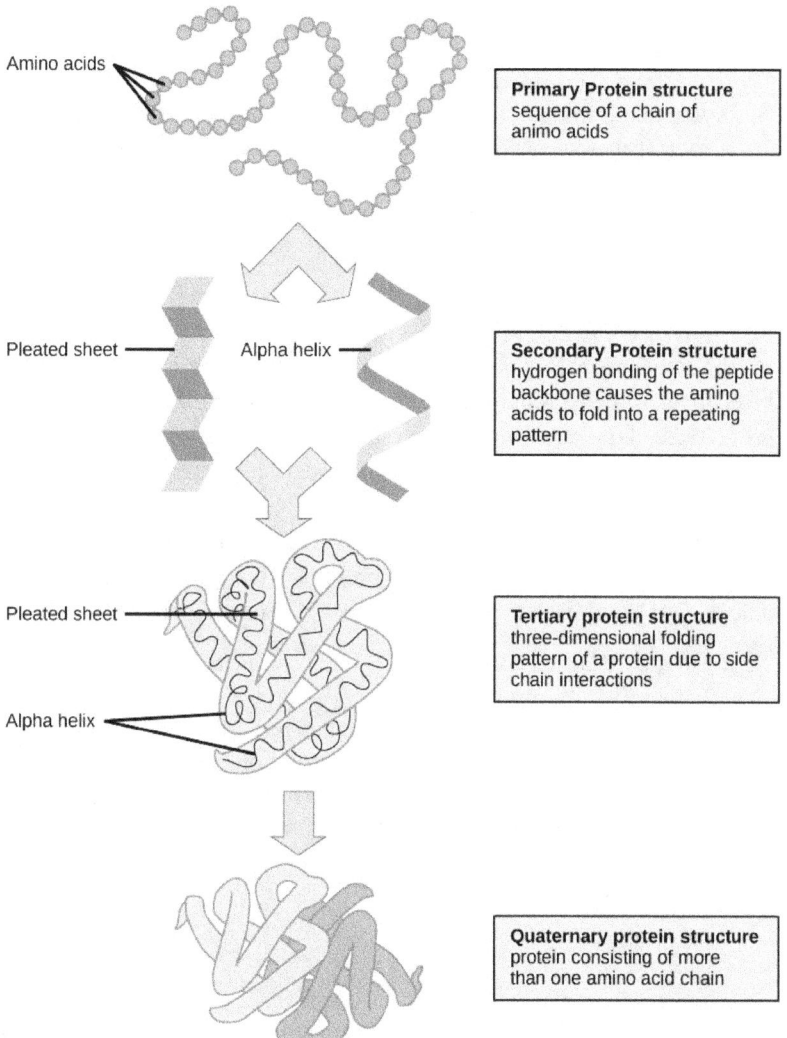

Fig. 5. Protein Folding.[192]

Computer scientist David Gelernter argues that the sequence specificity of protein chains poses a problem for blind-watchmaker evolution:

> A protein molecule is based on a chain of amino acids; 150 elements is a "modest-sized" chain.... The total count of *possible* 150-link chains, where each link is chosen separately from 20 amino acids, is 20^{150} [which] roughly equals 10^{195}.... What

---

192. https://commons.wikimedia.org/wiki/File:Figure_03_04_09.jpg.

proportion of these many polypeptides are useful proteins? Douglas Axe did a series of experiments to estimate how many 150-long chains are capable of stable folds—of reaching the final step in the protein-creation process (the folding) and of holding their shapes long enough to be useful.... He estimated that... 1 in 10^{74} will be capable of folding into a stable protein... your chances of hitting a stable protein that performs some useful *function*, and might therefore play a part in evolution, are even smaller.[193]

Indeed, according to physicist Brian Miller, later research "showed that the actual rarity [of operational proteins] is far more extreme," both for the relatively simple protein studied by Axe "and for many others."[194] While Axe "looked at the rarity in a region of sequence space close to a functional sequence," the "actual rarity is much more extreme when all of sequence space is considered."[195]

Stephen C. Meyer reports that "other studies using different methods of estimating the rarity of functional proteins have [given results comparable to] Axe's multiyear experimental study."[196] For example,

> [Branko] Kozulic and [Matti] Leisola ... concluded that even with very conservative conditions, the probability of finding ATP binding activity that would function in a cell, would be less than 1 in 10^{32}. Estimates like these depend on various factors, including the length of the proteins considered, and indicate that while the probability of finding a functional protein in sequence space can vary broadly it commonly remains far beyond the reach of Darwinian processes.[197]

Meyer observes,

---

193. Gelernter, "Giving Up Darwin," para. 25. In point of fact, most proteins are "250 to 300 amino acids in length." Dembski and Marks, "Life's Conservation Law," 9. See also Discovery Institute, "Biologist Douglas Axe on Evolution's Ability to Produce New Functions" (YouTube video); Hoover Institution, "Mathematical Challenges" (YouTube video); Axe, "Estimating the Prevalence of Protein Sequences Adopting Functional Enzyme Folds," 1295–1315; and "Losing the Forest by Fixating on the Trees"; McLatchie, "Joining the Conversation"; Miller, "Dentist in the Sahara"; "Mistakes Our Critics Make"; and "Engineering Principles," 178–79.

194. Miller, "Engineering Principles," 179.

195. Miller, "Engineering Principles," 179.

196. Meyer, *Return of the God Hypothesis*, 319.

197. Thorvaldsen, "Intelligent Design and Natural Theology." See Kozulic and Leisola, "Have Scientists Already Been Able?" See also Miller, "Engineering Principles," 178–79.

Protein scientist Dan Tawfik has shown that protein folds lose their structural and thermodynamic stability as more and more mutations accumulate. Experimentally, Tawfik found that he could completely destroy the stability of numerous different protein folds with between three and fifteen random mutational changes.... So just as a series of random changes to computer code will destroy the function of the software before a new program could arise, a small handful (typically between 3 and 15) of random changes to the amino acid sequence in a protein will destroy the stability of the protein fold well before enough mutations could accumulate to generate a novel fold.[198]

Axe and fellow biologist Ann Gauger took two bacterial enzymes with different functions but very similar structures and experimentally determined that shifting the function of one enzyme to that of the other required a minimum of seven mutations. They used population genetics to argue that this is "too many mutations to have occurred by an unguided neo-Darwinian process," noting that "The waiting time for seven coordinated neutral mutations to arise in a bacterial population is on the order of 10^{27} years."[199]

Moreover, as Luskin explains, "Proteins commonly interact with other molecules through a 'hand-in-glove' fit, but these interactions often require multiple amino acids to be 'just right' before they occur."[200] In 2004, Michael Behe and University of Pittsburgh physicist David Snoke published a paper modeling the evolution of protein-protein interactions. Their model suggested that evolving an interaction requiring two or more mutations in multicellular organisms would probably take more such organisms than have been available in the history of Earth.[201] In response, Cornell University biologists Rick Durrett and Deena Schmidt published a paper using a more optimistic model of population genetics. Their model suggested that for a double mutation to become fixed in the human population "would take > 100 million years."[202] On the assumption that humans share a common ancestor with chimpanzees about 6 million years ago, they conceded that such mutational events were "very unlikely to occur on a reasonable timescale."[203]

198. Meyer, *Return of the God Hypothesis*, 319.
199. Gauger, "Science and Human Origins," 20. See Gauger and Axe, "Evolutionary Accessibility"; Reeves et al., "Enzyme Families."
200. Luskin, "Problem 3," para. 14.
201. Behe and Snoke, "Simulating Evolution."
202. Durrett and Schmidt, "Waiting for Two Mutations," abstract.
203. Durrett and Schmidt, "Waiting for Two Mutations," 1507. See also Behe, "Waiting Longer for Two Mutations"; Hössjer et al., "On the Waiting Time"; LeMaster,

The fact that biological functions usually require multiple different proteins means that "the improbability of evolving such systems increases exponentially with each additional protein required."[204] As biologists Joseph W. Thornton and Rob DeSalle admit,

> it remains a mystery how the undirected process of mutation, combined with natural selection, has resulted in the creation of thousands of new proteins with extraordinarily diverse and well optimized functions. This problem is particularly acute for tightly integrated molecular systems that consist of many interacting parts . . .[205]

Cells are packed with multi-protein machines, like the bacterial flagellum (see Fig. 6 and Fig. 7), that exhibit an "irreducible complexity." This means that they can't serve their function without all of their many, tightly integrated, essential parts.[206]

"Evolution's Waiting-Time Problem"; Sanford et al., "Waiting Time Problem."

204. Swift, "Genetic and Biochemical Challenges," para. 29.

205. Thornton and DeSalle, "Gene Family Evolution and Homology."

206. See Williams, "Irreducible Complexity" (YouTube playlist); Behe, "Darwinism Gone Wild"; Behe, "Irreducible Complexity"; Behe, "'Resurrected' Flagella"; Dembski, "Irreducible Complexity Revisited"; Dembski, "Still Spinning Just Fine"; Evolution News, "Three Flagellum Updates"; Luskin, "Why the Type III Secretory System"; Luskin, "Study Challenges Evolutionary Relationship"; Behe, *Darwin's Black Box* (2nd ed.); "Appendix: Clarifying Perspective"; and "Appendix C"; Miller, "Advances in Biology"; Dembski, *No Free Lunch*; Dembski and Wells, *Design of Life*; Eberlin, *Foresight*, 77–82; Miller, "Engineering Principles," 206–9.

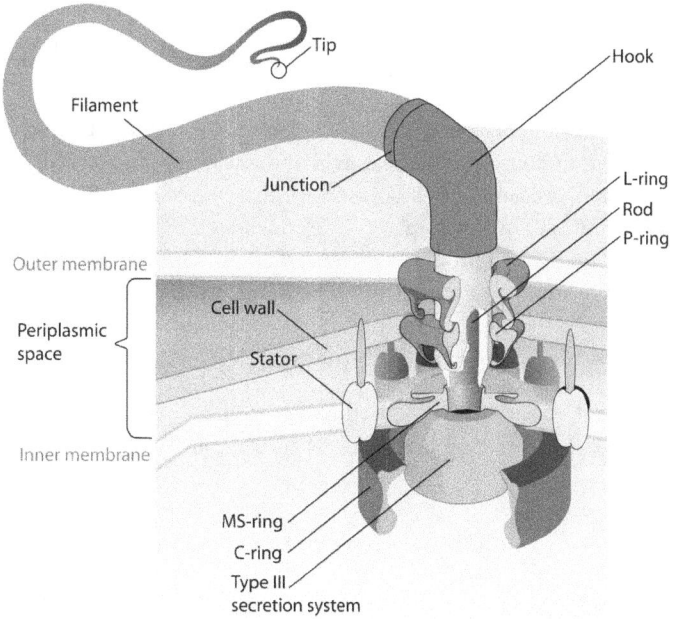

Fig. 6. A simplified conceptual diagram of a gram-negative bacterial flagellum.[207]

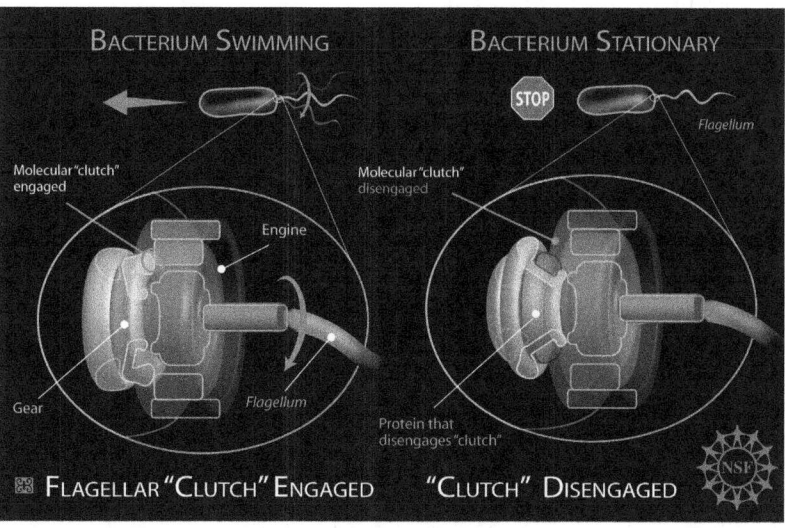

Fig. 7. Simplified conceptual diagram of a bacterial flagellum and motor assembly.[208]

207. https://en.wikiversity.org/wiki/File:Flagellum_base_diagram_en.svg (public domain image by LadyofHats).

208. "Insights Into the Workings of a Bacterium's Flagellum," https://commons.

Not only is the coordination of multiple interacting parts to achieve a function an obvious sign of design, but a blind evolutionary process can't plausibly explain such systems:

> An irreducibly complex system cannot be produced directly by numerous, successive, slight modifications of a precursor system, because any precursor . . . that is missing a part is by definition nonfunctional. . . . Although an irreducibly complex system can't be produced directly, one can't definitively rule out the possibility of an indirect, circuitous route. However, as the complexity of an interacting system increases, the likelihood of such an indirect route drops precipitously.[209]

At least some of these "irreducibly complex" machines are complex enough to count as examples of "specified complexity."[210]

Natural Genetic Engineering

One might think an explanation for at least some otherwise improbable mutations may lie with the discovery of "mechanisms by which organisms can 'rewrite' their own genomes, especially in response to stress."[211] For example, Brian Miller explains that

> plant genomes contain DNA segments known as transposable elements (TEs) that can move to new locations, allowing them to alter the activity of local genes. Specific environmental stimuli can initiate relocation to target locations . . . and stimuli can activate the TEs, resulting in adaptive benefits. For instance, TEs modify gene regulation in maize to confer drought tolerance, alter flowering time, and enable plants to grow in toxic aluminum soils . . .[212]

Then again, "Yeast cells respond to nutrient starvation by increasing the mutation rates at specific locations referred to as mutational hot spots."[213]

---

wikimedia.org/wiki/File:Insights_into_the_workings_of_a_bacterium%27s_flagellum_(12291548414).jpg (public domain image by Zina Deretsky, National Science Foundation).

209. Behe, "Evidence for Intelligent Design from Biochemistry."
210. See Dembski, "Irreducible Complexity Revisited"; Dembski, "Still Spinning Just Fine."
211. Luskin, "James Shapiro's *Evolution*."
212. Miller, "Nearly All of Evolution."
213. Miller, "Nearly All of Evolution."

University of Chicago biologist James A. Shapiro calls these "goal-orientated responses"[214] processes of "cell guided natural genetic engineering."[215] However, on the one hand, many biomolecular systems are so complex that stumbling upon novel functionality remains highly unlikely despite whatever additional resources might be directed to their discovery by mechanisms like that deployed by yeast. Indeed, many structures appear to be so complex that they remain highly unlikely even if one factors in all the probabilistic resources of the observable universe. On the other hand, while various "cellular functions for self-modification"[216] may aid in the ascent up Mount Improbable, the existence of such "goal-orientated responses"[217] is itself something that requires explanation, and as Casey Luskin points out, one "cannot invoke mechanisms of directed change to explain how those same mechanisms of directed change arose."[218]

Abiogenesis

Before any process of biological evolution by natural selection can get started, some form of life able to reproduce itself with variation must come into existence within the context of the lifeless conditions that existed many millennia ago.[219] Here's how British paleontologist and evolutionary biologist Henry Gee describes the origin of life in his book *A (Very) Short History of Life on Earth*:

> The earliest living things were no more than scummy membranes across microscopic gaps in rocks. They formed when the

---

214. Shapiro, "What Natural Genetic Engineering Does and Does Not Mean."
215. Shapiro, *Evolution*, 69.
216. Shapiro. *Evolution*, 146.
217. Shapiro, "What Natural Genetic Engineering Does and Does Not Mean."
218. Luskin, "James Shapiro's *Evolution*." See also McLatchie, "Joining the Conversation."
219. As Bradley Monton observes: "Darwinian evolution only comes into play once life already exists. Darwinian evolution doesn't explain (or even purport to explain) how life came to arise in the first place" (*Seeking God in Science*, 29). See Williams, "Origin of Life" (YouTube playlist); ID the Future, "RNA World" (Podcast); Berlinski, "On the Origins of Life"; Evolution News, "Could Blind Forces Build?"; Hedin, "Information and Life's Origin"; Luskin, "Presto!"; Meyer, "Of Molecules and (Straw) Men"; Meyer, "DNA and the Origin of Life"; Tour, "Are Present Proposals"; "We're Still Clueless"; "Animadversions of a Synthetic Chemist"; and "Two Experiments in Abiogenesis"; Tour et al., "Thermodynamic Limitations"; Abel, *Primordial Prescription*; Abel, *First Gene*; Eberlin, "Evidence of Foresight in Nature," 213–42; Meyer, *Signature in the Cell*; Tan and Stadler, *Stairway to Life*; Thaxton et al., *Mystery of Life's Origin: The Continuing Controversy*; Wedgwood, *DNA*.

> rising currents [in the depths of the ocean] became turbulent and diverted into eddies, and, losing energy, dumped their cargo of mineral-rich debris into gaps and pores in the rock. These membranes were imperfect . . . and, like sieves, allowed some substances to cross but not others. Even though they were porous, the environment inside the membranes became different from the raging maelstrom beyond, calmer, more ordered . . . The membranes made a virtue of their leakiness, using holes as gateways for energy and nutrients, and as exit points for wastes. Protected from the chemical clamour of the outside world, these tiny pools were havens of order. Slowly, they refined the generation of energy, using it to bud off small bubbles, each encased in its own portion of the parent membrane. This was haphazard at first, but gradually became more predictable, as a result of the development of an internal chemical template that could be copied and passed down to new generations of membrane-bound bubbles. This ensured that new generations of bubbles were, more or less, faithful copies of their parents. The more efficient bubbles began to thrive at the expense of those less well-ordered. These simple bubbles found themselves at the very gates of life, in that they found a way to halt—if temporarily, and with great effort—the otherwise inexorable increase in entropy. . . . These foamy lathers of soap-bubble cells stood as tiny clenched fists, defiant against the lifeless world.[220]

Readers who fail to follow up on Gee's endnotes will miss the following admission:

> As I am telling this tale more as a story than as a scientific exercise, some of the things I'll say have more evidential support than others. The circumstances of the origin of life are perhaps the least understood of anything else I'll discuss. This is the part that comes closest to Making Stuff Up.[221]

Indeed, Gee's tale of gradually developing membranes is a just-so story that appears to confuse being "ordered" with specified complexity, and that conspicuously lacks an explanation as to *how* nature's blind watchmaker was able ("with great effort") to make this ("well-ordered" and "defiant") stuff up! This lack is hardly surprising, for as science writer Jon Kelvey reports (from a perspective that excludes intelligent design),

---

220. Gee, *(Very) Short History*, 6–7.
221. Gee, *(Very) Short History*, 243.

The chemistry of life's emergence, the way merely organic, carbon-containing molecules begin linking up into large, self-replicating molecules like DNA and form life, remains a mystery . . .[222]

In the words of astrophysicist Ethan Siegel, "we still cannot describe, in any sort of detail, how life first emerged, naturally, from non-life in our Universe."[223] Fellow astrophysicist Paul Sutter comments that "We do not yet know how, where, or why life first appeared on our planet."[224] Astrobiologist Nathalie A. Cabrol, who is director of the Carl Sagan Center at the SETI Institute, confirms that "Life's origin is still uncertain today . . . . we are still trying to grasp . . . what led to the dawn of life."[225] John Bryant, emeritus professor of cell and molecular biology at the University of Exeter, acknowledges that "we have no idea about how those first organisms originated."[226] Likewise, Richard Dawkins somewhat begrudgingly admits that "we still don't know—yet—exactly how the process of evolution got started."[227]

Whilst the basic building blocks of life (e.g., sugars, fats, lipids, amino acids, peptides, and nucleotides) can be formed from simpler organic compounds,[228] Brian Miller cautions that "individual reactions in the chemical pathways to synthesize life's building blocks . . . require multiple, mutually exclusive reaction conditions, so no environment could support more than a few of them."[229] Miller goes on to explain that

The challenges faced in any origin-of-life scenario related to the formation of enzymes and other proteins are immense. First, any natural process which yielded amino acids would also have produced a myriad of other molecules which would have blocked the formation of long functional chains. Second, the probability of amino acids forming a chain in even the most ideal conditions drops exponentially with its length, so none would likely have formed on the early Earth sufficiently long to correspond to nearly any of the essential proteins in a minimally functional

222. Kelvey, "Scientists Find the 'Chemistry,'" para. 1.
223. Siegel, "What We Wish We Knew," para. 11.
224. Sutter, "Improbable Origins of Life On Earth," para. 1.
225. Cabrol, *Secret Life of the Universe*, 27 & 29.
226. John Bryant in Swinerd and Bryant, *From the Big Bang to Biology*, 135.
227. Dawkins, *Outgrowing God*, 268.
228. See Kelvey, "Scientists Find the 'Chemistry'"; Oba et al., "Identifying the Wide Diversity"; Service, "Researchers May Have Solved."
229. Miller, "Thermodynamic Challenges," 310. See Tour, "We're Still Clueless," 277–306.

cell. Third, even if the probability for long-chain formation were significantly higher, all realistic processes on the Early earth would have yielded both left-handed and right-handed amino acids. However, functional proteins require amino acids of only one chirality. Even if some process could generate a solution of homochiral amino acids, it would spontaneously racemize (move toward equal quantities of both versions).[230]

Crucially, even if natural processes could both produce all the right organic building blocks, and even if they could get those building blocks to the same location at the same time, research has not shown that they can assemble into complex, self-replicating molecules.[231] Nor has research shown that they can form an information storage and retrieval system able to specify and manufacture even the simplest functional protein.[232]

Moreover, as chemist Marcos Eberlin (a member of the Brazilian Academy of Sciences) points out:

> Living cells need membranes. . . . And not just membranes, but membranes with a myriad of phospholipids and channels that enable a cell to control its internal environment. Those channels require complex and specialized proteins to function. Yet in the absence of a skilled biochemist, the necessary proteins are made only in cells. . . . Without stable membranes loaded with protein-operated channels, there are no cells. But without cells there are no proteins to form membrane channels.[233]

Thus the state of play remains that described by Arizona State University astrobiologist and theoretical physicist Sara Imari Walker:

> While a number of proposals exist for possible starting points in the pathway from non-living to living matter, these have so far not achieved states of complexity that are anywhere near that of even the simplest living systems.[234]

Thomas Nagel correctly observes that

> the origin of life remains, in light of what is known about the huge size, the extreme specificity, and the exquisite functional

230. Miller, "Thermodynamic Challenges," 310–11.
231. See Anderson, "Origin Stories."
232. See the begrudging acceptance of these points in Charlesworth and Charlesworth, *Evolution*, 128. See also Thaxton et al., *Mystery of Life's Origin: The Continuing Controversy*.
233. Eberlin, *Foresight*, 138.
234. Walker, "Origins of Life."

> precision of the genetic material . . . an event . . . to which no significant probability can be assigned on the basis of what we know of the laws of physics and chemistry.[235]

As he notes in *Mind & Cosmos*,

> the coming into existence of the genetic code . . . together with mechanisms that can read the code and carry out its instructions—seems particularly resistant to being revealed as probable given physical law alone.[236]

Nagel's focus upon the "specificity" and negligible "probability" of any life arising from pre-biotic chemistry reminds me of Bernd-Olaf Küppers's observation that "The problem of the origin of life is clearly basically equivalent to the problem of the origin of information."[237] According to Walker, "the causal role of information in biology represents one of the hardest explanatory problems for solving the origins of life."[238] Indeed, Paul Davies admits that

> Chemistry alone, however complex, can never produce the genetic code or contextual instructions. Asking chemistry to explain coded information is like expecting computer hardware to write its own software.[239]

As Stephen C. Meyer argues,

> There is simply too much information in the cell to be explained by chance alone. The information in DNA (and RNA) has also been shown to defy explanation by forces of chemical necessity. Saying otherwise would be like saying a headline arose as the result of chemical attraction between ink and paper.[240]

Meyer calculates that "The odds of getting even one functional protein of modest length (150 amino acids) by chance from a prebiotic soup is no better than 1 chance in 10^{164}."[241] That's not the odds of getting a *particular* functional protein (of this length) by chance; it's the odds of getting *any functional protein at all* (of this length). Thus, he concludes,

235. Nagel, "Dawkins and Atheism," 25.
236. Nagel, *Mind & Cosmos*, 10.
237. Küppers, *Information and the Origin*, 170–72. See also Davies, *Origin of Life*.
238. Walker, "Origins of Life," quoted by Wedgwood, *DNA*.
239. Davies, *Demon in the Machine*, 167. See ID the Future, "Discussing an Unbelievable Conversation" (Podcast); Shedinger, "Hey, Paul Davies."
240. Meyer, "Intelligent Design Is Not Creationism," para. 14.
241. Meyer, *Signature in the Cell*, 212.

it is extremely unlikely that a random search through all the possible amino acid sequences could generate even a single relatively short functional protein in the time available since the beginning of the universe.[242]

Yet even the simplest conceivable non-parasitical organism would need *hundreds* of different functional proteins. Atheist molecular biologist Eugene Koonin estimates[243] the probability of just a coupled replication-translation system arising within the observable universe at 1 in 10^{1018}!

A POSITIVE CASE FOR DESIGN

> ID aims to adhere to the same standards of rational investigation as other scientific and philosophical enterprises, and is subject to the same methods of evaluation and critique.
>
> —STEINAR THORVALDSEN, PROFESSOR OF INFORMATION SCIENCE AT THE ARCTIC UNIVERSITY OF NORWAY[244]

Over the past seventy-odd years, science has revealed the existence of functionally specified biological structures so complex that explanatory appeals to the probabilistic resources of the observable universe are hopelessly inadequate. However, far from being content to rest on the laurels of a correctly assigned burden of proof, design theorists made a *positive* case for the thesis that

> intelligent agency, as an aspect of scientific theory making, has more explanatory power in accounting for the specified, and sometimes irreducible complexity of some physical systems, including biological entities, and/or the existence of the universe as a whole, than the blind forces of . . . matter.[245]

Setting aside the issue of whether intelligent design theory can legitimately be called "science," the positive case for intelligent design can be advanced as a single, logically valid syllogism:

1. **ID Premise 1)** There exist one or more reliable tests for detecting intelligent design.

---

242. Meyer, "Evidence for Design," 75.
243. Koonin, *Logic of Chance*, referenced by Behe, *Darwin Devolves*, 105.
244. Thorvaldsen, "Intelligent Design and Natural Theology," 75.
245. Beckwith, *Law, Darwinism, and Public Education*, xiii.

2. **ID Premise 2)** Nature exhibits empirical data that pass one or more tests for reliably detecting intelligent design.

3. **Core ID Conclusion)** Therefore, at least one aspect of nature reliably signals intelligent design.

Of course, as well as claiming that the "core argument" of intelligent design theory is sound, design theorists additionally affirm:

1. **ID Premise 3)** Inferring intelligent design from empirical evidence using reliable tests is a *scientific* enterprise.

If ID Premises 1–3 are true, then if follows that we can *scientifically* infer that at least one aspect of nature reliably signals intelligent design. Although I have argued that all three premises are defensible, it is worth underscoring the fact that the question of whether intelligent design theory may legitimately be called "science" is not the same question as whether the "core argument" of intelligent design theory is sound. Arguments may be sound without being scientific (and vice versa).

The viability of a positive, scientific argument for design from biological information first struck me during my MPhil studies as I read about the informational properties of life.[246] This positive argument for intelligent design establishes an "explanatory framework" that "leads to new research questions, some of which suggest specific predictions that are testable against observations or by laboratory experiments."[247]

Contrasting Predictions

The central predictions of evolutionary theory have consistently failed while the predictions of ID have been increasingly confirmed.

—BRIAN MILLER[248]

Brian Miller reports that "Despite the reticence of many to question the official scientific orthodoxy" biologists and engineers in the field of systems biology have found themselves "forced . . . to replace historic evolutionary

---

246. See Pearcey, "DNA."

247. Meyer, *Signature in the Cell*, 481. See Reeves, "Systems Biology" (YouTube video); Science—Faith—Reason, "Intelligent Design 3.0" (YouTube video); Evolution News, "Engineers Crash the Evolution Party"; Meyer, *Signature in the Cell*, epilogue and Appendix A.

248. Miller, "Engineering Principles," 209.

assumptions with design-based assumptions, language and methods of investigation."[249] Systems biologists

> More commonly today . . . reject [the] reductionist approach as it has failed to yield any significant understanding of the organisation of living systems. Instead, they now recognize that they must look at life as a collection of integrated systems composed of integrated components where the whole is greater than the sum of the parts.[250]

As Miller observes,

> Evolutionists have long stated that the key difference in predictions between evolutionary and design-based models is the extent to which biological systems demonstrate suboptimal (or non-functional) bottom-up design that resembles Rube-Goldberg machines verses optimal, top-down design that resembles human engineering. The latest research has continuously affirmed the design-based predictions.[251]

Indeed,

> In stark contrast to evolutionary predictions, mounting evidence demonstrates that life consistently demonstrates optimal design. . . . Purported examples of poor design usually represent opinions resulting from armchair critics' limited understanding of the technical literature and their lack of training in engineering . . . systems biologists increasingly recognise that assuming optimal design leads to the most productive research.[252]

In other words, the "optimal design" prediction is warranted by a) an analogy with human engineering, and/or b) an inference from the expanding data set of observed optimality exhibited by systems that pass a design inference, and/or c) by the heuristic value to research of the optimality assumption.

Of course, the concept of "optimal design" doesn't hold biology to an unrealistic standard of absolute, abstract perfection: "Many natural and artificial designs exhibit 'constrained optimality,' where parts have to work together against competing interests."[253] As philosopher Jay Richards points out using the example of a laptop computer,

---

249. Miller, "Engineering Principles," 180. See Evolution News, "Engineers Crash the Evolution Party"; Reeves, "Systems Biology."
250. Miller, "Engineering Principles," 181.
251. Miller, "Engineering Principles," 189.
252. Miller, "Engineering Principles," 184–85.
253. Evolution News, "DNA a Stupid Design?," para. 28.

You don't want the largest monitor, the biggest hard disk, and the fastest processor when you want a product that can fit in a shoulder bag or sit on a lap without starting the user's clothes on fire. You want the best all-around design—something that hits the "sweet spot" between competing design goals.[254]

The theory of entirely blind evolution predicts the prevalence of non-functional and suboptimal "designs," whereas intelligent design theory recognizes and predicts the prevalence of functional designs exhibiting constrained optimality, though accompanied by the generally degradative effects of natural processes.[255]

Evolutionary biologists predicted that the random nature of genetic mutations would mean genomes are swamped with non-functional "junk DNA."[256] This prediction appeared to be confirmed by the fact that only 2 percent of the human genome coded for proteins, leaving the other 98 percent to be labeled as "junk DNA." The existence of so much "junk DNA" was presented as an argument for the blind watchmaker thesis and against design. Thus, in a 1994 essay, evolutionary biologist Kenneth Miller wrote that:

> the human genome is littered with pseudogenes, gene fragments, "orphaned" genes, "junk" DNA, and so many repeated copies of pointless DNA sequences that it cannot be attributed to anything that resembles intelligent design.[257]

By contrast, in a 1998 essay, design theorist William A. Dembski commented,

> [Intelligent] design is not a science stopper. Indeed, design can foster inquiry where traditional evolutionary approaches obstruct it. Consider the term "junk DNA." Implicit in this term is the view that because the genome of an organism has been cobbled together through a long, undirected evolutionary process,

---

254. Example from Jay Richards, cited by Evolution News, "DNA a Stupid Design?," para. 28.

255. For a critique of Richard Dawkins's use of the "bad design" argument in general, and his claim that vertebrate eyes are poorly designed in particular, see Williams, *Outgrowing God?*, 170–74. See also Behe, "Malodorous Argument for Darwinian Evolution"; Burgess, "Why the Ankle-Foot Complex"; Evolution News, "Design Can Be Suboptimal on Purpose"; Glicksman and Laufmann, "Supposed Bad Design"; McLatchie, "Argument from Suboptimal Design"; Miller, "Why Systems Biologists Now Assume"; Nelson, "Jettison the Arguments, or the Rule?"; Behe, *Darwin Devolves*; Bergman, *Poor Design*; Laufmann and Glicksman, *Your Designed Body*; Wells, *Zombie Science*, chaps. 6 and 7.

256. See Miller, "Why Systems Biologists Now Assume."

257. Miller, "Life's Grand Design," 32.

> the genome is a patchwork of which only limited portions are essential to the organism. Thus on an evolutionary view we expect a lot of useless DNA. If, on the other hand, organisms are designed, we expect DNA, as much as possible, to exhibit function.... Design encourages scientists to look for function where evolution discourages it.[258]

In sum, while the Darwinian research paradigm predicted more junk than function, and readily assumed that genes that didn't code for proteins were genetic garbage, the intelligent design research paradigm predicted more function than junk, and assumed that further research would reveal functionality in so-called "junk DNA."

To quote a recent paper in *Genome Biology and Evolution*, "The days of 'junk DNA' are over."[259] As Casey Luskin reports: "Numerous examples of function have been discovered for so-called junk DNA ... the more we study the genome, the more we detect function for non-coding DNA."[260] A prime example of research demonstrating the functionality of so-called "junk DNA" came in 2012, when

> the journal *Nature* reported the results of a years-long research project, involving over 400 international scientists studying the functions of non-coding DNA in humans. Called the ENCODE Project, its set of 30 groundbreaking papers reported that the "vast majority" of the genome has function. The lead paper reporting ENCODE's results stated: *These data enabled us to assign biochemical functions for 80 [percent] of the genome, in particular outside of the well-studied protein-coding regions.* Ewan Birney, ENCODE's lead analysis coordinator commented in *Discover Magazine* that since ENCODE looked at only 147 types of cells, and the human body has a few thousand, "It's likely that 80 percent will go to 100 percent." The same article quoted Tom Gingeras, a senior scientist with ENCODE, noting that, "Almost every nucleotide is associated with a function of some sort or another, and we now know where they are, what binds to them, what their associations are, and more."[261]

Much of what was formerly dismissed as genetic "junk" has been shown to have functions in repairing DNA, assisting in DNA replication, regulating DNA transcription, aiding in the folding and maintenance of chromosomes,

---

258. Dembski, "Intelligent Science and Design," 21–27.
259. McGrath, "'Junk DNA' No More."
260. Luskin, "Problem 10." See also Wells, *Myth of Junk DNA*.
261. Luskin, "Problem 10." See Young, "ENCODE."

controlling RNA editing and splicing, helping to fight disease or regulating embryological development.²⁶² As Paul Davies comments,

> For a long while much of the non-coding DNA segments were dismissed as junk, as serving no useful biological function. But increasingly there is evidence that much of the "junk" plays a crucial role in the manufacture of other types of molecules, such as short strands of RNA, which regulate a whole range of cellular functions. Cells are beginning to look like bottomless pits of complexity.²⁶³

Biochemist Dan Graur ruefully muses that

> If the human genome is indeed devoid of junk DNA as implied by the ENCODE project, then a long, undirected evolutionary process cannot explain the human genome. If, on the other hand, organisms are designed, then all DNA, or as much as possible, is expected to exhibit function. If ENCODE is right, then evolution is wrong.²⁶⁴

THE SHADOW OF THE ALMIGHTY

The debate about intelligent design theory is often overshadowed by and/or conflated with the God debate. In the candid words of geneticist Richard Lewontin,

> It is not that the methods . . . of science somehow compel us to accept a material explanation of the . . . world, but, on the contrary, that we are forced by our . . . adherence to material causes to create . . . a set of concepts that produce material explanations, no matter how counterintuitive, no matter how mystifying. Moreover, that materialism is absolute, for we cannot allow a Divine foot in the door.²⁶⁵

---

262. Somewhat confusingly, non-protein-coding but functional genetic information is referred to as (and included within the concept of) "epigenetic" information. See Evolution News, "Caltech Finds Amazing Role"; Evolution News, "Next Phase of ENCODE"; Evolution News, "As Research Advances"; Luskin, "Paper Shows 'Mutational Load' Arguments"; Luskin, "Problem 10"; Evolution News, "Jonathan Wells Was Right"; Wells, *Myth of Junk DNA*.

263. Davies, *Demon in the Machine*, 113.

264. Graur, Dan (Slide 16), as cited by Miller, "Engineering Principles Explain Biological Systems," 185.

265. Lewontin, "Billions and Billions of Demons."

However, intelligent design theory is *not* an exercise in "creation science"[266] or even "theistic science."[267] Nor is it an exercise in "natural theology."[268] Rather, as Meyer explains,

> ID holds that there are tell-tale features of living systems and the universe that are best explained by a designing intelligence. The theory does not challenge the idea of evolution defined as change over time, or even common ancestry, but it disputes Darwin's idea that the cause of biological change is wholly blind and undirected.[269]

To quote Professor Steinar Thorvaldsen, professor of information science at the Arctic University of Norway:

> The designer that eventually emerges from ID-theory is an intelligence capable of originating the complexity and specificity that we find throughout the universe, especially in biological systems. The designer of ID is not the God of any particular philosophical reflection or the God of any particular religion, but merely an intelligent source that is capable of initiating certain features of the natural world.[270]

Just as philosophers are free to build metaphysical arguments for God upon the scientific theory of the Big Bang,[271] without thereby stripping cosmology of its scientific status, so they are free to build metaphysical arguments for God upon the scientific theory of intelligent design, without thereby stripping intelligent design theory of its scientific status.[272] After all, there's an obvious gap (a gap highlighted by David Hume, as discussed in the Preface) between the proposition that something in nature is designed

---

266. See Beckwith, *Law, Darwinism, and Public Education*; Dembski, "In Defence of Intelligent Design."

267. See Moreland, *"Theistic Science & Methodological Naturalism."*

268. See Beckwith, *Law, Darwinism, and Public Education*; Dembski, "Is Intelligent Design?"; Luskin, "Is Intelligent Design Theory?"

269. Meyer, "Intelligent Design Is Not Creationism."

270. Thorvaldsen, "Intelligent Design and Natural Theology."

271. See Turek et al., "Is the Cosmological Argument Still Sound?" (YouTube video); FOCLOnline, "Can We Believe in God in an Age of Science? The Big Bang & Cosmic 'Fine Tuning'" (YouTube video); FOCLOnline, "Can We Believe in God in an Age of Science? Cosmology and God" (YouTube video); Williams, "Christian Worldview and Science in Apologetic Perspective: Cosmos" (Podcast); Copan and Craig, *Kalam Cosmological Argument*, Vol 2; Meyer, *Return of the God Hypothesis*; Williams, *Faithful Guide to Philosophy*, chap. 5.

272. See Gordon, "Is Intelligent Design Science?"; Meyer, "Scientific Status."

and the conclusion that the designer was God! To quote British philosopher A. E. Taylor (1869–1945),

> An argument from the "marks of design" in nature . . . will never *of itself* amount to "proof of the being of *God*." To believe in God is to believe in something much more than the presence . . . of intelligence at work in nature. It must at least be a belief in a purposive intelligence which is supreme, and whose purposes are without qualification good. And this is something more than [design reasoning] will warrant.[273]

As neo-atheist Sam Harris observes, "Even if we accepted that our universe simply had to be designed by a designer, this would not suggest that this designer is the biblical God, or that He approves of Christianity."[274]

Filling in the gap between "intelligent design" and "designed by God" (let alone "designed by the God of a particular religious tradition") takes us beyond "the design inference" made by intelligent design theory and into the philosophical realm of "natural theology." That is, a logically valid argument for God can be based upon intelligent design theory, but *only by adding an additional, metaphysical premise to the core argument for ID*:

1. There exist one or more reliable tests for detecting intelligent design.
2. Nature exhibits empirical data that passes one or more tests for reliably detecting intelligent design.
3. Therefore, at least one aspect of nature reliably signals intelligent design.
4. The best explanation for intelligent design within nature is monotheistic.
5. Therefore, the presence of intelligent design within nature supports the case for monotheism.

The necessity for a premise that bridges the logical gap between steps 3 and 5 of this argument gives the lie to the claim that intelligent design theory is an inherently theological project.[275] Only those who think that premises 1, 2 and 4 are jointly more plausible than their denial will think that the above argument is sound.

---

273. Taylor, *Does God Exist?*, 90.

274. Harris, *Letter to a Christian Nation*, 73.

275. For example, see Williams, "Simulation Hypothesis" (YouTube playlist); Mines, "Simulation Hypothesis."

The question of design must be approached in what physicist turned theologian Sir John Polkinghorne (1930–2021) called a "bottom-up" manner. *First* we detect design, *then* we ask who the best designer candidate is in this particular case. Whatever answer we give to the latter question (and we may remain agnostic on the issue), the fact remains that we have evidence for design *by something capable of producing the design in question.* As Michael J. Behe insists,

> my argument is limited to design itself; I strongly emphasize that it is not an argument for the existence of a benevolent God . . . I recognize that philosophy and theology may be able to extend the argument. But a scientific argument for design in biology does not reach that far.[276]

ONE SHORT ARGUMENT

Nobel laureate Brian Josephson affirms that "intelligent design is valid science."[277] Danish biologist Jørn Dyerberg, Professor Emeritus in Human Nutrition at the University of Copenhagen, concurs that "Intelligent Design is a scientific discipline."[278] Although the scientific status of ID was the first question I settled in my own mind, it is really a secondary question; for if the core ID argument is unsound, according it scientific status would be a matter of relative insignificance; whereas, if the core ID argument is sound, it becomes implausible not to accorded it scientific status.

While it is gratifying to note that many atheistic scholars (e.g., Richard Dawkins, Bradley Monton, Thomas Nagel, Victor J. Stenger) agree with me in according scientific status to ID, the debate about whether or not intelligent design theory is science clearly isn't as important as the debate about whether or not it is *true*.

At its core, intelligent design theory advances a simple, logically valid argument. A variety of scholars who disagree with intelligent design theory accept the premise that there are one or more reliable tests for design.[279] The crucial question is actually whether any aspect of the natural world passes such a test. It seems to me that many aspects of the natural world do just that.

---

276. Behe, "Modern Intelligent Design Hypothesis," 165.

277. Josephson, from his cover endorsement to the 2023 paperback edition of Meyer, *Return of the God Hypothesis.*

278. Pultz, "Our Danish Correspondent."

279. See Williams, "Design Inference from Specified Complexity."

Chapter Two

Reflections on Natural Theology

the evidence for theism has never been so clear and so strong as it is now.
—Robert C. Koons[1]

I HAVE FAITH *IN* God; that is, I give my trusting allegiance to God.[2] I also believe *that* God exists. On the assumption that beauty is an objective value,[3] the God in whom I believe and trust can be defined as being not only unsurpassably beautiful, but as having a necessarily existing essential nature that exhibits the maximal beauty of having "the greatest possible array of compossible [i.e., possible together] great-making properties."[4] Moreover, I believe this God to be the very same Trinitarian God[5] revealed

1. Koons, "Science and Theism," 73.

2. See Williams, "Nature of Faith" (YouTube playlist); McKaughan and Howard-Snyder, "Faith"; McKaughan, "Value of Faith and Faithfulness"; Howard Snyder, "Does Faith Entail Belief?"; Pojman, "Faith Without Belief?"; Pruss, "Christian Faith and Belief"; Himma, "Christian Faith Without Belief"; Swinburne, *Faith and Reason*, Second Edition. On the interpretation of Heb 11:6 (a topic discussed in some of the above sources), see Williams, "Hebrews 11 and Faith" (Podcast); Hartley, "Reassessment of the Translation 'God Exists,'" 289–230.

3. See Williams, "Beauty" (YouTube playlist); Cowen and Spiegel, *Love of Wisdom*, chap. 9; DeWeese and Moreland, *Philosophy Made Slightly Less Difficult*, Second Edition, chap. 7; Groothuis, *Truth Decay*; Lewis, *Abolition of Man*; Taliaferro, *Aesthetics*; Tallon, "Theistic Argument from Beauty"; Williams, *Faithful Guide to Philosophy*, chap. 14; Williams, *I Wish I Could Believe*, chap. 6.

4. Morris, *Our Idea of God*, 37.

5. See Williams, "Trinity" (YouTube playlist); Williams, "Sermon: Revelation

in and through the Bible, "the God of Abraham, the God of Isaac, and the God of Jacob" (Exod 3:6) who is also "the God and Father of our Lord Jesus Christ" (1 Pet 1:3). Finally, I believe that the case for God's existence is stronger than the case against.[6]

This chapter introduces some of the positive philosophical reasons that can be given for belief in the existence of a being worthy of the name "God." Our third and final chapter will cover some of the reasons to believe that "God" is in fact the God of Christianity, as revealed in and by Jesus of Nazareth.

EXPLORING THE GOD QUESTION

The philosophical exploration of "the God question" and its worldview ramifications has been a consistent theme in my life and work. This is a topic of perennial interest that I've been privileged to write about in various books and journals, and to speak about and/or debate not only around the United Kingdom, but also in several other countries.

1:1–8" (Podcast); Copan, "Is the Trinity a Logical Blunder?"; Craig, "Doctrine of the Trinity"; Davies, "Somewhat Playful Proof of the Social Trinity"; Hasker, "Deception and the Trinity"; Hasker, "Objections to Social Trinitarianism"; Williams, "Understanding the Trinity"; Craig, *Philosophy of Religion*; Moreland and Craig, *Philosophical Foundations* (2nd edition); Morris, *Our Idea of God*; Morris, *Logic of God Incarnate*; Murray and Rea, *Introduction to the Philosophy of Religion*; Shumack, *Wisdom of Islam*; Senor, "Incarnation and the Trinity"; Swinburne, *Was Jesus God?*; Swinburne, *Christian God*; Richard of St Victor, *On the Trinity*.

6. See O'Leary-Hawthorn, "Arguments for Atheism"; Shalkowski, "Atheological Apologetics." For some responses specific to the "problem of evil" objection to theism, see Williams, "Problem of Evil" (YouTube playlist); "Practical Apologetics for a Christian Way of Life: The Evidential Problem of Evil" (YouTube video); and "Practical Apologetics for a Christian Way of Life: The Logical Problem of Evil" (YouTube video); Clark, "I Believe in God the Father"; Copan, "God Can't Possibly Exist"; Craig, "Problem of Evil"; Craig, *On Guard*, chap. 7; Williams, *Faithful Guide to Philosophy*, chap. 17. On the "Hiddenness of God" argument for atheism, see Beilby, "Divine Hiddenness"; Evans, *Natural Signs and Knowledge of God*, especially chap. 6.

Fig. 8. On a speaking trip to Athens in 2013, I visited the sixth-century B.C. Theatre of Dionysus, at the foot of the Parthenon, where the classical Greek plays I'd read in Classical Civilization back in college had originally been performed.

It seems to me that most arguments for God try to formalize, and so rationally and explicitly motivate, the recognition of relationships between God and creation. Each relationship uncovered adds to our understanding of God. Many of these relationships are intuitively perceived (as being at least plausible) by most people.

In this context I note with appreciation C. Stephen Evans's appropriation of Thomas Reid's concept of "natural signs" to articulating a nuanced understanding of the link between intuitions grounded in people's lived experience (i.e., phenomenology) and natural theology. For example, in discussing the cosmological argument, Evans suggests that:

> The perception of the world as contingent, as something that might never have been, is closely linked to the contrasting notion of something that lacks this character, something whose existence is in some way impervious to non-existence . . . a reality that has a deeper and firmer grasp on existence than the things we see around us.[7]

Intuition plays a key role in philosophy, and so in all intellectual pursuits. As C. S. Lewis observed: "You cannot produce rational intuition by argument, because argument depends upon rational intuition. Proof rests

---

7. Evans, *Natural Signs and Knowledge of God*, 62, 63.

upon the unprovable which just has to be 'seen.'"[8] This is one reason (contra the "New Atheists") it doesn't do to see reason and faith—taking the latter in the sense of *trust* and *allegiance*—as opposed to one-another by nature. Rationality requires faith. However, faith should be exercised with wisdom. While some intuitions (e.g., intuitions of the basic laws of logic, or of one's own existence) are indubitable, others carry varying degrees of *prima facie* warrant, such that "if one carefully reflects on something, and a certain viewpoint intuitively seems to be true, then one is justified in believing that viewpoint in the absence of overriding counterarguments (which will ultimately rely on alternative intuitions)."[9]

From childhood, I found it natural to trust the *prima facie* appearance of my irreducibly first-person experience, the appearance that I was an embodied but more than bodily self, and that I had a degree of freedom connected to a moral responsibility to think and to judge and to act well according to the interlinked objective values of truth, goodness and beauty (and their parasitical shadows of falsehood, evil and ugliness). It also seemed to me that I was part of a world of selves and other objects of intricate complexity and grandeur that had some meaningful purpose. And I found it natural to believe that behind all of this stood the reality of a divine Creator.

Now, I realize that (beyond indubitable intuitions) such appearances are the beginning of a philosophical conversation, rather than the end of the discussion. Nevertheless, I think it's important to recognize that this is where the conversation begins, and that the ensuing discussion proceeds on the basis of a principled credulity.

Of course, "an appeal to intuitions does not rule out the use of additional arguments that add further support to that appeal;"[10] and I think the arguments for accepting the above description of reality are stronger than those against—as atheist philosopher Thomas Nagel reminds us, "Philosophy has to proceed comparatively."[11] Concerning ultimate reality, I think

---

8. Lewis, "Why I am Not a Pacifist," 67.

9. Moreland and Craig, *Philosophical Foundations*, 422. See also CCA. "Phenomenal Conservatism"; Huemer, "Compassionate Phenomenal Conservatism"; Stoke, *Shot of Faith*.

10. Moreland and Craig, *Philosophical Foundations*, 422.

11. Nagel, *Mind and Cosmos*, 127.

there are sound and mutually re-enforcing cases against naturalism/materialism[12] and for monotheism.[13]

There's a far broader range of theistic arguments than most people realize. In his bestselling book *The God Delusion*, Richard Dawkins devotes just *thirty-seven pages* to rejecting just *ten* theistic arguments. Alvin Plantinga once presented a paper outlining "a couple of dozen or so" theistic arguments.[14] Not that I'd endorse *every* argument mentioned by Plantinga's paper, but the point stands.

Moreover, theistic arguments come in "families" that deal with the same general theme (e.g., teleological arguments deal with design, cosmological arguments deal with causality, axiological arguments deal with value, etc.) in different ways (e.g., appealing to different premises and/or using different argumentative forms).

Initial Thoughts

As a three-year-old, I surprised my mother by stopping in the middle of a road crossing to ask her: "If God made everything, who made God?" She doesn't remember her response, though it presumably satisfied me enough at the time to get me out of the road!

12. See Williams, "Problems with Materialism/Metaphysical Naturalism" (YouTube playlist); Williams, "Imagine Naturalism" (YouTube video); Craig and Moreland, *Naturalism*; Dennett and Plantinga, *Science and Religion*; Goetz and Taliaferro, *Naturalism*; Menuge, *Agents Under Fire*; Menuge, et al., eds., *Minding the Brian*; Moreland, *Recalcitrant Imago Dei*; Nagel, *Mind and Cosmos*; Reppert, *C. S. Lewis' Dangerous Idea*; Swinburne, *Mind, Brain, and Free Will*; Williams, *C.S. Lewis vs. the New Atheists*; Williams, *Faithful Guide to Philosophy*.

13. See Williams, "Natural Theology" (YouTube playlist); Williams, "Debating God" (YouTube playlist); Williams, "Arguing for God (Oslo, 2022)" (Podcast); Beck, "God's Existence"; Craig, "Five Arguments for God"; Evans, "Mystery of Persons and Belief in God"; Kreeft and Tacelli, "Twenty Arguments for God's Existence"; Plantinga, "Two Dozen (or so) Arguments for God"; Swinburne, "Evidence for God"; Willard, "Language, Being, God"; Beck, *Does God Exist?*; Copan, "Naturalists Are Declaring the Glory of God"; Copan and Taliaferro, *Naturalness of Belief*; Copan and Moser, *Rationality of Theism*; Craig and Moreland, *Blackwell Companion to Natural Theology*; Craig, *Does God Exist?*; Geivett and Sweetman, *Contemporary Perspectives on Religious Epistemology*; Meyer, *Return of the God Hypothesis*; Moreland, *Consciousness and the Existence of God*; Moreland and Craig, *Philosophical Foundations* (2nd edition); Sennett and Groothuis, *In Defence of Natural Theology*; Swinburne, *Is There a God?* rev. ed.; Swinburne, *Existence of God*, second edition; Walls and Dougherty, *Two Dozen (or so) Arguments*; Williams, *Universe From Someone*; *Outgrowing God?*; *Faithful Guide to Philosophy*; and *C.S. Lewis vs. the New Atheists*.

14. Plantinga, "Two Dozen (or so) Arguments for God." See Walls and Dougherty, *Two Dozen (or so) Arguments*.

Perhaps this early interest in the nature of God's existence explains the intellectual satisfaction I would later find in grappling with the cosmological argument (especially through reading philosophers like F. C. Copleston, W. David Beck, J. P. Moreland, Bruce Reichenbach, Richard Taylor and Dallas Willard).[15]

Of course, the answer to the question posed by my three-year-old self is that "God" isn't the sort of thing that needs to be made to exist by a cause outside of itself. On the contrary, "God" designates the uncreated, non-dependent (i.e., independent) Creator of all reality besides God, the non-contingent (i.e., necessary) cause of all contingent reality.[16]

This answer is *not* an exception to the logic of causality designed to smuggle God into the picture, but is both part-and-parcel of the traditional monotheistic concept of what's meant by "God," and a conclusion forced upon us *by* the logic of causality.

Suppose I ask you to loan me a certain book, but you say: "I don't have a copy right now, but I'll ask my friend to lend me his copy and then I'll lend it to you." Suppose your friend says the same thing to you, and so on. Two things are clear. First, if the process of asking to borrow the book goes on *ad infinitum*, I'll never get the book. Second, if I get the book, the process that led to me getting it can't have gone on *ad infinitum*. Somewhere down the line of requests to borrow the book, someone *had* the book *without having to borrow it*. Likewise, argues Richard Purtill, consider any contingent or dependent (e.g., physical) reality that receives its existence from something outside of itself:

> the same two principles apply. If the process of everything getting its existence from something else went on to infinity, then the thing in question would never [have] existence. And if the thing has . . . existence then the process hasn't gone on to

---

15. See Williams, "Cosmological Arguments for God" (YouTube playlist); Beck, "God's Existence"; Taylor, "Cosmological Argument"; Willard, "Language, Being, God"; Beck, *Does God Exist?*, chap. 2; Russell and Copleston, "Debate on the Existence of God"; Sadowsky, "Endless Regress of Causes?"; Moreland, *Scaling the Secular City*, chap. 1; Rasmussen, "Argument for a Supreme Foundation"; Reichenbach, *Cosmological Argument*.

16. See Williams, "Who Made God?" The distinctions between contingent (possible not to exist) and necessary (not possible not to exist) existence, and between dependent (having a cause outside of itself) and independent (having no cause outside of itself) existence, can and often do co-inside (e.g., physical things are contingent and thus dependent), but they are not synonymous. Something can have an existence that is both necessary and dependent if it is dependent upon something necessary that necessarily causes its existence.

infinity. There was something that had existence without having to receive it from something else . . .[17]

It is impossible for everything to be the sort of thing that needs to be caused to exist by something outside of itself. On the assumption that *everything* requires an external cause of its existence, since a thing must exist in order to cause anything, and since there is nothing outside of *everything*, it follows that nothing would exist. But something does exist. Therefore, it is not the case that everything requires an external cause, and that means there is something that exists without requiring an external cause of its existence. And, to quote Thomas Aquinas, "this we call God" (especially when we consider this particular argument in the context of the overall cumulative case for monotheism).

We cannot equate "God" with the universe because the universe is a physical reality, and physical realities are contingent, dependent realities. As philosopher Dallas Willard argued:

> the dependent character of all physical states, together with the completeness of the series of dependencies underlying the existence of any given physical state, logically implies at least one self-existent, and therefore nonphysical, state of being.[18]

A self-existent being explaining all of physical reality can't be a physical reality (since then it would have to be explanatorily prior to itself, which is impossible). The most credible remaining possibilities are an abstract object or an immaterial mind. But abstract objects (even granting their existence) are by definition causally impotent. Therefore, the best explanation of the physical universe is a "self-existent, and therefore nonphysical" Creative Mind.

Some might be tempted to think the need for a "self-existent, and therefore nonphysical" Creative Mind (i.e., "God") can be avoided by postulating that the causal regress behind the existence of any particular contingent thing is actually infinite (i.e., that "everything" is "A collection of definite and discrete members whose number is greater than any natural number"[19]). Indeed, the denial that anything has necessary existence combines with the acknowledgement that something exists to entail the existence of an actually infinite causal regress. But why think the postulate of an actually infinite causal regress does any useful explanatory work? Each supposed member of such an actually infinite series of contingent things is *a contingent thing that cannot exist unless it is caused to exist by a previous*

17. Purtill quoted by Taliaferro, *Contemporary Philosophy of Religion*, 358–359.
18. Willard, "Language, Being, God."
19. Beliefmap, "Infinity/Impossible/Paradoxes."

member of the series that actually exists, for only existing things can cause anything. However, *no* member of such a series can actually exist in order to cause the existence of any other member of the series *unless it is caused to exist by a previous member of the series that actually exists.* Each member of this hypothetically infinite causal series is in just as much of an existential bind as any and all of the others. As Bruce R. Reichenbach argues:

> Suppose we have an infinite series, such that a is caused by b, which in turn and at the same time is caused by c . . . and so on to infinity. The series is actually infinite, and each cause is in a transitive causal relation to another cause . . . . since the series continues indefinitely, the explanation of a is deferred indefinitely. Consequently, this type of series can never yield any sufficient reason for the existence of a . . . . the explanation is continually being deferred.[20]

W. David Beck illustrates Reichenbach's point by analogy with explaining the motion of a boxcar in a train:

> It is tempting to settle the problem of ultimate causal explanation by noting that each boxcar is being pulled by the one in front of it. But this is where transitivity becomes crucial. It may well be true that boxcar A is pulled by boxcar B. But B can pull A only because B is being pulled by C. The pulling action of B is transitive. It occurs only because B is, in turn, pulled by C. And so it is also true that A is being pulled by C. And C, and therefore A, is pulled by D, and so on . . . . An infinity of boxcars will still leave unsolved the problem of explaining why the first boxcar [boxcar A] is moving and hence why any are. The problem is not with the arrangement of boxcars, nor is it a matter of the number of boxcars. The problem is that no boxcar in the chain has the capacity to generate or initiate its own motion. It can pass on the pulling, but it does not initiate it. Likewise, the problem with everything we know of in the universe is its contingency. The supposition that the causal nexus is constituted by infinitely many contingent objects fails to be an ultimate explanation for the existence of any individual object in the nexus. There has been no full accounting for the existence of even the first item of the sequence currently under observation.[21]

Hence, to assume that if God exists then this can only be because something outside of God makes him exist, is not only to beg the question

---

20. Reichenbach, *Cosmological Argument*, 16–17.
21. Beck, "God's Existence."

against the traditional conception of God as the uncreated Creator, but to assume both the possibility and explanatory sufficiency of an actually infinite regress of causes. If reason suggests we shouldn't believe in the existence or explanatory sufficiency of an actually infinite regress of contingent causes, then reason suggests both that the "who made God" question is malformed, and that we have good reason to believe in "God."

In the Beginning

Having been born (in September 1974) to Christian parents who raised me within the community of a Baptist Church in the south-coast English city of Portsmouth, my spiritual maturation was (and is) a process of ratcheting understanding and ongoing re-commitment within "the faith that God has once for all given to his people" (Jude 1:3, CEV). My parents were both science teachers who encouraged me to think about everything, not least the relationship between science and theology,[22] so I didn't take Christianity lightly. I knew other people have different worldviews.[23] Moreover, my

---

22. See Williams, "Christianity and Science" (YouTube playlist); Williams, "Christian Worldview and Science in Apologetic Perspective: Introduction" (Podcast); Koons, "Science and Theism"; Lennox, *Cosmic Chemistry*; Pearcey and Thaxton, *Soul of Science*; Ratzsch, *Science and Its Limits*; Williams, *Faithful Guide to Philosophy*, chap. 16.

23. See Williams "Understanding Worldviews" (YouTube playlist); Sire, *Universe Next Door*.

parents had taught me to play chess by the time I was five, which probably encouraged my capacity for logical thought.

Fig. 9. Getting familiar with chess pieces at circa. fourteen months old, January/February 1976.

My mother began reading C. S. Lewis's *Narnia* books to me when I was five, and I was reading them for myself by *Prince Caspian* at six or seven. As I matured, I absorbed much of Lewis's non-fiction, beginning with the handful of volumes in my parent's book collection, including *Mere Christianity*, *The Problem of Pain*, and *Miracles*. Together with other books from the same source, especially Keith Ward's *The Battle for the Soul*, my interest in philosophy was kindled.[24]

At sixth-form college in the early 1990s I studied A Levels in English Literature, Music, and Classical Civilization. The latter subject introduced me to ancient Greek literature (including Plato's *Apology*) and stoked my interest in philosophy to the point that I wrote my dissertation on the

---

24. The "other books" included Hawthorne's *Windows on Science and Christian Faith*; Pine-Coffin's translation of *Saint Augustine's Confessions*; and Ramm's *Christian View of Science and Scripture*.

influence of polytheistic and monotheistic worldviews upon the development of "scientific" thought in Greek culture.

I was further stimulated to explore the intellectual dimension of faith by a friend from college. A student of the natural sciences as well as an excellent musician, David Bacon was "a bright cookie." Together, we helped lead the college Christian Union, and formed a band (mainly playing covers of Pink Floyd, Led Zeppelin, etc).[25] Having studied at Cambridge University, Dr. Bacon is now Professor and director of the Institute of Cosmology and Gravitation at the University of Portsmouth, and a fellow congregant of the Church of England.

University

When I went to Cardiff University in 1993, it was to study a joint degree in English Literature and Music. However, as a humanities student, I had to take three subjects in the first year, and chose philosophy as my third course. Here I discovered part of the University that actively invited rational discourse about the factuality and significance of God's existence or non-existence. While some of my teachers were atheists (e.g., Professor Christopher Norris, whom I'd later debate on God's existence[26]), I was taught Philosophy of Religion by an agnostic, and my personal tutor—Professor Michael Durrant (1934–2018)[27]—was a Christian.

Professor Durrant served as Head of Cardiff University's Department of Philosophy from May to September 1987, and then as Head of the Philosophy Section of Cardiff's School of English Studies, Journalism, and Philosophy until 1991. He was a member of the Executive Committee of the British Society for the Philosophy of Religion at its inception, and a founder-member and first President of the European Society for the Philosophy of Religion. As well as being my personal tutor, the pipe-smoking Professor (who spent some of his spare time as a church organist) taught my lecture course on Aristotle, and served as President of the Student Philosophical Society that I and some coursemates established. I recall Professor Durrant lecturing from memory, often with his eyes closed, and even from a recumbent position on the desk at the head of the lecture room!

---

25. For recordings of our band playing at our College leaver's day celebrations in 1993, see http://podcast.peterswilliams.com/e/utopia-in-concert-tracks-from-college-leavers-day-gig-1993/. For more information, see my "Musical Auto-Biography" at www.peterswilliams.com/composing/.

26. See Bradford, "Cardiff University 'Does God Exist?' Debate."

27. See "Obituaries: Michael Durrant."

Fig. 10. My room in my first-year halls of residence (University Hall) at Cardiff University. Yes, that is a CD/Audio-Cassette player on my desk, next to my extremely high-tech electronic word-processor.

Fig. 11. Playing a grand piano in the music department at Cardiff University.

During my first year at Cardiff, I experienced a growing frustration with the postmodernism of the English Literature department at that time, a frustration that bled in two directions. On the one hand, I found an outlet for enjoying creative writing in my philosophy assignments. For example, I wrote an essay on Aristotle's distinction between primary and secondary matter in the form of a dialogue between a man and a Sphinx, conducted in iambic pentameter. On the other hand, I wrote what was basically a philosophy essay for my English Literature course, critiquing French atheist philosopher and literary critic Roland Barthes's rejection of authorial intent.

The Resurrection of the Author

Barthes's "death of the author" was a self-contradictory rejection of objective meaning, both in literary texts and "the world as text" authored by God:

> We know now that a text is not a line of words releasing a single "theological" meaning (the "message" of the Author-God) . . . Once the Author is removed, the claim to decipher a text becomes quite futile. To give a text an Author is to impose a limit on that text, to furnish it with a final signified . . . writing ceaselessly posits meaning ceaselessly to evaporate it, carrying out a systematic exemption of meaning. In precisely this way literature (it would be better from now on to say writing), by refusing to assign a "secret", an ultimate meaning, to the text (and to the world as text), liberates what may be called an antitheological activity, an activity . . . that is truly revolutionary since to refuse to fix meaning is, in the end, to refuse God and his hypostases—reason, science, law.[28]

Barthes's "death of the author" was the application to literature of the existential philosophy that shrouds the acceptance of an objective nihilism with the subjective meanings of supposedly self-made people. The obvious question here is, did Barthes *intend* or *mean* to communicate this philosophy to his readers?

If removing the author renders any claim to decipher what a text signifies "quite futile," it necessarily renders quite futile any claim—even a claim on the part of a text's author—that one has *mis*interpreted what a text signifies. But as William Lane Craig wryly comments: "nobody adopts a Postmodernist view of literary texts when reading the labels on a medicine bottle or a box of rat poison!"[29]

28. Barthes, "Death of the Author," 142–48.
29. Craig, "Resurrection of Theism."

If denying God's existence means denying that "the world as text" has an objective meaning (the kind of meaning that we discover rather than invent), it follows that the only way to coherently affirm that the world has an objective meaning is to affirm the existence of God as its "Author." This is one justification for Mortimer J. Adler's statement that: "More consequences for thought and action follow the affirmation or denial of God than from answering any other basic question."[30] In other words—as atheist philosophers such as Friedrich Nietzsche, Bertrand Russell and Jean-Paul Sartre recognized—the question of God's existence is not a question of merely academic interest, but a question of existential import.[31] Indeed, if we embrace a properly basic rational intuition of the meaningfulness of reality, we can reverse Barthes's argument into an argument for God.[32]

During a Q&A time with our lecturers at the end of the first-year English Literature course, I asked for a response to a quotation that I thought skewered the claim of postmodern hermeneutics to "see through" authorial intent and objective meaning:

> You cannot go on seeing through things for ever. The whole point of seeing through something is to see something through it. It is good that the window should be transparent, because the street or garden beyond it is opaque. How if you saw through the garden too? It is no use trying to see through first principles. If you see through everything, then everything is transparent. But a wholly transparent world is an invisible world. To "see through" all things is the same as not to see.[33]

In reply, one of the lecturers asked who had written the passage in question. An interesting question given the supposed "death of the author!" This being the case, I should have responded that the origin of the argument was irrelevant to its cogency. Instead, I disclosed that the passage came from C. S. Lewis's *The Abolition of Man* (which was originally published in 1943, and which *National Review* chose as the seventh entry in their list of the "100 Best Nonfiction Books of the Twentieth Century"[34]). With this authorial information now in hand, my lecturer proceeded to ignore my application

---

30. Adler, *Great Books of the Western World*, 561.

31. See Evans, *Despair*; Nietzsche, "Parable of the Madman"; Russell, "Free Man's Worship"; Sartre, "Existentialism Is a Humanism"; Williams, *I Wish I Could Believe*.

32. See Williams, "Beginner's Guide to the Theistic Argument from Desire."

33. Lewis, *Abolition of Man*, 48.

34. Lewis, *Abolition of Man*. See Aeschliman, *Restoration of Man*, third edition; Mosteller and Anacker, *Contemporary Perspectives on C.S. Lewis'* The Abolition of Man; Ward, *After Humanity*.

of Lewis's argument to postmodern hermeneutics in favor of dismissing *The Abolition of Man* as a work authored in and to a society seeking certainty on account of the Second World War. This *ad hominem* attack, grounded in the supposed authorial intent of Lewis' work, not only constituted a genetic fallacy (attacking the source rather than the content of the argument) but contradicted the professed rejection of authorial intent!

Looking back, the whole situation puts me in mind of this passage from theologian D. A. Carson's book *The Gagging of God*:

> A few years ago I was teaching an evening course on hermeneutics. . . . I was trying to set out both what could be learned from the new hermeneutic, and where the discipline was likely to lead one astray. In particular, I was insisting that true knowledge is possible, even to finite, culture-bound creatures. A doctoral student from another seminary . . . quietly protested that she did not think I was escaping from the dreaded positivism of the nineteenth century. Deeper appreciation for the ambiguities of language, the limits of our understanding, the uniqueness of each individual, and the social nature of knowledge would surely drive me to a more positive assessment of the new hermeneutic. I tried to defend my position, but I was quite unable to persuade her. Finally, in a moment of sheer intellectual perversity on my part, I joyfully exclaimed, "Ah, now I think I see what you are saying. You are using delicious irony to affirm the objectivity of truth." The lady was not amused. "That is exactly what I am not saying," she protested with some heat, and she laid out her position again. I clasped my hands in enthusiasm and told her how delighted I was to find someone using irony so cleverly in order to affirm the possibility of objective knowledge. Her answer was more heated, but along the same lines as her first reply. I believe she also accused me of twisting what she was saying. I told her I thought it was marvelous that she should add emotion to her irony, all to the purpose of exposing the futility of extreme relativism, thereby affirming truth's objectivity. Not surprisingly, she exploded in real anger, and accused me of a lot of unmentionable things. When she finally cooled down, I said, rather quietly, "But this is how I am reading you." Of course, she saw what I was getting at immediately, and sputtered out like a spent candle . . . My example was artificial, of course, since I only pretended to read her in a certain way, but what I did was sufficient to prove the point I was trying to make to her. "You are a deconstructionist," I told her, "but you expect me to interpret your words aright. More precisely, you are upset because I seem

to be divorcing the meaning I claim to see in your words from your intent. Thus, implicitly you affirm the link between text and authorial intent. I have never read a deconstructionist who would be pleased if a reviewer misinterpreted his or her work: thus in practice deconstructionists implicitly link their own texts with their own intentions . . ." . . . in the real world, for all the difficulties there are in communication from person to person . . . we still expect people to say more or less what they mean (and if they don't, we chide them for it), and we expect mature people to understand what others say, and represent it fairly. The understanding is doubtless never absolutely exhaustive and perfect, but that does not mean the only alternative is to dissociate text from speaker, and then locate all meaning in the reader or hearer.[35]

Towards the end of the Q&A session, one of our lecturers told us that if we wanted to enjoy reading literature, we didn't need to *study* literature, just to read it. I thought she had a good point.

The Philosophical Turn

Walking towards the University library after the English Literature Q&A session had ended, I met a member of the philosophy faculty. They encouraged me to "come and join" the philosophers because they were "more sensible" than the English department! At the end of my first year, I followed his advice (and that of the tutor who marked my first-year essays) and switched to a single honors degree in philosophy.[36]

---

35. Carson, *Gagging of God*, 101–3 [Kindle location].

36. I'd come late to music (I studied GCSE Music in my final year at Secondary School), so didn't have the performance grades on multiple instruments required to progress with composition past the first year at Cardiff, which was the aspect of the course that most interested me. I had reached Grade 7 on the flute, and continued playing for many years. Later still, I returned to composing, as you can hear via my website's "Composing" page at www.peterswilliams.com/composing/.

Fig. 12. The library at Cardiff University (on the right) on the way to philosophy lectures in 1993.

Although I embarked upon philosophical study as someone who believed in God, I was willing to change my mind should I meet a strong enough case for doing so. I didn't come across one then and I haven't since. On the contrary, the more I studied philosophy—including that of atheists such as A. J. Ayer, J. L. Mackie, Michael Martin, Kai Nielson and Bertrand Russell—the more I came to appreciate the breadth and strength of the case for God. As David Bradshaw reports:

> The practice of natural theology goes back to Xenophanes and Anaximander and was developed in elaborate detail by Plato and Aristotle. It has a long and complex history stretching from antiquity through the Middle Ages and modern philosophy, one that was by no means brought to an end (as is sometimes supposed) by Hume and Kant. Although it went into eclipse in the first half of the twentieth century, owing to the dominance of phenomenology on the Continent and of positivism and ordinary language philosophy in the Anglophone world, it came roaring back with the revival of metaphysics that began in the 1960s. Today natural theology is a flourishing enterprise that includes a wide range of argument types and strategies, some of them drawing from classical sources and many others of more recent vintage.[37]

37. Bradshaw, "Introduction" in *Natural Theology in the Eastern Orthodox*

Talking of positivism, the anti-metaphysical philosophy of "[the] Vienna Circle, an influential group of scientifically oriented philosophers who flourished in Vienna from the early 1920s to the mid-1930s,"[38] A. J. Ayer's classic but self-refuting positivist polemic *Language, Truth and Logic* was a set text in my first year at Cardiff. I'm not sure if this was meant as an example of how to do philosophy, or an example of how not to do it, since philosophers had long since pointed out that Ayer's attempt to confine linguistic meaning to statements that were either true by definition or empirically verifiable was neither true by definition nor empirically verifiable.[39]

Despite the collapse of verificationism (which even Ayer went on to repudiate), atheist Kai Nielson, in his 1988 debate against J. P. Moreland, put all his philosophical eggs into arguing that definite descriptions such as "God is the maker of heaven and earth" and "The being transcendent to the world on whom all things depends and who depends on nothing himself" are "so problematic and so obscure that it turns out that we don't know what we are talking about when we use them."[40]

Commenting on the debate, philosopher Dallas Willard observed that Nielson's approach looked "awfully like warmed over Logical Positivism with superficial disclaimers"[41] and argued that "The overly-simple quasi-positivist models which, it seems to me, lie back of Nielson's remarks surely cannot do justice to the actual performances of language."[42]

In the debate itself, Moreland replied to Nielson that,

> It seems to me that it's possible to have ostensive knowledge of God. It's also possible to have knowledge of him as you infer a cause to explain a set of effects. I would further say that . . . miraculous acts of God could be baptismal events, to use Kripke's phrase, and meanings associated with those events . . . could be passed through salvation history in a way similar to a Kripkian ancestral chain view of reference. So . . . I believe that God-talk makes sense through ostentation, through the fact that [we have] been visited by Jesus of Nazareth, through a very similar

---

Tradition, 2. On Hume's critique of natural theology, see Sennett and Groothuis, *In Defence of Natural Theology*. See also Geivett and Habermas, *In Defence of Miracles*. On Kant, see Geisler, *Christian Apologetics* (2nd ed.), 5–6, 13.

38. Edwards, "Behaviorism." Nancy R. Pearcey and Charles B. Thaxton explain that according to positivists, "progress in science consists in its 'emancipation' from the confining fetters of religion and metaphysics." *Soul of Science*, xi, see also 46–49.

39. See Alston, "Religious Language and Verificationism."

40. Nielsen, "No! A Defence of Atheism," 51.

41. Willard, "Language, Being, God."

42. Willard, "Language, Being, God."

kind of meaning as is used in science, and through analogy with myself as I reflect upon my own faculties and form a conception of God as a being who has intellect, emotion, and will.[43]

Moreover, just as D. A. Carson argued that we "can understand what others say" despite the fact that our understanding is "never absolutely exhaustive and perfect," so Moreland argued that,

> Most people know very well what "God" means, and they use it to refer, even if they cannot give you a complete theory of reference and meaning to explain this. There is no philosophical topic of interest wherein philosophers are in universal agreement regarding how we talk about it or what its definition is. No philosopher to my knowledge has given a universally accepted definition of "knowledge." I couldn't for the life of me define "history." I'm not sure I could define "love;" I'm not sure that I could define to everyone's satisfaction what a number is. And I couldn't define to everyone's satisfaction what God is nor how I refer to any of these entities. Nonetheless, it does seem reasonable that I could know something about these things, whether or not I could give an exhaustive treatment of how those terms get meaning. We can know them truly without knowing them exhaustively.[44]

As the Cambridge University philosopher A. C. Ewing argued in his 1973 book *Value and Reality*,

> There are a number of intermediate degrees between a perfectly clear definite concept and no concept at all . . . It may be argued that the suggestion that there is such a being [as God] is groundless, but hardly that it has no meaning at all.[45]

In the end, as William Lane Craig concluded, "Nielsen fails to prove . . . that the concept 'God' is any more problematic than theoretical entities in science . . ."[46]

I *devoured* the 1993 published form of this debate,[47] being particularly impressed by the incisive debate review contributed by William Lane Craig,

---

43. Moreland, "Christian's Rebuttal," 59.
44. Moreland, "Christian's Rebuttal," 59.
45. Ewing, *Value and Reality*, 31.
46. Craig, "Defence of Rational Theism," 158.
47. See Moreland and Nielson, et al., *Does God Exist*? Moreland's *Scaling the Secular City: A Defence of Christianity* (Baker, 1987) was a major early influence on my philosophical thinking.

and by Dallas Willard's now classic essay "Language, Being, God, and the Three Stages of Theistic Evidence."[48]

Superseding Scientism

William Lane Craig describes how, during the 1950s and 60s:

> The overwhelmingly dominant mode of thinking was scientific naturalism. Physical science was taken to be the final, and really only, arbiter of truth. Metaphysics—that traditional branch of philosophy which deals with questions about reality which are beyond science (hence, the name "*meta*-physics," *i.e.*, "beyond physics")—had been vanquished, expelled from philosophy like an unclean leper . . . Any problem that could not be addressed by science was simply dismissed as a pseudo-problem.[49]

Whereas verificationism attributes the determination of linguistic *meaning* (outside of purely definitional truths) to empirical verifiability, the related epistemology (that is, theory of knowledge) known as "scientism" attributes exclusive rights over *knowledge* and/or *rational belief* to empirical verification. Whilst verificationism is an all-but-dead philosophy today, scientism is alive and kicking in contemporary culture.[50]

For example, leading neo-atheist and evolutionary biologist Richard Dawkins proclaims that "the only good reason to believe that something exists is if there is real evidence that it does . . . it always comes back to our senses, one way or another."[51] Likewise, neo-atheist chemist Peter Atkins affirms:

> I stand by my claim that the scientific method is the only means of discovering the nature of reality, and although its current views are open to revision, the approach, making observations and comparing notes, will forever survive as the only way of acquiring reliable knowledge.[52]

---

48. See Moreland and Nielson et al., *Does God Exist?*, 197–217. See also Willard, "Language, Being, God."

49. Craig, "Resurrection of Theism."

50. For an introduction to and critique of scientism, see Williams, "Scientism" (YouTube playlist); Deane, "Is Science the Only Means for Acquiring Truth?"; Moreland, *Scientism and Secularism*; Trigg, *Does Science Undermine Faith?*, chap. 1; West, *Magician's Twin*.

51. Dawkins, *Magic of Reality*, 16, 19.

52. Atkins, *Being*, xiii.

Neo-atheist philosopher and physicist Victor J. Stenger complained that: "critics accuse New Atheism of 'scientism,' which is the principle that science is the only means that can be used to learn about the world and humanity. They cannot quote a single new atheist who has said that."[53] Yet Stenger himself defined science as "belief in the presence of supportive evidence,"[54] affirming that "faith is belief in the absence of supportive evidence,"[55] that "Science . . . does not require nor does it use any metaphysics"[56] and that "reason is just the procedure by which humans ensure that their conclusions are consistent with the theory that produced them and with the data that test those conclusions,"[57] such that "Being rational just means that when you talk about some subject, the words you use are well defined and the statements you make are self-consistent."[58] In other words, Stenger held that while philosophical reason checks the *coherence* of propositions (to show if they could be true), it is only if there is (sufficient) "supportive evidence" (i.e., empirical data) for a proposition that belief in the truth of that proposition can be considered "scientific" rather than being a matter of blind faith. Sounds like scientism to me.

Of course, the scientistic demand that *rational belief must be justified by empirical evidence* is self-contradictory, in that it can't be justified by empirical evidence, and in that it entails an infinite regress that can't be satisfied (since the demand requires evidence for the existence and reliability of one's evidence, and so on *ad infinitum*). It's also open to obvious counter-examples (e.g., logical, metaphysical, moral and aesthetic knowledge).

On this last point I'm happy to agree with neo-atheist philosopher Sam Harris, who contradicts scientism (along with his own book's central thesis, that science can deal with morality) when he admits in *The Moral Landscape* that:

> Science cannot tell us why, *scientifically*, we should value [human] well-being . . . the demand for *radical* justification leveled by the moral skeptic could not be met by science. Science is defined with reference to the goal of understanding the processes at work in the universe. Can we justify this goal scientifically? Of

---

53. Stenger, *New Atheism*, 238–39.
54. Stenger, *New Atheism*, 15.
55. Stenger, *New Atheism*, 45.
56. Stenger, *New Atheism*, 21.
57. Stenger, *New Atheism*, 15.
58. Stenger, *New Atheism*, 71.

course not . . . What evidence could prove that we should value evidence?[59]

No *empirical* evidence of what is the case could justify believing that we "should" value evidence in the moral sense of "having an objective obligation" to do so; but the non-empirical, phenomenological evidence of moral experience does justify such a belief.[60] As atheist philosopher Mary Midgely warned: "Physical science . . . is not a separate, supreme champion outclassing history or philosophy. It has no private line to reality."[61] After all, there are second order philosophical questions about first order scientific issues, questions about science and the significance of scientific ideas, such that scientists have philosophical disagreements that can't be settled on scientific grounds but which affect how they do science. Furthermore, however detailed and accurate our scientific descriptions of physical realities become, such descriptions can't explain *why physical reality has the fundamental structure it has* or *why any physical reality described by that structure exists at all*. In other words, science makes metaphysical assumptions and raises metaphysical questions that require metaphysical answers. In my own view, as in the view of such leading lights of the scientific revolution as Kepler and Newton, the best understanding of those assumptions, and the best answers to many of those questions, make reference to God.

Science presupposes that the natural world isn't an illusion. Science presupposes that the natural world exhibits a rational order, despite this being an order that cannot simply be deduced from first principles (making observation and experiment useful scientific activities). Science presupposes that human cognitive and sensory faculties are both generally reliable; and it presupposes that there are knowable objective values of truth, goodness, and even beauty. These presuppositions are all at home within the Judeo-Christian worldview. This is hardly surprising, for as Stephen C. Meyer explains: "modern science was specifically inspired by the conviction that the universe is the product of a rational mind who . . . designed the human mind to understand it."[62] Indeed, sociologist of science Steve Fuller concedes that,

---

59. Harris, *Moral Landscape*, 37.

60. See Beckwith and Koukl, *Relativism*; Williams, *Faithful Guide to Philosophy*, chap. 8.

61. Midgley, *Are You an Illusion?*, 6

62. Meyer, *Return of the God Hypothesis*, 24. See Williams, "Theological Roots of Science" (YouTube playlist); Chapman, *Slaying the Dragons*; Grant, *History of Natural Philosophy*; Hannam, *Genesis of Science*; Keas, *Unbelievable*; Peterson, *Flat Earths and Fake Footnotes*.

> While I cannot honestly say that I believe in a divine personal creator, no plausible alternative has yet been offered to justify the pursuit of science as a search for the ultimate systematic understanding of reality . . . science . . . makes sense only if there is an overall design to nature that we are especially well-equipped to fathom, even though most of it has little bearing on our day-to-day animal survival. Humanity's creation in the image of God . . . provides the clearest historical rationale for the rather specialised expenditure of effort associated with science.[63]

As Fuller intimates, the assumption that rational thought can penetrate through *what works* in terms of survival to *what's true about reality* isn't merely an assumption that's at home within a monotheistic worldview, but an assumption ill at ease with a naturalistic worldview.[64]

Arguments About Meta-Ethics

Since the verification principle applies to moral propositions as well as to propositions about God, the collapse of verificationism opened up the metaphysical debate between moral subjectivists (also known as moral relativists) and moral objectivists.[65] This debate overlaps with the debate over scientism, because knowledge of objective moral facts lies beyond the reach of science,[66] such that a belief in moral facts that are knowable requires the rejection of scientism. As James Davidson Hunter and Paul Nedelisky explain:

> When it began, the quest for a moral science sought to discover the good. The new moral science has abandoned that quest and now, at best, tells us how to get what we want . . . Today's moral scientists no longer look to science to discover moral truths, for they believe there is nothing there to discover. As they see it, there are no such things as prescriptive moral or ethical norms; there are no moral "oughts" or obligations; there is no ethical good, bad, or objective value of any kind. Their view is . . . a kind of moral nihilism . . . In the end, as these thinkers see it, the

---

63. Fuller, *Dissent Over Descent*, 9, 70.

64. See Beck, "God's Existence"; Williams, *Faithful Guide to Philosophy*, chap. 12; Williams, *C.S. Lewis vs. the New Atheists*, chap. 4.

65. See Harman and Thomson, *Moral Relativism and Moral Objectivity*.

66. For a critique of Sam Harris's muddled claims to the contrary, see Williams, *C.S. Lewis vs. the New Atheists*, 153–60. See also: Hunter and Nedelisky, *Science and the Good*.

"good" is a social engineering project, the foundation of which is an unmitigated, though rarely acknowledged metaphysical scepticism.[67]

Many atheists—e.g., Friedrich Nietzsche, Jean-Paul Sartre, Paul Kurtz and J. L. Mackie (whose 1977 book *Ethics: Inventing Right and Wrong* was a set text in my undergraduate days)—argue that the existence of God is a prerequisite (or at least the best explanation) for the existence of objective moral values, such that the subjectivity (and hence relativity) of morality is entailed, or at least implied, by the truth of atheism.

Joel Marks, Professor Emeritus of Philosophy at the University of New Haven, takes this position, explaining that his atheism leads him to reject moral objectivism:

> the religious fundamentalists are correct: without God, there is no morality. But they are incorrect, I still believe, about there being a God. Hence, I believe, there is no morality . . . In sum, while theists take the obvious existence of moral commands to be a kind of proof of the existence of a Commander, i.e., God, I now take the non-existence of a Commander as a kind of proof that there are no Commands, i.e., morality.[68]

Conversely, many theistic philosophers agree with such atheistic colleagues as these that the existence of God is a prerequisite (or at least the best explanation) for the existence of objective moral values, but they use this premise in the service of natural theology by combining it with a defence of moral objectivism.

Of course, plenty of non-theistic philosophers argue for moral objectivism, whilst trying to fend off any suggestion that moral objectivism suggests anything positive about the existence of God.[69] This has the interesting consequence that both premises of the meta-ethical moral argument for God can be defended by quoting from non-theistic philosophers. It's just that non-theists can't consistently defend *both* of these premises!

According to John Cottingham: "the increasing consensus among philosophers today is that some kind of objectivism of truth and of value is correct . . ."[70] For example, drawing upon the "principle of credulity," atheist philosopher Peter Cave argues that:

---

67. Hunter and Nedelisky, *Science and the Good*, xv, 21.
68. Joel Marks, "Amoral Manifesto."
69. See Williams, "Can Moral Objectivism Do Without God?"
70. Cottingham, "Philosophers Are Finding Fresh Meanings in Truth, Goodness and Beauty."

whatever sceptical arguments may be brought against our belief that killing the innocent is morally wrong, we are more certain that the killing is morally wrong than that the argument is sound ... Torturing an innocent child for the sheer fun of it is morally wrong. Full stop.[71]

Likewise, atheist and moral philosopher Russ Shafer-Landau argues that:

some moral views are better than others, despite the sincerity of the individuals, cultures, and societies that endorse them. Some moral views are true, others false, and my thinking them so doesn't make them so. My society's endorsement of them doesn't prove their truth. Individuals, and whole societies, can be seriously mistaken when it comes to morality. The best explanation of this is that there are moral standards not of our own making.[72]

Atheist philosopher Colin McGinn comments that "we do not need to believe in God in order to find morality both important and binding."[73] However, as J. P. Moreland and William Lane Craig caution:

The question is *not*: Must we believe in God in order to live moral lives? There is no reason to think that atheists and theists alike may not live what we normally characterize as good and decent lives. Similarly, the question is *not*: Can we formulate a system of ethics without reference to God? If the non-theist grants that human beings do have objective value, then there is no reason to think that he cannot work out a system of ethics with which the theist would largely agree. Or again, the question is *not*: Can we recognize the existence of objective moral values without reference to God? The theist will typically maintain that a person need not believe in God in order to recognize, say, that we should love our children.[74]

Rather, the meta-ethical moral argument raises what philosopher Frank Jackson called a "location problem," namely, the problem of how to give objective moral value a coherent location or home within one's ontology (that is, one's theory of being). As Paul Copan urges, while "*Belief* in God

---

71. Cave, *Humanism*, 146.
72. Shaefer-Landau, *Whatever Happened to Good and Evil?*, viii.
73. McGinn, *Ethics, Evil and Fiction*, vii.
74. Moreland and Craig, *Philosophical Foundations*, 492.

isn't a requirement for being moral . . . the *existence* of a personal God is crucial for a coherent understanding of objective morality."[75]

In other words, although the non-theist can *do* the objectively right thing because they *know* what the objectively right thing to do is, their worldview can't provide *an adequate ontological account of* the objective moral values they know and obey.[76] As Welsh philosopher H. P. Owen argued:

> On the one hand [objective moral] claims transcend every human person . . . On the other hand . . . it is contradictory to assert that impersonal claims are entitled to the allegiance of our wills. The only solution to this paradox is to suppose that the order of [objective moral] claims . . . is in fact rooted in the personality of God.[77]

Russell's False Dilemma

In Plato's *Euthyphro* dialogue, Socrates asks: "Is what is holy holy because the gods approve it, or do they approve it because it is holy?"[78] This question is popularly, but inaccurately, said to show that "God" is a redundant explanation for the objectivity of moral values. On the one hand, it is correctly observed that if we ground morality in nothing but God's commands, morality becomes arbitrary (for if something is good simply because God commands it, he could just have easily commanded the opposite). On the other hand, if we don't ground morality in God's commands, morality must be *independent of God's commands*, and thus — so it is mistakenly suggested — *independent of God*. As Bertrand Russell argued:

---

75. Copan, *True for You, but Not for Me*, 45.

76. See Williams, "Moral Argument For God" (YouTube playlist); Kreeft, "Refutation of Moral Relativism" (Audio); Anscombe, "Modern Moral Philosophy"; Beckwith, "Why I Am Not a Moral Relativist"; Williams, "Can Moral Objectivism Do Without God?"; Baggett and Walls, *Good God*; Beck, *Does God Exist?*, chap. 4; Beckwith and Koukl, *Relativism*; Copan, "God, Naturalism, and the Foundations of Morality"; Copan, "Hume and the Moral Argument"; Evans, *Natural Signs and Knowledge of God*, chap. 5; Garcia and King, *Is Goodness Without God Good Enough?*; Owen, "Why Morality Implies the Existence of God"; Shaefer-Landau, *Whatever Happened to Good and Evil?*; Sorley, *Moral Value and the Idea Of God*; Williams, *Outgrowing God?*, chap. 4; Williams, *Faithful Guide to Philosophy*, chap. 8; Williams, *Case For God*, chap. 2.

77. Owen, "Why Morality Implies the Existence of God," 648.

78. Plato, *Euthyphro*, 10a, Plato, *The Collected Dialogues of Plato*, 178.

if you are quite sure there is a difference between right and wrong, you are then in this situation: is that difference due to God's fiat or is it not? If it is due to God's fiat, then for God himself there is no difference between right and wrong, and it is no longer a significant statement to say that God is good. If you are going to say, as theologians do, that God is good, you must then say that right and wrong have some meaning which is independent of God's fiat, because God's fiats are good and not bad independently of the mere fact that He made them. If you are going to say that, you will then have to say that it is not only through God that right and wrong came into being, but that they are in their essence logically anterior to God.[79]

However, Russell's *Euthyphro*-inspired objection rests upon a false dilemma. As Keith E. Yandell warns:

> The Euthyphro argument nicely raises some issues, but it does not settle anything. There are alternatives in addition to the two that the Euthyphro argument considers. The argument would succeed only if there were not.[80]

Granted, objective moral values cannot be grounded in divine commands issued according to an arbitrary divine "fiat." However, there's more to God that his commands, or his supposedly arbitrary "fiat" in issuing them. In the words of philosopher Francis J. Beckwith:

> God's commands are good, not because God commands them, but because God is *good*. Thus, God is not subject to a moral order outside of himself, and neither are God's moral commands arbitrary.[81]

As William Lane Craig observes:

> Plato himself saw the solution to this objection: you split the horns of the dilemma by formulating a third alternative, namely, God is the Good. The Good is the moral nature of God himself. That is to say, God *is* necessarily holy, loving, kind, just, and so on, and these attributes of God comprise the Good. God's moral character expresses itself towards us in the form of certain commandments, which become for us our moral duties. Hence

---

79. Russell, quoted in Peterson et al., *Reason and Religious Belief*, 85.
80. Yandell, "Theology, Philosophy, And Evil," 240.
81. Beckwith, "Moral Law, the Mormon Universe, and the Nature of the Right," 232.

God's commandments are not arbitrary, but necessarily flow from his own nature.[82]

Neutralizing Methodological Naturalism

In the nineteenth century, the French empiricist philosopher Auguste Compt (1798–1857) "insisted that science properly practiced could make no reference to divine action to explain any events or phenomena."[83] Subsequent thinkers have sometimes expanded Compt's rule to exclude from science reference to any intelligence that might be suspected of being irreducibly mental. Hence the U.S. *National Academy of Science* asserts that: "The statements of science must invoke only natural things and processes."[84] This "methodologically naturalistic" conception of science remains prevalent amongst scientists, though it is controversial among philosophers of science.[85]

Inferring the activity of "intelligence" as the best explanation for empirical data within archaeology, cryptography, forensic science, or the search for extra-terrestrial intelligence, is an avowedly scientific venture, even if a philosopher might argue—perhaps correctly—that the intelligence in question is best conceived in terms of substance dualism (a subject to which we will return). In the same way, inferring the activity of "intelligence" as the best explanation for empirical data within biology or cosmology should count as a scientific venture, whether the intelligence in question appears to be an immanent extra-terrestrial intelligence that a philosopher might think of in terms of a naturalism-busting substance dualism, or a transcendent intelligence best conceptualized in equally naturalism-busting metaphysical terms. As philosopher of science Bruce L. Gordon writes:

> When generating scientific conclusions in cryptography or forensics, the design inference is not controversial. The sticking point is with the philosophical issue of methodological naturalism. What happens if the design inference, applied to certain

---

82. Craig, *God, Are You There?*, 38–39.
83. Meyer, *Return of the God Hypothesis*, 53.
84. *Teaching about Evolution*, 2.
85. See Williams, "Scientific Status of Intelligent Design Theory" (YouTube playlist); Gordon, "Is Intelligent Design Science?"; Gordon, "Scientific Status of Design Inferences"; Larmer, "Science, Methodological Naturalism, and Question-Begging"; Meyer, "Sauce for the Goose"; Monton, "Is Intelligent Design Science?"; Moreland, *Scientism and Secularism*, chap. 11; Moreland "Design and the Nature of Science"; Plantinga, "Should Methodological Naturalism Constrain Science?"

natural phenomena, yields the conclusion that there is an intelligent cause that might transcend our universe? There seems to be an illegitimate double standard operative in barring such a conclusion when design inferences are otherwise scientifically acceptable.[86]

Strictly speaking, a methodological refusal to allow evidentially supported design inferences to count as "science" *if and when the inferred intelligence is most plausibly interpreted in irreducibly mental terms* means *either* (a) refusing to follow the evidence where it leads, or (b) excluding study of the relevant empirical data from "science" and thus from "scientific" institutions.[87] The latter option entails a willingness to transfer resources to some "non-scientific" institution (which we might call an institution of "natural philosophy") in order to understand the truth about the relevant aspect of physical reality on the basis of empirical evidence! It seems to me that such a move is pragmatically less appealing than simply recognizing that "natural science" is a first-order discipline demarcated by its object of study (physical reality) and its intellectual goals (to rationally explain and/or predict as much as we can about physical reality), rather than by its adherence to such a "methodological naturalism." As J. P. Moreland argues: "The most important thing about a scientific theory . . . is that it explains things."[88]

In any event, Thomas Nagel is surely right when he observes that "a purely semantic classification of a hypothesis or its denial as belonging or not to science is of limited interest to someone who wants to know whether the hypothesis is true or false."[89] Hence, whether or not intelligent design is semantically classified as a "scientific" hypothesis, design inferences can be made on the basis of empirical evidence (e.g., cosmic fine-tuning), and the subsequent discussion about the best way to think about the nature of the inferred designing intelligence may well be thought to add some weight to the cumulative philosophical case for the existence of God.

The Collapse of Verificationism and the Renaissance of Natural Theology

Basil Mitchell observes that,

---

86. Gordon, "Scientific Status of Design Inferences."
87. See Kojonen, "Methodological Naturalism and the Truth Seeking Objection."
88. Moreland, "Intelligent Design and the Nature of Science," 57.
89. Nagel, *Secular Philosophy and the Religious Temperament*, 48.

the Logical Positivist movement started as an attempt to make a clear demarcation between science and common sense on the one hand, and metaphysics and theology on the other. But work in the philosophy of science convinced people that what the Logical Positivists had said about science was not true, and, by the time the philosophers of science had developed and amplified their accounts of how rationality works in science, people discovered that similar accounts applied equally well to the areas which they had previously sought to exclude, namely theology and metaphysics.[90]

As Craig explains:

> The collapse of this Verificationism was perhaps the most important philosophical event of the twentieth century. Its downfall meant a resurgence of metaphysics, along with other traditional problems of philosophy which Verificationism had suppressed. Accompanying this resurgence came something altogether unanticipated: a renaissance of Christian philosophy.[91]

So startling was this renaissance that *Time* magazine, which had famously used its cover to ask "Is God Dead?" in 1966, ran a cover story entitled "Modernizing the Case for God" in 1980:

> In a quiet revolution in thought and argument that hardly anyone could have foreseen only two decades ago, God is making a come-back. Most intriguingly, this is happening not among theologians or ordinary believers—most of whom never accepted for a moment that he was in any serious trouble—but in the crisp, intellectual circles of academic philosophers, where the consensus had long banished the Almighty from fruitful discourse.
>
> Now it is more respectable among philosophers than it has been for a generation to talk about the possibility of God's existence. The shift is most striking in the Anglo-American academies of thought, where strict forms of empiricism have reigned. . . A. J. Ayer, on behalf of logical positivism, decreed that "all utterances about the nature of God are nonsensical." The accepted wisdom was that the only valid statements were those verifiable through the senses. Today even atheistic philosophers

---

90. Mitchell, "Reflections on C. S. Lewis," 19.
91. Craig, "Does God Exist?"

agree that Ayer's rigid rule is inadequate to deal with human experience.[92]

Moreover, as Craig also notes:

> The renaissance of Christian philosophy has not been merely defensive ... it has also been accompanied by a resurgence of interest in natural theology ... All of the traditional arguments for God's existence, such as the cosmological, teleological, moral, and ontological arguments, not to mention creative, new arguments, find intelligent and articulate defenders on the contemporary philosophical scene.[93]

Science and Natural Theology

The philosophical resurgence of interest in natural theology began around the same time that scientists were making a series of breakthroughs in our understanding of the physical universe that gave added impetus to reflection upon cosmic and biological origins.

For example, while "few physicists and astronomers at the beginning of the twentieth century doubted the infinite age of the universe,"[94] the cosmic background radiation discovered in 1964 by American physicist Arno Penzias and radio-astronomer Robert Wilson solidified the "Big Bang" model of a finite cosmic past advanced in 1927 by Belgian physicist (and Catholic priest) Georges Lemaître. This development made its way into widespread philosophical discussion via William Lane Craig's *The Kalam Cosmological Argument* (1979).[95]

The significance of the scientific picture of a cosmic beginning can be measured by the impact it had upon Antony Flew (1923–2010), whom

---

92. *Time*, "Modernizing the Case for God."

93. Craig, "Resurrection of Theism." On the ontological argument, see Williams, "Ontological Argument for God" (YouTube playlist); Craig, "Ontological Argument"; Plantinga, "Ontological Argument"; Williams, "Modern Ontological Argument"; Williams, *Faithful Guide*, chap. 9.

94. Meyer, *Return of the God Hypothesis*, 73.

95. See Hackett, *Resurrection of Theism* (a major influence upon Craig); Craig, *Kalam Cosmological Argument*. See also FOCLOnline, "Can We Believe in God in an Age of Science? The Big Bang & Cosmic 'Fine Tuning'" (YouTube video); Cerebral Faith, "Why the Divisibility of Time Is Irrelevant to The Kalam Cosmological Argument"; Copan and Craig, *Kalam Cosmological Argument*, Vol. 1; Copan and Craig, *Kalam Cosmological Argument*, Vol. 2; Meyer, *Return of the God Hypothesis*; Williams, *Faithful Guide to Philosophy*, chap. 5.

philosopher Craig J. Hazen called "arguably the world's foremost philosophical atheist."[96] In 1992 Flew admitted to being "embarrassed by the contemporary cosmological consensus . . . that the universe had a beginning."[97] He recognized that the Big Bang's description of cosmic history was in tension with the naturalistically comfortable idea that the existence of the universe "without beginning," together with "whatever are found to be its most fundamental [physical] features," should be accepted as our "explanatory ultimates."[98] Flew conceded that "it is certainly neither easy nor comfortable to maintain this position in the face of the Big Bang story."[99] In 2004, Flew publicly announced his intellectual conversion to a belief in God (though not to belief in any particular divine revelation), in part because "There does seem to be a reason for a First Cause."[100]

In my own view, the *kalam* cosmological argument is best viewed as highlighting the need to explain the existence of the first physical, and therefore contingent, event; a physical event that, by definition, cannot be explained by reference to a prior physical event, and which must therefore be explained in terms of a transcendent, non-physical cause.[101]

Cosmic Fine Tuning

As discussed in chapter 1, since the 1950s scientists have come to recognize that the existence of complex material states, up to and including organic life, and especially "embodied conscious agents (ECAs)"[102] with the opportunity to "develop scientific technology and discover the universe,"[103] depends upon a staggering degree of cosmic "fine tuning." (Life on Earth also relies upon, or benefits from, various contingent "local" conditions concerning properties of our galaxy, solar system, planet, moon and sun that are, at the very least, atypical.[104])

   96. Flew in Hazen et al., "Pilgrimage from Atheism to Theism."
   97. Flew in *Cosmos, Bios, Theos*, 241.
   98. Flew in Hazen et al., "Pilgrimage from Atheism to Theism.
   99. Flew in *Cosmos, Bios, Theos*, 241.
   100. Flew in Hazen et al., "Pilgrimage from Atheism to Theism."
   101. See Williams, "ELF 2023: Can We Believe in God in an Age of Science? The Big Bang" (Podcast); Williams, *Faithful Guide to Philosophy*, chap. 5.
   102. Holder, *Ramified Natural Theology*, 56.
   103. Collins, "Anthropic Fine-Tuning: Three Approaches," 173–91. See also Collins, "Argument from Physical Constants: The Fine-Tuning for Discoverability"; Denton, *Miracle of Man*; Gonzalez and Richards, *Privileged Planet*, chap. 10.
   104. See Williams, "Rare Earth Hypothesis" (YouTube playlist); ID the Future, "Problem of Earth Privilege" (Podcast); ID the Future, "Privileged Place for Life and

As previously noted, there are multiple aspects to cosmic "fine-tuning," including physical constants such as the force of gravity, and initial conditions such as the amount of entropy in the early universe. Multiplying together the odds of these individually unlikely factors *all* falling by chance within the specification provided by the narrow, life-permitting range of possible values gives an improbability that's literally beyond astronomical. Hence cosmic fine-tuning appears to be an example of specified complexity that is best explained by the activity of intelligence.[105] Three attempted rebuttals of this argument (Richard Dawkins's complexity objection, the hypothesis of "dynamical parameters," and the multiverse hypothesis) were considered, and rejected, in chapter 1.

Reflecting upon the evidence for cosmic fine-tuning, agnostic cosmologist Paul Davies recognizes that: "the impression of design is overwhelming."[106] Atheist philosopher of science Bradley Monton reflects that the fine-tuning argument:

> doesn't stop me from being an atheist, but I don't have any completely definitive objections to it – and I have problems with all the objections that are presented as completely definitive . . . This is why I consider the fine-tuning argument to be somewhat plausible.[107]

Even neo-atheist Christopher Hitchens once commented that:

Discovery" (Podcast); Denton, *Miracle of Man*; Denton, *Nature's Destiny*; Gonzalez, "Local Fine-Tuning"; Gonzalez and Richards, *Privileged Planet*; Eberlin, *Foresight*, chap. 2; Waltham, *Lucky Planet*; Ward and Brownlee, *Rare Earth*.

105. See FOCLOnline, "Can We Believe in God in an Age of Science? The Big Bang & Cosmic 'Fine Tuning'" (YouTube video); FOCLOnline, "Can We Believe in God in an Age of Science? Cosmology and God" (YouTube video); Williams, "Christian Worldview and Science in Apologetic Perspective: Cosmos" (Podcast); "Cosmic Fine Tuning: Design or Multiverse?" (Podcast); "Introduction to An Informed Cosmos" (Podcast); "Veritas 2022: Outgrowing God?" (Podcast); and *Outgrowing God?*, chap. 9. See also Williams, "Cosmic Fine Tuning" (YouTube playlist); Mind Matters, "Universe Is so Fine Tuned" (Podcast); Barnes, "Fine-Tuning in the Context of Bayesian Theory Testing"; Collins, "Argument from Physical Constants"; "Exploration of the Fine-Tuning of the Universe"; "Teleological Argument: An Exploration"; and "Teleological Argument"; Craig, "Richard Dawkins on Arguments for God"; Díaz-Pachón et al., "Is it Possible to Know Cosmological Fine-Tuning?"; Díaz-Pachón et al., "Is Cosmological Tuning Fine or Coarse?"; Gordon, "Balloons on a String"; Holder, *God, The Multiverse, And Everything*; Holder, *Big Bang, Big God*; Løkhammer, "Fine-Tuning Argument"; Lewis and Barnes, *A Fortunate Universe*; Meyer, *Return of the God Hypothesis*; Moreland and Craig, *Philosophical Foundations* (2nd edition), 493–500.

106. Davies, *Cosmic Blueprint*, 203.

107. Monton, *Seeking God in Science*, 86.

> At some point, certainly, we [Neo-Atheists] are all asked which is the best argument you come up against from the other side. I think every one of us picks the fine-tuning one as the most intriguing... It's not a trivial [argument]. We all say that.[108]

The philosophical impact of the scientific discovery of cosmic fine tuning can be seen in a fascinating turn of events that followed my debate about God's existence with Norwegian agnostic philosopher Professor Einar Bøhn, which took place at the Norwegian University of Science and Technology, in Trondheim, in 2018.[109]

During the period allotted for interaction with audience questions after the formal debate, an atheist student objected to the argument from cosmic fine-tuning that I'd presented. Before I could respond, Professor Bøhn stepped in to defend the argument as being worthy of serious attention. He used philosopher John Leslie's analogy, of a man sentenced to execution by firing squad who survives when every member of the squad misses him, to show that although we wouldn't exist to be surprised by cosmic fine-tuning if no finely tuned cosmos existed, this fact does nothing to explain why a finely tuned cosmos exists. The fact that the sentenced man wouldn't exist to be surprised if the firing squad hadn't missed him doesn't explain *why* they missed him. The fact that an event is a pre-condition of its being observed doesn't explain the occurrence of the event in question.

Moreover, Bøhn used Leslie's analogy to argue that fine-tuning does naturally suggest an explanation framed in terms of an intentionality behind the cosmos, *if one thinks that life is something special*. While one could cash this specialness out in terms of metaphysical values, it could also be cashed out in terms of the special type of complexity known as "specified complexity."[110]

---

108. Hitchens, "Christopher Hitchens Makes a Shocking Confession."

109. For video of this debate, see Apologikk, "Peter S Williams vs Einar Duenger Bøhn." An audio recording of this debate is available from my podcast: "Debate: Does God Exist? Peter S. Williams vs. Einar Bohn at the Norwegian University of Science and Technology in Trondheim." With respect to Professor Bøhn's comments about simplicity, see Flannagan, "Is Naturalism Simpler than Theism?"

110. See Williams, "Intelligent Design, Aesthetics and Design Arguments." See also Williams, "Specified Complexity" (YouTube playlist); Mind Matters, "Run the Gambit of Complexity" (Podcast); Dembski, "Specification"; Meyer, "Yes, Intelligent Design Is Detectable"; Montañez, "Unified Model"; Williams "Design Inference from Specified Complexity"; Dembski and Ewert, *Design Inference*; Dembski and Wells, *Design of Life*, chap. 7.

Biological Fine-Tuning

In the same year that Hoyle predicted the resonance state in the carbon 12 nucleus (i.e., 1953), Francis Crick and James Watson announced their discovery of the three-dimensional, double helical structure of DNA.[111] In 1958, Crick theorized that "the sequence specificity of amino acids in proteins derives from a prior specificity of arrangement in the nucleotide bases on the DNA molecule,"[112] which "functioned just like alphabetic letters in an English text or binary digits in software or a machine code."[113] A series of experiments in the 1960s established that the sequential arrangement of amino-acids that determine the folding and thus the function of proteins is indeed encoded within the rungs of the twisting DNA ladder. It has consequently become apparent that, as origin-of-life researcher Bernd-Olaf Küppers observed: "The problem of the origin of life is clearly basically equivalent to the problem of the origin of information."[114] This problem poses a significant challenge to the naturalistic/materialistic worldview.[115] As William Lane Craig comments:

> Most of us were probably taught... that life originated in the so-called primordial soup by chance chemical reactions, perhaps fueled by lightning strikes. All of these old, chemical origin of life scenarios have broken down and are now rejected by the scientific community. Today there are a plethora of competing, speculative theories with no consensus on the horizon.[116]

Starting with scientist-philosopher Michael Polanyi's 1967 paper "Life Transcending Physics and Chemistry,"[117] the scientific recognition that information lies at the root and heart of biology has formed the basis for increasingly sophisticated arguments against reductive explanations of life in terms of chance and/or physical necessity, and for the need to incorporate an appeal to intelligence into any causally adequate explanation of organic life.[118] As philosopher of science Stephen C. Meyer argues:

---

111. See Pray, "Discovery of DNA Structure and Function."
112. Meyer, *Signature in the Cell*, 101.
113. Meyer, *Signature in the Cell*, 100.
114. Küppers, *Information and the Origin of Life*, 170–72.
115. See Davies, *Origin of Life*; Nagel, *Mind and Cosmos*.
116. Craig in Caruso, *Science and Religion: 5 Questions*, 36.
117. Polanyi, "Life Transcending Physics and Chemistry," 54–69.
118. See Williams, "Origin of Life" (YouTube playlist); Bracht, "Natural Selection as an Algorithm"; Meyer, "DNA and the Origin of Life"; Abel, *First Gene*; Abel, *Primordial Prescription*; Dembski and Ewert, *Design Inference*; Johnson, *Programming of*

Experience shows that large amounts of specified complexity (especially in codes and languages) invariably originate from an intelligent source – from a mind or personal agent. Since intelligence is the only known cause of specified information (at least starting from a nonbiological source), the presence of specified information-rich sequences in even the simplest living systems points definitely to the past existence and activity of a designing intelligence.[119]

Not only is complex and functionally specified information[120] an essential aspect of life with respect to the production of proteins considered individually, but of the many "irreducibly complex" molecular machines composed of multiple interacting protein parts upon which the functions of cells depend,[121] and of the different cell-types and arrangements that specify different basic body-plans.[122] In other words, organic life turns out to be a matter of interdependent, hierarchically nested information. And while there is a philosophical gap between an argument for design and an identification of the source of design as divine (as discussed in chapter 1), the former obviously offers grist to the mill of arguments within the field of natural theology that seek to bridge this gap.[123]

The Best Explanation for Design

The discovery of fine-tuning within physics and biology laid the foundations for a renaissance of design arguments in science and philosophy. As Fred Hoyle commented in 1982:

Life; Klinghoffer, *Signature of Controversy*; Overman, *Case Against Accident and Self-Organization*; Meyer, *Return of the God Hypothesis*; Meyer, *Signature in the Cell*; Pullen, *Intelligent Design or Evolution?*; Tan and Stadler, *Stairway to Life*; Thaxton et al., *Mystery of Life's Origin: The Continuing Controversy*; Williams, *Outgrowing God?*, chap. 7.

119. Meyer, *Signature in the Cell*, 343.

120. See Williams, "Specified Complexity" (YouTube playlist); Dembski, "Specification"; Meyer, "Yes, Intelligent Design Is Detectable"; Montañez, "Unified Model"; Williams "Design Inference from Specified Complexity"; Dembski and Ewert, *Design Inference*; Dembski and Wells, *Design of Life*, chap. 7.

121. See Williams, "Irreducible Complexity" (YouTube playlist); Behe, "Irreducible Complexity: Obstacle to Darwinian Evolution"; Dembski, "Irreducible Complexity Revisited"; Behe, *Darwin's Black Box*, 10th anniversary edition; "Appendix: Clarifying Perspective"; "Appendix C: Assembling the Bacterial Flagellum"; and *Mousetrap for Darwin*; Dembski, *No Free Lunch*; Dembski and Wells, *Design of Life*.

122. See Meyer, *Darwin's Doubt*; Klinghoffer, *Debating Darwin's Doubt*.

123. See Meyer, *Return of the God Hypothesis*.

> A common sense interpretation of the facts suggests that a super-intellect has monkeyed with physics, as well as with chemistry and biology, and that there are no blind forces worth speaking about in nature. The numbers one calculates from the facts seem to me so overwhelming as to put this conclusion almost beyond question.[124]

Likewise, atheist philosopher of science Bradley Monton notes that "intelligent design" arguments (in combination with the Kalam cosmological argument): "make me less certain of my atheism that I would be had I never heard the arguments."[125] He admits: "I think that there is some evidence for an intelligent designer, and in fact, I think that there is some evidence that that intelligent designer is God."[126]

Note how Monton carefully distinguishes between "evidence for an intelligent designer" and "evidence that that intelligent designer is God."[127] Any move from the design inference to the conclusion that the design in question was ultimately produced by God requires justification (as discussed in the Preface and at the end of chapter 1). After all, "God" is not the only potential candidate for Hoyle's "super-intellect." So, why think the designer is God? Because one can make an argument to the best explanation for this conclusion.

Given that specified complexity is a reliable marker of intelligent design, it follows that any design hypothesis featuring a designer whose nature either essentially exhibits specified complexity, and/or is dependent upon any preconditions that exhibit specified complexity, will point beyond itself to an external source of design. And so on, *ad infinitum*. Given that we reckon an infinite regress of causes to be impossible, vacuous as an explanation, or both,[128] we are compelled to recognize the existence of a designer with an essential nature that can halt this regress, and that means a designer that doesn't essentially exhibit, or depend upon, specified complexity.

---

124. Hoyle, "Universe: Past and Present."

125. Monton, *Seeking God in Science*, 39.

126. Monton, *Seeking God in Science*, 39. See also: Luskin, "Interview With Bradley Monton."

127. Monton, *Seeking God in Science*, 39. See also: Luskin, "Interview With Bradley Monton."

128. See Williams, "Cosmological Arguments for God" (YouTube playlist); Beck, "God's Existence"; Russell and Copleston, "Debate on the Existence of God"; Sadowsky, "Endless Regress of Causes?"; Taylor, "Cosmological Argument"; Willard, "Language, Being, God"; Beck, *Does God Exist?*, chap. 2; Moreland, *Scaling the Secular City*, chap. 1; Rasmussen, "Argument for a Supreme Foundation"; Reichenbach, *Cosmological Argument*.

Consequently, the traditional monotheistic concept of God as a being the existence of which is necessary, i.e., a being with an essential nature that lacks contingency, *and which therefore lacks complexity*, fits the explanatory bill in a way that other design candidates fail to do.

Indeed, in a comparative analysis with alternative design hypotheses - whether involving hypothetical aliens,[129] viewing the cosmos as a computer simulation,[130] positing a creator along the lines of Plato's "Demiurge" (a being Plato conjectured to have imposed order upon the material world without being responsible for the creation *ex nihilo* of its fundamental constituents), or polytheism[131] (as in Mormonism[132]) - some kind of monotheism turns out to be the best explanation of the fine-tuning data.[133]

THINKING ABOUT MIND

I don't think a naturalistic account of the mind-body problem has been offered, and I am frankly doubtful as to whether one could be offered

—MICHAEL RUSE IN CARUSO, ED. *SCIENCE & RELIGION*, 193.

The fall of verificationism also precipitated a revitalization of interest in the philosophy of mind. Under the positivist paradigm of philosophical behaviorism, which was popular in the middle of the twentieth century, talk about "mind" was held to be ultimately translatable into talk about physical behavior caused by a physical response to physical stimuli. As philosopher

---

129. See Rana, "Is the Intelligent Designer Alien?" For problems with positing aliens as even a proximate cause of life on Earth, see Mind Matters, "Why Is There Fine Tuning Everywhere?" (Podcast); Williams, *Behold the Man*, chap. 6.

130. See Williams, "Simulation Hypothesis" (YouTube playlist); Mind Matters, "Why Is There Fine Tuning Everywhere?" (Podcast); Mines, "Simulation Hypothesis."

131. See Craig, "How Can Christians Engage with Polytheists?" (YouTube video); Geisler, *Baker Encyclopedia of Christian Apologetics*, 602–6; Geisler, *Christian Apologetics* (2nd ed.), chap. 13; Geisler and Watkins, *Worlds Apart* (2nd ed.), chap. 7.

132. See Williams, "Mormon View of God" (YouTube playlist); Geisler and Watkins, *Worlds Apart* (2nd ed.), chap. 7; Jackson, "Many Worlds and Many Gods"; Beverley, *Mormon Crisis*, 103–111; Parrish, "Tale of Two Theisms." For a critique of Mormonism, see Williams, "Mormonism" (YouTube playlist); BeliefMap, "About Mormonism"; Beckwith et al., *New Mormon Challenge*; Beverley, *Mormon Crisis*; Bowman, *Jesus' Resurrection and Joseph's Visions*; Burningham, *An American Fraud*; Larson, *Quest for the Golden Plates*.

133. See Craig, "How Can Christians Engage with Polytheists?" (YouTube video); Mind Matters, "Why Is There Fine Tuning Everywhere?" (Podcast); Geisler, *Christian Apologetics* (2nd ed.), part 2; Geisler and Watkins, *Worlds Apart* (2nd ed.); Meyer, *Return of the God Hypothesis*.

C. E. M. Joad explained in his 1942 *Guide to Modern Thought*, according to the behaviorists

> a living organism must in the last resort be presumed to be of the same character as an automatic machine. It will, that is to say, only "behave" in so far as it is caused to do so by a specific stimulus; and this stimulus must be a physical stimulus. It is the object of the Behviourist, therefore, to describe all behaviour in terms of responses to stimuli.[134]

On the positivist philosophy of the Vienna Circle that lay behind behaviorism, "All sentences about reality must be measurable; and if you cannot measure something then it does not exist."[135] Hence Rudolph Carnap asserted that: "All sentences of psychology describe physical occurrences, namely, the physical behaviour of humans and other animals."[136] To give an example from Gilbert Ryle:

> If we now raise the epistemologist's question, "How does a person find out what mood he is in?" we can answer that . . . he does not groan "I feel bored" because he has found out that he is bored. . . Rather, somewhat as the sleepy man finds out that he is sleepy by finding that, among other things, he keeps on yawning, so the bored man finds out that he is bored, if he does find this out, by finding that among other things he glumly says to others and to himself "I feel bored" . . .[137]

However, as Rem B. Edwards reports: "First-person self-knowledge based on direct introspective experience has been a great obstacle to the acceptance of behaviorism."[138] A. C. Ewing makes this point with a vivid example:

> In order to refute such views I shall suggest your trying an experiment. Heat a piece of iron red-hot, then put your hand on it, and note carefully how you feel. You will have no difficulty in observing that it is quite different from anything which a psychologist could observe, whether he considered outward behavior or you brain processes . . . The behaviorists pride themselves on being empiricist, but in maintaining their view they

---

134. Joad, *Guide to Modern Thought*, 53.
135. Latham, *Enigma of Consciousness*, 13.
136. Carnap, "Psychology in Physical Language", quoted by Latham, *Enigma of Consciousness*, 9.
137. Ryle, *Concept of Mind*, 102–3.
138. Edwards, "Behaviorism: II. Philosophical Issues."

are going clean contrary to experience. We know by experience what feeling pain is like and we know by experience what the physiological reactions to it are, and the two are quite unalike.[139]

Moreover, as Edwards points out: "Purposive acts, like trying to persuade psychologists that behavior is the only proper subject matter of psychology, cannot be redescribed as nonpurposive behaviors without losing essential meaning . . ."[140]

According to behaviorism, a thought just is a piece of physical behavior, a bodily event caused by physical stimuli; but as Joad argued:

> it would be meaningless to ask whether a bodily event, for example, the state of my blood pressure or the temperature of my skin, was true. These are things which occur and are real; they are facts. But they are not and cannot be true, because they do not assert anything other than themselves.[141]

In contemporary philosophical parlance, Joad is pointing out that physical behavior lacks the intrinsic "aboutness," "intentionality" or "ofness" that characterizes the "directedness of a mental state towards its object."[142] As atheist philosopher and one-time clinical neuroscientist Raymond Tallis acknowledges: "Intentionality . . . points in the direction opposite to causation . . . it is incapable of being accommodated in the materialistic world picture as it is currently constructed."[143] Consequently, on the hypothesis that behaviorism is true, no one could actually believe that behaviorism is true, because no one could have a mental state that was *about* behaviorism. In other words, along with any physicalist account of the mind, behaviorism is self-contradictory.[144]

American philosopher of science Carl Hempel announced his defection from behaviorism in 1966, rightly declaring that: "In order to characterize . . . behavioral patterns, propensities, or capacities . . . we need not only a suitable behavioristic vocabulary, but psychological terms as well."[145] George Graham reports that: "Contemporary psychology and philosophy

139. Ewing, *Fundamental Questions of Philosophy*, 101–2.
140. Edwards, "Behaviorism: II. Philosophical Issues."
141. Joad, *Guide to Philosophy*, 535.
142. Moreland, *Recalcitrant Imago Dei*, 91.
143. Tallis, *Aping Mankind*, 359.

144. For more on this and other aspects of "the argument from reason," see Willard, "Knowledge and Naturalism"; Menuge, *Agents Under Fire*; Moreland, *Recalcitrant Imago Dei*, 91–95; Reppert, *C. S. Lewis' Dangerous Idea*; Williams, *Faithful Guide to Philosophy*, chap. 12; Williams, *C.S. Lewis vs. the New Atheists*, chap. 4.

145. Hemple, *Philosophy of Natural Science*, 110.

largely share Hempel's conviction that the explanation of behavior cannot omit invoking a creature's representation of its world."[146] As Charles Taliaferro observes:

> generally, philosophers have come to abandon the project of eliminating consciousness. The denial of our mental life simply flies in the face of every waking moment. The subsequent philosophical task has been to explain, rather than to explain away, consciousness.[147]

Of course, many philosophers assume that a creature's subjective, intentional "representation of its world" must ultimately be explained, if not explained away, in terms that are consistent with a materialistic worldview. Yet, as William Lycan admits, even among theorists who are committed to materialism, "many see a deep principled difficulty for the materialist in giving a plausible account of consciousness."[148] This difficulty is what David Chalmers famously dubbed "the hard problem of consciousness"[149] in 1995. As Anthony O'Hear explains:

> Evolutionary biology and psychology can give partial accounts of particular mental functions . . . But these explanations, such as they are, assume that we do have consciousness, thought and experience . . . What they do not explain . . . is how consciousness, thought and experience can be produced by material processes at all. The most we can do is to correlate these mental phenomena with brain activity. But however fine-grained these accounts get, they do nothing to solve the basic enigma, which is how mental states and experience can emerge from physical matter . . .[150]

When I was introduced to the philosophy of mind by Dr. Alessandra Tanesini at Cardiff University, the subject was dominated by discussion of mind-brain identity and functionalism, materialist theories of mind that appeared fundamentally mistaken to me in their rejection of the mental as such.[151] As philosopher Keith Ward argues, the attempt to fit mind within a materialistic worldview

---

146. Graham, "Behaviorism."
147. Taliaferro, "Where Do Thoughts Come From?," 156–7.
148. Lycan, quoted by Iredale, "Putting Descartes Before the Horse," 40.
149. Chalmers, "Facing up to the Problem of Consciousness," 207.
150. O'Hear, *Philosophy*, 87.
151. See Williams, "Mind-Body Dualism, Free Will and Related Issues" (YouTube playlist); Goetz and Taliaferro, *Naturalism*; Moreland and Craig, *Philosophical*

is immensely counter-intuitive. It conflicts with our commonsense view that all human knowledge begins from personal experience, that we have thoughts and feelings that no one else can experience, that we are free to plan the future, and that our intentions make a real difference to the world. In short, materialism has a major problem with consciousness . . . It looks as though there is a clear distinction between the spiritual and the material, that they are different in kind.[152]

By 1998, naturalistic philosopher of mind John Heil was reporting that "in recent years, dissatisfaction with materialist assumptions has led to a revival of interest in forms of dualism."[153]

Panpsychism

More recently, this dissatisfaction with materialist assumptions has also led to a revival of interest in panpsychism, especially in a form that avoids suggesting that all things have subjective experience, but which seeks to explain human and animal consciousness by theorizing that the basic constituents of the physical realm (be they particles, strings, or whatever) either have, or intrinsically are, a very "simple" form of (vaguely defined) phenomenal consciousness (that is to say, there is "something it is like" to be these things).[154]

Panpsychism doesn't explain the convenient hypothetical proclivity of simple consciousnesses to coalesce into more complex forms of consciousness in the case of creatures with brains, but not in the case of computers, or rocks. As philosopher of mind Colin McGinn complains, pansychism

---

Foundations (2nd edition); Taliaferro, *Consciousness and the Mind of God*; Williams, *Faithful Guide to Philosophy*, chap. 11.

152. Ward, *Big Questions in Science and Religion*, 28 & 134.

153. Heil, *Philosophy of Mind*, 53. See Göcke, *After Physicalism*; Koons and Bealer, *Waning of Materialism*; Loose et al., *Blackwell Companion to Substance Dualism*; Menuge et al., eds., *Minding the Brian*; Rickabaugh and Moreland, *Substance of Consciousness*.

154. See Williams, "Panpsychism" (YouTube playlist); In Our Time, "Panpsychism" (Podcast); Mind Matters, "Dr. Angus Menuge: Models of Consciousness" (Podcast); Mind Matters, "Panpsychism Is, in Angus Menuge's View, a Desperate Move" (Podcast); Baysan, "Does Panpsychism Explain Mental Causation?"; Leidenhag, "How to Be a be a Theological Panpsychist"; Levine, "Panpsychism"; Leidenhag, *Minding Creation*; Moreland, *Consciousness and the Existence of God*, chap. 6; Robinson, "Qualia, Qualities, and Our Conception of the Physical World"; Rickabaugh and Moreland, *Substance of Consciousness*. There has also been some revived interest in the "idealist" hypothesis that *only* minds and their contents exist (See Menuge et al., eds., *Minding the Brian*).

can't even explain why a brain is conscious and a rock isn't! Even if all matter is agreed to be conscious, we still need something else to explain the facts about (macro) consciousness, specifically its distribution.[155]

Moreover, the hypothesis that the rich and unified consciousness of human subjects (a consciousness that includes cognitive mental states, such as beliefs and desires, that contemporary panpsychists generally don't attribute to "simple" consciousness) somehow emerges from, or is somehow constituted by, conjunctions of simple consciousnesses, lacks explanatory adequacy. As McGinn argues:

> The claim is that the mini minds in particles explain the maxi minds in animals. . . . Here the panpsychist faces a dilemma: either the mini minds are just like the maxi minds or they are not; the claim that they are thus alike is absurd, so it must be that they are not; but then how do they explain the maxi minds? . . . . What kind of consciousness is possessed by electrons? Presumably it is nothing like ours . . . But then how can it explain *our* consciousness? . . . . If electrons experience sensations of attraction and repulsion, how does that convert into the normal range of animal sensations? Some sort of magical transformation would need to be posited, just what panpsychism is supposed to avoid.[156]

At the very least, as Raymond Tallis points out, the panpsychist faces some important questions:

> If all stuff has mind as one of its aspects, what is special about the brain such that it—and not say rocks and trees—is aware of a world in virtue of being aware of itself? What is it about a brain that enables the mind-like aspect of things to manifest itself? If even the smallest things have very basic kinds of experiences, how is the macroscopic consciousness of organisms such as birds and beasts and people built up out of these elementary constituents? What the consciousness of these constituents would amount to and how the consciousness of a vast assembly of such constituents would throw in their lot with each other to generate an agreed upon continuous, world-supporting viewpoint of a macroscopic conscious being like you and me is entirely obscure.[157]

155. McGinn, "Problems With Panpsychism," para. 3.
156. McGinn, "Problems with Panpsychism," para. 6.
157. Tallis, "Against Panpsychism," para. 11.

Consciousness and God

Despite the growing popularity of dualism and panpsychism, many people continue to find themselves torn between acknowledging the reality of subjective mental realities on the one hand, and the modernistic assumption that minds must ultimately be explained in physical terms lacking mental properties on the other hand. Of course, as atheist Julian Baggini admits: "we do not have a rational explanation for how consciousness can be produced in physical brains."[158] However, for many scholars and lay-people alike, mind-body physicalism isn't a conclusion supported by evidence, but a deduction from their pre-commitment to a materialistic worldview. As philosopher Michael Lockwood revealed:

> I count myself a materialist . . . I take consciousness to be a species of brain activity. Having said that, however, it seems to me evident that no description of brain activity of the relevant kind, couched in the currently available language of physics . . . is remotely capable of capturing what is distinctive about consciousness. So glaring, indeed, are the shortcomings of all the reductive programmes currently on offer, that I cannot believe that anyone with a philosophical training, looking dispassionately at these programmes, would take any of them seriously for a moment, were it not for the deep-seated conviction that . . . *something* along the lines of what the reductionists are offering *must* be true.[159]

Those whose thinking isn't constrained by the same reductive conviction might find something persuasive in arguments for God that recommend monotheism as offering the best explanatory framework for panpsychism,[160] or that frame a dualistic response to the hard problem of consciousness by noting that while "it is hard to see how finite consciousness could result from the rearrangement of brute matter; it is easier to see how a conscious Being could produce finite consciousness."[161]

---

158. Baggini, *Atheism*, 77.

159. Lockwood, "Consciousness and the Quantum World," 447.

160. See Cutter and Crummett, "Psychophysical Harmony"; Leidenhag, "Why a Panpsychist Should Adopt Theism"; Moreland, *Consciousness and the Existence of God*, chap. 6.

161. Moreland, "Physicalism, Naturalism and the Nature of Human Persons," 225. See also Moreland, *Consciousness and the Existence of God*; Williams, *Faithful Guide to Philosophy*, chap. 12.

MOVING ONWARDS AND UPWARDS

Towards the end of my time at Cardiff University, an unravelling romantic relationship led me into what a flat-mate who was studying psychology recognized as clinical depression. Soon after my finals, the relationship in question ended, leading to a summer of selective serotonin reuptake inhibitors (SSRIs) and sessions with a Christian counsellor.

Despite my trying personal circumstance, I graduated with a "2:1" degree just a few marks off a "First," and was accepted onto a one year taught MA in Philosophy at Sheffield University, where my studies encompassed the Philosophy of Mind, of Time, and of Religion.

I recall writing about the contingency form of the cosmological argument (discussed earlier in this chapter) whilst taking in the view over the landscape beyond Sheffield as seen from high up in the modernist architecture of the Arts Tower, with its constantly moving paternoster lifts.[162]

Fig. 13. The Arts Tower, University of Sheffield, viewed from almost due East on Bolsover Street in 2013.[163]

---

162. See "Arts Tower."
163. https://en.wikipedia.org/wiki/File:Arts_Tower_S_2013.jpg.

Fig. 14. Paternoster lift in the Arts Tower, University of Sheffield, top floor.[164]

Alongside my taught courses, I attended a study group that worked its way through Aquinas's famous "Five Ways" of arguing for God.[165] I also served on the Committee of the Joint Chaplaincy Society, which broadened the boundaries of my ecclesiology, and through which I discovered solace in some close friendships as I continued my slow trek out of depression.

From Sheffield, I went to the University of East Anglia (UEA) in Norwich, where I wrote an interdisciplinary MPhil thesis cashing out perfect being theology in terms of the classical "transcendental values" of objective truth, goodness and beauty. Parts of my thesis were inspired by Mortimer J. Adler's defence of the objectivity of these values, a taped lecture by Norman L. Geisler on "The Issue of Beauty," and Alvin Plantinga's *Warrant and Proper Function* (Oxford, 1993).

My primary supervisor was atheist philosopher Nicholas Everett, but he spent some time away during my sojourn in Norwich (I think he was teaching abroad), leaving me with a stand-in supervisor who, as a Wittgensteinian, was not supportive of my project. During my oral thesis defence, Dr. Everett ended up "going to bat" for me against his colleague's criticism of my essentially Anselmian project!

---

164. https://en.wikipedia.org/wiki/File:Paternoster_Arts_Tower_2013.jpg.

165. See Aquinas, "Five Ways"; Kreeft, "Thomistic Cosmological Argument"; Copleston, "Commentary on the Five Ways," 86–93.

I remember Professor Everett phoning me with the news that my thesis had been passed "subject to minor correction." The correction in question was the deletion of a single footnote. I got the distinct impression that this requirement hadn't been imposed by him . . . To save me the effort and expense of having to reprint and resubmit my manuscript, Dr. Everett offered to apply some tip-ex to the offending footnote on my behalf. As this merely meant not saying something I believed, rather than saying something I didn't believe, I accepted his offer with thanks.

Beside my studies at Norwich, I helped lead the Christian Union and the Anglican Theological Society. The latter was set up by the Anglican chaplain, the Revd. Dr. Garth Barber, an astrophysicist and cosmologist who would discuss his research with me. Somehow, I also found time to hang out with friends, to participate in a short published debate on God's existence with the American atheist philosopher Michael Martin (in the pages of *The Philosopher's Magazine*[166]), and to write my first book—*The Case For God* (Monarch, 1999). Quantum physicist turned theologian Revd. Dr. John Polkinghorne KBE FRS (1930–2021)[167] described this volume as "A scrupulous and wide-ranging survey of the arguments for the existence of God . . ."[168]

Fig. 15. Playing flute in a worship band in the Chaplaincy church on campus at UEA, in Norwich.

166. See Martin and Williams, "Is There a Personal God?"

167. See McGrath, "John Polkinghorne (1930–2021)."

168. From Dr. Polkinghorne's endorsement on the front cover of *The Case For God* (Monarch, 1999). I was fortunate enough to meet Dr Polkinghorne in person at a couple of Christian conferences, and to have him sign my copy of his book *Science & Christian Belief* (SPCK, 1994).

From Being a Student to Working with Students

After UEA, I spent three years as a "student pastor" at Holy Trinity, a Church of England congregation in Leicester, before moving to Southampton to spend about fifteen years working with a (now defunct) Christian educational charity called the Damaris Trust.

My role at Damaris included presenting, and eventually producing and training a team of presenters for "Philosophy and Ethics" conferences aimed at upper year school students. Our conferences aimed to equip participants with the critical thinking tools to think for themselves about their worldview, helping them to explore questions about the meaning of life, moral responsibility, and the existence of God.

Though Damaris I found myself teaching Norwegian students from Gimlekollen College in Kristiansand on their annual UK study tour, and then teaching at the College in Norway as well. I became a part-time "Assistant Professor in Communication and Worldviews," and then Gimlekollen became part of NLA University College, where my teaching encompassed logic, the philosophy of science, natural theology and Christian apologetics.

Due to financial constraints resulting from changes in the research funding formula for Universities used by the Norwegian Government, my part-time employment with NLA came to an end in June 2025, after which I took up the role of an "Adjunct Lecturer in Communication and Worldviews."[169]

CONCLUDING THOUGHTS

Two things struck me with particular force in the writing of this chapter. The first is how so many highly influential ideologies promulgated by atheists, from modernistic verificationism, scientism and philosophical behaviourism, to postmodern death-of-the-author hermeneutics, are self-contradictory. It suggests that there's a measure of truth to the hyperbolic witticism (widely attributed to G. K. Chesterton) that: "When men stop believing in God they don't believe in nothing; they believe in anything."[170]

The second thing is how the twentieth-century revival of metaphysics coincided and combined with a string of important discoveries in various

---

169. See Williams, "Newsletter, June 2025."

170. According to Ratcliffe, *Oxford Essential Quotations* (fourth edition), this saying is "Widely attributed to G. K. Chesterton, although not traced in his works; first recorded as 'The first effect of not believing in God is to believe in anything' in Emile Cammaert's *Chesterton: The Laughing Prophet* (1937)."

sciences (from discoveries pointing to the Big Bang and Cosmic Fine Tuning, to the discovery that complex specified information lies at the core of life) to produce a renaissance in the field of natural theology, a renaissance that points with greater strength than ever before to the conclusion that our universe depends upon the uncreated, necessary and independent existence of an intelligent and wholly good personal Creator. In the words of philosopher Robert T. Lehe:

> The classical "proofs" of the existence of God are widely assumed to have been decisively discredited since the days of Hume and Kant, but they have made a comeback in the last half of the twentieth century. There has been a resurgence of Christian philosophy since the 1960s, which has benefitted from scientific developments in the last hundred years that seem to be consistent with the idea that the universe was created by a supremely powerful, intelligent being.[171]

---

171. Lehe, *God, Science, and Religious Diversity*, [Kindle loc. 1506].

Chapter Three

Reflections on the Historical Jesus

> What I have noticed is that the people around me, my awkward generation, just now on our way out of youth, have started discussing faith more seriously than we once did
>
> —Lamorna Ash, *Don't Forget We're Here Forever*, 288.

As a "way of life" or "spirituality," Christianity includes a philosophical worldview,[1] and the principle component in that worldview is the existence of "God." Within this context, "God" refers to the tri-personal, uncreated creator of all reality besides God; a being that can perhaps be best described as having a maximally beautiful essential nature that exhibits "the greatest possible array of compossible [i.e., possible together] great-making properties."[2]

There are two reasons why there's more to the Christian idea of God than can be gathered from the arguments of a traditional, non-ramified [i.e., non-expanded] natural theology (even granting the purely philosophical case for God's trinitarian nature[3]). The first reason is that Christianity identifies God as the self-revealing, historically involved God of the Jewish scriptures; "the God of Abraham, the God of Isaac, and the God of Jacob." (Ex 3:6, ESV.) The second reason is that, according to the Christian worldview,

---

1. See Williams, "Understanding Worldviews" (YouTube playlist); Sire, *Universe Next Door* (6th ed.); Williams, *Apologetics in 3D*.
2. Morris, *Our Idea of God*, 37.
3. See Williams, "Understanding the Trinity."

the messiah promised by the Jewish scriptures was none other than Jesus of Nazareth, who was not only a human, but also, as the fourth century Nicene Creed asserts, "the only Son of God, eternally begotten of the Father, God from God, Light from Light, true God from true God, begotten, not made . . ."[4] On both counts, the Christian worldview is tied to claims about events in the historical past (not in some once upon a time, never-never land); events that are in principle open to historical investigation.[5]

Of course, the Bible contains a variety of ancient languages and literary genres, and contemporary readers of biblical narratives that make historical claims can be led astray if they fail to appreciate they are reading *ancient history* rather than a work in the genre of contemporary historical scholarship.[6] Nevertheless, as noted lawyer and theologian Professor John Warwick Montgomery observes:

> Christianity . . . declares that the truth of its absolute claims rests squarely on certain historical facts open to ordinary investigation. These facts relate essentially to the man Jesus, his presentation of himself as God in human flesh, and his resurrection from the dead as proof of His deity.[7]

Or, to highlight the other side of the same historical coin, as atheist John Gray says in a comment that echoes the thinking of the apostle Paul (see 1 Cor 15:14): "If Jesus was not crucified and did not return from the dead the Christian religion is seriously compromised . . . Christianity is liable to falsification by historical fact."[8]

MY HISTORY WITH HISTORY

Being raised in a Christian home, the historical dimension of the Christian worldview was apparent to me from an early age. My interest in the history directly relevant to the claims contained in the Christian scriptures

---

4. See The Church of England, "Nicene Creed."

5. See Williams, "Christianity and Archaeology" (YouTube playlist); Williams, "Historical Jesus" (YouTube playlist); Williams, "Archaeological Evidence and Jesus (ELF 2025)" (Podcast); Armstrong, *Word Set in Stone*; Hoffmeier et al., "*Did I Not Bring Israel Out of Egypt?*"; Kitchen, *On the Reliability of the Old Testament*; Provan et al., *Biblical History of Israel*; Williams, *Behold the Man*; Williams, *Getting at Jesus*.

6. See Beale, *Erosion of Inerrancy*; Copan, *Is God a Moral Monster?*; Lamb, *God Behaving Badly*; LeFebvre, *Liturgy of Creation*.

7. Montgomery, *History, Law, and Christianity*, 48.

8. Gray, *Seven Types of Atheism*, 14–15.

was interwoven with a parentally and environmentally encouraged general interest in the past.

For example, as I explored my parent's bookshelves, I came across my mother's copy of classicist F. F. Bruce's *The New Testament Documents: Are They Reliable?*,[9] which introduced me to New Testament studies. Another early influence was German science-writer Werner Keller's best-selling *The Bible as History: Archaeology Confirms the Book of Books* (published in English in 1956, with the revised second edition following in 1980), which introduced me to an archaeological perspective on biblical history.[10]

As a child I was especially interested in medieval history. I often visited Portsmouth's Tudor-era Southsea Castle,[11] and nearby Porchester Castle, a medieval fortress with an eleventh century keep that developed within the walls of the third century Roman "Saxon Shore" fort of Portus Adurni.[12] I also enjoyed visiting medieval Cathedrals, especially those at Winchester and Salisbury.[13]

King Henry VIII was stood on Southsea Castle during the Battle of the Solent against the French in 1545, when he witnessed the sinking of his flagship The Mary Rose.[14] I recall watching in-person as the remaining hull of the Mary Rose was slowly raised from the sea in 1982; and later I spent a summer volunteering as a tour guide for the vessel as it was being preserved at Portsmouth's Navel Dockyard (which is also home to Lord Nelson's eighteenth century flagship H. M. S. Victory[15]).

I remember watching a repeat broadcast of the landmark 1969 BBC television series *Civilisation: A Personal View by Kenneth Clark*. Perhaps it was this series that set me on the road towards studying history as one of my GCSE (General Certificate in Secondary Education) subjects, and then Classical Civilization as one of my A-Level subjects. Indeed, whilst attending Mayfield Secondary School, I did my "work placement" week at what

---

9. Bruce, *New Testament Documents*.

10. Keller, *Bible as History*. For a more up-to-date introduction to Biblical archaeology, see Williams, "Christianity and Archaeology" (YouTube playlist); Williams, "Archaeological Evidence and Jesus (ELF 2025)" (Podcast); Armstrong, *Word Set in Stone*; Evans, *Jesus and the Remains of History*; Evans, *Jesus and His World*; Kitchen, *On the Reliability of the Old Testament*; Williams, *Digging for Evidence*.

11. See https://southseacastle.co.uk/.

12. See Snow, "Portchester Castle" (YouTube video); Wikipedia, "Portchester Castle."

13. See Wikipedia, "Winchester Cathedral"; Wikipedia, "Salisbury Cathedral."

14. See https://maryrose.org/.

15. Wikipedia, "H. M. S. Victory."

was then Portsmouth's "City Records Office," and for a while I considered a career in archaeology.

In short, I've had a long standing interest in history, especially as it relates to the Bible; and while I didn't become an archaeologist or historian, I have published several papers and books, and delivered a number of lectures and conference talks, that discuss historical issues of relevance to Christianity.

A PROPERLY SKEPTICAL HISTORICAL INVESTIGATION

As philosopher and atheist Bradley Monton recognizes:

> a key part of Christian doctrine is that God became flesh in the form of Jesus Christ, and that Christ acted in the world in such a way that we can get evidence of his existence, and of his divinity.[16]

The truth or falsehood of this doctrine is something that matters, and which therefore deserves to be the subject of some skepticism.

The Christian literature from the first century affirms both Jesus's humanity and his divinity, and preserves the first Christian's testimony about the experiences upon which this belief was based. This "New Testament" literature, as well as the early extra-biblical creeds, both contain attempts to state this doctrine using a combination of figurative language and the philosophical terminology of their era.

There are, naturally, a host of *metaphysical* issues that attend the claim that Jesus is simultaneously human and divine. Much scholarship has been devoted over the centuries to elucidating different philosophical understandings of "the incarnation," as well as the related doctrine of God's trinitarian nature. As philosopher Peter van Inwagen affirms, this work has shown that "these doctrines can be formulated in a way that allows no formal contradiction to be deduced from them."[17] These are very deep waters into which we cannot stray here.[18]

---

16. Monton, *Seeking God in Science*, 71.

17. Inwagen, *God, Knowledge & Mystery*, 221.

18. For philosophical explorations of the Incarnation and the Trinity, see Williams, "Trinity" (YouTube playlist); Copan, "Is the Trinity a Logical Blunder?"; Craig, "Doctrine of the Trinity"; Davies, "Somewhat Playful Proof of the Social Trinity"; Hasker, "Objections to Social Trinitarianism"; Williams, "Understanding the Trinity"; Craig, *Philosophy of Religion*; Moreland and Craig, *Philosophical Foundations* (2nd edition); Morris, *Our Idea of God*; Morris, *Logic of God Incarnate*; Murray and Rea, *Introduction*

The central concern of this chapter is what a properly skeptical *historical* investigation has to contribute to our thinking about the key Christian claim "that God became flesh in the form of Jesus Christ, and . . . acted in the world in such a way that we can get evidence of his existence, and of his divinity."[19] However, to undertake such an investigation, we need to think critically not only about how to collect relevant historical *evidence*, but how to choose the best *explanation* of that evidence, and how to carefully consider the worldview *expectations* that impinge upon these tasks.

Indeed, thinking critically about our worldview "expectations" (that is, our worldview beliefs and/or assumptions) is the most fundamental aspect of this project. We not only need to ensure that our investigative "expectations" will help to reveal, rather than to obscure, the truth about Jesus; we also need to allow the possibility that historical inquiry might lead us to adjust elements of our worldview, even to the extent that we end up holding a different worldview.

Depending upon the reader and their current worldview, this may be an unsettling prospect, or an exciting one, or both. In any case, it is of paramount importance that our investigation is not aimed at any predetermined result, besides discerning the truth.

Any reader who chafes at the notion that "discerning the truth" is a goal to be held in high esteem might profitably consider the perilous state of democracy when those who seek or possess political power routinely flout the truth in its pursuit, especially when voters are either taken in by their lies or are prepared to live as if political power rather than reality is the foundation of truth.[20]

CONTEMPORARY WORLDVIEWS & THE QUEST FOR THE HISTORICAL JESUS

A growing dissatisfaction with "modernism," and its "postmodern" terminus, is currently stimulating a quest for a "post-postmodern" or "metamodern" worldview more in line with human experience and more conducive to human flourishing. Many of those engaged in this quest are deeply reticent

---

to the Philosophy of Religion; Shumack, *Wisdom of Islam*; Senor, "Incarnation and the Trinity"; Swinburne, *Was Jesus God?*; Swinburne, *Christian God*.

19. Monton, *Seeking God in Science*, 71.

20. See Williams, "President Trump and Nationalism" (YouTube playlist); Cheney, *Oath and Honor*; Karl, *Tired of Winning*; Kessler et al., *Donald Trump and His Assault*; Rucker and Leonnig, *Very Stable Genius*; Osborn, *Assault on Truth*; Sider, *Spiritual Danger of Donald Trump*; Woodward, *Rage*.

about the idea that any contemporary version of a "pre-modern" or "traditional" worldview, such as Christianity, might have the key answers they are seeking. Nevertheless, there's an acknowledged existential hunger for things that modernism and/or postmodernism reject but which a Christian worldview can supply.[21] In this context, a properly skeptical historical investigation into the truth of the Christian doctrine "that God became flesh in the form of Jesus Christ"[22] may be seen anew as a matter of both cultural and personal consequence.

Pre-Modern Skepticism

As the website of *Skeptical Inquirer: The Magazine for Science and Reason* reminds us:

> The word "skepticism" comes from the ancient Greek *skepsis*, meaning "inquiry." Skepticism is, therefore, not a cynical rejection of new ideas, as the popular stereotype goes, but rather an attitude of both open mind and critical sense [that requires] . . . mindful cultivation of critical thinking, and an honest attitude toward intellectual inquiry.[23]

Hence, to say that Christian claims about Jesus deserve to be the subject of some skepticism is to say that they deserve to be met by an attitude of open-minded critical thought, and should be the subject not of cynical rejection, but of an honest attitude of intellectual inquiry.[24]

Of course, one person's "critical sense" can be another's "cynical rejection." As Egyptologist James K. Hoffmeier observes:

> "Critical" biblical scholars are averse to speaking of possibilities or probabilities when it comes to the Pentateuch [the first five books of the Old Testament] as a witness to history, owing to modern and postmodern skepticism.[25]

Clearly, what goes for the Pentateuch goes for *any* literature that has been gathered into the Bible, including the New Testament literature referring to Jesus.

---

21. See Williams, "Reading Culture in 3D." (Podcast.)
22. Monton, *Seeking God in Science*, 71.
23. *Skeptical Inquirer*, "What Is Skepticism?," §1, 5.
24. See Williams, "Critical Thinking" (YouTube playlist); Sinnott-Armstrong, *Think Again*; Williams, *Faithful Guide to Philosophy*, chaps. 2 and 3.
25. Hoffmeier, "Hoffmeier Rejoinder," 133.

The mere fact that the pre-modern concept of "skepticism" can now be qualified as being either "modern" or "postmodern" highlights the fact that different scholars bring different worldview expectations into their pursuits. Indeed, as Hoffmeier points out, while so-called "critical" scholars "often believe that [so-called] conservative scholars err because of flawed philosophical or theological assumptions,"[26] it is only fair to recognize that "everyone interprets texts, especially the Bible, through their political, theological, worldview, and experiential lenses."[27] Philosophical expectations *per se* are a necessary component of scholarship; but the cannons of "modern" and "postmodern" skepticism should be just as open to skeptical review as the assumptions of so-called "conservative" scholars.[28]

Worldview Expectations

> Historical judgement exercises itself within a framework of faith . . .
>
> —SCOT MCKNIGHT[29]

In the words of Hanzi Freinacht, fictional political philosopher and author of *The Listening Society: A Metamodern Guide to Politics*:

> A lot of people think that philosophy is a certain activity: that you write books about it . . . or discuss with friends. But philosophy is more than that—it is: How you view the world (ontology, "what is really real" and epistemology, "how to know stuff"); and your place in it (your idea of a "self"), and what is right and wrong (ethics or ideology). So everybody has a philosophy. When someone prays, or doesn't pray, or saves money, or helps a stranger, or works to end animal slavery, all of these things are rooted in the philosophy of that person.[30]

---

26. Hoffmeier, "Hoffmeier Rejoinder," 133.

27. Hoffmeier, "Hoffmeier Rejoinder," 133.

28. On the Old Testament as a witness to history, see FOCLOnline, "Evidence for Old Testament History" (YouTube video); Williams, "Christianity and Archaeology" (YouTube playlist); "Exodus" (YouTube playlist); "King David" (YouTube playlist); "King Solomon" (YouTube playlist); Hill, "Noachian Flood: Universal or Local?"; Armstrong, *Word Set in Stone*; Hoffmeier et al., "*Did I Not Bring Israel Out of Egypt?*"; Kitchen, *On the Reliability of the Old Testament*; Provan et al., *A Biblical History of Israel*.

29. McKnight, "Jesus of Nazareth," 161.

30. Freinacht, *Listening Society*, 15. As Jules Evans explains: "Hanzi Freinacht is a made-up character invented by two people—Emil Ejner Friis, a Danish philosopher and activist in the Danish Alternative Party; and Daniel Gortz, a PhD student in sociology at Lund University in Sweden" (Evans, "New World of Metamodernism," §5).

The philosophy that underpins a person's actions is their "worldview." As co-authors Tawa J. Anderson, W. Michael Clark, and David K. Naugle explain:

> The English term worldview is derived from the German Weltanschauung, a compound word (Welt = world + Anschauung = view or outlook) first used by Immanuel Kant to describe an individual's sensory perception of the world. . . . German philosophers used Weltanschauung increasingly for the concept of answering pivotal questions regarding life, the universe, and everything. Very quickly, other German thinkers—von Ranke (history), Wagner (music), Feuerbach (theology), and von Humboldt (physics)—applied Weltanschauung to their own disciplines. Furthermore, Weltanschauung was quickly adopted in other European countries, either as a loanword or translated into the local language.[31]

While Freinacht draws attention to the link between worldview assumptions and actions, he overlooks the connective role of motivating attitudes. Properly functioning humans develop a "way of life" or "spirituality" that aims to ingrate their worldview *assumptions* (i.e., the philosophical "expectations" they believe and/or act upon), *attitudes* (a term that here includes commitments as well as emotions), and *actions*. In other words, a person's spirituality is a way of life that tries to coherently combine their head, heart, and hands.[32]

Worldview assumptions ground spiritual attitudes to jointly sustain spiritual activities. Spiritual activities are part and parcel of a positive feedback loop. This is obvious when one thinks of the practices involved in liturgical worship, for example, but "spiritual activities" encompass the whole of one's practical life *insofar as it is coherently lived out of one's worldview assumptions and accompanying attitudes*. Our attitudes not only reflect our worldview assumptions, they can restrict the range of propositions we will even consider believing or assuming. Spiritual practices are not just the practical outworking *of* faith, but positive aids *to* faith.[33] In light of this fact, it is appropriate to represent spirituality as a dynamic loop:

---

31. Anderson et al., *Introduction to Christian Worldview*, 9.

32. See Williams, "Christian Leadership in 3D"; Williams, *Apologetics in 3D*.

33. Following philosophers Daniel Howard-Snyder and Daniel McKaughan (see their article on "Faith" in *Encyclopedia of Philosophy of Religion*), I would suggest that we can define what it means for someone's "faith/spirituality/way of life" to include faith *that* some proposition p is true, or faith *in* some proposition or person p, as: a) for them to have a positive (doxastic or non-doxastic) cognitive attitude toward the truth or trustworthiness of p (e.g., to believe that p is probably true or trustworthy, or

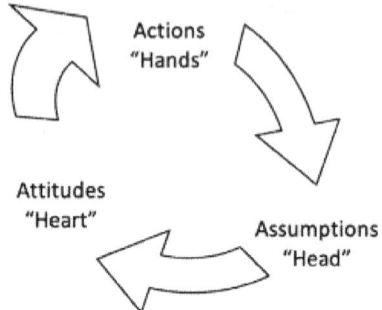

Fig. 16. Spirituality as a loop.

As theologian Mark Earey observes:

> It is not just that we express with our bodies or voices what we think in our minds or feel in our hearts: on the contrary, what we do with our bodies or say with our mouths can change or influence how we feel and what we think, as individuals and communities.[34]

That said, spirituality is more firmly rooted in worldview than in attitudes or actions, for as philosopher Dallas Willard argues: "Thoughts determine the orientation of everything we do and evoke the feelings that frame our world and motivate our actions."[35] In general one "can't evoke thoughts by feeling a certain way. However, we can evoke—and to some degree control—our feelings by directing our thoughts."[36] Hence: "what we think, imagine, believe, or guess sets boundaries to what we can or will choose, and therefore to what we can create."[37]

Spirituality is intimately bound up with the sort of people we see ourselves as being and/or becoming. As psychologist Joanna Collicutt explains:

> Our idealized self-image . . . is expressed in terms of certain principles, which are in their turn expressed in action programs. A less technical way of describing this is as who I want to be;

---

to assume p whilst neither believing nor disbelieving p), b) for them to have a positive conative attitude toward p (seeing p as worthy of choice and/or admiration), and c) for them to be disposed to live in light of their cognitive and conative stance towards p (e.g., being disposed to act on this basis, trusting and/or giving allegiance to p, whilst being disposed to be appropriately resilient in the face of challenges to living in this way).

34. Earey, *Liturgical Worship*, 65.
35. Willard, *Renewing the Christian Mind*, 4.
36. Willard, *Renewing the Christian Mind*, 4.
37. Willard, *Renewing the Christian Mind*, 4.

rules for living this out; and what I actually try to do in order to keep to those rules.[38]

That is, our worldview includes a vision of the sort of people we want to be (a matter of both "head" and "heart"), and this vision leads us to make commitments to various "rules for living," commitments we translate into actions that, over time, can become habitual or "second nature." Generally speaking, it's easier to find a different way of acting upon a given rule for living than it is to commit to a different rule, and harder still to change our idealized self-image. This aspect of spirituality must be diagrammatically represented in a hierarchical manner:

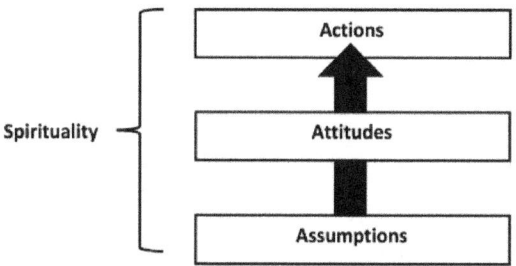

Fig. 17. Spirituality is Rooted in Worldview.

When a spirituality is shared, it sustains a "culture." In the words of Professor Walter Leirman:

By culture we mean three related aspects:
– a culture contains a vision of man and society, with a set of values and norms
– a culture is a living community of people with a certain identity
– a culture is a social and institutional practice which reflects to a certain degree the vision and the community.[39]

Leirman's "vision of man and society, with a set of values and norms" is grounded in the worldview concepts of philosophical anthropology and axiology. To quote British philosopher C. E. M. Joad:

Civilization . . . is bound up with the development of those qualities and the practice of those activities which distinguish

---

38. Collicutt, *Psychology of Christian Character Formation*, 16.
39. Leirman, *Cultures of Learning and Education*, 4.

us from the animals.... Our reason, our perception of the difference between right and wrong, our sense of beauty.[40]

The notion of "a culture" may be captured by Raymond Williams's phrase "a structure of feeling,"[41] or Charles Taylor's concept of a "social imaginary":

> our "social imaginary," that is, the way that we collectively imagine, even pre-theoretically, our social life.... What I'm trying to get at with this term is something much broader and deeper than the intellectual schemes people may entertain when they think about our social reality in a disengaged mode. I am thinking rather of the ways in which they imagine their social existence, how they fit together with others, how things go on between them and their fellows, the expectations which are normally met, and the deeper normative notions and images which underlie these expectations ... this is often not expressed in theoretical terms, it is carried in images, stories, legends, etc.... the social imagery is that common understanding which makes possible common practices.... It incorporates a sense of the normal expectations that we have of each other; the kind of common understanding which enables us to carry out the collective practices which make up our social life.[42]

I agree with Freinacht that "spirituality has little or nothing to do with specific religious content or belief."[43] Spirituality *per se* is a matter of having *some content or other* that fills out the generic spiritual structure of assumptions, attitudes, and actions. A spirituality may be Muslim or Hindu. It may be Marxist or Secular Humanist. However, content does matter! Assumptions can be true or false, attitudes can be beautiful or ugly, actions can be good or bad, and a specific spirituality can have a more or less integrative or disintegrative effect upon its adherents, depending upon whether or not it tends towards the virtuous and coherent integration of their assumptions, attitudes, and actions.[44]

Freinacht lays out the historical sequence in which different spiritualities have become culturally prominent:

---

40. Joad, *Joad's Opinions*, 120.
41. See Akker and Vermeulen, "Periodising the 2000s," 6–7.
42. Taylor, *Secular Age*, 146 and 171–72.
43. Freinacht, *Listening Society*, 265.
44. See Williams, "Reading Culture in 3D" (Podcast); Williams, "Christian Leadership in 3D"; Williams, *Apologetics in 3D*.

very roughly: First you have pre-modern society, like in medieval Europe. Then you have modern society. Then you have a postmodern criticism of modern society.[45]

Freinacht is a major voice in the contemporary quest to establish a "metamodern" worldview, spirituality, and culture.

Pre-Modernisms

There are a wide variety of "pre-modern" or "traditional" spiritualities in the contemporary world. Many—notably those rooted in classical and/or historic near-eastern cultures—celebrate the existence of objective truth, goodness, and beauty (in their axiology), believe in a cosmos of both material and spiritual realities (in their ontology), and think (in their epistemology) that humans can have and communicate knowledge (albeit in an often limited and fallible way) about those values and that cosmos, because (in their anthropology) they view humans as embodied but fundamentally immaterial selves with capacities for rational thought, reliable perception, and morally significant choice.[46]

Most contemporary pre-modernists are monotheists, including (as of 2022) "at least 3.8 billion . . . followers of Abrahamic religions."[47] According to philosopher Charles Taliaferro, in addition to "philosophical theists" with no religious affiliation:

> Hindu tradition includes important strands in which ultimate reality is described in theistic terms and there is an acknowledged distinction between Brahman (conceived of as the creator of the cosmos) and the cosmos itself.[48]

That said, comparative religions scholar Gavin Denis Flood cautions that:

> If by monotheism we mean the idea of a single transcendent God who creates the universe out of nothing (*creatio ex nihilo*), as in the Abrahamic religions, then it is open to question

---

45. Freinacht, *Listening Society*, 361.

46. See Holmes, *Contours of a Worldview*; Williams, *Faithful Guide to Philosophy*.

47. Koch, "How Many Monotheists Are There?" On Abraham, see Kitchen, *On the Reliability of the Old Testament*, chap. 7. For a critique of Islam, see Williams, "Islam" (YouTube playlist); Craig, "Concept of God in Islam and Christianity"; Beverley and Evans, *Getting Jesus Right*; Licona, *Paul Meets Muhammad*; Nicholls, *Understanding & Answering Islam*; Qureshi, *No God but One*; Small, *Textual Criticism and Qur'an Manuscripts*.

48. Taliaferro, *Philosophy of Religion*, 147.

whether or not that idea is found in the history of Hinduism. But if we mean a supreme, transcendent deity who impels the universe (whether created from nothing or not), sustains it, and ultimately destroys it before causing it to emerge once again, who is the source of all other gods who are her or his emanations, then this idea does develop within that history.[49]

As Keith Ward explains:

> *Creatio ex nihilo* (Latin for "creation from nothing") refers to the view that the universe, the whole of space-time, is created by a free act of God out of nothing, and not either out of some preexisting material or out of the divine substance itself. This view was widely, though not universally, accepted in the early Christian Church, and . . . is now almost universally accepted by Jews, Christians, and Muslims.[50]

Interestingly, a substantial percentage of religiously unaffiliated people (known to pollsters as "nones") say they believe in some sort of God, "even if they largely dislike organized religion."[51] In a 2023 poll of American adults:

> Forty-three percent of all nones professed belief in God or a higher power—including 61 [percent] of nothings in particular, 40 [percent] of agnostics and 4 [percent] of atheists. Overall, 79 [percent] of U.S. adults professed faith in God.[52]

The existence of an uncreated, personal God who created the cosmos *ex nihilo* and conserves it in being is a key element in the ontology of Abrahamic forms of monotheism, and one that arguably offers the best overall explanation for the other pre-modern worldview claims (about axiology, ontology, epistemology, and anthropology) enumerated above.

However, the "pre-modern" label encompasses a plethora of different worldviews. While space precludes a comprehensive treatment of pre-modern worldviews here, I will pass some comments about a selection of non-Abrahamic perspectives.[53]

---

49. Flood, "Introduction," 3.
50. Ward, "Creatio Ex Nihilo." See Craig, "Creation Ex Nihilo."
51. Smith, "Highlights from AP-NORC poll."
52. Smith, "Highlights from AP-NORC poll."
53. See Williams, "Buddhism" (YouTube playlist); Williams, "Pantheism/New Age Spirituality" (YouTube playlist); Collins, "Eastern Religions"; Geisler, *Christian Apologetics* (2nd ed.); Pemberton, "Are We Really All Hindus Now?"; Sire, *Universe Next Door* (6th ed.).

Polytheistic worldviews (a category that includes Mormonism, for all its Abrahamic aspects[54]) postulate the existence of multiple "gods" who emerge from within the cosmos.[55] However, as Norman L. Geisler observes: "The idea of an eternal universe posited by polytheism has . . . serious philosophical and scientific objections."[56] Indeed, past-eternal or not, polytheism lacks an adequate explanation for the existence of the physical cosmos,[57] especially one whose laws and initial conditions exhibit a chemistry and biology-permitting "fine tuning,"[58] within which the gods are said to emerge. Polytheism also faces the same problems as naturalism with respect to accounting for the existence of rational, conscious minds,[59] and to providing an adequate grounding for objective moral and aesthetic values.[60]

The pantheistic or panentheistic identification of the cosmos with divinity has stark axiological implications, as C. S. Lewis observes:

> If you do not take the distinction between good and bad very seriously, then it is easy to say that anything you find in this world is a part of God. But, of course, if you think some things really bad, and God really good, then you cannot talk like that.[61]

---

54. See Williams, "Mormon View of God" (YouTube playlist); Geisler and Watkins, *Worlds Apart* (2nd ed.), chap. 7; Jackson, "Many Worlds and Many Gods"; Beverley, *Mormon Crisis*, 103–111; Parrish, "Tale of Two Theisms." For a critique of Mormonism, see Williams, "Mormonism" (YouTube playlist); BeliefMap, "About Mormonism"; Beckwith et al., *New Mormon Challenge*; Beverley, *Mormon Crisis*; Bowman, *Jesus' Resurrection and Joseph's Visions*; Burningham, *American Fraud*; Larson, *Quest for the Golden Plates*.

55. See Geisler, *Baker Encyclopedia of Christian Apologetics*, 602–6.

56. Geisler, *Baker Encyclopedia of Christian Apologetics*, 605. See Copan and Craig, *Kalam Cosmological Argument*, Vol. 1, *Philosophical Arguments*; Copan and Craig, *Kalam Cosmological Argument*, Vol. 2, *Scientific Evidence*; Meyer, *Return of the God Hypothesis*.

57. See Craig, "How Can Christians Engage with Polytheists?" (YouTube video); Beck, "God's Existence"; Williams, *Universe From Someone*; Williams, *Faithful Guide to Philosophy*, chap. 4.

58. See Craig, "How Can Christians Engage with Polytheists?" (YouTube video); Meyer, *Return of the God Hypothesis*.

59. See Craig and Moreland, *Naturalism*; Goetz and Taliaferro, *Naturalism*; Moreland, *Recalcitrant Imago Dei*; Williams, *Faithful Guide to Philosophy*.

60. See Beckwith, "Why I Am Not a Moral Relativist"; Beckwith, "Moral Law, the Mormon Universe, and the Nature of the Right"; Beckwith and Koukl, *Relativism*; Lewis, *Abolition of Man*; Williams, *Faithful Guide to Philosophy*.

61. Lewis, *Mere Christianity*, 33. See also, Anderson, "Why I Am Not a Panentheist."

The problems with "absolute pantheism" (i.e., idealistic monism) are particularly severe. As philosopher Robin Collins explains:

> As traditionally interpreted, the Sankara school [of Hinduism] claims that there is ultimately only one reality, *Brahman*, with which each of us is absolutely identical. Moreover . . . Brahman is pure consciousness, without any internal differentiation or characteristics whatsoever. . . . Since Brahman comprises all of reality, and since there are no internal distinctions within Brahman, it follows that ultimately the world of separate entities, distinctions, and characteristics is an illusion [*maya*].[62]

However, if there's "a unity of all things," the distinction between true and false must then itself be "*maya*," and statements such as "Brahman comprises all of reality" and "the world of separate entities, distinctions, and characteristics is an illusion" *cannot be advanced as being true rather than false*. Hence:

> Sankara's philosophy . . . seems to be self-contradictory. As advocates of other Hindu schools of thought have pointed out, if the only reality is Brahman, and Brahman is pure, *distinctionless* consciousness, then there cannot exist any real distinctions in reality. But the claim that this world is an illusion already presupposes that there is an actual distinction between illusion and reality.[63]

A related problem is that, since Brahman is supposedly pure and complete knowledge:

> ignorance cannot exist in Brahman. But, since nothing exists apart from Brahman, ignorance cannot exist apart from Brahman either. Thus, it follows that ignorance could not exist, contrary to the assertion that our perception of the world of distinct things is a result of ignorance.[64]

Therefore, as Collins observes:

> It seems that one could never have any satisfactory experiential basis for believing in Sankara's philosophy. . . . even if we assume that the entire material world does not exist, but is merely a dream, experience would still overwhelmingly testify against

---

62. Collins, "Eastern Religions," 187.
63. Collins, "Eastern Religions," 188.
64. Collins, "Eastern Religions," 189.

Sankara's claim: for, within our dream itself there are innumerable distinct experiences.[65]

Mahayana Buddhists fall foul of the same problem, because they likewise "deny that any distinctions exist in reality."[66] On the assumption that there is "a unity of all things," it follows that no distinction between good and evil (or between beauty and ugliness) can truly exist, and that no statement about good or evil (or about beauty and ugliness) can be advanced as being either true or false.

James W. Sire presents the following *reductio ad absurdum* argument against any claim that there is a unity of all things: "the One is beyond duality. . . . language requires duality; several dualities in fact (speaker and listener, subject and predicate); ergo, language cannot convey truth about reality."[67] Sire's point is that this deduction, from the supposed "unity of all things" to the conclusion that "language cannot convey truth about reality," is made using language, and is thus self-contradictory.

According to *The Upanishads*: "The ignorant think that Brahman is known, but the wise know him to be beyond knowledge."[68] However, as philosophers Norman L. Geisler and William D. Watkins argue:

> The very claim that "God is unknowable in an intellectual way" seems to be either meaningless or self-defeating. For if the claim itself *cannot* be understood in an intellectual way, then it is a meaningless claim. If the claim *can* be understood in an intellectual way, then it is self-defeating, since it affirms that nothing can be understood about God in an intellectual way.[69]

According to the Madhyamika school of Mahayana Buddhism: "anything that can be spoken of or thought about is empty of content or substantial reality; indeed . . . all statements are empty of meaning."[70] Likewise, Yogacara and Zen Buddhists alike

> assert that human reason, thought, and language are ultimately invalid and indeed self-contradictory. . . . After all, Zen Buddhists argue, if we are to experience the absolute oneness (or emptiness) of all things, we must get beyond language and reason, for the business of thought and language is to make

---

65. Collins, "Eastern Religions," 189.
66. Collins, "Eastern Religions," 210.
67. Sire, *Universe Next Door*, 155.
68. "Kena," in *Upanishads*, 31, quoted in Geisler and Watkins, *Worlds Apart*, 80.
69. Geisler and Watkins, *Worlds Apart*, 104.
70. Collins, "Eastern Religions," 211.

distinctions and is thus directly opposed to the experience of enlightenment.[71]

In each case, these views are self-refuting, for "if, as they claim, all statements are empty of meaning, then the statement that all statements are empty of meaning is itself empty of meaning, and thus does not assert anything about reality."[72]

If a worldview excludes the idea that reality can be rationally understood *to any extent at all*, and/or denies that there are any real distinctions in reality, then that worldview cannot differentiate between fact and fantasy, between the objectively good and evil, beautiful and ugly, or between personal and impersonal realities. As anthropologist David Burnett explains, for Sankara Hinduism:

> Individuality and human consciousness are just a part of the total illusion of Maya. The individual soul, atman, is in fact the divine self, which is identical with "Brahman." The focus of human achievement therefore becomes world-denying rather than world-affirming. . . . To realize one's true oneness with the cosmos is to pass beyond personality.[73]

Likewise, "The Mahayana Buddhist's stress on loving others is inconsistent with their overall worldview, because ultimately their worldview implies that there is no one to love."[74]

By contrast with these (broadly) pantheistic worldviews, the world and human affirming idea "that God became flesh in the form of Jesus Christ"[75] underpins Christianity's trinitarian form of monotheism, and its call to embrace a spirituality of inter-personal love that virtuously influences and integrates our assumptions, attitudes, and actions *through faithfulness to Jesus as Lord* (Mark 8:34; Matt 11:29).[76]

---

71. Collins, "Eastern Religions," 212.
72. Collins, "Eastern Religions," 213.
73. Burnett, *Clash of Worlds*, 72.
74. Collins, "Eastern Religions," 214.
75. Monton, *Seeking God in Science*, 71.
76. On the nature of Christian faith and spirituality, see Williams, "Discipleship in 3D" (YouTube video); "Nature of Faith" (YouTube playlist); "Discipleship and Spiritual Formation" (YouTube playlist); and "Faith and Rationality" (Podcast); Howard-Snyder and McKaughan, "Faith"; Williams, "Christian Leadership in 3D"; Austen, *Humility*; Edwards, *Humility Illuminated*; McGrath, *Mere Discipleship*; McGrath, *Passionate Intellect*; Moreland, *Love the Lord with All Your Mind*; Williams, *Apologetics in 3D*.

As suggested by its earliest self-description as "The Way,"[77] Christianity is *a way of life centered upon following Jesus Christ as* "the way, the truth and the life" (John 14:6; see 1 Cor 4:16–17 and 1 Pet 3:16). The fact that Christian spirituality stems from factual claims about a historical person opens the door to confirming or disconfirming the Christian "way" (including the Christian worldview) through historical investigation, an opportunity that does not arise with respect to spiritualities that are not derived from historical events in this way. As theoretical physicist turned theologian Sir John Polkinghorne commented, as "a historically orientated religion," the "foundational stories" of Christianity "are not simply symbolic tales," but are "mediated through particular persons and events."[78] Consequently, "there is an evidential aspect to what we are told in the Bible."[79]

Caveats about Pre-modernism

It is important to note that recommending a Jesus-centered way of life, or recommending the basic ontology, axiology, epistemology, and anthropology of monotheistic pre-modernism, is *not* the same thing as rejecting everything that comes under the labels of the "modern" or the "postmodern." To borrow some words from sociologist Christian Smith:

> While I adhere to many modern ideas, I also find certain pre-modern ideas insightful and illuminating. In fact, I believe that some of them are true. Our criterion for adjudicating ideas should not be whether they are modern or premodern, but rather how well they seem to illuminate and explain reality for us.[80]

The same goes for anything the monotheistic pre-modernist may coherently consider to be "genuine insights of postmodernism."[81]

We can certainly grant that Danish economist and philosopher Lene Rachel Andersen (who describes herself as "a practicing, doubting"[82] Jewish convert) has a point when she warns:

---

77. "Christian" was originally an outsider term of abuse meaning "Christ-slave." See Acts 11:26 and 22:4.
78. Polkinghorne, *Encountering Scripture*, x–xi.
79. Polkinghorne, *Encountering Scripture*, xi.
80. Smith, *To Flourish or Destruct*, 15.
81. Dempsey, *Metamodernism*, 8.
82. Rutt, "Lene Rachel Andersen on Polymodernity," 30:12–14.

Pre-modern cultural code is the source of fundamentalism, authoritarianism, totalitarianism, and institutionalized violence, torture, oppression, persecution of minorities and freethinkers, violent enforcement of obedience and conformity, and the creation of order out of chaos through patriarchy, dogmatism and narrowmindedness.[83]

However, one cannot assume that every pre-modernist endorses everything that comes under the expansive label of the "Pre-modern cultural code." Even if one focuses upon Jewish, Christian, or Islamic pre-modernism, one finds plenty of "in-house" disagreements about the specifics of their cultural code (not to mention the "inter-house" disagreements)! Moreover, Andersen's examples seem to be "cherry picked." On the one hand, the "modern" and "postmodern" cultural codes are obviously able to produce their own share of social ills (including authoritarianism, totalitarianism, etc.).[84] On the other hand, the Judeo-Christian "Pre-modern cultural code" is the source of many socially beneficial outcomes, including such cultural institutions as hospitals, universities, experimental science, and human rights.[85] In the words of atheist philosopher Jürgen Habermas:

> Universalistic egalitarianism, from which sprang the ideals of freedom and a collective life in solidarity, the autonomous conduct of life and emancipation, the individual morality of conscience, human rights and democracy, is the direct legacy of the Judaic ethic of justice and the Christian ethic of love. This legacy substantially unchanged, has been the object of continual critical appropriation and reinterpretation. To this day, there is no alternative to it. And in light of the current challenges of a postnational constellation, we continue to draw on the substance of this heritage. Everything else is just idle postmodern talk.[86]

---

83. Andersen, *Metamodernity*, 106.

84. See Carson, *Intolerance of Tolerance*; Kramer, *Black Book of Communism*; Weikart, *Hitler's Ethic*; Weikart, *From Darwin to Hitler*.

85. See Williams, "Is Christianity Good for Society?" (YouTube playlist); Williams "Theological Roots of Science" (YouTube playlist); Hannam, "How Christianity Led to the Rise"; Brierley, *Surprising Rebirth of Belief in God*, chap. 3; Cavanaugh, *Myth of Religious Violence*; Chamberlain and Hall, *Realized Religion*; Chapman, *Slaying the Dragons*; Dickson, *Bullies and Saints*; Hannam, *God's Philosophers*; Harrison, *Bible, Protestantism and the Rise of Natural Science*; Hill, *What Has Christianity Ever Done for Us?*; Holland, *Dominion*; Mangalwadi, *Book That Made Your World*; Scrivener, *Air We Breathe*; Ward, *Is Religion Dangerous?*

86. Habermas, "Conversation about God," 150–51.

One may question whether this egalitarian legacy can be coherently sustained once it has been extracted from the ontology, axiology, epistemology, and anthropology of the Judeo-Christian pre-modernism that gave it birth. A contemporary worldview that embraces at least *some* pre-modern assumptions is actually a prerequisite for any robust critique of the social ills listed by Andersen.

Modernism

> Nearly all that I loved I believed to be imaginary; nearly all that I believed to be real I thought grim and meaningless.
>
> —C. S. Lewis[87]

The cultural dominance of worldviews that are "pre-modern" in the sense explored above waned with the growth of agnosticism and secular atheism in the (self-described) "modern" era of the nineteenth and twentieth centuries.[88] Ironically, as Alvin Plantinga points out, the "modernist" worldview has "pre-modern" roots stretching back:

> to Epicurus, Democritus, and others in the Ancient world and finds magnificent expression in Lucretius' poem, *De Rerum Natura*. . . . it is also to be found in the medieval world, perhaps among some of the Averroists, for example. It was left to modernity, however, to display the most complete and thorough manifestations of this perspective.[89]

Broadly speaking, modernity embraced an ontology of materialism/physicalism or metaphysical naturalism,[90] an epistemology of (either "hard" or "soft") scientism,[91] and an axiology that ejected moral and aesthetic value from the realm of facts.[92] As philosopher Jonathan Rowson explains, modernism has generally been opposed to the pre-modern, transcendental triad of objective truth, goodness, and beauty[93] as such:

87. Lewis, *Surprised by Joy*, 197.
88. See Walker, *Seven Atheisms*; McGrath, *Twilight of Atheism*; Spencer, *Atheists*.
89. Plantinga, "Augustinian Christian Philosophy," 296–97.
90. See Rosenberg, *Atheist's Guide to Reality*, chap. 2.
91. See Williams, "Scientism" (YouTube playlist); Williams, "Distinguishing Science from Scientific Naturalism" (Podcast); Moreland, *Scientism and Secularism*.
92. See Baggini, *Atheism*, chap. 3 (especially page 51); Mackie, *Ethics*; Rosenberg, *Atheist's Guide to Reality*.
93. On this triad, see Williams, "Thinking in 3D" (Podcast); Wattles, "C. S. Lewis,

> it . . . broke them apart—so you have a . . . scientific truth severed from the . . . ethics and aesthetics of the good and the beautiful.[94]

From a pre-modern Abrahamic perspective, the resultant modernist anthropology is dehumanizing. As Plantinga explains, according to the typical worldview of modernism,

> there is no God, nor anything else beyond nature; and we human beings are insignificant parts of a vast cosmic machine that proceeds in majestic indifference to us, our hopes and aspirations, our needs and desires, our sense of fairness or fittingness.[95]

True, a number of thinkers who are "modernists" in the sense of being agnostic or atheistic reject scientism and/or make philosophical arguments for objective moral values, and/or for a non-materialistic anthropology (e.g., David Chalmers, Donald Hoffman, Mary Midgley, Thomas Nagel, Russ Shafer-Landau, Eric Wielenberg). Nevertheless, the culturally dominant strand of "modernism" remains that summed up in Richard Dawkins's assertion that:

> The universe that we observe has precisely the properties we should expect if there is, at bottom, no design, no purpose, no evil and no good, nothing but blind, pitiless indifference.[96]

As C. S. Lewis explained, "some people believe that nothing exists except Nature . . . a vast process in space and time which is *going on of its own accord.*"[97] Given this materialistic worldview, the natural "process" which is "going on of its own accord" is a "meaningless play of atoms in space and time."[98] To quote Freinacht: "'Modernism', in this sense, is the standard worldview we get in secular Western societies today."[99]

To put matters more formally, whilst making allowance for some in-house disagreement, the "modernist" worldview says that:

Peter Kreeft,"; Adler, *Adler's Philosophical Dictionary*; Adler, *Six Great Ideas*; Cowan and Spiegel, *Love of Wisdom*; Lewis, *Abolition of Man*; Turley, *Awakening Wonder*; Williams, *Faithful Guide to Philosophy*; Williams, *Apologetics in 3D*.

94. Quoted in Perspectiva, "What Is Metamodernism?"
95. Plantinga, "Augustinian Christian Philosophy," 296.
96. Dawkins, *River out of Eden*, 133. See Baggini, *Atheism*; Rosenberg, *Atheist's Guide to Reality*. See also Williams, "Sorting the Chaff from the Wheat."
97. Lewis, *Miracles*, 4–5.
98. Lewis, "On Living in an Atomic Age," 73–80.
99. Freinacht, *Listening Society*, 372.

- *The physical world is an uncreated, and therefore unintended, closed system* (i.e., every effect within the system has a cause within the system).

- *The fundamental elements of the physical world are "blind"* (i.e., they lack conscious awareness or intentionality).

- *If anything exists that can't be described in the terms used by the naturalistic physical sciences*—something denied by the standard materialism described by Lewis—*then it "supervenes" on* (i.e., depends upon and is wholly determined by) *something that can be so described* (and it is thus causally *effete*).

A classic statement of the standard modernist ontology and anthropology was laid out by British philosopher and mathematician Bertrand Russell (1872–1970), in a famous essay published under the title "The Free Man's Worship" in 1903:

> That Man is the product of causes which had no prevision of the end they were achieving; that his origin, his growth, his hopes and fears, his loves and his beliefs, are but the outcome of accidental collocations of atoms; that no fire, no heroism, no intensity of thought and feeling, can preserve an individual life beyond the grave; that . . . the whole temple of Man's achievement must inevitably be buried beneath the debris of a universe in ruins—all these things, if not quite beyond dispute, are yet so nearly certain, that no philosophy which rejects them can hope to stand. Only within the scaffolding of these truths, only on the firm foundation of unyielding despair, can the soul's habitation henceforth be safely built.[100]

As for the axiology and epistemology of modernism, Russell affirmed elsewhere that:

> While it is true that science cannot decide questions of value, that is because they cannot be intellectually decided at all, and lie outside the realm of truth and falsehood. Whatever knowledge is attainable, must be attained by scientific methods; and what science cannot discover, mankind cannot know.[101]

More recently, atheist philosopher Alex Rosenberg presented a modernist creed in his book *The Atheists' Guide to Reality*:

> Is there a God? No. What is the nature of reality? What physics says it is. What is the purpose of the universe? There is none.

100. Russell, "Free Man's Worship," 2.
101. Russell, *Religion and Science*, §27.

> What is the meaning of life? Ditto. Why am I here? Just dumb luck... Is there a soul? Is it immortal? Are you kidding? Is there free will? Not a chance. What happens when we die? Everything pretty much goes on as before, except us. What is the difference between right and wrong, good and bad? There is no moral difference between them.[102]

With respect to the axiology leading Rosenberg to affirm that there is "no moral difference" between right and wrong, philosopher Nancy Pearcey comments that

> The strict separation of facts from values is the key to unlocking the history of the modern Western mind. . . . people have always known that there is a distinction between is and ought . . . between descriptive statements and normative statements. In earlier ages, however, people thought both types of statement dealt with questions of truth. If you made a moral statement about what someone ought to do, it was either true or false.[103]

The strict separation of objective facts from subjective values is entailed both by modernism's ontology and by the epistemology of "hard scientism" expressed in Rosenberg's statement that "we trust science as the only way to acquire knowledge."[104]

Of course, the philosophical claim that "science" is "the only way to acquire knowledge" is self-defeating. In the words of philosopher of science Del Ratzsch:

> science cannot validate either scientific method itself or the presuppositions of that method. . . . Those who claim either that science is competent for dealing with all matters or that science is the only legitimate method for dealing with any matter are seriously confused.[105]

Moreover, the claim that science is either the only way to acquire knowledge ("hard scientism"), or even that it is the best way to acquire knowledge ("soft scientism"), is refuted by counter-examples concerning intuitively known, properly basic truths, such as our knowledge of modal logic, or of certain ethical and aesthetic values (e.g., "the holocaust was evil," "rainbows are beautiful"). As neo-atheist Sam Harris rightly observes:

---

102. Rosenberg, *Atheists' Guide to Reality*, 2–3.
103. Pearcey, *Saving Leonardo*, 25 and 27.
104. Rosenberg, *Atheists' Guide to Reality*, 20.
105. Ratzsch, *Science and Its Limits*, 93.

"intuition"... denotes the most basic constituent of our faculty of understanding. While this is true in matters of ethics, it is no less true in science. When we can break our knowledge of a thing down no further, the irreducible leap that remains is intuitively taken. Thus, the traditional opposition between reason and intuition is a false one: reason is itself intuitive to the core, as any judgement that a proposition is "reasonable" or "logical" relies on intuition to find its feet.... The point, I trust, is obvious: we cannot step out of the darkness without taking a *first* step. And reason, without knowing how, understands this axiom if it would understand anything at all. The reliance on intuition, therefore, should be no more discomforting for the ethicist than it has been for the physicist.[106]

However, once we widen our epistemology beyond the self-contradictory confines of hard scientism, we come face-to-face with metaphysical realities that refuse to fit within the parameters of modernism. As William Lane Crag and J. P. Moreland explain, using terminology that originated with philosopher Frank Jackson:

given that naturalists are committed to a fairly widely accepted physical story about how things came to be and what they are, the location problem is the task of locating or finding a place for some entity (for example, semantic contents, mind, agency) in that story.[107]

The apparent existence of realities including consciousness, intentionality, rational thought, libertarian free will and objective values pose "location problems" that many philosophers and scientists argue break the strictures of the modernist worldview.[108] Besides which, scientific inquiry over the

---

106. Harris, *End of Faith*, 183.

107. Craig and Moreland, *Naturalism*, xii.

108. See Williams, "Imagine Naturalism" (YouTube video); "Problems with Materialism/Metaphysical Naturalism" (YouTube playlist); and "Christian Worldview and Science in Apologetic Perspective: Anthropos" (Podcast); Koons, "Incompatibility of Naturalism and Scientific Realism"; Lewis, "Cardinal Difficulty of Naturalism"; Menuge, "Dennett Denied"; Menuge, "Libertarian Free Will"; Plantinga, "Evolutionary Argument against Naturalism"; "Content and Natural Selection"; and "Against Materialism"; Reppert, "Argument from Reason"; Willard, "Knowledge and Naturalism"; Craig and Moreland, *Naturalism*; Goetz and Taliaferro, *Naturalism*; Menuge, *Agents Under Fire*; Menuge et al., eds., *Minding the Brian*; Midgley, *Are You an Illusion?*; Moreland, *Consciousness and the Existence of God*; Moreland, *Recalcitrant Imago Dei*; Moreland and Rickabaugh, *Substance of Consciousness*; Nagel, *Mind and Cosmos*; O'Hear, *Philosophy in the New Century*; O'Hear, *After Progress*; Reppert, *C. S. Lewis's Dangerous Idea*; Taliaferro, *Consciousness and the Mind of God*; Williams, *Universe from Someone*; *Faithful*

past century has uncovered various aspects of physical reality (from the finitude of the cosmic past to the specified complexity of cosmic and biological fine-tuning) that constitute *empirically grounded* "location problems" for the belief that the cosmos can be adequately described as nothing but "a vast process in space and time which is *going on of its own accord*."[109]

Modernism and History

When the modernists at *Skeptical Inquiry* say that "proper skepticism promotes scientific inquiry, critical investigation, and the use of reason in examining controversial and extraordinary claims,"[110] you may be tempted to simply nod in agreement. However, there are questions about what it means to say an inquiry is "scientific,"[111] how particular truth-claims are and others are not assigned the label of being "controversial and extraordinary," and what all of that might imply when it comes to critically assessing the Christian view of Jesus; and these questions are themselves matters deserving proper skepticism. It is all too easy for the modernist skeptic to build their conclusion into their method of inquiry. For example, many modernists are persuaded by David Hume's skepticism about miracles, but as William Lane Craig writes: "those who are familiar with contemporary philosophy . . . know that Hume's arguments are today widely rejected as fallacious."[112]

A key point worth making here is that Hume wrote before probability calculus was well understood. As philosopher Angus Menuge explains:

> That Hume is mistaken in applying the probability of frequency to historical cases is clearly shown by Bayesian probability theory. According to Bayes's theorem . . . even if an event initially seems unlikely, new evidence can rationally convince us that the event occurred. . . . As applied to miracles, Bayes's theorem shows that even if the prior probability of a miracle (M) is low based on our background knowledge (B), there may be evidence (E) that is very unlikely if no miracle occurred (Not-M) but very

---

Guide to Philosophy; *C. S. Lewis vs. the New Atheists*; and *I Wish I Could Believe*.

109. Lewis, *Miracles*, 5.

110. *Skeptical Inquirer*, "What Is Skepticism?"

111. See Monton, *Seeking God in Science*; Ratzsch, *Science and Its Limits*; Williams, *Informed Cosmos*.

112. Craig, "Christ and Miracles," 142. See Williams, "Miracles" (YouTube playlist); Beckwith, "Theism, Miracles, and the Modern Mind"; Beckwith, *David Hume's Argument against Miracles*; Earman, *Hume's Abject Failure*; Geivett and Habermas, *In Defence of Miracles*; Houston, *Reported Miracles*; Larmer, *Legitimacy of Miracle*; McGrew, "Arguments from Providence and Miracles"; Williams, *Getting at Jesus*, chap. 1.

likely if there was a miracle (M). This is the relative likelihood. When multiplied by the prior probability, this is sufficient to give a high posterior probability for M.[113]

As a case study in modernist assumptions predetermining the conclusion historical investigation is allowed to reach, consider the approach taken by atheist philosopher Daniel Dennett, who said of his naturalism that: "It's defeasible. I could learn to abandon it if I encountered insuperable difficulties in carrying out the naturalist program."[114] Despite this apparent openness to falsification, Dennett rejected the possibility that evidence for a miraculous act of divine revelation might pose an "insuperable" difficulty to "carrying out the naturalist program," on the *a priori* basis that "historical arguments simply cannot be introduced into serious investigation [of God], since they are manifestly question begging."[115] Yet, far from begging the question of God's existence, historical arguments for miracles need only presuppose *the possibility of* God's existence. Moreover, historical arguments for miracles might play a significant part in a cumulative case for God in which other arguments establish a measure of plausibility for monotheism.

Hence, it was actually *Dennett* who begged the question here. Indeed, Dennett invoked "the scientific method, with its assumption of no miracles"[116] as a bulwark against considering evidence for miraculous defeaters to his "naturalist program." According to Dennett: "saying something is a miracle is a failure of imagination."[117] On the contrary, saying that naturalism "is defeasible," while simultaneously rejecting evidentially motivated arguments for miracles on *a priori* grounds, is an exercise in smuggling the modernist conclusion into one's investigative method. All of which highlights the importance of Richard Dawkins's call for making "disciplined precautions against personal bias, confirmation bias, pre-judgement of issues before the facts are in."[118]

---

113. Menuge, "Justified Belief in the Resurrection," 131–32.
114. Dennett and Spencer, "Mounting Disbelief," 13.
115. Dennett, *Breaking the Spell*, 240.
116. Dennett, *Breaking the Spell*, 26.
117. Dennett and O'Malley, "Q&A."
118. Dawkins, *Science in the Soul*, 7.

An Enlightened Understanding of Jesus?

Many people (including academics) have modernist worldview commitments that preclude a Christian understanding of Jesus. For example, according to New Testament scholar Helen K. Bond:

> modern *academic study* of the historical Jesus only really began in the wake of the eighteenth-century Enlightenment, with . . . its rejection of a God who intervenes in history in supernatural ways. The emergence of historical criticism in the nineteenth century allowed distinctions to be made between the "Christ of faith" and the "Jesus of history," distinctions that have underpinned the Quest [for the historical Jesus] ever since.[119]

This received, modernist "wisdom" deserves some skeptical unpicking. First, "the Enlightenment" was not the monolithic movement portrayed by Bond. According to historian Helena Rosenblatt:

> The term "Christian Enlightenment" no longer raises eyebrows. . . . A widespread consensus used to exist that the very essence of the Enlightenment . . . was its attack on religion. . . . Many scholars . . . described the Enlightenment as being—by its very nature—anti-Christian, anti-Church and even antireligious. We now know, however, that the relationship between Christianity and the Enlightenment was far more complex and interesting. We realize that these previous interpretations were overly focused on France, and erroneously tended to posit a single Enlightenment. . . . we now see it not so much as a unified and Francophone phenomenon, but rather as a "family of discourses" with many regional and national variations across Europe and in America. It has become clear that earlier interpretations were based on an impoverished view of religious traditions and perhaps even an outright disdain for them.[120]

As historian Rodney Stark explains:

> The single most remarkable and ironic thing about the "Enlightenment" is that those who proclaimed it made little or no contribution to the accomplishments they hailed. . . . Voltaire, Rousseau, Diderot, Hume, Gibbon, and the rest were literary men, while the primary revolution they hailed as the "Enlightenment" was scientific. Equally misleading is the fact that although the literary men who proclaimed the "Enlightenment"

---

119. Bond, *Historical Jesus*, 7.
120. Rosenblatt, "Christian Enlightenment," 283.

were irreligious, the central figures in the scientific achievements of the era were deeply religious. So much then for the idea that suddenly in the sixteenth century, enlightened secular forces burst the chains of Christian thought and set the foundation for modern times. What the proponents of "Enlightenment" actually initiated was the tradition of angry secular attacks on religion in the name of science.... Presented as the latest word in sophistication, rationalism, and reason, these assaults are remarkably naïve and simplistic—both then and now. In truth, the rise of science was inseparable from Christian theology, for the latter gave direction and confidence to the former.[121]

Likewise, many of the Enlightenment's leading philosophers were Christians (e.g., Immanuel Kant, Gottfried Leibniz, John Locke, Thomas Reid, Mary Wollstonecraft, etc.). Hence Terry Eagleton observes both that "the Enlightenment . . . was not especially anti-religious"[122] and that "the Enlightenment was deeply shaped by values which stemmed from the Christian tradition."[123] As historian Allan Chapman concludes, in the skewed sense that modernists often attach to the phrase, "the Enlightenment" turns out to be "the creation of scholars with their own cultural and usually anti-Christian axes to grind."[124]

Second, and more importantly for our present purposes, the Enlightenment did *not* draw a line of demarcation between scholars whose rejection of miracles left them free to engage in a respectably critical, properly skeptical historical study of the "Jesus of history," and un-critical scholars whose religious beliefs condemn them to blind adherence to the "Christ of faith." Indeed, the rejection of the supernatural expressed in the traditional, anti-religious conception of "the Enlightenment" does not *allow* the distinction between the "Christ of faith" and the "Jesus of history" as Bond says. Rather, it *requires* that distinction, and does so *regardless of the evidence*! Philosopher C. Stephen Evans calls out the modernist critics on this game bait and switch:

> Critics . . . raise objections to historical religious knowledge that are apparently empirical in nature, and thus should presuppose [a] conception of religious knowledge that is open in principle to such historical knowledge. When we look more deeply, however, we find that these empirical objections are a smokescreen

---

121. Stark, *Triumph of Christianity*, 252.
122. Eagleton, *Culture and the Death of God*, 5.
123. Eagleton, *Reason, Faith, and Revolution*, 68.
124. Chapman, *Slaying the Dragons*, 67.

> for covert [philosophical] presuppositions.... Why should we assume that whatever religious knowledge takes as its object... can't manifest itself in the natural world at all? While it may be a genuinely empiricist claim to say that empirical religious knowledge is difficult to attain or can only be attained under certain conditions, empiricism provides no real support for the thesis that empirical religious knowledge is impossible.[125]

Being open to the evidence means being open to whatever theory is best supported by the evidence. A miraculous explanation should never be our *first* port of call (even people who believe in miracles think they are exceptional events); but, absent a knock-down proof against miracles, neither should our theory of knowledge preclude accepting a miracle *regardless of the evidence*. Hence, when it comes to claims about miracles, there's no avoiding the need *to examine and explain the evidence.*

From Modernism to Post-Modernism

> What then is the postmodern?... It is undoubtedly part of the modern.
> —JEAN-FRANÇOIS LYOTARD[126]

Modernism's main claim to superiority as a worldview is that it offers the supposed explanatory simplicity of a monistic ontology.[127] However, the monism of modernism forces it to deny the existence of apparent realities (ontological, epistemological, axiological, and anthropological) that most people think they are warranted in acknowledging. At the turn of the twenty-first century, British philosopher Anthony O'Hear articulated the incongruity of this situation:

> There are key aspects of human life and experience which cannot be seen in purely materialistic terms. Our search for knowledge, our moral sense and the appreciation of beauty all extend our horizons beyond those of survival and reproduction. The phenomenon of consciousness is hard to even describe in terms drawn from the physical sciences. So central is consciousness to our life that it is impossible to see it as a mere by-product of physical forces and events.... In the past these intimations of value have typically been expressed in and understood

---

125. Evans, *Historical Christ*, 176 and 177.
126. Quoted in Rudrum, "Note on the Supplanting," 337.
127. See Gage, "Is the God Hypothesis Improbable?," 59–76.

> religiously.... with the advance of materialism, formal religion has declined. But the intimations of value survive, and they are resistant to being explained away in materialistic fashion.... Together, consciousness and our attitudes to logic and knowledge suggest that seeing ourselves as biological survival machines is woefully inadequate. Similarly, the moral sense which permeates our lives... suggests the limitations of naturalistic accounts for human existence.... And so does our aesthetic interest.[128]

Orthodox modernists recognize that their worldview commits them to a form of nihilism that ejects pre-modern notions of objective goodness and beauty from their axiology, and pre-modern notions of personhood from their anthropology.[129] They profess this a metaphysical price worth paying, because they believe modernism to be both grounded in, and a royal road to, objective truth about reality discovered through naturalistically defined sciences.

Postmodernists argue that modernists have not taken their ontological commitment to naturalism seriously enough, and that the logical outcome of this commitment is a deeper form of nihilism that forces objective truth into the outer darkness formerly reserved for objective goodness and beauty. Hence postmodernism has its roots deep within modernism and belongs "to a long post-Nietzschean tradition of despair about reason."[130] As philosopher Douglas Groothuis comments:

> Postmodernism is so often presented as a radical departure from modernism that it is easy to miss the insight that postmodernism is, in many ways, modernism gone to seed, carried to its logical conclusion and inevitable demise.[131]

---

128. O'Hear, *Philosophy in the New Century*, 146, 153, and 159.

129. See Baggini, *Atheism*; Rosenberg, *Atheist's Guide to Reality*. See also Williams, "Sorting the Chaff from the Wheat"; *C.S. Lewis vs. the New Atheists*; and *I Wish I Could Believe*.

130. Butler, *Postmodernism*, 115.

131. Groothuis, *Truth Decay*, 40.

Taking the Darwinian Saw to the Modernist Branch

> If philosophy is to have a future in the twenty-first century, it must not sacrifice rigour. But to retain relevance and significance, it must turn away from scientism and cultural nihilism, the philosophical dead-ends of the twentieth century.
>
> —Anthony O'Hear[132]

Postmodern philosopher Richard Rorty (1931–2007) wrote that "keeping faith with Darwin" means realizing that "our species, its faculties and its current scientific and moral languages, are as much products of chance as are tectonic plates and mutated viruses."[133] Why trust the cognitive capacities of a creature cobbled together by "chance" events winnowed by the axiomatic restriction that the results of those events must work with respect to survival?[134] As Steven Pinker observes, according to philosophical Darwinism: "Our brains were shaped for fitness, not for truth."[135] Following this logic, atheist John Gray argues that modernists should *not* treat science as a quest for truth:

> Now and then, perhaps, science can cut loose from our practical needs, and serve the pursuit of truth. But to think that it can ever embody that quest is pre-scientific—it is to detach science from human needs, and make of it something that is not natural but transcendental. To think of science as the search for truth is to renew a mystical faith, the faith of Plato and Augustine, that truth rules the world, that truth is divine . . . . Modern humanism is the faith that through science humankind can know the truth—and so be set free. But if Darwin's theory of natural selection is true this is impossible. The human mind serves evolutionary success, not truth. To think otherwise is to resurrect the pre-Darwinian error that humans are different from all other animals. . . . Darwinian theory tells us that an interest in truth is not needed for survival or reproduction . . . Truth has no systematic evolutionary advantage over error.[136]

---

132. O'Hear, *Philosophy in the New Century*, viii.

133. Rorty, "Untruth and Consequences."

134. See Dennett and Plantinga, *Science and Religion*; Plantinga, *Where the Conflict Really Lies*, part 4; Williams, *Faithful Guide to Philosophy*, chap. 12; Williams, *C.S. Lewis vs. the New Atheists*, chap. 4.

135. Pinker, *How the Mind Works*, 305.

136. Gray, *Straw Gods*, 20, 26, and 27.

Hence Rorty argued *on modernist grounds* that:

> The idea that one species of organism is, unlike all the others, oriented not just towards its own increased propensity but toward Truth, is as un-Darwinian as the idea that every human being has a built-in moral compass.[137]

Again, it was on the basis of the *modernist* philosophy, "which denies that we are related to the world in anything other than causal terms,"[138] that Rorty concluded he had to explain "rationality and epistemic authority by reference to what society lets us say, rather than the latter by the former."[139]

David Rudrum hits the nail on the head when he comments that postmodernism:

> is not an epoch that follows the modern, but a moment of crisis, fissure, or rupture within it, and it is part of the very fabric of modernity that such moments will come back up again (and again).[140]

This being so, it follows that *to deviate from postmodern skepticism about reality we must simultaneously deviate from the core commitments of modernism.* Fortunately, this is a deviation urged upon us by reason itself, for as atheist philosopher Thomas Nagel recognizes: "Evolutionary naturalism provides an account of our capacities that undermine their reliability, and in doing so undermines itself."[141]

Incredulity towards the Postmodern Metanarrative

Oxford University literary scholar Christopher Butler (1940–2020) explains that "the basic attitude of postmodernists was a scepticism about the claims of any kind of overall, totalizing explanation."[142] French philosopher Jean-François Lyotard "argued in his *La condition postmoderne* (published

---

137. Rorty, "Untruth and Consequences," 36.
138. Ramberg and Dieleman, "Richard Rorty."
139. Rorty, *Philosophy and the Mirror of Nature*, 174. See C. S. Lewis Essays, "C. S. Lewis - De Futilitate" (YouTube video); Koons, "Incompatibility of Naturalism and Scientific Realism"; Menuge, "Role of Agency in Science"; Menuge, "Libertarian Free Will"; Willard, "Knowledge and Naturalism"; Lewis, *Miracles*; Reppert, *C. S. Lewis's Dangerous Idea*; Williams, *Faithful Guide to Philosophy*, chap. 12; Williams, *C.S. Lewis vs. the New Atheists*, chap. 4.
140. Rudrum, "Note on the Supplanting," 337.
141. Nagel, *Mind and Cosmos*, 27.
142. Butler, *Postmodernism*, 15.

in French in 1979 . . .) that we now live in an era in which legitimizing 'master narratives' are in crisis and in decline."[143] Lyotard famously commented that: "simplifying to the extreme, I define postmodern as incredulity towards metanarratives."[144] For postmodernists:

> This heralded a pluralist age, in which . . . even the arguments of scientists and historians are to be seen as no more than quasi narratives which compete with all the others for acceptance. They have no unique or reliable fit to the world, no certain correspondence with reality. They are just another form of fiction.[145]

To quote metamodern writer Brendan Graham Dempsey:

> Postmodern theories divorced language from reality, positing signs as arbitrary abstractions whose meaning only derives through contrast to other abstract signs in a linguistic system. In this way, language never quite refers to the world, only to other signs, which are always pointing elsewhere, leading to an infinite deferral of meaning.[146]

As Butler wryly observes, postmodernism "is certain of its uncertainty, and often claims that it has seen through the sustaining illusions of others," so that it "has grasped the 'real' nature of the cultural and political institutions which surround us."[147] Butler critiques the way in which French philosopher Jacques Derrida and his followers:

> seem to be committed to one fairly clear historical proposition: that philosophy and literature in the Western tradition had for too long falsely supposed that the relationship between language and world was . . . well founded and reliable. . . . This is Derrida's own grand metanarrative. . . . However, it is logically obvious that you can't demonstrate how language always "goes astray" without at the same time having a secret and contradictory trust in it. For without a pretty confident notion of the truth, how can we show that any particular stretch of language has "gone astray" or fallen into contradiction?[148]

---

143. Butler, *Postmodernism*, 13.
144. Butler, *Postmodernism*, 13.
145. Butler, *Postmodernism*, 15.
146. Dempsey, *Metamodernism*, 125.
147. Butler, *Postmodernism*,
148. Butler, *Postmodernism*, 17–18.

Literary scholar and cultural theorist Terry Eagleton likewise skewers the self-referential incoherence of postmodernism with respect to political (and hence moral) discourse:

> Who needs to launch a detailed critique of left-wing thought when you can argue, much more grandiosely, that all social discourse is blinded and indeterminate, that the "real" is undecidable, that all actions beyond a timorous reformism will proliferate perilously beyond one's control, that there are no subjects sufficiently coherent to undertake such actions in the first place, and that there is no total system to be changed in any case, that any apparently oppositional stance has already been pre-empted by the ruse of power, and that the world is no particular way at all, assuming we can know enough about it to assert even that? But in seeking to cut the ground from under its opponents feet, postmodernism finds itself unavoidably pulling the rug out from under itself, leaving itself with no more reason why we should resist fascism than the feebly pragmatic plea that fascism is not the way we do things in Sussex or Sacramento.[149]

Postmodernism and History

As Christopher Butler observes, postmodern deconstruction: "supported a general move towards relativist principles in postmodernist culture. It left postmodernists not particularly interested in empirical confirmation and verification in the sciences."[150] Naturally, this "de-constructive" attitude carried over into the study of history. However: "there is such a thing as a more or less adequately descriptive narrative. A large amount of correspondence between language and reality is possible."[151] It is an eminently reasonable form of (pre-modern) skepticism that cautions us to be more aware of "the theoretical assumptions which support the narratives produced by all historians;"[152] but "if anyone says that everything is 'really' just constituted by a deceiving image, and not by reality, how does he or she know? They presuppose the very distinctions they attack."[153]

Historian Richard J. Evans reckons that:

---

149. Eagleton, *Illusions of Postmodernism*, 27–28.
150. Butler, *Postmodernism*, 28.
151. Butler, *Postmodernism*, 35.
152. Butler, *Postmodernism*, 35.
153. Butler, *Postmodernism*, 118.

> the most far-reaching, comprehensive and explicit challenge to history as a discipline . . . has been mounted by the French linguistic theorist Roland Barthes and the philosopher Jacques Derrida. As early as 1968 Barthes charged that historians' claim to reconstruct past reality . . . was . . . "an inscription on the past pretending to be a likeness of it, a parade of signifiers masquerading as a collection of facts." Objectivity was "the product of what might be called the referential illusion." . . . Historians' own understanding of what they did remained, as Jacques Derrida noted, stubbornly "logocentric," that is, they imagined they were rational beings engaged in a process of discovery. But this too was an illusion, like all forms of "logocentrism."[154]

Of course, when Barthes wrote about the claims made by historians, he did so with reference to claims that historians *had* made, and he was therefore acting as a historian offering his readers a reconstruction of past reality (albeit the recent past). Hence, Barthes's critique of historians was self-referentially incoherent. Likewise, Derrida's objection to the idea that anyone can engage in a rational process of discovery has no force unless it is itself offered up as the conclusion of a rational process of discovery, in which case it contradicts itself.

Evans explains that, according to Derrida:

> the meaning of a text changes every time it is read. Meaning is put into it by the reader, and all meanings are in principle equally valid. In history, meaning cannot be found in the past; it is merely put there, each time differently, and with equal validity, by different historians. There is no necessary or consistent relationship between the text of history [i.e., the past] and the texts of historians.[155]

Of course, if Derrida is correct, then reading Derrida doesn't enable anyone (including Evans, and including Derrida himself) to correctly understand what Derrida wrote!

In his famous essay "The Death of the Author" Roland Barthes issued a self-contradictory rejection of the link between authorial intent and the meaning of a text, both with respect to literary texts and to "the world as text" authored by God:

> We know now that a text is not a line of words releasing a single "theological" meaning (the "message" of the Author-God). . . . Once the Author is removed, the claim to decipher a text

---

154. Evans, *In Defence of History*, 94.
155. Evans, *In Defence of History*, 95.

> becomes quite futile. To give a text an Author is to impose a limit on that text, to furnish it with a final signified . . . writing ceaselessly posits meaning ceaselessly to evaporate it, carrying out a systematic exemption of meaning. In precisely this way literature (it would be better from now on to say writing), by refusing to assign a "secret," an ultimate meaning, to the text (and to the world as text), liberates what may be called an anti-theological activity, an activity . . . that is truly revolutionary since to refuse to fix meaning is, in the end, to refuse God and his hypostases—reason, science, law.[156]

The obvious question here is: Did Barthes *intend* or *mean* to communicate this philosophy to his readers?! If the "death of the author" renders any claim to decipher what a text signifies "quite futile," it necessarily renders "quite futile" any claim—even a claim on the part of a text's author—that one has *mis*interpreted what a text signifies. But as William Lane Craig wryly comments: "nobody adopts a Postmodernist view of literary texts when reading the labels on a medicine bottle or a box of rat poison!"[157]

Responding to postmodern scholars who reject the very possibility of historical knowledge, Evans comments:

> The fundamental problem with this kind of extreme relativism is . . . that it inevitably falls foul of its own principles when they are applied to itself. Why, after all, if all theories are equally valid, should we believe postmodernist theories of history rather than other theories? If all knowledge is relative, if it is impossible to give an accurate summary of a discourse without at the same time projecting one's own reading on to it, then why should we not give to the work of Barthes, or Derrida . . . any significance that we wish to give it?[158]

As theologian D. A. Carson remarks:

> I have never read a deconstructionist who would be pleased if a reviewer misinterpreted his or her work: thus in practice deconstructionists implicitly link their own texts with their own intentions . . . in the real world, for all the difficulties there are in communication from person to person . . . we still expect people to say more or less what they mean (and if they don't, we chide them for it), and we expect mature people to understand what others say, and represent it fairly. The understanding is

156. Barthes, "Death of the Author," 146.
157. Craig, "Resurrection of Theism."
158. Evans, *In Defence of History*, 231.

doubt-less never absolutely exhaustive and perfect, but that does not mean the only alternative is to dissociate text from speaker, and then locate all meaning in the reader or hearer.[159]

If denying God's existence means denying that "the world as text" has an objective meaning (the kind of meaning that is discovered rather than invented), it follows that the only way to coherently affirm that the world has an objective meaning is to affirm the existence of God as its "Author." In other words, as many atheist philosophers recognize, the question of God's existence is not a question of merely academic interest, but a question of existential import.[160] Indeed, if we embrace a properly basic rational intuition of the meaningfulness of reality, we can reverse Barthes's argument into an argument for theism.

Of course, "Postmodernists are right to say that readers bring to history . . . their own beliefs and purposes. The point, however, is that these no more completely shape their reading of the book than do the intentions of the author."[161] Hence: "The first prerequisite of the serious historical researcher must be the ability to jettison dearly-held interpretations in the face of the recalcitrance of the evidence."[162] In other words, *contra* postmodernism, historical "interpretations really can be tested and confirmed or falsified by an appeal to evidence."[163] The past:

> really happened, and we really can, if we are very scrupulous and careful and self-critical, find out how it happened and reach some tenable though always less than final conclusions about what it all meant.[164]

While "modernist" skeptics all too often succumb to a question-begging failure to seriously engage with the historical case for the Christian picture of Jesus, "postmodern" skeptics all to often slide into an "extreme relativism"[165] that expects us to take their texts seriously when their texts assert that texts don't assert anything. But as Evans complains: "even the most

---

159. Carson, *Gagging of God*, 101–3.

160. See Evans, *Despair*; Nietzsche, "Parable of the Madman"; Russell, "Free Man's Worship"; Sartre, "Existentialism Is a Humanism"; Williams, *I Wish I Could Believe*.

161. Evans, *In Defence of History*, 107.

162. Evans, *In Defence of History*, 120.

163. Evans, *In Defence of History*, 128.

164. Evans, *In Defence of History*, 253.

165. Evans, *In Defence of History*, 231.

extreme deconstructionists do not really accept that their own theories can be applied to their own work."[166]

CULTURE IN FLUX

In the assessment of Lene Rachel Andersen:

> modernity is not complex enough to handle our inner spiritual needs.... Postmodernism is good at deconstructing culture and society, but it is terrible at bringing people together; it is only good at taking things apart.... The postmodern world with its deconstruction of almost everything and constant relativizing, has prevented a lot of honest, deep emotional connection to cultural heritage and other people. There is always this "distance." It has left many morally alone, as Fromm called it; we are massively in an existential vacuum, and it feels horrible.[167]

Likewise, literary theorists David Rudrum and Nicholas Stavris protest that postmodern "scepticism about reality is not a strategy that is conducive to a sense of respect for others' identities or for the planet at large."[168] As eminent literary critic and writer Ihab Hassan (1925–2015) warned: "If truth is dead, then everything is permitted—because its alternatives, now more than ever, are rank power and rampant desire."[169]

Fortunately, truth is not dead, and postmodernism is a culturally waning force. As Brendan Graham Dempsey comments:

> the cultural vanguard has long since moved on from the played-out tropes and predictable strategies of "postmodernism." That story is old, and there is, by now, over a decade's worth of academic literature devoted not just to postmodernism's decline but to what has arisen to succeed it since the early 2000s. While the legacy of postmodernism will of course live on and continue to permeate society, it is hardly the spearpoint anymore of cultural innovation. Something new is afoot.[170]

---

166. Evans, *In Defence of History*, 231. For a further critique of postmodernism, see Groothuis, *Truth Decay*; Köstenberger, *Whatever Happened to Truth?*; Moreland, "Postmodernism and Truth"; Moreland, "Four Degrees of Postmodernism"; Scruton, *Intelligent Person's Guide to Culture*, chap. 11.
167. Andersen, *Bildung*, 90 and 152.
168. Rudrum and Stavris, "Introduction to Ihab Hassan," 13.
169. Hassan, "Beyond Postmodernism," 20.
170. Dempsey, *Metamodernism*, 7.

In his 2002 introduction to postmodernism, Butler wrote that "the period of its greatest influence is now over. Its founding fathers are in their turn encountering the scepticism of a new generation."[171] In 2006, British cultural critic Alex Kirby commented:

> Buy novels published in the last five years, watch a twenty-first-century film, listen to the latest music—above all just sit and watch television for a week—and you will hardly catch a glimpse of postmodernism. Similarly, one can go to literary conferences. . . and sit through a dozen papers which make no mention . . . of Derrida, Foucault, Baudrillard.[172]

In 2007, John McGowan (professor emeritus of English and comparative literature at the University of North Carolina at Chapel Hill) noted that:

> The term "postmodernism" is still with us as a vague reference to French theory, historical meta-fiction, and eclectic hybrid forms in architecture and art. But the theoretical debate represented by "postmodernism" has, for better and worse, passed from the scene.[173]

In 2015, Rudrum and Stavris cautioned that while "postmodernism is in decline . . . calling time on postmodernism is still a work in progress."[174] The "work in progress" nature of postmodernism's "decline" reflects the fact that, having followed modernism through to its nihilistic terminus, and having "deconstructed" deconstruction itself, "it is not clear whether the 'present history' of the early twenty-first century actually has a 'general sense of a cultural dominant.'"[175] The so-called "New Atheism" was big in the early 2000s, but crumpled under the weight of external critiques and internal divisions.[176] In its wake, the quest to define a "post-postmodern" worldview and spirituality with the capacity to supplant both modernism and postmodernism as a new "cultural dominant" has become an

---

171. Butler, *Postmodernism*, 127.
172. Kirby, "Death of Postmodernism and Beyond," 52.
173. McGowan, "They Might Have Been Giants," 63.
174. Rudrum and Stavris, *Supplanting the Postmodern*, xiii and xviii.
175. Rudrum, "Note on the Supplanting," 344.

176. See Brierley, *Surprising Rebirth of Belief in God*, chap. 1. For an assessment of the New Atheism, see Williams, "'New Atheism'" (YouTube playlist); Craig, "Dawkins' Delusion"; Bannister, *Atheist Who Didn't Exist* (Tenth Anniversary Edition); Craig and Meister, *God Is Great*; Ganssle, *Reasonable God*; Gilson and Weitnauer, *True Reason*; Glass, *Atheism's New Clothes*; Hart, *Atheist Delusions*; Rasmussen and Vallier, *New Theist Response to the New Atheism*; Williams, *Outgrowing God?*; *Getting at Jesus*; and *C.S. Lewis vs. the New Atheists*.

increasingly prominent part of both academic and popular culture. As British writer and freelance journalist Lamorna Ash (b. 1994) comments,

> We are leagues away from the New Atheist movement . . . which repudiated religion on supposedly intellectual grounds – though the straw-man version of religion Richard Dawkins and his ilk chose to burn down was the most pallid simplistic form they could devise. Our feelings about faith are distinct, too, from the broad strokes of apathy or indifference towards belief which often characterised the 2000s. . . . The conversations about faith I have with friends and acquaintances of a similar age to me are characterised by a mood of increased tolerance and openness to religious frames of mind. This, I think, speaks to the kind of world in which we have come of age.[177]

What has this growing disenchantment with modernism-cum-postmodernism, and its concomitant search for a new "cultural dominant," have to do with the quest for the historical Jesus? Despite the overwhelming evidence for the historical existence of Jesus of Nazareth,[178] our culture's worldview expectations have led to a cultural moment in which an astonishing 46 percent of the UK population are either uncertain of, or even actively refute, Jesus's status as a historical figure![179] The quest to transcend the modern-cum-postmodern worldview could create a space within which to reinvent the quest for the historical Jesus along evidential and truth-oriented lines. If so, we may find that historical investigation can, in a partial yet adequate way, put us in touch with a Jesus whose historical life and teaching invites us to reshape our spirituality and culture in fruitful ways.

Metamodernism

> The word metamodernism is basically a term that describes that which comes after modern society (and after the "postmodern" critique of it).
>
> —HANZI FREINACHT[180]

177. Ash, *Don't Forget We're Here Forever*, 16.

178. As Craig L. Blomberg observes, by combining evidence from first-to-third-century Greco-Roman writers: "one can clearly accumulate enough evidence to refute the fanciful notion that Jesus never existed" (*Historical Reliability of the Gospels*, 251). See Williams, "Existence of Jesus" (YouTube playlist); Casey, *Jesus*; Ehrman, *Did Jesus Exist?*; Habermas, *Historical Jesus*; Holding, *Shattering the Christ Myth*; Williams, *Getting at Jesus*.

179. Talking Jesus, *What People in the UK*.

180. Freinacht, *Listening Society*, 361.

Hanzi Freinacht lays out three different meanings for the term *metamodern*:

> the most commonly used in other sources thus far, is metamodernism as a certain cultural phase in matters such as art, architecture, media, philosophy and politics.... In that sense "metamodernism" is comparable to things such as the Romantic period ... the Enlightenment ... and postmodernism. If you ever studied arts, philosophy or literature you are familiar with this way of thinking in cultural phases.[181]

The second meaning, which relates to political philosophy:

> is metamodernism as a developmental stage. This is very different from a cultural phase. The idea of a phase, like Romanticism, which came after the Enlightenment ... simply states that this phase came after that one (for instance, because the German idealists wanted to distance themselves from French rationalism). Stage theories are different. They claim, for instance, that adulthood comes after childhood.... Or that industrial civilization comes after traditional, agricultural civilization.[182]

The third meaning is: "a philosophical paradigm ... a fundamental worldview."[183] A philosophical paradigm or worldview underpins the shared spirituality of a culture and finds expression in that culture's architecture, art, institutions, etc.

In Search of a Worldview

Little appears to be settled about metamodernism, whether as a cultural phase or stage, or as a worldview. Different academics offer different definitions of what they think metamodernism is and/or should be, and even whether *metamodern* is the best term to use for it. Nevertheless, one central metamodern theme seems to be the need to take personhood, and those things which make personhood existentially meaningful, with a seriousness that is undermined by modernism and postmodernism. As literary critic and intellectual historian Patricia Waugh observes:

> In the current cross-disciplinary quest to recover from what Raymond Tallis calls "neuromania" and "Darwinitis" as well as

---

181. Freinacht, *Listening Society*, 361.
182. Freinacht, *Listening Society*, 362.
183. Freinacht, *Listening Society*, 362.

from postmodernism, there seems to be a renewed interest in retrieving the self.[184]

Indeed, according to cultural theorist Greg Dember:

> the essence of metamodernism is a (conscious or unconscious) motivation to protect the solidity of felt experience against the scientific reductionism of the modernist perspective and the ironic detachment of the postmodern sensibility.[185]

Thus literary theorist and poet Alexandra Dumitrescu defines metamodernism as:

> the struggle to find meaning, and in searching for meaning, it is the tendency to re-establish that connection or those connections that would render life and creation, love and expression meaningful.[186]

This resonates with Freinacht's call for a metamodern spirituality (and hence worldview) that takes "philosophical, cultural and aesthetic matters very seriously, as they are seen as inherent dimensions of reality, not just 'additional woo-woo' on top of physics."[187]

Hollow Metamodernism

Unfortunately, Freinacht's proposals concerning the content of a metamodern worldview "that is not yet established, but we are trying to establish,"[188] are an incoherent mixture of beliefs grounded in the debatable proposition "that God is dead and humanism dying."[189] On the one hand, Freinacht affirms a need "to take ontological questions very seriously, i.e., to let questions about 'what is really real' guide us in science and politics."[190] On the other hand, he affirms a need "to be anti-essentialist, not believing in 'ultimate essences' such as matter, consciousness, goodness, evil."[191] Indeed, Freinacht affirms a need "to accept and thrive in the paradoxical,

---

184. Quoted in Stavris, "Anxieties of the Present," 354. See Tallis, *Aping Mankind*.
185. Dember, "After Postmodernism," §8.
186. Dumitrescu, "Interconnections in Blakean and Metamodern Space," §69.
187. Freinacht, *Listening Society*, 367.
188. Freinacht, *Listening Society*, 362.
189. Freinacht, *Listening Society*, 363.
190. Freinacht, *Listening Society*, 365.
191. Freinacht, *Listening Society*, 365.

self-contradictory."[192] Accepting paradox is one thing. Accepting self-contradiction is quite another.

According to an influential essay by cultural critic Timotheus Vermeulen and philosopher Robin van den Akker: "Metamodernism . . . oscillates between a modern enthusiasm and a postmodern irony, between hope and melancholy."[193] Cultural theorists Linda Ceriello and Greg Dember describe metamodernism in similar terms, using a different image:

> "metamodernist works" engage the conflicts between modernist conviction and postmodern relativism, in part by embodying an aesthetic that braids the various epistemic perspectives with an emphasis on felt experience.[194]

However, one cannot escape the problems inherent within modernism and postmodernism merely by oscillating between them, or by braiding them together.

Metamodern writer Brendan Graham Dempsey proposes a unifying account of metamodernism in the idea of "going meta,"[195] arguing that just as "Postmodernists come after, objectify, reflect upon, critique, and transcend modernism," so "metamodernists come after, objectify, reflect upon, critique, and transcend postmodernism."[196] Dempsey illustrates the idea of "going meta" by describing a series of nested perspectives:

> Going meta never means diminishing one's scope of perspectives, but always increasing it. By definition, it is what allows one to step outside a given frame to see more of the picture. It's like a person in a painting climbing out of the painting and then looking back at where they had been encased. Now they can see the whole context of their former position: it was just a painting! They can also see their old context within the broader context of their new vantage: an art gallery![197]

Dempsey describes the process of "going meta" as "iterative," such that:

> before long it becomes clear that the "reality" in which they currently stand is also limited. Transcending again, imagine the person now climbs out of a television, and can see that the art gallery was itself just in their TV as the painting was in the art

---

192. Freinacht, *Listening Society*, 363.
193. Vermeulen and Akker, "Notes on Metamodernism."
194. What Is Metamodern? "About the Authors."
195. Dempsey, *Metamodernism*, 7.
196. Dempsey, *Metamodernism*, 7.
197. Dempsey, *Metamodernism*, 8.

gallery! . . . The context of the TV "contains more" than the context of the painting, allowing one a broader view of (provisional) reality. In short, higher vantages provide more information than lower ones.[198]

The principle problem with Dempsey's portrait of metamodernism is that, unlike the coherently nested perspectives of "the picture" of painting, gallery, and TV show, the worldviews of modernism and postmodernism *contradict each other* on various matters. Dempsey asserts that "the modern and the postmodern need not be antagonistic opposites,"[199] but in light of the contradictions between them as worldviews, the best one could say along these lines is that they are both partially true perspectives with something to contribute to a "broader" meta-perspective on "the picture" of reality. To assert with Dempsey that "the metamodern perspective . . . contains the postmodern, as well as the pre-postmodern, as enduring modalities available to it,"[200] is incoherent. This incoherence pervades Dempsey's description of the "metamodern sensibility" as:

> a multi-perspectival one, able to move through the various levels of reflection it contains. So, while the postmodern has foreclosed the possibility of idealism in reaction to the modern, the metamodern can toggle between both, holding modern aspirational enthusiasm one minute, then checking this with a more reflective awareness the next.[201]

If modernistic "idealism" and "aspirational enthusiasm" was something "foreclosed" by postmodernism, is it "foreclosed" by metamodernism, or is it not? Either it is, or it isn't. The proposal of a meta-perspective that contains multiple *compatible* perspectives is one thing; the proposal of a meta-perspective that "toggles" between *incompatible* perspectives is quite another. Toggling between incompatible perspectives does not synthesize them into a more informative perspective. According to Dempsey:

> While postmodernism had recognized plurality, metamodernism recognizes the nested nature of this plurality, the Russian doll structure that allows the metamodernist to relate multiple perspectives to each other and to its own vantage.[202]

---

198. Dempsey, *Metamodernism*, 8.
199. Dempsey, *Metamodernism*, 15.
200. Dempsey, *Metamodernism*, 14.
201. Dempsey, *Metamodernism*, 14.
202. Dempsey, *Metamodernism*, 18.

Russian dolls are able to nest one inside of the other because they have compatible forms. This doesn't apply to the contradictory aspects of pre-modernism, modernism, and postmodernism.

Fig. 18. Russian Matryoshka Dolls.[203]

Another problem with Dempsey's theory of metamodernism is his assertion that: "like all theories and all knowledge, it is provisional."[204] One has to ask, is *this statement itself* presented as a "provisional" claim? Is "all" knowledge, or are "all" knowledge claims, really "provisional"? What about the reader's first person knowledge of their own existence? What about our knowledge of the basic laws of logic?

Moreover, according to Dempsey, "going meta" is not an epistemological movement towards an increased knowledge of the way things are, but "towards a continually receding horizon."[205] In his view:

> There is no final Absolute, rendering all gains relative. . . . This sort of paradoxical advance I call infinitesimal progress (movement by means of infinitely diminishing strides). . . . How does one reach a destination when the ground one must cover is recursively divisible into smaller and smaller parts? The metamodernist, appeasing both modernists and postmodernists, assures: "All progress is relative." Progress is real, but it lies in the going.[206]

Presumably, this will appease neither the modernist nor the postmodernist! As for the Abrahamic pre-modernist, they would reply that while humans lack the omniscience of God, they do have a God-given ability to know truth and to make genuine progress in their knowledge about reality, a progress

203. Credit: TanTanika, https://pixabay.com/photos/matryoshka-souvenir-russia-toy-879751/.
204. Dempsey, *Metamodernism*, 21.
205. Dempsey, *Metamodernism*, 11.
206. Dempsey, *Metamodernism*, 11.

that doesn't merely lie "in the going" because it isn't merely a matter of "never-ending approximation."[207] Dempsey appears to confuse genuine knowledge with *comprehensive* knowledge; but knowledge is knowledge, even if one knows one can always see one's knowledge in the context of additional knowledge. One can know (absolutely!) that one's present knowledge is partial, without this knowledge devaluing or contradicting what one presently knows (just as one can know that one's claims to knowledge, or to warranted belief, often remain open to sufficiently warranted challenge without thereby opening the door to the epistemological despair of postmodernism).

Nothing Matters Anywhere at Any Time, but All You Need Is "Love"?

The problem with these attempts to present metamodernism as a worldview is exemplified by the message of the 2023 multi-Oscar winning metamodern film *Everything Everywhere All at Once*,[208] summarized here by critic Calum Russell:

> Refusing to deny nihilism outright, *Everything Everywhere All at Once* argues that the feeling of worthlessness and apathy that comes with the philosophical concept can be combatted by embracing absurdity . . . and finding empathy in this shared mortal connection. In such a meaningless universe, the love Evelyn shares with her daughter and husband is the source of true meaning, finding mutual understanding and acceptance in their shared experience of the absurdity of modern life.[209]

Everything Everywhere All at Once is a prime example of a metamodern attempt to "protect the solidity of felt experience against the scientific reductionism of the modernist perspective and the ironic detachment of the postmodern sensibility"[210] that ultimately rings hollow. Faced with the postmodern, nihilistic entailments of its modernistic worldview assumptions, the film advocates a knowingly absurd choice to focus upon love.[211] Of course, love is a paradigm example of something that *seems* to matter (not only in a subjective, "to us" sense, but in an objective sense). However,

---

207. Dempsey, *Metamodernism*, 28.
208. See Dember, "Everything Metamodern All at Once."
209. Russell, "Everything Everywhere All at Once," §5–6.
210. Dember, "After Postmodernism," §8.
211. See Breedlovecraft, "Absurd Philosophy"; Films Prophet, "Everything Everywhere All at Once."

if one believes that, objectively speaking, "nothing matters,"[212] and that the way love subjectively *appears* to matter is an illusion one has seen through, can choosing to love really allow one to "transcend" the despair of nihilism *even as one continues to affirm the nihilism that evacuates love of all objective meaning*? Doesn't such an absurd act of "let's pretend" undermine itself? How is this any better than Alex Rosenberg's resolutely modernistic advice that:

> human life is meaningless, without purpose, and without ultimate moral value. . . . So, what should we scientific folks do when overcome with *Weltschmertz* (world-weariness)? Take two of whatever neuro-pharmacology prescribes.[213]

Humans have an innate desire for meaning, and nihilism renders this desire "absurd" in the technical sense defined by Albert Camus when he wrote in *The Myth of Sisyphus* that: "the absurd is born of this confrontation between the human need and the unreasonable silence of the world."[214] The innate desire for meaning is rendered absurd by the modernist assumptions that underpin nihilism, such that trusting that desire would entail overthrowing those assumptions. Indeed, the very existence of that desire arguably constitutes a reason for doubting those modernist assumptions.[215] At the very least, isn't it worth keeping an open mind as to whether there might be a more viable way to "protect the solidity of felt experience" than engaging in an absurdist act of pretense? As Marcelle Couto writes:

> In the case of "Everything Everywhere All at Once," love itself, particularly the choice to love, serves as the ultimate weapon against despair. While this perspective may seem liberating . . . what is love in a meaningless universe? . . . . why should I sacrifice my desires for the sake of another (which I will do if I truly love someone) in a meaningless universe? Why should I choose suffering, and vulnerability, when egoism offers a much greater reward under utilitarian arithmetic? Yes, I can feel

---

212. Hup, "Everything Everywhere All at Once."

213. Rosenberg, *Atheist's Guide to Reality*, 18 and 282.

214. Camus, *Myth of Sisyphus*.

215. See Williams, "Argument from Desire" (YouTube playlist); Dougherty, "Argument from Desire"; Hoyler, "Argument from Desire"; Kreeft, "Argument from Desire"; Simek, "Bayesian Exploration of C. S. Lewis's 'Argument from Desire'"; Williams, "Beginner's Guide to the Theistic Argument from Desire"; "C. S. Lewis as a Central Figure"; and "Re-Defending Arguments from Desire"; Bassham, *C. S. Lewis's Christian Apologetics*; Boethius, *Consolation of Philosophy*, book 3; Buras and Cantrell, "C. S. Lewis's Argument from Nostalgia"; Haldane, "Philosophy, the Restless Heart"; Puckett, *Apologetics of Joy*.

affection toward my friends and family, but why in the world would I choose to forgive, to love persistently amidst failure and disappointment? In [a meaningless] universe, love is an empty attitude.[216]

However, maybe love itself is a sign that nihilism is mistaken about reality:

> But I think love . . . is never a vain thing. I would dare say we all know this, intuitively. "Everything Everywhere All at Once" knows this, too, and therein lies its tremendous influence. Audiences have frequently been left in tears—and not without reason—after observing the mother-daughter reconciliation central to the plot. This very scenario contradicts the movie's philosophy because it calls for an unspoken understanding of what true love should actually look like. Love is an inherent good, and an inherent good cannot exist under nihilism no matter how much we attempt to fabricate it. In other words, "Everything Everywhere All at Once" has not earned the right to use the word "love." Its philosophy does not allow for there to be anything remarkable about whatever combination of atoms consists of "love," or any other neurological phenomenon for that matter.[217]

Such "hollow metamodernism" is a doomed attempt to have one's cake while eating it.[218]

Knock, Knock . . .

Timotheus Vermeulen describes metamodernism as a response to the combination of what he calls a postmodern "claustrophobia of the chest," and the perception of "a knocking sound" from an unknown source that could, possibly, be "something out there"[219] beyond the confines of our currently dominant modern-cum-postmodern worldview. In a fascinating lecture entitled "Knock, Knock," Vermeulen diagnoses the human condition of life lived within the precincts of the modern-cum-postmodern "mall," or worldview, as one in which "we suffer from a kind of 'asthma of the soul,'" (i.e.,

---

216. Couto, "Reflecting on the Philosophy," §3–4. See Mavrodes, "Religion and the Queerness of Morality."

217. Couto, "Reflecting on the Philosophy," §5 See also Gospel Coalition Australia, "Love."

218. For those who have seen *Everything Everywhere All at Once*, perhaps I should say it is a doomed attempt to have one's bagel while eating it!

219. What Is Metamodern?, "Talking Metamodernism with Tim Vermeulen."

those who live within this worldview feel is too constricting to accommodate "the solidity of felt experience"[220]) and in which there is consequently "this feeling of dissatisfaction . . . with the world around you."[221] This sense of suffocating dissatisfaction awakes within us a desire for *something more*. Since the 1990s, says Vermeulen:

> we're hearing knocks . . . on the walls of the mall . . . and we begin to think . . . what if there are still big questions, what if, even if we shouldn't believe in grand narratives . . . the mess that has left us in necessitates us to reimagine the possibility of an outside, the possibility of an alternative, the possibility that things could be different; and so people begin to run for the doors, to find that there are no doors in this mall, that they have been barricaded with all those books . . . that my [modern and postmodern] philosophy teachers at university used to speak about . . . and so we look for windows and there aren't any windows, and so this is the metamodern situation, the moment that we realize . . . that this shopping mall, this end of history . . . may not be the end state; and how do you create an alternative, how do you start from there, how do you begin to think, how do you kick start history . . . when you only have that inside, when you only have that enclosed space?[222]

One way to answer Vermeulen's question is to suggest exploring the possibility that we might be able to critically dismantle that barricade of books his modern and postmodern philosophy teachers used to speak about, thereby clearing a path that allows people to journey outside the mall. Might it not at least be worth reading some of those books on the dustier shelves of the university library, the ones written by philosophers (ancient and contemporary) with a pre-modern worldview? Vermeulen laments:

> We have no idea what the alternative looks like, because I grew up in a generation that was told there is no alternative, and I grew up in a generation where if in school I would say "But this is the truth" then my teacher would say "Yeah, come on, this is *your* truth, right, the other kid has also his own truth." And so you think, "Ah, shit, there is no truth." And so how do you think the alternative when all your options, all the tools . . . which we used to create alternatives, have been taken away from you? When all the horizons have been wiped out, then how do you

---

220. Dember, "After Postmodernism," §8.
221. Vermeulen, "Knock Knock."
222. Vermeulen, "Knock Knock."

begin to think about how stuff could be different? And I think this is the difficult moment that metamodernism as a vernacular, as a heuristic label tries to capture.[223]

However, as British philosopher Roger Scruton once commented, anyone "who says that there are no truths, or that all truth is 'merely relative,' is asking you not to believe him. So don't."[224] The only coherent response to Vermeulen's woes rests in recovering the concept of truth denied to him by his teachers. Without the pursuit of truth, as Vermeulen observes:

> what is happening now . . . is that we are both trying to create new narratives like those moderns (especially here "moderns" as a system of thought, as a philosophy) used to do, but of course because of all the postmodern knowledge . . . you are also stuck in that postmodern doubt, in a postmodern reflective stance. . . . I would say this is the ontological state of our present moment.[225]

The "ontological state" of this simultaneously modern and postmodern "present moment" both drives and undermines the quest for a better worldview. The result is an existential tantalization that breeds a desire it can never satisfy. But what if that presumed "postmodern knowledge" is not actually knowledge, but only *falsely perceived to be knowledge*? What if we ditch the self-contradictory doubt of the "postmodern reflective stance," while embracing a properly (pre-modern!) skeptical reflective stance aimed at discovering the truth about reality?

The metamodern quest to retrieve the self requires what Nicholas Stavris describes as "a realigned focus on truth which deviates from postmodern scepticism about reality."[226] Ironically, as we have seen, postmodern skepticism about reality is driven by modernist worldview commitments. Hence, the metamodern quest to retrieve the self requires us to ditch those commitments.

The only hope for a better worldview lies in a willingness to doubt Vermeulen's assumption that "all the tools" for creating alternative worldviews have "been taken away" by "postmodern knowledge." At the very least, we have the critical tools to know that anything "outside" of the "mall" cannot be a replica of the inside. Nor can it be an oscillation, or braiding together, or toggling between its key modernist and postmodernist worldview "architectures." Furthermore, we know what the philosophical tools of critical

---

223. Vermeulen, "Knock Knock."
224. Scruton, *Modern Philosophy*, 12.
225. Vermeulen, "Knock Knock."
226. Stavris, "Anxieties of the Present," 353.

thinking, and the classical concept of truth at which they aim, look like.[227] And we have good reason to believe that the "outside" has to be a worldview that can accommodate those experienced realities that pose serious "location problems" to the worldviews that delimit "the mall."

Hungry Metamodernism

Metamodernism is a return to fundamental questions that define our being in the world.... It is a search for the meaning and beauty of the present.... Metamodernism is a bold assertion of the human being as a spiritual entity, rather than a forlorn person inhabiting his or her detached island of individualism.... Metamodernism is the expression of the self's search for home.

—Alexandra Dumitrescu[228]

To successfully "protect the solidity of felt experience," escape the modern-cum-postmodern "claustrophobia of the chest," recover "the connection between the good, the true and the beautiful," and free ourselves to respond to the perceived "knocking" of transcendent reality upon the walls of Vermeulen's worldview "mall," we must reject both the destructive essence of postmodernism *and* its distinctively modernistic roots.

This is *not* to say our culture needs to reject *everything* that comes under the multivalent labels of modernity and postmodernity. Nor is it to say that we need to uncritically embrace everything associated with premodernism. It is to say that we should keep an open but appropriately skeptical mind as we ask whether some form of premodernism might provide the core worldview concepts and tools for sifting and integrating the good aspects of modernism and postmodernism into a coherent contemporary spirituality and culture.

In this cultural moment, says Jonathan Rowson: "metamodernism is called for because we need to wake up to being in a time between worlds."[229]

---

227. See Williams, "Critical Thinking" (YouTube playlist); Alston, *Realist Conception of Truth*; Audi, *Epistemology*; Cowan and Spiegel, *Love of Wisdom*, chaps. 1 and 2; Geisler and Feinberg, *Introduction to Philosophy*, chaps. 3, 4, and 16; Groothuis, *Truth Decay*; Köstenberger, *Whatever Happened to Truth?*; Sinnott-Armstrong, *Think Again*; Moreland, "Postmodernism and Truth"; Moreland, "Four Degrees of Postmodernism"; Williams, *Faithful Guide to Philosophy*, chaps. 1 and 2.

228. Dumitrescu, "Metamodernism."

229. Quoted in Perspectiva, "What Is Metamodernism."

The cultural world we will eventually settle within after the present moment of cultural flux is ours to shape. In Rowson's judgment:

> We're not going to go back to pre-modern religion, but nor are we going to stay stuck in a kind of flatland postmodern context where the notion of the sacred struggles to be heard . . . where arguably there is a meaning crisis . . . We have to question the entire meaning and purpose of life.[230]

The phrase "meaning crisis" was coined by psychologist John Vervaeke to describe:

> the sense of alienation people experience as they move through life feeling disconnected from each other and the world. Most especially they feel disconnected from a purpose to live for, or a story that makes sense of who they are. . . . Vervaeke sees a range of symptoms to this crisis, including "the rise in suicide, even suicide independent of clinical depression right now, which is a very telling sign. A loneliness epidemic, the mental health crisis . . . depression and anxiety disorders, the addiction crisis, the opioid crisis.[231]

Rowson talks of "the mystic beyond,"[232] and recognizes that:

> modernity [arguably] severed the connection between the good, the true and the beautiful—it . . . broke them apart—so you have a . . . scientific truth severed from the . . . ethics and aesthetics of the good and the beautiful; and one of the things metamodernism has to do is to take the responsibility of bringing these back together . . . The truth that I'd be looking for is one that contains goodness and beauty as a kind of integral part of it.[233]

Of course, a divine truth "that contains goodness and beauty as a kind of integral part of it" is at the core of every monotheistic pre-modern worldview! Isn't it possible, then, that a contemporary version of monotheistic premodernism might turn out to *be* the post-postmodernism our culture is longing for? Isn't it possible that solving the "meaning crisis" requires us to recover "the connection between the good, the true and the beautiful," to protect "the solidity of felt experience," and to escape the modern-cum-postmodern

---

230. Perspectiva, "What Is Metamodernism."
231. Quoted in Brierley, *Surprising Rebirth of Belief in God*, 192.
232. Quoted in Perspectiva, "What Is Metamodernism."
233. Perspectiva, "What Is Metamodernism."

"claustrophobia of the chest" by allowing the "sacred ... to be heard" thorough a contemporary version of a monotheistic spirituality?

Metamodernism and History

If there might be "something out there"[234] in "the mystic beyond,"[235] don't we have to be open to the possibility that, far from being content to knock at the borders of our perceived reality, it might be the sort of thing that can take, and could have already taken, the initiative, even in a historically accessible act of self-revelation?

Simone Stirner argues that whereas "postmodernism announced the death of the subject"[236] metamodernism heralds "a paradigm shift. The subject reappears and it comes with other dismissed categories such as trust, belief, coherence and even love."[237] Such a paradigm shift seems to imply we should be prepared to exercise trust (albeit a duly skeptical trust, alert to any indications of unreliability) in the apparently sincere testimony of our fellow humans. And that includes the testimony that reaches us through the documents that were subsequently gathered together into the New Testament.[238] To strike the appropriate critical combination of trust and skepticism in examining and explaining such evidence is the task of the historian.

Can such a critical combination of trust and skepticism be achieved? Gregg Henriques, Marcia Gralha, Brendan Graham Dempsey, and Layman Pascal jointly affirm that:

> While the metamodern sensibility embraces the modernist ability to ground knowledge in true claims about reality through empirical methods, it also acknowledges its limitations due to social and subjective elements of human culture.[239]

Note that acknowledging these "limitations" does not mean rejecting the reality of "knowledge" grounded "in true claims about reality" gained through "empirical methods." Note, too, that the philosophical assumptions held by a culture or an individual needn't be assumptions that encourage

---

234. What Is Metamodern?, "Talking Metamodernism with Tim Vermeulen."

235. Perspectiva, "What Is Metamodernism?"

236. Stirner, "Notes on the State of the Subject," §1.

237. Stirner, "Notes on the State of the Subject," §5.

238. On why various writings made it into the New Testament, see Williams, "New Testament Canon" (YouTube playlist); Comfort and Driesbach, *Many Gospels of Jesus*; Hill, *Who Chose the Books of the New Testament?*; Hill, *Who Chose the Gospels?*

239. Henriques et al., "What Is Metamodern Spirituality?"

gullibility or that obfuscate truth. Instead, they can be properly skeptical assumptions that discourage gullibility and disclose truth. Acknowledging and addressing the limitations of searching for "true claims about reality through empirical methods" is the province of a properly formulated skepticism that critically considers the criteria by which we collect *evidence*, the criteria by which we choose the best *explanation* of that evidence, and how our worldview *expectations* impinge upon these tasks.

If everyone brings worldview expectations to the task of historical inquiry, does this mean that we are doomed to talk past each other from hermetically sealed scholarly silos? I don't believe so, because at least some of us are able to agree on a common commitment to critical standards such as: rejecting internally incoherent theories of knowledge, refusing to use less than indubitable worldview expectations as the basis for begging the question against a historical claim regardless of the evidence in its favor, and revising our historical beliefs under the weight of sufficient counter-evidence according to carefully formulated criteria of evidence and explanation. Commitment to scholarly standards such as these does not mean that historical arguments will always, or even usually, be resolved; but they do at least mean that scholarly arguments can be engaged in and that progress, even resolution, is possible.

GETTING AT THE JESUS OF HISTORY

If we use "the historical Jesus" as a phrase designating the flesh and blood person who was born in Israel under the auspices of the Roman Empire ca. 5 BC,[240] and who was killed by crucifixion[241] and entombed[242] just outside the walls of Jerusalem in AD 33 (or perhaps 30),[243] in all of his feeding-trough-to-borrowed-grave particularities, then we may use "the Jesus of history" as a phrase designating the somewhat vague and more or less approximate "picture" of the historical Jesus that we believe the application of a "properly skeptical" process of historical inquiry warrants.[244]

Once upon a time (from 1936–67 in the UK), televisions displayed moving pictures in "black and white" at a resolution of 405 lines;[245] but that

240. See Humphreys, "Star of Bethlehem"; Maier, "Date of the Nativity."
241. See Bishop, "Historical Problems with Islam's View"; Williams, *Getting at Jesus*, 257–68 and 310–14.
242. See Craig, "Historicity of the Empty Tomb"; Evans, "Resurrection of Jesus."
243. See Köstenberger, "April 3, AD 33"; Köstenberger et al., *Final Days of Jesus*.
244. See Craig, *Reasonable Faith*, 296–97.
245. Baird, "Beginning of the End."

was and is enough to let people witness the coronation of Queen Elizabeth II in 1953.[246] Likewise, for all that the above definition of "the Jesus of history" highlights the gap between past actuality on the one hand and the present-day results of historical research on the other, even a vague and approximate "picture" can be enough to reliably bring us face to face with significant realities.

Fig. 19. Philip, Duke of Edinburgh, giving allegiance to his wife, Queen Elizabeth II, during her coronation ceremony in 1953.[247]

Of course, we are surrounded by many different and often mutually exclusive portraits of Jesus (for example, Jewish, Christian, and Islamic portraits of Jesus overlap but are fundamentally incompatible); and many of these portraits, including the incompatible ones, lay claim to historical warrant. Much of the difference between attempts to offer a historically warranted description of "the historical Jesus" can be explained by differences between: (1) the worldview *expectations* that are brought to bear in this venture, (2) the methodological approaches taken to establishing what will count as *evidence* that needs to be taken into account, and (3) the methodological approaches taken to establishing the best *explanation* of that evidence.

---

246. See Archive of Recorded Church Music, "BBC TV Coronation."

247. Credit: https://en.wikipedia.org/wiki/Coronation_of_Elizabeth_II#/media/File:Philip,_Duke_of_Edinburgh,_giving_allegiance_to_his_wife,_Queen_Elizabeth_II,_during_her_coronation_ceremony.jpg.

Establishing Evidence

> A historical fact is something that happened in history and can be verified as such through the traces history has left behind.
>
> —RICHARD J. EVANS[248]

In his signature work *Christian Apologetics* (second edition, Baker, 2013), Christian philosopher and apologist Norman L. Geisler (1932–2019) exemplifies what we might call the "traditional" approach to establishing the evidence to be taken into account by any historically warranted description of the historical Jesus. According to Geisler:

> The reliability of the New Testament records is a crucial link in the apologetic argument . . . if the New Testament records are historically reliable, then we can examine them to see if Jesus claimed to be . . . the Son of God.[249]

What Geisler means by "historically reliable" here is clearly something like "generally speaking historically reliable"; which we might take as an affirmation that the New Testament's historical testimony is truth-preserving to such an extent that we have *prima facie* reason to believe any historical testimony contained therein, in the absence of a sufficient counter-argument.

The Traditional Approach: Textual Reliability

> The earliness and the number of manuscripts for most of the Christian documents, is unusually great. . . . [That's] very good authority for the accuracy of the text that is provided in translation in the New Testament.
>
> —ANTONY FLEW[250]

Geisler's case for the general historical reliability of the New Testament has two steps. First, he argues for the *general textual reliability* of the New Testament, on the basis that:

> there are (1) more manuscripts, (2) earlier manuscripts, and (3) better copied manuscripts for the New Testament than for any other book from the ancient world. This [establishes] beyond

---

248. Evans, *In Defence of History*, 76.
249. Geisler, *Christian Apologetics* (2nd ed.), 371.
250. In Habermas et al., *Did Jesus Rise from the Dead?*, 66.

reasonable doubt the reliability of the New Testament writings as an accurate copy of the original text.[251]

The text of the NT currently comes to us through about 23,980 manuscripts, including some 10,000 Latin manuscripts, 975 Coptic manuscripts, 350 Syriac manuscripts, and 5,700 Greek manuscripts:[252]

> The number of Greek New Testament manuscripts (fragments or complete) as of October 2023 is 5,700. There are 135 papyri, 283 majuscules, 2,860 minuscules, and 2,422 lectionary (i.e., the New Testament text is divided into separate pericopes) manuscripts.[253]

Theologians Andreas J. Köstenberger, Darrell L. Bock, and Joshua D. Chatraw jointly comment that: "in almost every case even the most widely accepted works from ancient philosophers and historians are considered verifiable with only a small handful of available sources to vouch for them."[254] According to Geisler (writing with Frank Turek), many ancient works survive "on fewer than a dozen manuscripts [and the average is about twenty manuscripts], yet few historians question the historicity of the events those works describe."[255] Homer's ca. eighth-century BC *Iliad* provides the closest comparison to the New Testament on this score, with recent discoveries pushing the number of manuscripts from the oft-quoted 643 up to about 1900.[256] However, classical literature only offers a very rough point of comparison, as unlike NT scholars (who count every manuscript), classicists don't count any manuscript that's clearly copied from another member of the same textual family tree. That said, the point stands that "there are a good number of manuscripts that attest to the text of the NT compared to classical authors."[257]

Of course, the New Testament manuscripts are spread across a wide range of dates, from the second to the sixteenth century (with numbers

---

251. Geisler, *Christian Apologetics* (2nd ed.), 363. On the *textual* reliability of the New Testament, see Williams, "Textual Reliability of the New Testament" (YouTube playlist); Mounce, *Why I Trust the Bible*; Williams, *Getting at Jesus*.

252. See Geisler, "Updating the Manuscript Evidence"; GreekNewTestament,net; Fernandes and Larson, *Hijacking the Historical Jesus*, 73; McDowell and McDowell, *Evidence That Demands a Verdict*, 46–68.

253. GreekNewTestament.net, §9.

254. Köstenberger et al., *Truth Matters*, 112.

255. Geisler and Turek, *I Don't Have Enough Faith*, 225.

256. See Geisler, "Updating the Manuscript Evidence"; Jones, "Bibliographical Test Updated"; McDowell and McDowell, *Evidence That Demands a Verdict*, 56.

257. Potter, "Revised Approach to Defending," 9.

dropping off after the fifteenth-century invention of the printing press). However, as Don Stewart and Joseph M. Holden observe: "The entire New Testament text is accounted for in manuscript from within 300 years of the original writing."[258] Major early witnesses to the NT text include:

- *Codex Alexandrinus*, which contains almost the entire Bible ca. AD 400.
- *Codex Sinaiticus*, which contains the whole NT (and about half of the Old Testament) ca. AD 350.
- *Codex Vaticanus*, which contains most of the Bible, including complete copies of the four Gospels, ca. AD 325–350.
- *The Chester Beatty Papyri*, which contains major portions of all four Gospels and Acts ca. AD 250.
- *The Bodmer Papyri*, which contains several pages of Luke and most of John ca. AD 200.

There are various NT Gospel manuscript fragments from within about 50 to 200 years of the autographs, and whole pages of the NT Gospels from within about 100 to 150 years. There are "at least 120 Greek manuscripts that date to within three centuries of the original composition of the New Testament."[259] Since we know "a manuscript could survive [in use for] 150 to 200 years as a norm,"[260] some of these could be first generation copies of the autographs!

Consider the temporal gap between the original autographs and the earliest surviving *complete* manuscript in the following representative cases from ancient literature:

---

258. Stewart and Holden, "Were the New Testament Manuscripts Copied," 193.
259. Holden and Stewart. "Were the New Testament Manuscripts Copied," §9.
260. Mounce, *Why I Trust the Bible*, 131.

Fig. 20. Temporal Gap until Our Earliest Complete Manuscript of Ancient Literature.[261]

Ancient Literature	Temporal Gap Until Our Earliest Complete Manuscript
Homer's *Iliad* (epic poem from the 8th century BC)	ca. 1800 years.
Roman Poet Gaius Valerius Catullus	ca. 1,500 years.
The plays of Sophocles	ca. 1,500 years.
The works of Aristotle	ca. 1,400 years.
The histories of Herodotus	ca. 1,350 years.
The works of Plato	ca. 1,300 years.
Thucydides's *History of the Peloponnesian War*	ca. 1,300 years.
The plays of Aristophanes	ca. 1,200 years.
Josephus's *Jewish War*	ca. 900 years.
The poetry of Horace	ca. 900 years.
The histories of Suetonius	ca. 800 years.
The surviving books of the *Annals* of Tacitus	ca. 800 years.
The writings of Pliny the Younger	ca. 750 years.
Pliny the Elder's *Historia Naturalis*	ca. 400 years.
Gaius's *Institutes of Roman Law*	ca. 300 years.

Note that whereas Homer's *Iliad* was the closest textual comparison to the NT in terms of the sheer number of available manuscripts, it fares poorly in terms of this "time gap" metric. Apologist David Cloud reports that "the oldest entire manuscripts of Homer's writings are from the 10th and 11th centuries AD, at least 1,800 years later."[262] Moreover, according to Lynnette Wofford: "Our earliest extant papyrus fragments of the *Iliad* are from the Ptolemaic period (fourth and third century BC) and thus reflect some degree of editorial intervention by Alexandrian scholars."[263]

Figure 21 compares the gap between the autograph and *the earliest extant complete manuscript copies* for both the NT Gospels and a dozen representative ancient literary examples.

261. Data taken from various sources including: Geisler, "Updating the Manuscript Evidence"; Collins, *Defendable Faith*, 98; Köstenberger et al., *Truth Matters*, 115; McDowell and McDowell, *Evidence That Demands a Verdict*; Moreland, *Scaling the Secular City*, 135; Morrow, *Questioning the Bible*, 96.

262. Cloud, "Illiad vs the New Testament," §2.

263. Wofford, "When Was Homer's Iliad Written?," §4.

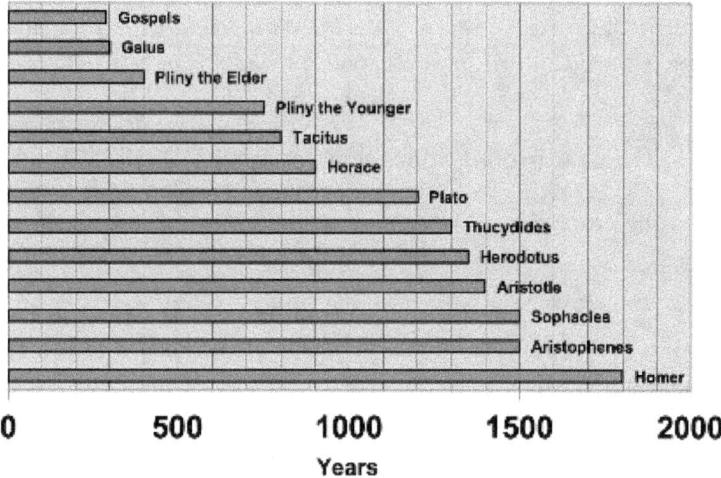

Fig. 21. Temporal Gap between Autographs and Earliest Extant Complete Copies.

As Geisler (writing with Peter Bocchino) notes: "The average time span between the original and earliest [complete] copy of the other ancient texts [those outside the New Testament] is over 1,000 years."[264]

In sum, there is a wealth of manuscript evidence that allows textual critics to reconstruct the original wording of the New Testament with a high degree of confidence:

> the abundance of manuscripts and the antiquity of manuscripts, when run through the mill of text-critical methodology, allows us to know with a very high level of probability what the evangelists and other New Testament authors wrote.[265]

As theologian Timothy Paul Jones explains:

> The 5,700 or so [Greek] New Testament manuscripts that are available to us may differ from one another in as many as 400,000 places—and there are only 138,000 or so words in the Greek New Testament in the first place.... [However] Most of these 400,000 variations stem from differences in spelling, word order, or the relationships between nouns and definite articles — variants that are easily recognizable and, in most cases, virtually unnoticeable in translations.... Most important, *none* of the differences affects any central element of the Christian faith.[266]

264. Geisler and Bocchino, *Unshakable Foundations*, 257.
265. Roberts, *Can We Trust the Gospels?*, 37.
266. Jones, *Misquoting Truth*, 42, 43, and 44.

Hence, as Bart Ehrman concludes: "Scholars are convinced that we can reconstruct the original words of the New Testament with reasonable (although probably not 100 percent) accuracy."[267]

The Traditional Approach: Testimonial Reliability

> The New Testament is a basically reliable source of information about the life of Jesus.
>
> —RICHARD SWINBURNE[268]

Having established the *general textual reliability* of the New Testament, Geisler proceeds to argue for the *general testimonial reliability* of the New Testament:

> As for the reliability of the New Testament writers as conveyers of the truth of the events of which they spoke . . . we have more writers, whose accounts are based on more eyewitnesses . . . which possesses more internal evidence . . . supported by more archaeological evidence, and attested by more non-Christian writers than any book from ancient times that the world has ever seen![269]

As William Lane Craig comments:

> Radical critics still get a free pass from the press today for their sensational assertions, but they are being increasingly marginalized within the academy, as scholarship has come to a new appreciation of the historical reliability of the New Testament documents.[270]

As philosopher Lydia McGrew observes, this appreciation comes from simply "holding the Gospels [and other NT literature] up to the standards that are applicable to other ancient works."[271]

---

267. Bart Ehrman, *New Testament: Historical Introduction to the Early Christian Writings* (3rd ed.), 481, quoted in Stewart, *Reliability of the New Testament*, 31.

268. Swinburne, *Was Jesus God?*, 99.

269. Geisler, *Christian Apologetics* (2nd ed.), 363–364. On the *testimonial* reliability of the New Testament, see McGrew, *Testimonies to the Truth*; McGrew, *Hidden in Plain View*; Williams, Peter J., *Can We Trust the Gospels?*; Williams, *Behold the Man*; Williams, *Getting at Jesus*.

270. Craig, *On Guard*, 183.

271. McGrew, *Testimonies to the Truth*, ix.

McGrew sorts evidence for the reliability of any source of putatively historical testimony into two categories: internal evidence and external evidence. Applied to literature such as the New Testament Gospels, internal evidences mostly concern:

> ways in which the books look truthful by corresponding to what we know about how truthful people talk and write. They include undesigned coincidences, unnecessary details, unexplained allusions, reconcilable variation, and unity of personalities.[272]

External evidences concern the use of:

> information from outside the canonical books of the Bible to support factual statements made within the biblical books. These include information about geography, archaeology, customs, and rulers.[273]

The tight connection between the NT Gospels and their testimonial sources is confirmed by research summarized by Cambridge New Testament scholar Peter J. Williams in his book *Can We Trust the Gospels?* (Crossway, 2018), which documents "a plethora of ways in which the Gospel writers show that they are clearly familiar with the times, places, and customs of Jesus's day, including the local geography."[274] In short, the NT exhibits a historical verisimilitude that would in all likelihood be lacking in material written by authors informationally detached from the life and times of Jesus.

Again, the New Testament's testimony has been the subject of extensive *archaeological* confirmation.[275] In my own research into the currently available archaeological evidence, I have been fascinated to discover material evidence able to demonstrate and/or confirm (with varying degrees of plausibility) that:

- Jesus, son of Joseph and brother of James (who was buried in Jerusalem in the middle of the first century), existed within the early to mid first century period.
- Jesus was crucified (which probably killed him).
- Victims of Roman crucifixion could be interred.

---

272. McGrew, *Testimonies to the Truth*, vii–viii. See Williams, "Undesigned Coincidences in the Gospels" (YouTube playlist).

273. McGrew, *Testimonies to the Truth*, vii.

274. Brierley, *Surprising Rebirth of Belief in God*, 117.

275. See Evans, *Jesus and the Remains of History*; Evans, *Jesus and His World*.

- Jesus was entombed (a process that probably confirms his death) in a disused quarry that was also used for gardening, just outside the first-century city walls of Jerusalem.

- Grave robbery was an offence that may have been particularly associated with Nazareth, where the NT says Jesus lived, by the middle of the first century AD (lending credence to Jesus's empty tomb, and thus to his entombment).

- Despite the shameful stigma of crucifixion, Jesus was considered to be divine, in the Judeo-Christian sense, by some people in the near east within ca. 170 years of his execution.

- The New Testament Gospels have been repeatedly verified by archaeological discoveries relating to places, people, culture, and beliefs, which encourages us to trust them on matters we can't independently verify in this way.[276]

Of course, historians may well use a combination of internal and external data to determine something like the date and/or authorship of a historical document (and the strongest argument for the historical reliability of a document is the cumulative case made by all of the internal and external evidences taken together).

The internal and external evidence taken together indicates that the canonical Gospels compare favorably with other ancient works of history in terms of the temporal interval between their date of publication and the events they claim to report (see figure 22). The average gap between a historical event and a published report of that event for the non-biblical sources listed in figure 22 is about eighty-eight years. Even if we exclude Plutarch's *Lives*, the average temporal gap for the remaining non-biblical texts is about fifty-nine years. The average lapse between the four Gospels and the events they report is (on the dating I assign to them) just over forty-five years. This drops to about thirty-eight years for the Synoptic Gospels, and less if we exclude Matthew and Luke's stories about Jesus's infancy. Indeed, one can see that even on a "liberal" dating of the canonical Gospels (which would place Mark ca. 60–75, Matthew ca. 65–85, and Luke ca. AD 65–95[277]), they would still count as relatively "early" sources by the standards of ancient historiography.

---

276. See FOCLOnline, "Archaeological Evidence for Jesus" (YouTube video); Williams, "Archaeological Evidence and Jesus (ELF 2025)" (Podcast); Williams, *Behold the Man*, 89–91; *Digging for Evidence*; and *Getting at Jesus*.

277. See Roberts, *Can We Trust the Gospels?*, 58.

Fig. 22. Temporal Interval between Events and Reports.[278]

Author/ Work	Reported Events	Report Published	Lapse between Events & Report	Average Lapse
Mark	ca. AD 30–33	ca. AD 49	ca. 16–19 yrs	ca. 17.5 yrs
Luke	ca. 6 BC–AD 33	ca. AD 60	ca. 27–66 yrs	ca. 46.5 yrs
Matthew	ca. 6 BC–AD 33	ca. AD 65	ca. 32–71 yrs	ca. 51.5 yrs
John	ca. AD 30–33	ca. AD 98	ca. 65–68 yrs	ca. 66.5 yrs
Pliny, *Letters*	AD 97–112	AD 100–112	0–3 yrs	1.5 yrs
Thucydides, *History*	431–411 BC	410–400 BC	0–30 yrs	15 yrs
Xenophon, *Anabasis*	401–399 BC	385–375 BC	15–25 yrs	20 yrs
Polybius, *History*	200–120 BC	150 BC	20–70 yrs	45 yrs
Tacitus, *Annuls*	AD 14–68	ca. AD 100–110	ca. 32–96 yrs	ca. 64 yrs
Heroditus, *History*	546–478 BC	430–425 BC	48–121 yrs	84.5 yrs
Suetonius, *Lives*	50 BC–AD 95	ca. AD 120	ca. 25–170 yrs	ca. 97.5 yrs
Josephus— *War*	200 BC–AD 70	ca. AD 80	ca. 10–280 yrs	ca. 145 yrs
Plutarch, *Lives*	500 BC–AD 70	ca. AD 100	ca. 30–600 yrs	ca. 315 yrs

Much more could be said along these lines, but in sum: "the available evidence from a variety of angles confirms the strong foundation on which we can base the general reliability of the New Testament reports of the historical Jesus."[279] A plethora of standard tests for historical authenticity find application to the New Testament's historical testimony and warrants an inference to the conclusion that this testimony is, at least generally speaking, historically reliable.

278. For a justification of the Gospel dates used for the synoptic gospels in this table, see Williams, *Getting at Jesus*. On dating the Fourth Gospel, see chaps. 2 and 3 of Williams, *Behold the Man*. Some data in this table was sourced from Newman, "Miracles", 443.

279. Habermas, "Recent Perspectives on the Reliability," §13.

Geisler's "traditional" approach constructs a historical argument for the *general* textual and testimonial reliability of the New Testament before using the New Testament's testimony to warrant a historical portrait of Jesus as someone who both laid claim to divinity and provided miraculous confirmations of that claim. Again, the case for this historical portrait has two parts.

The Traditional Approach: Evidence That Jesus Promulgated a "High Christology"

First, according to Geisler:

> After reviewing these historically reliable documents for what Jesus actually taught concerning his own origin and nature, we find both indirect implications and explicit statements that Jesus claimed to be God Almighty, the Creator of the universe in human flesh.[280]

The New Testament testifies to a variety of ways in which Jesus laid claim to divinity through a combination of his words and deeds.[281] N. T. Wright summarizes this data by stating that "Jesus was aware of a call, a vocation, to do and be what, according to the scriptures, only Israel's God gets to do and be."[282] Theologian Michael F. Bird explains that

> Jesus identified himself as a divine agent with a unique authority and a unique relationship with Israel's God. In addition, he spoke as one who speaks for God in an immediate sense and believed himself to be embodying the very person of God in his mission to renew and restore Israel.[283]

---

280. Geisler, *Christian Apologetics* (2nd ed.), 391.

281. See Williams, "Christology" (YouTube playlist); Craig, "Who Was Jesus of Nazareth?"; Bird et al., *How God Became Jesus*; Bock, *Who Is Jesus?*; Bowman and Komoszewski, *Incarnate Christ and His Critics*; Craig, *Reasonable Faith*, chap. 7; Grindheim, *Christology in the Synoptic Gospels*; Gruneler, *New Approaches to Jesus and the Gospels*; Habermas, *Risen Jesus and Future Hope*, chap. 3; Komoszewski et al., *Reinventing Jesus*; Loke, *Origin of Divine Christology*; Loke, *Studies on the Origin*; Overman, *Case for the Divinity of Jesus*; Williams, *Getting at Jesus*, chap. 2; Witherington, *Christology of Jesus*.

282. Wright, *Simply Christian*, 101.

283. Bird, "Did Jesus Think He Was God?," 46.

As J. P. Moreland concludes, "a high Christology [that is, the view that Jesus is divine in a sense that stems from and is compatible with Jewish monotheism] goes back to Jesus himself."[284]

A separate line of argumentation that supports the same conclusion comes from considering the view of Jesus formed by the first generation of Christians. The New Testament letters "date mainly from the period AD 49–69, and provide confirmation of the importance and interpretations of Jesus in this formative period."[285] These letters prove that "a concept of a divine Jesus was already present, at the latest, within sixteen to twenty years after the crucifixion."[286]

For example, the epistle of James (which plausibly dates from ca. 45–47 AD) displays an early "high Christology" in a strongly Jewish milieu, not only through its reference to "our glorious Lord Jesus Christ" (Jas 1:1), but through its application *to Christians* of Old Testament language about Israel being "called upon" by God's name, when it references "the ones who are blaspheming the good name called upon you" (Jas 2:7).[287]

Paul's mid-first-century epistles contain creeds and hymns (e.g., Rom 1:3–4; 1 Cor 11:23 ff.; 15:3–8; Phil 2:6–11; Col 1:15–18; 1 Tim 2:8) that had become "standard, recognized creeds and hymns well before their incorporation into Paul's letters."[288] These creeds and hymns "consistently present a portrait of a miraculous and divine Jesus who rose from the dead."[289] For example, the letter to the Colossians dates from ca. 60–62 AD, and affirms of Jesus that "in him all things were created: things in heaven and on earth, visible and invisible . . . all things have been created through him and for him." (Col 1:15, NIV.) Like the end-of-century opening verses of the fourth gospel (John 1:1–3),[290] this passage places Jesus firmly on the divine side of the key Jewish distinction between the creator and the created (Gen 1:1). The same can be said of Paul's statement, in 1 Cor 8:6 (ca. 54–55 AD), that

---

284. Moreland, *God Question*, 111.

285. McGrath, *Jesus*, 69.

286. Moreland, *Scaling the Secular City*, 148.

287. My translation. For a detailed argument for high Christology in the epistle of James, see Williams, "Epistle of St. James" (available online), or the revised version of this paper in Williams, *Behold the Man*, chap. 2.

288. Moreland, *Scaling the Secular City*, 148–49.

289. Moreland, *Scaling the Secular City*, 149.

290. On the dating of the fourth gospel, see Williams, *Behold the Man*, chaps. 3 and 4.

> for us there is one God, the Father, from whom are all things and for whom we exist, and one Lord, Jesus Christ, through whom are all things and through whom we exist.

Likewise, the letter/sermon of Hebrews (ca. 49–70 AD) affirms that God

> has spoken to us by his Son, whom he appointed the heir of all things, through whom also he created the world. He is the radiance of the glory of God and the exact imprint of his nature, and he upholds the universe by the word of his power. (Heb 1:2–3, ESV.)

In short, belief in the divinity of Jesus stems from the first generation of Jesus's followers, and this belief is indirect evidence that Jesus himself "claimed to be God Almighty, the Creator of the universe in human flesh."[291]

Now, as Paul Copan observes: "Orthodox Jews considered worshipping a mere human blasphemous and detestable (Acts 10:25–26; 14:11–15), so the church's without-controversy acceptance of Christ-worship is stunning."[292] The most plausible explanation of this early belief in the divinity of Jesus is that Jesus himself encouraged people to relate to him in these terms, and did so in a manner sufficiently compelling to convince them that this theological innovation was warranted. As philosopher Anthony O'Hear argues:

> We should remember that [Jesus's] first followers were pious Jews, to whom the claims being made would have seemed blasphemous had they not been given strong reason to believe them—and where better than from Jesus himself?[293]

The Traditional Approach: Evidence for Divinity

Second, Geisler seeks to verify Jesus's claim to divinity on purely historical grounds, arguing that the best explanation of the relevant evidence is that Jesus's claims were genuinely verified by a convergence of miracles:

> Miracles associated with Christ's claim to be God are acts of God that confirm him to be the Son of God . . . . And in Jesus's case there is a convergence of three great miraculous happenings—prophecy, his sinless life and miraculous deeds, and his

---

291. Geisler, *Christian Apologetics* (2nd ed.), 391.
292. Copan, *True for You but Not for Me*, Rev. ed., 167.
293. O'Hear, *Jesus for Beginners*, 84.

resurrection—that lead forthrightly to the conclusion that he alone is the unique Son of God.[294]

As Michael F. Bird affirms: "Jesus made extravagant claims about himself as to his authority, mission, and origin, and the resurrection was a divine affirmation that those claims were good."[295]

Secular philosopher Michael Ruse says he can "agree on the fairly uncontroversial claim that if the miracles of the Gospels did occur, then we have some pretty strong evidence for the truth of Christianity."[296] In particular, Ruse affirms that "if Jesus was really dead on Friday and really alive on Sunday, then I for one will be satisfied."[297] I submit that the principle obstacle in attempting to satisfy someone like Ruse as to the truth of Christianity is not historical, but philosophical. As R. T. France observed:

> At the level of their literary and historical character we have good reason to treat the gospels seriously. . . . Beyond that point, the decision as to how far a scholar is willing to accept the record they offer is likely to be influenced more by his openness to a "supernaturalist" worldview than by strictly historical considerations.[298]

Assessing Geisler's Traditional Approach

As a "classical" apologist,[299] Geisler explicitly constructs his historical case for a Christian understanding of the historical Jesus within the context of a theistic worldview for which he has already argued on philosophical grounds. Geisler outlines his overall argument as follows:

---

294. Geisler, *Christian Apologetics* (2nd ed.), 393. On Jesus's other miraculous deeds and his fulfilment of prophecy, see Williams, *Understanding Jesus*, chaps. 4 and 6.

295. Bird, "Did Jesus Think He Was God?," 67.

296. Ruse, *Atheism*, 161.

297. Ruse, *Atheism*, 161.

298. France, "Gospels as Historical Sources for Jesus," 86.

299. To explore different apologetic methodologies, see Williams, "Apologetic Methodology" (YouTube Playlist); Williams, "Apologetics in 3D (Norway, 2024)" (Podcast); Bannister, *How to Talk about Jesus*; Boa and Bowman, *Faith Has Its Reasons* (2nd edition); Burson and Walls, *C. S. Lewis & Francis Schaeffer*; Cowan, *Five Views on Apologetics*; Gould, *Cultural Apologetics*; Gould and McLean, *Primer on Cultural Apologetics*; Jones, *Understanding Christian Apologetics*; Koukl, *Tactics* (10th Anniversary Edition); Morley, *Mapping Apologetics*; Morris, *Francis Schaeffer's Apologetics*; Williams, *Apologetics in 3D*.

> We have shown the following: (1) truth is knowable . . . (2) the opposite of true is false . . . (3) in opposition to all other views of God . . . a theistic God exists . . . (4) in a theistic world, miracles are possible . . . (5) miracles can be used to confirm a truth claim within a theistic worldview . . . (6) the New Testament documents are historically reliable . . . (7) those documents report that Jesus claimed to be God in human flesh. . . . Now we will show that (8) those documents provide multiple lines of miraculous evidence that Jesus is God, as he claimed to be.[300]

Geisler's approach to the historical Jesus has much to recommend it. However, while the historical case for Jesus is undoubtedly at its strongest within the context of a monotheistic worldview, historical argumentation for a Christian understanding of Jesus only requires the assumption that miracles *might* occur in a knowable way because God *might* exist and *might* perform miracles.[301] Moreover, having established the *textual reliability* of the NT, one can sidestep Geisler's focus on the *general testimonial reliability* of the NT by using various "criteria of historical authenticity" to argue directly for the *particular testimonial reliability* of various historical facts about Jesus.

The Criteria of Authenticity Approach to Testimonial Reliability

While the historical criteria of authenticity used by "Tradition Criticism"[302] cannot *guarantee* the historicity of data to which they apply, they do provide reasons to take such data with greater seriousness than would otherwise be the case.[303] All things being equal, the more criteria of authenticity a saying or event passes, the more seriously we must take it. As William Lane Craig explains:

> It is somewhat misleading to call these "criteria," for they aim at stating sufficient, not necessary, conditions of historicity . . . what the criteria really amount to are statements about the effect of certain types of evidence upon the probability of various sayings or events . . . all else being equal . . . the probability of

---

300. Geisler, *Christian Apologetics* (2nd ed.), 391.
301. See Evans, *Historical Christ*; Williams, *Getting at Jesus*, chap. 1.
302. Bock, *Studying the Historical Jesus*, 199.
303. On historical criteria of authenticity, see Williams, "Historical Criteria of Authenticity" (YouTube playlist); Craig, *Reasonable Faith*, 298; Habermas, *On the Resurrection*, Vol. 1, chap. 2; Stein, "Criteria for the Gospel's Authenticity"; Williams, *Getting at Jesus*, 242–48.

some event or saying is greater given, for example, its multiple attestation than it would have been without it ... these "criteria" ... focus on a particular saying or event and give evidence for thinking that specific element of Jesus' life to be historical, regardless of the general reliability of the document in which the particular saying or event is reported.[304]

Thus, as theologian Darrell L. Bock observes: "One should remember that failure to meet the criteria does not establish a text's inauthenticity, because the criteria cover only a limited amount of assessment factors,"[305] such that "these criteria serve better as a supplemental argument for authenticity."[306] After all: "The Gospels are prima facie evidence for what the historical Jesus said and did."[307]

Then again, the criteria of early sources may find application to a whole document and/or to sources within a document. The New Testament connects us to multiple early sources that can be dated to within two decades of the crucifixion. For example, on the basis of internal evidence, most New Testament scholars infer the existence of a written source of some 250 verses shared by the Gospels of "Matthew" and "Luke," a source that therefore pre-dates both Gospels (which are themselves relatively "early," first-century sources). Named after the German word for source/spring (*Quelle*), "Q" may even have been written during the lifetime of Jesus, perhaps by Matthew the tax collector.[308] As Paul Barnett notes: "'Q' texts are cited or echoed in letters of Paul written in the mid-fifties."[309] Indeed, Dale Allison "concludes that Paul knew material from Mark, material common to Luke and Matthew ("Q"), material unique to Luke "L," and perhaps material unique to Matthew ("M")."[310]

Several early sources are to be found in Luke's Gospel sequel, known as "Acts." As James Dunn explains: "Luke has sought out much earlier material and has incorporated it into the brief formalized expositions which he attributes to Peter, Stephen, Paul, etc."[311] Hugh Montefiore comments:

---

304. Craig, *Reasonable Faith*, 298.
305. Bock, *Studying the Historical Jesus*, 202–3.
306. Bock, *Studying the Historical Jesus*, 202–3.
307. Wenham and Walton, *Exploring the New Testament*, 139. For a discussion of the epistemology of testimony in relation to the New Testament, see Williams, *Understanding Jesus*, chap. 2.
308. See Williams, *Getting at Jesus*, 204–205.
309. Barnett, *Birth of Christianity*, 147.
310. Barnett, *Birth of Christianity*, 125.
311. Dunn, *Why Believe in Jesus' Resurrection?*, 22.

> These speeches have been examined in considerable detail, and there are indications that the author did use sources for them ... there is the presence of Semitisms in the speeches. ... It is held by many that these speeches represent the primitive *kerygma* (preaching of the Gospel in the early Church).[312]

Bart Ehrman concurs that:

> the speeches in Acts are particularly notable because they are, in many instances, based ... on oral traditions ... these speeches incorporate materials from the traditions about Jesus that existed long before Luke put pen to papyrus.[313]

Moreover, remember that Paul's letters contain creeds and hymns (e.g., Rom 1:3-4; 1 Cor 11:23 ff.; 15:3-8; Phil 2:6-11; Col 1:15-18; 1 Tim 2:8) that had become "standard, recognized creeds and hymns well before their incorporation into Paul's letters,"[314] and which "consistently present a portrait of a miraculous and divine Jesus who rose from the dead."[315] A prime example of this material is the list of resurrection appearances in 1 Cor 15.[316] Jake O'Connell comments that:

> the pre-Pauline material of 1 Corinthians 15:3-8, which surely dates to within years of the resurrection, and is nearly universally regarded as summarising extremely early material, ensures that the appearances enumerated there cannot be legendary.[317]

Jewish NT scholar Pinchas Lapide writes of the 1 Cor 15 creed that:

> this unified piece of tradition which soon was solidified into a formula of faith may be considered as *a statement of eyewitnesses* for whom the experience of the resurrection became the turning point of their lives.[318]

---

312. Montefiore, *Womb and the Tomb*, 134. See also Habermas, *On the Resurrection*, Vol. 1, 418.
313. Ehrman, *Did Jesus Exist?*, 109 and 111.
314. Moreland, *Scaling the Secular City*, 148-49.
315. Moreland, *Scaling the Secular City*, 149.
316. Habermas, "Tracing Jesus' Resurrection," 202-16.
317. O'Connell, "Jesus' Resurrection and Collective Hallucinations," 75.
318. Lapide, *Resurrection of Jesus*, 99, my italics.

Atheist New Testament scholar James Crossley concludes that in the 1 Cor 15 creed we have "reliable reports"[319] from "eyewitnesses"[320] that "must be taken very seriously."[321]

The canonical Gospels alone provide four first century sources relating to Jesus's death, burial, empty tomb, and resurrection appearances. Adding the *extremely* early information from Peter and Paul in speeches from Acts, from Paul in his own letters, and from the creed quoted by Paul in 1 Cor 15, gives us *seven early sources* of testimony about the death, burial, and resurrection of Jesus (Fig. 23). This *early* testimony (the earliest of which are tabulated in Fig. 24) is presented in *multiple forms* and includes *several eyewitness sources*.

Fig. 23. Seven Early Sources on the Resurrection.

	Peter in Acts	1 Corinthians 15 Creed	Mark's Passion Source	Paul in Acts & Letters	L	M	John
Death	2:23 & 36; 10:39	15:3	15:37	13:28–29	Luke 23:46	Matt 27:24	19:30
Burial		15:4	15:46	13:29	Luke 23:53	Matt 27:64	19:42
Empty Tomb			16:6		Luke 24:2, 10, 12, 23	Matt 27:59	20:2, 6
Appearances	2:32; 10:40–42	15:4–5	16:7	13:31, 22:6–9 & 26: 13–14; 1 Cor 9:1 & 15:8; Gal 1:13–17	Luke 24:12, 15, 36	Matt 28:9–10 & 16–17	20:14–29 & 21:1–25

Fig. 24. The Earliest Sources on the Resurrection

Acts 2:23–32	1 Cor 15:3–5	Mark 15:37 – 16:7	Acts 13:28–31
Peter's Pentecost sermon from AD 33.	Early Creed, ca. A.D. 33–34.	Pre-Marcan passion narrative, ca. AD 33–37.	Paul's Pisidian Antioch sermon, ca. AD 45.

319. Crossley, *Date of Mark's Gospel*, 140.
320. Crossley, "Against the Historical Plausibility," 171.
321. Crossley, "Against the Historical Plausibility," 186.

you ... put him to death by nailing him to the cross.	Christ died ...	Jesus breathed his last.	they asked Pilate to have him executed.
	he was buried	Joseph bought some linen cloth, took down the body, wrapped it in the linen, and placed it in a tomb ...	they took him down from the tree and laid him in a tomb.
God has raised this Jesus to life ...	he was raised [which implies the empty tomb]	He has risen! [which implies the empty tomb]	But God raised him from the dead ... [which implies the empty tomb]
we are all witnesses of the fact.	he appeared	He is going ahead of you into Galilee. There you will see him ...	for many days he was seen

Hence a historical case for Jesus's claims,[322] and his miracles,[323] including his resurrection,[324] can be made by "arguing from a critical perspective."[325]

---

322. See FOCLOnline, "Defending Early High Christology" (YouTube video); Williams, "Christology" (YouTube playlist); Williams, "Archaeological Evidence and Jesus (ELF 2025)" (Podcast); Craig, "Who Was Jesus of Nazareth?"; Bird et al., *How God Became Jesus*; Bock, *Who Is Jesus?*; Bowman and Komoszewski, *Incarnate Christ and His Critics*; Craig, *Reasonable Faith*, chap. 7; Grindheim, *Christology in the Synoptic Gospels*; Gruneler, *New Approaches to Jesus and the Gospels*; Habermas, *Risen Jesus and Future Hope*, chap. 3; Komoszewski et al., *Reinventing Jesus*; Loke, *Origin of Divine Christology*; Loke, *Studies on the Origin*; Overman, *Case for the Divinity of Jesus*; Williams, *Behold the Man*, 89–91; *Digging for Evidence*; and *Getting at Jesus*, chap. 2; Witherington, *Christology of Jesus*.

323. See Habermas, "Did Jesus Perform Miracles?"; Williams, *Getting at Jesus*, chap. 5.

324. See Williams, *Getting at Jesus*; Williams, *Behold the Man*, chap. 5 and appendix 1. See also Williams, "Resurrection of Jesus" (YouTube playlist); Williams, "Debating the Resurrection" (YouTube playlist); Craig, "Jesus' Resurrection"; "Bodily Resurrection of Jesus"; "Dale Allison on Jesus' Empty Tomb"; and "Dale Allison on the Resurrection of Jesus"; Habermas, "Dale Allison's Resurrection Skepticism"; Craig, *Did Jesus Rise?*; *Reasonable Faith*; and *Assessing the New Testament Evidence*; Davis, *Risen Indeed*; Dunn, *Why Believe in Jesus' Resurrection?*; Habermas, "Resurrection Appearances of Jesus," 262–75; *Risen Indeed*; and *On the Resurrection*; Habermas and Licona, *Case for the Resurrection of Jesus*; Hansen, "Tactile and True," 207–28; Licona, *Resurrection of Jesus*; Loke, *Studies on the Origin*; O'Connell, *Jesus' Resurrection and Apparitions*; Swinburne, *Resurrection of God Incarnate*; Wright, *Resurrection of the Son of God*.

325. Habermas, *Risen Jesus and Future Hope*, 96.

on the basis of evidence gathered using standard historical methods, such as making arguments using data from multiple early sources. For example:

> Of the five independent sources often recognized in the Gospel accounts—Mark, the Q sayings, the material unique to Matthew (M), the material unique to Luke (L), and John—Jesus's miracles are reported in all five layers, with some specific miracle claims being included in more than one of the sources. Jesus's crucial "Son of Man" statements are also confirmed in all five Gospel sources . . . . the story of the empty tomb is reported in at least three . . . of the Gospel sources.[326]

As historian Paul L. Maier observes: "Many facts from antiquity rest on just one ancient source, while two or three sources in agreement generally render the fact unimpeachable."[327]

The Criteria of Authenticity and "Minimal Facts" Approaches to the Resurrection of Jesus

In his PhD thesis and subsequent related research, philosopher Gary R. Habermas sets aside questions about the *general testimonial reliability* of the New Testament by using standard criteria of historical authenticity to argue *directly* for a set of *specific historical facts* about Jesus that can underpin a case for his resurrection.[328]

To construct what he calls "the minimal facts argument" for the resurrection, Habermas additionally sifts and categorizes these facts in terms of their acceptance by critical scholars in relevant academic fields:

> The Minimal Facts Argument proposes that even by using only those few historical data that are attested by many evidences each and that are therefore accepted as historical by a high percentage of scholars in the field, we have enough of a basis to show that Jesus' resurrection happened.[329]

Habermas explains that:

---

326. Habermas, *On the Resurrection*, Vol. 1, 46.
327. Maier, *Genuine Jesus*, 264.
328. See Williams, "'Minimal Facts' Approach to the Resurrection" (YouTube playlist); Habermas, *On the Resurrection*, Vol. 1, and *Risen Indeed*; Habermas and Licona, *Case for the Resurrection of Jesus*.
329. Habermas, "My Magnum Opus on the Minimal Facts Argument."

> My Minimal Facts Argument in favor of Jesus' resurrection . . . has two requirements for the historical facts that are used: each must be confirmed by several strong and independent arguments, plus the vast majority of even critical scholars must recognize the occurrence's historical nature. The critical scholars can be liberal, skeptical, agnostic, or even atheist, as long as they are specialists in a relevant field of study, such as New Testament. Of these two requirements . . . the initial standard concerning strong evidential back-up is by far the most crucial.[330]

Habermas uses his secondary requirement as a rhetorical move to deflect accusations of bias by showing that even scholars with non-Christian worldviews accept the "minimal facts," presumably due to the strength of the historical arguments for them. Indeed, Habermas describes his twin requirements for "events . . . established by an abundance of strong evidences,"[331] and accepted by "the vast majority of published contemporary scholars with credentials in relevant fields of study"[332] as "methodological moves" that "have the benefit of bypassing much of the often-protracted preliminary discussions which frequently take place regarding which data are permissible by beginning with a sort of 'lowest common denominator' approach."[333]

Habermas insists that well supported data beyond those admitted by the "vast majority" of relevant scholars can and should be taken into account as part of a supplementary argument, or as a tiebreaker between otherwise evenly matched hypotheses. So, in Habermas's "minimal facts" methodology, while a high level of common consent is *desirable*, good evidence marshalled by the criteria of authenticity is *essential*.[334] As Habermas observes: "If the case for historicity already has been resolved, this is an independent conclusion that stands regardless of whether any particular head count of scholars agrees."[335]

In his balanced and broadly sympathetic critique of "Habermas's Minimal Facts Argument," philosopher and theologian Robert B. Stewart comments that:

> In historical investigation, one should take note of all the relevant data. . . . [The "minimal facts"] method, with its insistence

---

330. Habermas, "Minimal Facts on the Resurrection."
331. Habermas, *On the Resurrection*, Vol. 1, 91.
332. Habermas, *On the Resurrection*, Vol. 1, 91.
333. Habermas, *On the Resurrection*, Vol. 1, 94.
334. See Stewart, "On Habermas's Minimal Facts Argument."
335. Habermas, *On the Resurrection*, Vol. 1, 91.

upon 90-percent or higher consensus, may be too clever by half. By requiring at least 90-percent agreement, it may force historians to ignore facts that are potentially even more helpful in discovering the truth than those that Habermas accepts as minimal facts. Habermas's method demands that he ignore propositions for which he has good reasons to believe—indeed, propositions that he does believe. I think this is why Habermas and Licona insist on mentioning... "Second Order" facts.... Having more true beliefs rather than fewer is almost always advantageous, *so long as one doesn't just believe irresponsibly*.[336]

We can distinguish between a historical methodology that uses criteria of authenticity from a "minimal facts" approach that combines the "criteria of authenticity" with the requirement that "the vast majority of even critical scholars must recognize the occurrence's historical nature."[337] Furthermore, one can deploy a "minimal facts" approach with different degrees of strictness with respect to the required scholarly majority, and with or without appealing to well supported data beyond those admitted by that majority, as the rhetorical situation dictates.

Habermas lists some of the facts that are generally acknowledged by the relevant community of scholars, regardless of their personal worldview:

> The vast majority of critical scholars... whatever their personal beliefs, espouse or at least concede that Jesus died by Roman crucifixion and that his disciples experienced grief and disillusionment at his death, usually allowing that Jesus' burial tomb was later found empty. Then, due to experiences that they believed were appearances of the risen Jesus, the disciples were transformed, even to the point of being willing to die for their faith. At a very early date they began to proclaim the death and resurrection of Jesus Christ, and the church was born shortly afterward, founded on this gospel message. Even a few former sceptics, such as James, the brother of Jesus, and Paul, became believers after they, too, believed that they had seen the risen Jesus.[338]

---

336. Stewart, "On Habermas's Minimal Facts Argument," 6, 7, and 9. For additional critiques of the "minimal facts" approach, see McGrew, "On the Minimal Facts Case for the Resurrection"; McGrew, *Eye of the Beholder*, chap. 8.

337. Habermas, "Minimal Facts on the Resurrection." For examples of a more criteria-centric approach, see Craig, *Did Jesus Rise from the Dead?*; *Reasonable Faith*, chap. 8; and *Son Rises*.

338. Habermas, "Resurrection and Agnosticism," 281–82.

Writing with New Testament historian Michael L. Licona, Habermas notes that:

> although the empty tomb lacks the nearly universal acceptance by critical scholars that these other events enjoy, the majority of scholars still clearly seem to think that it is probably also a historical fact.[339]

Licona categorizes the empty tomb as a "second order" historical fact[340] (a fact of the type Habermas says can and should be used as part of a supplementary argument, or as a tiebreaker between otherwise evenly matched hypotheses); yet chooses to argue for the resurrection without resting any weight on the historicity of the empty tomb.[341]

With respect to the testimony concerning purported resurrection appearances, as Licona comments:

> that subsequent to Jesus' execution, a number of his followers had experiences, in individual and group settings, that convinced them that Jesus had risen from the dead and had appeared to them in some manner . . . is granted by a nearly unanimous consensus of modern scholars. . . . Scholars differ, however, on the perceived nature of the experiences.[342]

Licona and Habermas address "the perceived nature of the experiences," and argue in favor of Jesus's physical resurrection, when they consider various theories which accept that a number of Jesus's followers "had experiences, in individual and group settings, that convinced them that Jesus had risen from the dead and had appeared to them in some manner."[343]

In my own published work on the resurrection, I have used criteria of authenticity not only to argue for the "minimal" fact that a number of Jesus's followers "had experiences, in individual and group settings, that

---

339. Habermas and Licona, *Case for the Resurrection of Jesus*, 74. See Williams, "Jesus' Tomb Was Empty" (YouTube playlist); Craig, "Historicity of the Empty Tomb"; "Disciples' Inspection of the Empty Tomb"; and "Reply to Evan Fales"; Habermas, "Empty Tomb of Jesus"; National Geographic Partners, "Unsealing of Christ's Reputed Tomb"; Williams, *Getting at Jesus*, 272–78.

340. Licona, *Resurrection of Jesus*, 469.

341. See Licona, *Resurrection of Jesus*, 461–63.

342. Licona, *Resurrection of Jesus*, 372–73. As Habermas writes: "The nearly unanimous consent of critical scholars is that, *in some sense*, the early followers of Jesus thought that they had seen the risen Jesus" ("Resurrection Research from 1975," 151), my italics.

343. Licona, *Resurrection of Jesus*, 372. See Habermas and Licona, *Case for the Resurrection of Jesus*, chap. 9; Licona, *Resurrection of Jesus*, chap. 5 and appendix.

convinced them that Jesus had risen from the dead and had appeared to them in some manner,"[344] but to supplement the traditional historical case for a series of specific, multi-sensory experiences in which both disciples and non-disciples, in individual and group settings, *see*, *hear* or *talk with*, and even *touch* Jesus.[345]

Fig. 25 lists specific post-interment appearances of Jesus referenced by the NT, in their apparent historical order, and notes the sensory modes reportedly involved in these appearances.[346]

Fig. 25: Post-interment Appearances of Jesus.

Resurrection Witnesses	Location	Senses Specified	Sources
Mary Magdalene	Empty Tomb	Saw and talked with Jesus (perhaps touching him)	John 20:11–18
At least five other women, including Joanna & Mary the mother of James	Jerusalem	Saw, heard and touched Jesus	Matt 28:1–10 (see Luke 24:8–11)
Cleopas & Mary	Emmaus Road	Saw and talked with Jesus	Luke 24:13–32
Peter	Unspecified	Saw Jesus	1 Cor 15:5a; Mark 16:7 & Luke 24:34
Ten disciples (and others)	Unspecified room in Jerusalem	Saw and talked with Jesus	John 20:19–23 & Luke 24:36–44
Eleven disciples including Thomas	Unspecified room	Saw, talked with and touched Jesus	John 20:24–29; see 1 Cor 15:5b
Seven disciples	Along the sea of Galilee (Tiberius)	Saw and talked with Jesus	John 21:1–23
500 individuals at once	Unspecified/ Galilee	Saw Jesus	1 Cor 15:6; Mark 16:7
Eleven disciples	Galilee	Saw and heard Jesus	Matt 28:16–20
Eleven disciples	Jerusalem	Saw and heard Jesus	Luke 24:45–49 & Acts 1:4–5

344. Licona, *Resurrection of Jesus*, 372.

345. See Williams, *Getting at Jesus*, 278–82.

346. Based on Miller, *Did Jesus Really Rise?*, 106; Wilkins, "Gospel of Matthew," 190–91.

Eleven disciples	Jerusalem & Mount of Olives	Saw and heard/talked with Jesus	Luke 24:50–53 & Acts 1:6–11
Saul	Road to Damascus	Saul saw a bright light and talked with Jesus, seeing Jesus within the light, in the presence of companions who saw the light and heard, but did not understand, Jesus's voice[347]	1 Cor 1:9; 1 Cor 9:1 & 15:8; Acts 9:1–19, 22:1–21 & 26:1–32

From this data, it appears we should take notice of eleven or twelve distinct reports of post-mortem appearance events (depending on whether the appearance to the five hundred at once is the same event as the appearance to the eleven disciples in Galilee, as some commentators suggest). These reports feature post-mortem appearances of Jesus to two individuals and to nine or ten groups. These appearance reports all qualify as *early* reports[348] that pass the criterion of *memorability*.[349] In addition:

- We have *multiple early, independent sources*[350] *for at least one* individual and three group appearances.
- The (unfortunately detail-free) reported appearance to Peter is *multiply attested in different forms*[351] and additionally passes the criterion of

---

347. See Habermas and Flew, "Did Paul Actually see the Risen Jesus" (YouTube video); BeliefMap, "Did Paul Simply Hallucinate Jesus's Appearing to Him?"; Quarles, "Paul as a Witness to the Resurrection of Jesus"; Marshall, *Acts*, 178–79 and 375; Williams, *Getting at Jesus*, 282–87.

348. As classical historian Mark D. Smith avers: "In particular, there is a significant watershed between first-generation sources, written during the lifetime of at least some who knew the person or experienced the event in question, and sources from subsequent generations" (*Final Days of Jesus*, 29).

349. As J. Warner Wallace says: "When witnesses experience something that's unique, unrepeated, and personally important or powerful, they're much more likely to remember it" (Strobel, *Case for Miracles*, 197).

350. For a discussion of the nature of independence between sources, see Williams, *Getting at Jesus*, 243–45.

351. According to John P. Meier: "The criterion of multiple attestation focuses on those saying or deeds of Jesus that are attested in more than one independent literary source and/or in more than one literary form or genre. The force of this criterion is increased if a given motif or theme is found in both literary sources and different literary forms" (*Marginal Jew*, 175).

historical verisimilitude[352] (see 1 Cor 15:5's use of the Aramaic *Cephas* instead of the Greek *Petros*[353]).

- The appearance to Mary Magdalene passes the criteria of *embarrassment*[354] and *historical verisimilitude* (note the popularity of the name Mary, and the Aramaic *Rabboni* in John 20:16).

- The *group* appearance to the other women likewise passes the criteria of *embarrassment* and *historical verisimilitude* (the most common female name at the time was *Mary*).

- The appearance to the two disciples on the Road to Emmaus (husband and wife Cleopas and Mary[355]) also passes the criteria of *embarrassment* (Luke 24:25) and *historical verisimilitude*.[356]

- The appearance to the *group* of ten male disciples[357] (plus others) is *multiply attested in different forms*, and is reported by an *eyewitness* (i.e., John[358]).

- The *multiply attested* group appearance to the eleven including Thomas passes the criteria of *embarrassment*, and is likewise reported by an *eyewitness* (i.e., John).

---

352. As James A. Beverley and Craig A. Evans explain: "One of the most important indications of an ancient document's veracity is something historians call verisimilitude. That is, do the contents of the document match with what we know of the place, people and period described in the document?" (*Getting Jesus Right*, 22). According to Thomas R. Yoder Neufeld, the criterion of verisimilitude includes "linguistic and cultural features that fit what we know of first-century Palestine" (*Recovering Jesus*, 44).

353. Both names mean "rock."

354. As Graham Stanton notes: "traditions which would have been an embarrassment to followers of Jesus in the post-Easter period are unlikely to have been invented" (*Gospels and Jesus*, 175). On why testimony from female witness passes the criterion of embarrassment, see Williams, *Getting at Jesus*, 273–74.

355. Boice, "Who Were the Disciples on the Road to Emmaus?"

356. Note the hospitality culture and the meal etiquette of prayer and bread breaking.

357. Luke employs a figurative synecdoche when he writes that "the eleven" were assembled with those with them: "because Judas was now gone from them, and dead; and this being their whole number, it is used, though every one might not be present, as particularly Thomas was not; see John 20:19" (*Gill's Exposition of the Entire Bible*, "Luke 24:33"). See also Jackson, "Does the Expression 'the Eleven.'"

358. On John as the eyewitness behind the Fourth Gospel, see Williams, *Behold the Man*, chap. 4. See also, Blomberg, *Historical Reliability of John's Gospel*; McGrew, *Eye of the Beholder*.

- The *group* appearance to seven disciples by the Sea of Galilee is reported by an *eyewitness* (i.e., John). Moreover, the specific count of fish (John 20:11) is an *unintentional sign of historicity*.[359]

- The group appearance to the eleven disciples (and perhaps others) in Galilee passes the criteria of *embarrassment* due to its mention that although "they worshiped [Jesus], some doubted" (Matt 28:17).

- The appearance to Saul is *multiply attested in different forms*, including a source containing the Aramaic of Saul's name ("Saoul, Saoul, why do you persecute me?" Acts 9:4; 22:7; 26:14), and the *eyewitness* testimony of the formerly hostile Saul himself. This testimony reaches us second-hand through Paul's sometime travelling companion Luke in his book of "Acts," but also first-hand (albeit without the narrative details given in Acts) through the first of Paul's undisputed letters to the Corinthians (i.e., 1 Cor 9:1; 1 Cor 15:8).

As for the multi-sensory content of these reports:

- Jesus was reportedly *seen* on at least eleven occasions.[360]

- At least nine reports concern appearances to *groups* of two, four, seven, ten, eleven, and even five hundred people.

- While Jesus purportedly appeared to Saul rather than to his travelling companions, they nevertheless both saw the bright light and *heard a voice without understanding it*. Perhaps they didn't speak Aramaic (see Acts 26:14); or perhaps they simply couldn't make out what the voice said.[361]

- On ten occasions, it is reported that people either *heard* Jesus or *talked with Jesus* (i.e., held a conversation involving both hearing and speaking to Jesus).

- Matthew reports an appearance in which the women *touch* Jesus.

- Luke and John narrate additional appearances in which various people might be taken to touch Jesus.

---

359. This criterion "argues that particularly vivid details of an eyewitness can demonstrate accurate knowledge of the environment and the event. This contributes to the credibility of a text" (Beverley and Evans, *Getting Jesus Right*, 201).

360. See Davis, *Christian Philosophical Theology*, 136–37.

361. See Marshall, *Acts*, 178–79 and 375; Williams, *Behold the Man*, 175–78, 189–236 and *Getting at Jesus*, 282–87.

Fig. 26. Criteria of Authenticity that Nine Reported Resurrection Appearances Pass (*in addition* to being *early*, historically *coherent* reports of *memorable* events).

Appearance witnesses	Report	Eyewitness Testimony	Multiple Literarily Independent Sources	Multiple Forms	Embarrassment	Verisimilitude	Unintentional Signs of History
Mary Magdalene	John 20:11–18				X	X	X
At least five other women (incl. Joanna, Salome & Mary the mother of James)	Matt 28:1–10 (see Luke 24:8–11)		X		X	X	
Cleopas and Mary	Luke 24:13–32				X	X	
Peter	1 Cor 15:5; Luke 24:34		X	X		X	X
Ten disciples (and others)	John 20:19–23 & Luke 24:36–44	X	X				
Eleven disciples including Thomas	John 20:24–29; 1 Cor 15:5b	X	X	X	X		
Seven disciples	John 21:1–25	X					X
Eleven disciples (at least)	Matt 28:16–20				X		
Saul (& others)	1 Cor 15:8 & Acts 9:1–19; 22:1–21 & 26:1–32	X	X	X		X	

Using criteria of authenticity to validate specific historical evidence that can underpin one's explanation of the Jesus of history is compatible with thinking that the sources containing that evidence are generally unreliable.[362] As Gary R. Habermas and Terry L. Miethe comment:

---

362. Note that a source being unreliable is not necessarily the same thing as its being deliberately misleading.

> Our arguments [for the resurrection are] based on a *limited number* of knowable historical facts and *verified by critical procedures*. Therefore, contemporary scholars should not spurn such evidence by referring to "discrepancies" in the New Testament texts or to its general "unreliability."[363]

However, *the greater application these criteria find in those sources, the more they indicate their general reliability*. As Lydia McGrew argues:

> If you sample a loaf of bread on both ends and at several points in the middle and find it good, it would be caviling [i.e., unreasonably sceptical] to say that perhaps just the parts you haven't tasted happen to be the moldy ones.[364]

While there's a much broader case for the historical reliability of the New Testament witness to the historical Jesus than is covered by the criteria of tradition criticism,[365] as Habermas affirms: "Both may be pursued together and can complement each other."[366]

Whether by using the "traditional," "criteria of authenticity" or "minimal facts" approaches, or by using a "criteria of authenticity" or "minimal facts" approach to lay the ground for a more maximal "traditional" approach, or by combining the "criteria of authenticity" approach with the "traditional" approach, one can use properly skeptical historical methods to *establish evidence* about Jesus that should be taken into account by any academically responsible historical *explanation* thereof.

EXPLAINING THE HISTORICAL EVIDENCE PERTAINING TO JESUS

> Historians are seldom if ever interested in discrete facts entirely for their own sake; they have almost always been concerned with . . . the "interconnectedness" of those facts.
>
> —Richard J. Evans[367]

---

363. Miethe and Habermas, *Why Believe?*, 273–74. On the topic of "discrepancies," see Williams, "Gospel Contradictions?" (YouTube playlist); Wenham, *Easter Enigma*; Williams, *Behold the Man*, 163–170.

364. McGrew, *Hidden in Plain View*, 225.

365. See McGrew, *Testimonies to the Truth*; Williams, Peter J., *Can We Trust the Gospels?*; Williams, *Getting at Jesus*.

366. Habermas, *On the Resurrection*, Vol. 1, 128.

367. Evans, *In Defence of History*, 76.

With the evidence in hand, one can turn to the task of assessing different competing theories of how best to explain that evidence. Was Jesus a liar or a madman? Were the disciples deceivers, deceived, or deluded? Did someone steal Jesus's body from the tomb? Were Jesus's reported post-mortem appearances hallucinations? And so on. As philosopher Angus Menuge explains:

> Historians do not use *induction* (which applies to generalizations of repeatable effects) but *abduction*, an inference to the best explanation of a singular event. According to the logic of abduction, given the available data, we are to select the best of competing explanations.[368]

The evidence shows that Jesus repeatedly said and did things that, when taken together in their cultural context, communicated a Divine self-image. While anyone can make such claims, there is a solid abductive case for inferring that the best *explanation* of the relevant historical *evidence* pertaining to Jesus is that he had an *accurate* self-image of being Divine with a capital D, a cumulative convergence of evidences "that lead forthrightly to the conclusion that he alone is the unique Son of God."[369]

The warrant of any historical explanation (including the Christian doctrine of the incarnation) depends on a combination of explanatory factors, including its *simplicity*, *explanatory scope* (covering the relevant facts), *explanatory power* (the degree to which it raises the probability of the facts to be explained), *explanatory plausibility* (the degree to which our background knowledge implies an explanatory hypothesis), degree of *explanatory disconfirmation* (avoiding conflict with our background knowledge), and degree of *explanatory ad hoc-ness* (the fewer contrived, un-evidenced hypotheses, the better).[370]

For example, the resurrection hypothesis offers a relatively simple[371] explanation of the historical evidence pertaining to Jesus's death, burial, empty tomb, reported appearances, and the origins of Christianity; an explanation that combines excellent explanatory scope (i.e., *if* the resurrection happened, it would explain "why the tomb was found empty, why the disciples saw post-mortem appearances of Jesus, and why the Christian faith came into being"[372]) and explanatory power (i.e., *if* God chose to resurrect

---

368. Menuge, "Justified Belief in the Resurrection," 131.
369. Geisler, *Christian Apologetics* (2nd ed.), 393.
370. See Williams, *Getting at Jesus*, chap. 5.
371. See Richards, "Divine Simplicity."
372. Craig, "Resurrection of Jesus."

Jesus, *then* the otherwise unlikely facts of his empty tomb, reported post-mortem appearances, and the early origin of belief in Jesus's resurrection all become highly probable) with a *fair* degree of plausibility and *low* degrees of *disconfirmation* and *ad-hoc-ness* (especially if one already accepts theism).

Indeed, it seems to me that in a comparative analysis with alternative explanations, the relevant evidence is best explained by the hypothesis that *Jesus was physically resurrected* (indeed, trans-physically resurrected) *by God*.[373] As N. T. Wright argues, the resurrection hypothesis "possesses unrivalled power to explain the historical data at the heart of early Christianity."[374]

Moreover, although the resurrection hypothesis posits an explanation that's miraculous—and therefore unusual, and in this respect unlikely *a priori*—the hypothesis gains plausibility from our background knowledge about the (comparative and cumulative) case for theism, about Jesus's fulfillment of prophecy,[375] about the miracles[376] and exorcisms[377] associated with his ministry, and about his claims in the context of his character.

Aut Deus Aut Malus Homo

If Jesus was not who he claimed to be, then he was either a charlatan or a madman, neither of which is plausible.

—William Lane Craig[378]

However one goes about establishing Jesus's claims about himself, those claims were astonishing enough to invite charges of insanity (if his claim was sincere) or blasphemy (if his claim was insincere). But the evidence

---

373. See Williams, *Getting at Jesus*, especially chap. 5; Williams, *Behold the Man*, chap. 5 and appendix 1.

374. Wright, *Resurrection of the Son of God*, 718. See also Swinburne, *Resurrection of God Incarnate*; Williams, *Behold the Man*, chap. 5 and appendix 1; Williams, *Getting at Jesus*, chap. 5.

375. See FOCLOnline, "Arguments for and from Fulfilled Biblical Prophecies" (YouTube video); Geisler, "Miraculous Bible Prophecy Fulfillments"; Scott, *Is Jesus of Nazareth the Predicted Messiah?*; Kaiser, *Messiah in the Old Testament*; Williams, *Understanding Jesus*, chap. 6; Williams, *Getting at Jesus*, chap. 5.

376. See Williams, "Did Jesus Perform Miracles?" (YouTube playlist); Habermas, "Did Jesus Perform Miracles?"; Williams, *Getting at Jesus*, chap. 5.

377. See Williams, "Do Angels Really Exist?"; Williams, "New Testament Criticism and Jesus the Exorcist"; Gallagher, *Demonic Foes*; Guthrie, *Gods of This World*; Williams, *Case for Angels*.

378. Craig, *Reasonable Faith*, 327.

appears to show that Jesus was *both sane and sincere*. This paradox, which is more to be expected on the hypothesis of the incarnation than on atheism, lies at the heart of an ancient argument for the divinity of Jesus summarized in Latin as "*aut deus aut malus homo*," that is "either God or a bad man."[379] As philosopher Peter Kreeft explains:

> The first premise is that Christ must be either God, as he claims to be, or a bad man, if he wasn't who he claims to be. The second premise is that he isn't a bad man. The conclusion is that he is God . . . he either believes his claim to be God, or he doesn't. If he does [and the claim is false], then he is intellectually bad . . . because that's a pretty large confusion! And if he does not believe his claim, then he is morally bad: a deceiver and a terrible blasphemer.[380]

Philosopher Stephen T. Davis comments:

> Virtually everyone who reads the Gospels . . . comes away with the conviction that Jesus was a wise and good man . . . Jesus shows none of the character traits usually associated with those who have delusions of grandeur or "divinity complexes." Such people are easily recognizable by their egotism, narcissism, inflexibility, predictable behaviour, and inability to relate understandingly and lovingly to others . . . We live in an age when scholars confidently make all sorts of bizarre claims about the historical Jesus. But few scripture scholars of any theological stripe seriously entertain the possibility that Jesus was either a lunatic or a liar.[381]

Davis formalizes these observations into what he calls the "Mad, Bad, or God" argument:

1. Jesus claimed, either explicitly or implicitly, to be divine.
2. Jesus was either right or wrong in claiming to be divine.
3. If Jesus was wrong in claiming to be divine, Jesus was either mad or bad.
4. Jesus was not bad.

---

379. See Williams, "'Lunatic, Liar or Lord' Argument" (YouTube playlist); Davis, "Mad/Bad/God Trilemma"; Kreeft, "Jesus"; Davis, "Was Jesus Mad, Bad or God?"; Horner, "Aut Deus Aut Malus Homo"; Kreeft, *Between Heaven and Hell*; Lewis, "What Are We to Make?"; Williams, Donald T., "Validity of Lewis's Trilemma"; Williams, *Behold the Man*, chap. 2 and *Getting at Jesus*, chap. 2.

380. Kreeft, *Between Heaven and Hell*, 38–39.

381. Davis, *Christian Philosophical Theology*, 154.

5. Jesus was not mad.
6. Therefore, Jesus was not wrong in claiming to be divine.
7. Therefore, Jesus was right in claiming to be divine.
8. Therefore, Jesus was divine.[382]

The main challenge to this argument comes from those who question the first premise. For example, while Richard Dawkins affirms that Jesus was "a great moral teacher,"[383] and concedes that "there's no evidence Jesus himself was barking mad," he reckons "the evidence that Jesus claimed any sort of divine status is minimal."[384] (Note that even Dawkins doesn't deny there is *some* evidence that Jesus claimed *some sort of* divine status!) Contra Dawkins, sufficient warrant for accepting that Jesus did indeed claim "either explicitly or implicitly, to be divine" (premise 1 of the "Mad, Bad, or God" argument) comes from a combination of direct evidence, concerning Jesus's explicit and implicit claims *about himself*, and indirect evidence, concerning the need to explain what other people believed *about Jesus*.

Dawkins's risible suggestion that the "Mad, Bad, or God" argument overlooks the possibility that Jesus was merely "honestly mistaken"[385] about his divinity constitutes a backhanded compliment to the strength of the argument. As Davis comments: "It is not easy to see how any sane religious first-century Jew could sincerely but mistakenly hold the belief: *I am divine.*"[386]

At the very least, then, the "Mad, Bad, or God" argument seems to provide *some* warrant for the conclusion that Jesus "was . . . who he claimed to be."[387] In other words, the "Mad, Bad, or God" argument should at least chip away a certain amount of skepticism about the Christian view of Jesus, making those who know it more open to additional arguments for the same conclusion. As I have emphasized elsewhere,[388] the arguments concerning the paradox of Jesus's claims in the context of his character, his fulfilment of prophecy, his exorcisms and miracles, and most especially the miracle of his resurrection from the dead, combine to form a *cumulative*, historically grounded case for the incarnation.

---

382. Davis, *Christian Philosophical Theology*, 152.
383. Dawkins, "Sorry Liberal Christians", §6.
384. Dawkins, *God Delusion*, 117.
385. Dawkins, *God Delusion*, 117.
386. Davis, "Mad/Bad/God Trilemma" 490.
387. Craig, *Reasonable Faith*, 327.
388. See Williams, *Understanding Jesus*.

CONCLUSION

I hope that the preceding "stepping stones"—of evidence for design in nature, evidence for the existence of God, and evidence for the Christian doctrine "that God became flesh in the form of Jesus Christ . . ."[389]—will have given readers sufficient reason to reflect seriously upon the affirmation by British theologian Rowan Williams that

> The story of Jesus . . . is not just an epiphany—a revelation of glory and no more—and it's not just a commandment or a set of instructions dropped down from heaven. It's a manifestation of radiant beauty that lands in our world in the form of a profound moral challenge, because it's a revelation of active love that dissolves fear, a revelation of an action of love into which you are invited to come, with which you are invited to cooperate.[390]

---

389. Monton, *Seeking God in Science*, 71.
390. Williams, Rowan, *What Is Christianity?*, 36.

Recommended Resources

My website has a page dedicated to this book, with various free resources: https://www.peterswilliams.com/publications/books/stepping-stones-to-christianity-reflections-on-intelligent-design-natural-theology-and-the-historical-jesus/

PETER S. WILLIAMS

Website: http://www.peterswilliams.com

Composing: http://www.peterswilliams.com/composing/

Podcast: http://peterswilliams.podbean.com/?source=pb

YouTube Channel: https://www.youtube.com/@peterswilliamsvid/featured

YouTube Channel Playlists: http://www.youtube.com/user/peterswilliams-vid/ playlists?view=1&flow=grid

Resources for Chapter 1

My website has a page dedicated to the book from which chapter 1 was adapted (*An Informed Cosmos: Essays on Intelligent Design Theory*, Wipf & Stock, 2023), with various free resources:

http://www.peterswilliams.com/publications/books/an-informed-cosmos-essays-on-intelligent-design-theory/

WEBSITES

Access Research Network: https://www.arn.org/
Michael J. Behe: https://michaelbehe.com
BioCosmos: https://norge.biocosmos.se/page/about-us
Biologic Institute: http://www.biologicinstitute.org/
Discovery Institute Centre for Science & Culture: https://www.discovery.org/id/
Evolution News: https://evolutionnews.org/
Evolution Under the Microscope: https://evolutionunderthemicroscope.com/home.html
Evolutionary Informatics Lab: https://evoinfo.org/
The God Question: http://www.thegodquestion.tv/
IntelligentDesign.org: https://intelligentdesign.org/
ID 3.0 Research Program: https://www.discovery.org/id/research/
Stephen C. Meyer: https://stephencmeyer.org/
The Privileged Planet: http://www.theprivilegedplanet.com/
UK Centre for Intelligent Design: http://www.c4id.org.uk/Groups/277253/Homepage_Resources.aspx

WATCH

Williams, Peter S. "Can We Believe in God in an Age of Science?" YouTube playlist. https://www.youtube.com/playlist?list=PLQhh3qcwVEWgusJHSKEHY-MZ9Tcd11IIm.

———. "Christianity and Science." YouTube playlist. https://youtube.com/playlist?list=PLQhh3qcwVEWjeYJfOKB1YYXsInZ5GIPL_.
———. "Cosmic Fine Tuning." YouTube playlist. https://youtube.com/playlist?list=PLQhh3qcwVEWj4aeE76A1vjLvPqWieH8tE.
———. "Debating Intelligent Design." YouTube playlist. https://youtube.com/playlist?list=PLQhh3qcwVEWhO4mPNzA-K41C7VfvSvkQW.
———. "Evolution & the Waiting Time Problem." YouTube playlist. https://youtube.com/playlist?list=PLQhh3qcwVEWjjyp6iQmdv4fTkysKEiAtB.
———. "The Fossil Record." YouTube playlist. https://youtube.com/playlist?list=PLQhh3qcwVEWjbYPLl33A3aF_W4TSAjcaF.
———. "The 'Immaterial Genome' Hypothesis." YouTube playlist. https://www.youtube.com/playlist?list=PLQhh3qcwVEWj3Oz-YTXv3Qzu54P2FE3UQ.
———. "Inside the Cell." YouTube playlist. https://youtube.com/playlist?list=PLQhh3qcwVEWiddQNZ6pQhCtF06TPYXwKQ.
———. "Intelligent Design." YouTube playlist. https://youtube.com/playlist?list=PLQhh3qcwVEWjckJb0K1rfuBKPcHiMFTSO.
———. "Introduction to Intelligent Design Theory." YouTube playlist. https://youtube.com/ playlist?list=PLQhh3qcwVEWhNWeZ2LxPUa5j2afVcG-B6.
———. "Irreducible Complexity." YouTube playlist. https://youtube.com/playlist?list=PLQhh3qcwVEWh3orLA2I3KySSxUoIXAdZ3.
———. "Is ID Creationism?" YouTube playlist. https://youtube.com/playlist?list=PLQhh3qcwVEWiGWPngKUzJoQ9v6hS4LNxh.
———. "The Origin of Life." YouTube playlist. https://youtube.com/playlist?list=PLQh3qcwVEWggFeEP9H7k1LyccfxzvoSr.
———. "Physical Pre-Conditions of Science & Technology." YouTube playlist. https://youtube.com/playlist?list=PLQhh3qcwVEWiEbtcuD5f8bK0DHH31Lg6Y.
———. "Protein Synthesis." YouTube playlist. https://youtube.com/playlist?list=PLQhh3qcwVEWg6lDvvo2GVv2-Y_kIcpjoi.
———. "The Rare Earth Hypothesis." YouTube playlist. https://youtube.com/playlist?list=PLQhh3qcwVEWiLU4H5kBr2JzSAzflITRst.
———. "The Scientific Status of Intelligent Design Theory." YouTube playlist. https://youtube.com/playlist?list=PLQhh3qcwVEWhq9Tl1f9UdqL6ZFNPLsc8P.
———. "The Simulation Hypothesis." YouTube playlist. https://youtube.com/playlist?list=PLQhh3qcwVEWhfgH84u_JzPzB4B8RPT5ca.
———. "Specified Complexity." YouTube playlist. https://youtube.com/playlist?list=PLQhh3qcwVEWiQrIEmUwrpyxVxVaZMc4i_.
———. "Who Designed the Designer?/Who Caused God?" YouTube playlist. https://youtube.com/playlist?list=PLQhh3qcwVEWiHxfFWcRQzOZmdZV5AEHei.
———. "Young Earth Creationism." YouTube playlist. https://youtube.com/playlist?list=PLQhh3qcwVEWitFuSuMLz5fmhRGBHR8-_O.

LISTEN

IDQuest. "Atheists Who Defend Intelligent Design: Interview with Bradley Monton." YouTube video, April 30, 2011. http://youtu.be/Et2VTJ1UBC4.

Luskin, Casey. "Atheist Philosopher of Physics Bradley Monton on Intelligent Design Debate, Part One." *ID the Future* (podcast), November 6, 2008.

https://www.podomatic.com/podcasts/intelligentdesign/episodes/2008-11-06T09_16_15-08_00.

Mind Matters. "The Universe Is so Fine Tuned." *Mind Matters* Podcast, September 16, 2021. https://mindmatters.ai/podcast/ep152/.

———. "Run the Gambit of Complexity." *Mind Matters* Podcast, September 2, 2021. https://mindmatters.ai/podcast/ep150/.

———. "Why Is There Fine Tuning Everywhere?" *Mind Matters* Podcast, September 23, 2021. https://mindmatters.ai/podcast/ep153/.

Unbelievable? "Signature in the Cell: Stephen C. Meyer vs. Keith Fox." February 22, 2022. https://www.premier.plus/unbelievable/podcasts/episodes/classic-replay-signature-in-the-cell-stephen-c-meyer-vs-keith-fox.

Williams, Peter S. "A Christian Worldview and Science in Apologetic Perspective: Bios (a) Introduction to Darwinism." *The Peter S. Williams Podcast*, October 25, 2021. http://podcast.peterswilliams.com/e/a-christian-worldview-and-science-in-apologetic-perspective-bios-a-introduction-to-darwinism/.

———. "A Christian Worldview and Science in Apologetic Perspective: Bios (b) Intelligent Design Theory." *The Peter S. Williams Podcast*, October 25, 2021. http://podcast.peterswilliams.com/e/a-christian-worldview-and-science-in-apologetic-perspective-bios-b-intelligent-design-theory/.

———. "A Christian Worldview and Science in Apologetic Perspective: Cosmos." *The Peter S. Williams Podcast*, October 25, 2021. http://podcast.peterswilliams.com/e/a-christian-worldview-and-science-in-apologetic-perspective-cosmos/.

———. "Cosmic Fine Tuning: Design or Multiverse?" *The Peter S. Williams Podcast*, April 23, 2021. http://podcast.peterswilliams.com/e/cosmic-fine-tuning-design-or-multiverse/.

———. "The Design Argument from Cosmic Fine Tuning." *The Peter S. Williams Podcast*, May 1, 2019. http://podcast.peterswilliams.com/e/the-design-argument-from-cosmic-fine-tuning/.

———. "The Design Argument in Biology after Darwin." *The Peter S. Williams Podcast*, May 1, 2019. http://podcast.peterswilliams.com/e/the-design-argument-in-biology-after-darwin/.

———. "Distinguishing Science from Scientific Naturalism." *The Peter S. Williams Podcast*, October, 2024. http://podcast.peterswilliams.com/e/distinguishing-science-from-scientific-naturalism/.

———. "Introduction to *An Informed Cosmos*: Essays on Intelligent Design Theory." *The Peter S. Williams Podcast*, English L'Abri, October, 2023. http://podcast.peterswilliams.com/e/introduction-to-an-informed-cosmos-essays-on-intelligent-design-theory/.

———. "Veritas 2022: Outgrowing God? Learning from Dawkins's Failed Arguments." *The Peter S. Williams Podcast*, November 1, 2022. http://podcast.peterswilliams.com/e/outgrowing-god-learning-from-dawkins-s-failed-arguments/.

PEER-REVIEWED PAPERS ONLINE

The Evolutionary Informatics Lab. "Main Publications." https://evoinfo.org/publications.html.

"Peer-Reviewed Articles Supporting Intelligent Design." https://www.discovery.org/id/peer-review/.

Axe, Douglas D. "Estimating the Prevalence of Protein Sequences Adopting Functional Enzyme Folds." *Journal of Molecular Biology* 341 (2004) 1295–1315. https://www.sciencedirect.com/science/article/abs/pii/S0022283604007624.

———. "Extreme Functional Sensitivity to Conservative Amino Acid Changes on Enzyme Exteriors." *Journal of Molecular Biology* 301 (2000) 585–95. https://www.sciencedirect.com/science/article/abs/pii/S0022283600939974?via%3Dihub.

Axe, Douglas D., and Ann K. Gauger. "Model and Laboratory Demonstrations That Evolutionary Optimization Works Well Only if Preceded by Invention: Selection Itself Is Not Inventive." *BIO-Complexity* 2 (2015) 1–13. https://bio-complexity.org/ojs/index.php/main/article/viewArticle/BIO-C.2015.2.

Barnes, Luke. "Fine-Tuning in the Context of Bayesian Theory Testing." *European Journal for Philosophy of Science*, 8(2):253–269, 2018. https://arxiv.org/pdf/1707.03965.

Behe, Michael J. "Experimental Evolution, Loss-of-Function Mutations, and 'the First Rule of Adaptive Evolution.'" *The Quarterly Review of Biology* 85 (2010) 419–45. https://www.discovery.org/a/experimental-evolution-loss-of-function-mutations-and-the-first-rule-of-adaptive-evolution/.

———. "Waiting Longer for Two Mutations: Published Letter in Response to Durrett & Schmidt." *Genetics* 181 (2009) 819–20. https://pmc.ncbi.nlm.nih.gov/articles/PMC2644969/.

Behe, Michael, and David Snoke. "Simulating Evolution by Gene Duplication of Protein Features That Require Multiple Amino Acid Residues." *Protein Science* 13 (2004) 2651–2664. https://www.ncbi.nlm.nih.gov/pmc/articles/PMC2286568/.

Dembski, William A. "Specification: The Pattern That Signifies Intelligence." *Philosophia Christi* 7 (2005) 299–343. https://billdembski.com/documents/2005.06.Specification.pdf.

Díaz-Pachón, Daniel Andrés, et al. "Is it Possible to Know Cosmological Fine-Tuning?" *The Astrophysical Journal Supplement Series*, Volume 271:56, Number 2 (2024). https://iopscience.iop.org/article/10.3847/1538-4365/ad2c88#apjsad2c88s5.

Díaz-Pachón, Daniel Andrés, et al. "Is Cosmological Tuning Fine or Coarse?" *Journal of Cosmology and Astroparticle Physics* 07, Article 20 (2021). https://doi.org/10.1088/1475-7516/2021/07/020.

Gauger, Ann K., and Douglas D. Axe. "The Evolutionary Accessibility of New Enzyme Functions: A Case Study from the Biotin Pathway." *BIO-Complexity* 1 (2011) 1–17. https://www.researchgate.net/publication/272177811_The_Evolutionary_Accessibility_of_New_Enzymes_Functions_A_Case_Study_from_the_Biotin_Pathway.

Gordon, Bruce R. "Balloons on a String: A Critique of Multiverse Cosmology." In *The Nature of Nature: Examining the Role of Naturalism in Science*, edited by William A. Dembski and Bruce L. Gordon, 558–601. Wilmington, DE: ISI, 2011. https://philpapers.org/archive/GORBLG.pdf.

Hill, Carol A. "The Noachian Flood: Universal or Local?" *Perspectives on Science and Christian Faith* 54 (2002). https://www.csun.edu/~vcgeo005/Carol%201.pdf.

Hössjer, Ola, Günter Bechly, and Ann Gauger. "On the Waiting Time Until Coordinated Mutations get Fixed in Regulatory Sequences." *Journal of Theoretical Biology* Volume 524, 7 September 2021. https://pubmed.ncbi.nlm.nih.gov/33675769/.

Kofoed, Jens Bruun. "Approaching Genesis and Science: Hermeneutical Principles and a Case Study." *Theofilos* 12 (2020) 4–23. https://theofilos.no/wp-content/uploads/2020/12/Theofilos-vol-12-nr-1-2020-Supplement-academia-1.pdf.

LeMaster, James C. "Evolution's Waiting-Time Problem and Suggested Ways to Overcome It—A Critical Survey." *BIO-Complexity* 2 (2018) 1–9. http://bio-complexity.org/ojs/index.php/main/article/viewArticle/BIO-C.2018.2.

Meyer, Stephen C. "DNA and the Origin of Life: Information, Specification and Explanation." In *Darwinism, Design, & Public Education*, edited by John Angus Campbell and Stephen C. Meyer, 223–85. East Lansing, MI: Michigan State University Press, 2003. https://www.discovery.org/f/1026/.

———. "The Origin of Biological Information and the Higher Taxonomic Categories." *Proceedings of the Biological Society of Washington.* 117 (2004) 213–39. https://intelligentdesign.org/articles/origin-biological-information/.

———. "A Scientific History—and Philosophical Defence—of the Theory of Intelligent Design." *Religion—Staat—Gesellschaft: Journal for the Study of Beliefs and Worldviews* 7 (2008) 1–33. http://www.discovery.org/a/7471.

Meyer, Stephen C., et al. "The Cambrian Explosion: Biology's Big Bang." In *Darwinism, Design, and Public Education*, edited by John Angus Campbell and Stephen C. Meyer, 323–402. East Lansing, MI: Michigan State University Press, 2003. https://www.discovery.org/m/2019/04/Darwin-Cambrian-Explosion.pdf.

Minnich, Scott, and Stephen C. Meyer. "Genetic Analysis of Coordinate Flagellar and Type III Regulatory Circuits in Pathogenic Bacteria." In *Proceedings of the Second International Conference on Design & Nature, Rhodes Greece*, edited by M. W. Collins and C. A. Brebbia, 295–304. Southampton, UK: WIT Press, 2004. http://www.discovery.org/a/2181/.

Montañez, George D. "A Unified Model of Complex Specified Information." *BIO-Complexity* 2018 (2018) 1–26. https://bio-complexity.org/ojs/index.php/main/article/view/BIO-C.2018.4/BIO-C.2018.4.

Montañez, George, et al. "Multiple Overlapping Genetic Codes Profoundly Reduce the Probability of Beneficial Mutation." *Biological Information: New Perspectives* (2013) 139–67. https://www.worldscientific.com/doi/epdf/10.1142/9789814508728_0006.

Niekerk, Frederik van, and Nico Vorster, eds. *Science and Faith in Dialogue. Reformed Theology in Africa 10.* Oxford: AOSIS, 2022. https://books.aosis.co.za/index.php/ob/catalog/book/334.

Plantinga, Alvin. "Methodological Naturalism?" *Perspectives on Science and Christian Faith* 49 (1997) 143–54. https://www.asa3.org/ASA/PSCF/1997/PSCF9-97Plantinga.html.ori.

———. "When Faith and Reason Clash: Evolution and the Bible." *Christian Scholar's Review* 21 (1991) 8–33. https://www.freddoso.com/courses/43150/plantinga.pdf.

Reeves, Mariclair A., et al. "Enzyme Families—Shared Evolutionary History or Shared Design? A Study of the GABA-Aminotransferase Family." *BIO-Complexity* 4 (2014) 1–16. https://bio-complexity.org/ojs/index.php/main/article/view/BIO-C.2014.4.

Sanford, John, et al. "The Waiting Time Problem in a Model Hominin Population." *Theoretical Biology and Medical Modelling* 12 (2015). https://tbiomed.biomedcentral.com/articles/10.1186/s12976-015-0016-z.

Sewell, Granville. "Entropy and Evolution." *BIO-Complexity* 2013 (2013) 1–5. http://dx.doi.org/10.5048/BIO-C.2013.2.

Thorvaldsen, Steinar. "Intelligent Design and Natural Theology." *Theofilos* 12 (2020) 66–84. https://theofilos.no/wp-content/uploads/2021/02/Theofilos-vol-12-nr-1-2020-Supplement-academia-5-NY-210211.pdf.

Thorvaldsen, Steinar, and Ola Hössjer. "Using Statistical Methods to Model the Fine-Tuning of Molecular Machines and Systems." *Journal of Theoretical Biology* 501 (2020). https://www.sciencedirect.com/science/article/pii/S0022519320302071.

Thorvaldsen, S., Øhrstrøm, P. and Hössjer, O. "The Representation, Quantification, and Nature of Genetic Information." *Synthese*, 204, 15 (2024). https://doi.org/10.1007/s11229-024-04613-z.

Tour, James M., et al. "Thermodynamic Limitations on the Natural Emergence of Long Chain Molecules: Implications for Origin of Life." *BioCosmos*, Volume 5 (2025): Issue 1 (January 2025) 64–71. https://sciendo.com/article/10.2478/biocosmos-2025-0010?tab=abstract.

Trevors, J. T., and D. L. Abel. "Three Subsets of Sequence Complexity and their Relevance to Biopolymeric Information." *Theoretical Biology and Medical Modelling* 2 (2005) 29. https://pubmed.ncbi.nlm.nih.gov/16095527/.

Voie, Øyvind Albert. "Biological Function and the Genetic Code Are Interdependent." *Chaos, Solutions and Fractals* 28 (2006) 1000–1004. https://www.sciencedirect.com/science/article/abs/pii/S0960077905008052.

Williams, Peter S. "The Design Inference from Specified Complexity Defended by Scholars Outside the Intelligent Design Movement—A Critical Review." *Philosophia Christi* 9 (2007) 407–28. https://www.epsociety.org/articles/the-design-inference-from-specified-complexity-defended-by-scholars-outside-the-intelligent-design-movement/.

OTHER ONLINE READING

Essays on Intelligent Design by Peter S. Williams @ https://www.arn.org/authors/williams.html.

Essays on Intelligent Design by Peter S. Williams @ https://www.c4id.org.uk/publisher/search.aspx?searchString=Peter%20S%20Williams.

Essays on Intelligent Design by Peter S. Williams @ https://www.peterswilliams.com/publications/articles/intelligent-design-articles/.

Barnes, Luke. "Why I'm No Longer a Young Earth Creationist." *Premier Christianity*, July 29, 2021. https://www.premierchristianity.com/features/why-im-no-longer-a-young-earth-creationist/5288.article.

Berlinski, David. "The Deniable Darwin." *Commentary* 101 (1996). https://www.arn.org/docs/berlinski/db_deniabledarwin0696.htm.

Craig, William Lane. "Scepticism about the Neo-Darwinian Paradigm." *Reasonable Faith* (blog), November 10, 2008. http://www.reasonablefaith.org/writings/question-answer/scepticism-about-the-neo-darwinian-paradigm.

———. "Scepticism about the Neo-Darwinian Paradigm—Re-Visited." *Reasonable Faith* (blog), November 24, 2008. https://www.reasonablefaith.org/writings/question-answer/scepticism-about-neo-darwinism-re-visited.

Dembski, William A. "In Defence of Intelligent Design." In *Oxford Handbook of Religion and Science*, edited by Philip Clayton, 715–31. Oxford: Oxford University

Press, 2006. https://www.scribd.com/document/251639529/William-a-Dembski-In-Defense-of-Intelligent-Design.

———. "Intelligent Design is Not Optimal Design." *Intelligent Design*, February 2, 2000. https://www.discovery.org/a/86/.

———. "Irreducible Complexity Revisited." https://billdembski.com/documents/2004.01.Irred_Compl_Revisited.pdf.

———. "The Logical Underpinnings of Intelligent Design." In *Debating Design: From Darwin to DNA*, edited by William A. Dembski and Michael Ruse, 311–30. Cambridge: Cambridge University Press, 2004. https://billdembski.com/wp-content/uploads/2020/02/Logical-Underpinnings-of-ID.pdf.

Fodor, Jerry. "Why Pigs Don't Have Wings." *London Review of Books*, October 18, 2007. https://www.lrb.co.uk/the-paper/v29/n20/jerry-fodor/why-pigs-don-t-have-wings.

Garvey, Jon. "Does it Follow?" *The Hump of the Camel* (blog), November 6, 2018. https://potiphar.jongarvey.co.uk/2018/06/11/does-it-follow/.

Gelernter, David. "Giving Up Darwin: A Fond Farewell to a Brilliant and Beautiful Theory." *Claremont Review of Books*, Spring 2019. https://claremontreviewofbooks.com/giving-up-darwin/.

Gordon, Bruce L. "The Scientific Status of Design Inferences." https://www.namb.net/apologetics/resource/the-scientific-status-of-design-inferences/.

Hunter, Cornelius. "False Science: A Claim to Simulate Protein Evolution." *Evolution News and Science Today*, August 6, 2025. https://evolutionnews.org/2025/08/false-science-a-claim-to-simulate-protein-evolution/.

Hyers, Conrad. "The Narrative Form of Genesis 1: Cosmogonic, Yes; Scientific, No." *Journal of the American Scientific Affiliation* 36.4 (1984) 208–15, https://biblicalelearning.org/wp-content/uploads/2022/01/Hyers_Gen1_JASA.pdf.

Jones, Michael. "The Origins of Young Earth Creationism." https://peacefulscience.org/prints/origns-yec/.

Keathley, Kenneth D. "The Confessions of a Disappointed Young-Earther." https://peacefulscience.org/prints/confessions-disappointed-young-earther/.

Koons, Robert C. "The Incompatibility of Naturalism and Scientific Realism." https://www.leaderu.com/offices/koons/docs/natreal.html.

Marks, Robert J., II. "Evolutionary Computation: A Perpetual Motion Machine for Design Information?" https://www.namb.net/apologetics/resource/evolutionary-computation/.

Marston, Paul. "Understanding the Biblical Creation Passages." Leyland, UK: Lifesway, 2007. https://www.asa3.org/ASA/topics/Bible-Science/understanding_the_biblical_creation_passages.pdf.

Meyer, Stephen C. "The Scientific Status of Intelligent Design." In *Science and Evidence for Design in the Universe*, edited by Michael J. Behe et al., 151–211. San Francisco: Ignatius, 2000. *Discovery Institute*, November 13, 2005. https://www.discovery.org/a/2834/.

Monton, Bradley. "Is Intelligent Design Science? Dissecting the Dover Decision." http://philsci-archive.pitt.edu/archive/00002583/01/ Methodological_Naturalism_2.pdf & https://www.arn.org/docs/monton/is_intelligent_design_science.pdf.

Nelson, Paul. "Intelligent Design." *Nucleus*, Winter 2005. https://archive.cmf.org.uk/resources/publications/content/?context=article&id=1303.

———. "Jettison the Arguments, or the Rule? The Place of Darwinian Theological Themata in Evolutionary Reasoning." https://www.discovery.org/a/104/.

Plantinga, Alvin. "Why Darwinist Materialism is Wrong." *The New Republic*, November 16, 2012. https://newrepublic.com/article/110189/why-darwinist-materialism-wrong.

Ruse, Michael. "Nonliteralist Antievolution." AAAS Symposium, "The New Antievolutionism," Boston, MA, February 13, 1993. https://www.leaderu.com/orgs/arn/orpages/or151/mr93tran.htm.

Tour, James. "Animadversions of a Synthetic Chemist." *Inference*, May 2016. https://inference-review.com/article/animadversions-of-a-synthetic-chemist.

———. "Two Experiments in Abiogenesis." *Inference*, September 2016. https://inference-review.com/article/two-experiments-in-abiogenesis.

———. "We're Still Clueless about the Origin of Life." In *The Mystery of Life's Origin: The Continuing Controversy*, by Charles B. Thaxton et al., 323–58. Seattle: Discovery Institute Press, 2020. https://www.discovery.org/m/securepdfs/2021/02/Tour-MeyerMOLO.pdf.

West, John G. "Darwin in the Dock: C.S. Lewis's Doubts about the Creative Power of Natural Selection." *Evolution News and Science Today*, November 21, 2013. https://evolutionnews.org/2013/11/darwin_in_the_d_2.

Williams, Peter S. "Atheists Against Darwinism: Johnsons' 'Wedge' Breaks Through." https://www.peterswilliams.com/wp-content/uploads/2013/07/Atheists-Against-Darwinism-May-09.pdf.

———. "Intelligent Designs on Science: A Surreply to Denis Alexander's Critique of Intelligent Design Theory." https://www.peterswilliams.com/wp-content/uploads/2016/02/Intelligent-Designs-on-Science.pdf.

———. "A Naturalist on The Edge of Evolution: Why Thomas Nagel Should Embrace ID." https://www.peterswilliams.com/wp-content/uploads/2013/07/A-Naturalist-on-The-Edge-of-Evolution.pdf.

Witt, Jonathan. "Panning God: Darwinism's Defective Argument Against Bad Design." https://www.namb.net/apologetics-blog/panning-god-darwinism-39-s-defective-argument-against-bad-design/.

BOOKS

Abel, David L., ed. *The First Gene*. New York: Long View Press—Academic, 2011.

———. *Primordial Prescription: The Most Plaguing Problem of Life Origin Science*. New York: Long View Press—Academic, 2015.

Axe, Douglas. *Undeniable: How Biology Confirms Our Intuition That Life is Designed*. San Francisco: HarperOne, 2017.

Bartlett, Jonathan, and Eric Holloway, eds. *Naturalism and Its Alternatives in Scientific Methodologies*. Broken Arrow, OK: Blyth Institute Press, 2017.

Beckwith, Francis J. *Law, Darwinism, and Public Education: The Establishment Clause and the Challenge of Intelligent Design*. Lanham: Rowman & Littlefield, 2003.

Behe, Michael J. *A Mousetrap for Darwin: Michal J. Behe Answers His Critics*. Seattle, WA: Discovery Institute, 2020.

———. *Darwin Devolves: The New Science about DNA That Challenges Evolution*. San Francisco: HarperOne, 2020.

———. *Darwin's Black Box: The Biochemical Challenge to Evolution*. 2nd ed. New York: Free Press, 2006.

———. *The Edge of Evolution: The Search for the Limits of Darwinism*. New York: Free Press, 2007.

Behe, Michael J., et al. *Science and Evidence for Design in the Universe*. San Francisco: Ignatius, 2000. https://www.discovery.org/scripts/viewDB/index.php?command=view&id=1780.

Bergman, Jerry. *Poor Design: An Invalid Argument against Intelligent Design*. Tulsa, OK: BP Books, 2019.

Berlinski, David. *The Deniable Darwin*. Seattle, WA: Discovery Institute, 2009.

Bethell, Tom. *Darwin's House of Cards: A Journalist's Odyssey through the Darwin Debates*. Seattle, WA: Discovery Institute, 2016.

Broom, Neil. *How Blind is the Watchmaker? Theism or Atheism: Should Science Decide?* London: Routledge Revivals, 2020.

Campbell, John Angus, and Stephen C. Meyer, eds. *Darwinism, Design, and Public Education*. East Lansing, MI: Michigan State University Press, 2003.

Collins, C. John. *Science and Faith: Friends or Foes?* Wheaton, IL: Crossway, 2003.

Dembski, William A. *The Design Revolution: Answering the Toughest Questions about Intelligent Design*. Downers Grove, IL: InterVarsity, 2004.

———. *No Free Lunch: Why Specified Complexity Cannot Be Purchased Without Intelligence*. Lanham, MD: Rowman & Littlefield, 2002.

Dembski, William A., ed. *Darwin's Nemesis: Phillip Johnson and the Intelligent Design Movement*. Downers Grove, IL: IVP Academic, 2006.

Dembski, William A., ed. *Uncommon Dissent: Intellectuals Who Find Darwinism Unconvincing*. ISI, 2004. https://docplayer.net/161847585-Uncommon-dissent-intellectuals-who-find-darwinism-unconvincing.html.

Dembski, William A., and Jonathan Wells. *The Design of Life: Discovering Signs of Intelligence in Biological Systems*. Richardson, TX: Foundation for Thought and Ethics, 2008.

Dembski, William A., and Jonathan Witt. *Intelligent Design: Uncensored*. Downers Grove, IL: InterVarsity, 2010.

Dembski, William A., and Sean McDowell. *Understanding Intelligent Design: Everything You Need to Know in Plain Language*. Eugene, OR: Harvest, 2008.

Dembski, William A., and Winston Ewert. *The Design Inference: Eliminating Chance through Small Probabilities*. 2nd edition. Seattle, WA: Discovery Institute, 2023.

Denton, Michael. *Evolution: A Theory in Crisis*. Bethesda, MD: Adler & Adler, 1986.

———. *Evolution: Still a Theory in Crisis*. Seattle, WA: Discovery Institute Press, 2018.

———. *Nature's Destiny: How the Laws of Biology Reveal Purpose in the Universe*. New York: Free Press, 1998.

DeWolf, David K., et al. *Traipsing into Evolution: Intelligent Design and the Kitzmiller vs. Dover Decision*. Seattle, WA: Discovery Institute, 2006.

Fodor, Jerry, and Massimo Piattelli-Palmarini. *What Darwin Got Wrong*. London: Profile Books, 2010.

Gonzalez, Guillermo, and Jay W. Richards. *The Privileged Planet: How Our Place in the Cosmos is Designed for Discovery*. Reprint, with a new foreword. New York: Gateway Editions, 2024.

Gordon, Bruce L., and William A. Dembski, eds. *The Nature of Nature: Examining the Role of Naturalism in Science*. Wilmington, DE: ISI, 2011.

Holder, Rodney D. *God, the Multiverse, and Everything.* London: Routledge, 2016.
———. *Big Bang, Big God: A Universe Designed for Life?* Oxford: Lion, 2013.
Hunter, Cornelius G. *Darwin's Proof: The Triumph of Religion Over Science.* Grand Rapids, MI: Brazos, 2003.
Johnson, Donald E. *Programming of Life.* Sylacauga, AL: Big Mac, 2010.
Johnson, Phillip E. *Darwin on Trial.* 20th anniversary edition. Downers Grove, IL: InterVarsity, 2010.
Klinghoffer, David, ed. *Debating Darwin's Doubt.* Seattle, WA: Discovery Institute Press, 2015.
Klinghoffer, David, ed. *Signature of Controversy: Responses to Critics of Signature in the Cell.* Seattle, WA: Discovery Institute Press, 2010.
Latham, Antony. *The Naked Emperor: Darwinism Exposed.* London: Janus, 2005.
Leisola, Matti, and Jonathan Witt. *Heretic: One Scientist's Journey from Darwin to Design.* Seattle, WA: Discovery Institute, 2018.
Lennox, John C. *Cosmic Chemistry: Do God and Science Mix?* Oxford: Lion, 2021.
Lewis, Geraint F., and Luke Barnes. *A Fortunate Universe: Life in a Finely Tuned Cosmos.* Cambridge: Cambridge University Press, 2016.
Lo, Thomas Y., et al. *Evolution and Intelligent Design in a Nutshell.* Seattle, WA: Discovery Institute, 2020.
Marks, Robert J., et al. *Introduction to Evolutionary Informatics.* New Jersey: World Scientific, 2017.
Menuge, Angus. *Agents Under Fire: Materialism and the Rationality of Science.* Lanham, MD: Rowman & Littlefield, 2004.
Meyer, Stephen C. *Darwin's Doubt: The Explosive Origin of Animal Life and the Case for Intelligent Design.* Rev. ed. Boulder, CO: Bravo, 2014.
———. *Signature in the Cell: DNA and the Evidence for Intelligent Design.* San Francisco: HarperOne, 2010.
Monton, Bradley. *Seeking God in Science: An Atheist Defends Intelligent Design.* Toronto, Ontario: Broadview, 2009.
Moreland, J. P. *Scientism and Secularism: Learning to Respond to a Dangerous Ideology.* Wheaton, IL: Crossway, 2018.
Nagel, Thomas. *Mind and Cosmos: Why the Materialist Neo-Darwinian Conception of Nature is Almost Certainly False.* Oxford: Oxford University Press, 2012.
———. *Secular Philosophy and the Religious Temperament.* Oxford: Oxford University Press, 2010.
Newman, Robert C., et al. *What's Darwin Got to Do with It? A Friendly Conversation about Evolution.* Downers Grove, IL: InterVarsity, 2000.
Niekerk, Frederik van, and Nico Vorster, eds. *Science and Faith in Dialogue.* Reformed Theology in Africa Series 10. Oxford: AOSIS, 2022. https://books.aosis.co.za/index.php/ob/catalog/book/334.
Pearcey, Nancy R., and Charles B. Thaxton. *The Soul of Science: Christian Faith and Natural Philosophy.* Wheaton, IL: Crossway, 1994.
Pullen, Stuart. *Intelligent Design or Evolution? Why the Origin of Life and the Evolution of Molecular Knowledge Imply Design.* Raleigh, NC: Intelligent Design Books, 2005.
Ratzsch, Del. *Science & Its Limits: The Natural Sciences in Christian Perspective.* Downers Grove, IL: InterVarsity, 2000.

Shedinger, Robert F. *The Mystery of Evolutionary Mechanisms: Darwinian Biology's Grand Narrative of Triumph and the Subversion of Religion*. Eugene, OR: Cascade, 2019.

Stewart, Robert B., ed. *Intelligent Design: Dembski, William A. & Michael Ruse in Dialogue*. Minneapolis: Fortress, 2007.

Stump, J. B., ed. *Four Views on Creation, Evolution and Intelligent Design*. Grand Rapids, MI: Zondervan, 2017.

Swift, David. *Evolution under the Microscope: A Scientific Critique of the Theory of Evolution*. Stirling, UK: Leighton Academic Press, 2002.

Tan, Chance Laura, and Rob Stadler. *The Stairway to Life: An Origin-of- Life Reality Check*. N.p.: Evorevo, 2020.

Thaxton, Charles B., et al. *The Mystery of Life's Origin: The Continuing Controversy*. Seattle, WA: Discovery Institute Press, 2020.

Thomas, Neil. *Taking Leave of Darwin: A Longtime Agnostic Discovers the Case for Design*. Seattle, WA: Discovery Institute, 2021.

Ward, Keith. *God, Chance & Necessity*. Oxford: OneWorld, 1996.

Wells, Jonathan. *The Myth of Junk DNA*. Seattle, WA: Discovery Institute Press, 2011.

———. *Zombie Science: More Icons of Evolution*. Seattle, WA: Discovery Institute, 2017.

West, John G., ed. *The Magician's Twin: C. S. Lewis on Science, Scientism, and Society*. Seattle, WA: Discovery Institute Press, 2012.

William, Peter S. *A Faithful Guide to Philosophy: A Christian Introduction to the Love of Wisdom*. Eugene, OR: Wipf & Stock, 2019.

———. *I Wish I Could Believe in Meaning: A Response to Nihilism*. Southampton, UK: Damaris, 2004.

———. *Outgrowing God? An Introduction to Richard Dawkins And The God Debate*. Eugene, OR: Cascade, 2020.

Woodward, Thomas. *Darwin Strikes Back: Defending the Science of Intelligent Design*. Grand Rapids, MI: Baker, 2006.

———. *Doubts about Darwin: A History of Intelligent Design*. Grand Rapids, MI: Baker, 2003.

Woodward, Tom, and James P. Gills. *The Mysterious Epigenome: What Lies Beyond DNA*. Grand Rapids, MI: Kregel, 2012.

Resources for Chapter 2

My website has a page dedicated to the book from which chapter 2 was adapted (*A Universe From Someone: Essays on Natural Theology*, Wipf & Stock, 2022), with various free resources:

http://www.peterswilliams.com/publicationsbooks/a-universe-from-someone-essays-on-natural-theology/

WEBSITES

BeliefMap: https://www.beliefmap.org
BeThinking: https://www.bethinking.org
Discovery Institute Centre for Science & Culture: https://www.discovery.org/id/
Evangelical Philosophical Society: https://www.epsociety.org/
Faith and Philosophy: https://place.asburyseminary.edu/ faithandphilosophy/
Forum of Christian Leaders: https://foclonline.org
J.P. Moreland: http://www.jpmoreland.com/
Joshua L. Rasmussen's "Worldview Design" YouTube channel: https://www.youtube.com/c/WorldviewDesignChannel/videos
Paul Copan: https://www.paulcopan.com/
Stephen C. Meyer: https://stephencmeyer.org/
The God Question: https://www.thegodquestion.tv/
Theofilos: https://theofilos.no/
Unbelievable?: https://www.premierradio.org.uk/shows/saturday/unbelievable.aspx?mod_page=0
William Lane Craig - Reasonable Faith: https://www.reasonablefaith.org

WATCH

Against the Tide: Finding God in an Age of Science. Pensmore Films, 2021.
The God Question. https://www.thegodquestion.tv/
C. S. Lewis Doodle. "The Poison of Subjectivism by C.S. Lewis Doodle." https://www.youtube.com/watch?v=bo_NNTRKjRQ.

Williams, Peter S. "The Argument from Desire." YouTube playlist. https://www.youtube.com/playlist?list=PLQhh3qcwVEWj3nK3TBydEVAFRtdqfrpW2.

———. "Can We Believe in God in an Age of Science?" YouTube playlist. https://www.youtube.com/playlist?list=PLQhh3qcwVEWgusJHSKEHY-MZ9Tcd11IIm.

———. "Cosmic Fine Tuning." YouTube playlist. https://youtube.com/playlist?list=PLQhh3qcwVEWj4aeE76A1vjLvPqWieH8tE.

———. "Cosmological Arguments for God." YouTube playlist. https://www.youtube.com/playlist?list=PLQhh3qcwVEWjEXjiEjnCCbr_Qnu-1UbAa.

———. "Debating God." YouTube playlist. https://www.youtube.com/playlist?list=PLQhh3qcwVEWiY3UmTAiRdj2OW4SBGoy_W.

———. "Imagine Naturalism - C.S Lewis' Atheism and His Escape From the Closed Universe." YouTube video, Jan 3, 2024. https://www.youtube.com/watch?v=H74iTqdQa7w.

———. "The Moral Argument for God." YouTube playlist. https://www.youtube.com/playlist?list=PLQhh3qcwVEWhOfs_uQrFceuBRfMF1asf4.

———. "Mind-Body Dualism, Free Will and Related Issues." YouTube playlist. https://www.youtube.com/playlist?list=PLQhh3qcwVEWhoMdW-hlHBPyLRWgFjzhPT.

———. "Natural Theology." YouTube playlist. https://www.youtube.com/playlist?list=PLQhh3qcwVEWiDA8QN4h8wLrrbm49fLzPN.

———. "The Ontological Argument for God." YouTube playlist. https://www.youtube.com/playlist?list=PLQhh3qcwVEWjE7hqAz3D6jp7MWjChVYKn.

———. "Panpsychism." YouTube playlist. https://www.youtube.com/playlist?list=PLQhh3qcwVEWgqvHToCegBMgssUAf0AO9j.

———. "Practical Apologetics for a Christian Way of Life: A Brief History of Natural Theology." YouTube video, Jun 22, 2025. https://www.youtube.com/watch?v=iO3l_geJId8&t=88s.

———. "Practical Apologetics for a Christian Way of Life: Introducing Natural Theology." YouTube video, Jun 22, 2025. https://www.youtube.com/watch?v=Sh57U1dDB5Y&t=19s.

———. "Practical Apologetics for a Christian Way of Life: The Evidential Problem of Evil." YouTube video, Jun 22, 2025. https://www.youtube.com/watch?v=BlZ886YTFsk&t=13s.

———. "Practical Apologetics for a Christian Way of Life: The Logical Problem of Evil." YouTube video, Jun 22, 2025. https://www.youtube.com/watch?v=CCdAqSKJmag&t=7s.

———. "The Problem of Evil." YouTube playlist. https://www.youtube.com/playlist?list=PLQhh3qcwVEWjSOz8xsGXuS_VahByzSzhe.

———. "Problems with Materialism/Metaphysical Naturalism." YouTube playlist. https://www.youtube.com/playlist?list=PLQhh3qcwVEWgolWsfZnhQvzNfRT_jHLJA.

———. "Religious Experience." YouTube playlist. https://www.youtube.com/playlist?list=PLQhh3qcwVEWjccogWzetsujJ_3BtcyLJT.

LISTEN

Bentsen, Børge Elliot and Peter S. Williams. *The Question of God Podcast*. https://www.peterswilliams.com/media/the-question-of-god-podcast/.

Capturing Christianity. "Exploring the Contingency Argument with Dr. Josh Rasmussen." (Part 1.) https://capturingchristianity.com/cc014-exploring-the-contingency-argument-with-dr-josh-rasmussen-part-1/.

C. S. Lewis Essays. "C. S. Lewis - De Futilitate." https://www.youtube.com/watch?v=-4N5ZrMiRLw&t=167s.

Mind Matters. "Why is there Fine Tuning Everywhere?" *Mind Matters* Podcast, September 23, 2021. https://mindmatters.ai/podcast/ep153/.

Williams, Peter S. "Arguing for God (Oslo, 2022)." *The Peter S. Williams Podcast*, October 29, 2022. http://podcast.peterswilliams.com/e/arguing-for-god-oslo-2022/.

———. "Escaping the Closed Universe: C.S. Lewis vs. Naturalism." *The Peter S. Williams Podcast*, October, 2023. http://podcast.peterswilliams.com/e/escaping-the-closed-universe-cs-lewis-vs-naturalism/.

———. "Four Reasons God Won't Go Away." *The Peter S. Williams Podcast*, October 31, 2022. http://podcast.peterswilliams.com/e/four-reasons-why-god-won-t-go-away/.

———. "Veritas 2022: Outgrowing God? Learning from Dawkins's Failed Arguments." *The Peter S. Williams Podcast*, November 1, 2022. http://podcast.peterswilliams.com/e/outgrowing-god-learning-from-dawkins-s-failed-arguments/.

ONLINE PAPERS

Aquinas, Thomas. "The Five Ways" from *Summa Theologica*, https://homepages.uc.edu/~martinj/The%20Infinite/Aquinas%20-%20the%20Five%20Ways%20-%20SummaTheologica%20P1Q2A3.pdf.

Beck, W. David. "God's Existence." In *In Defence of Miracles: A Comprehensive Case for God's Action in History*, edited by R. Douglas Geivett and Gary R. Habermas, 149–62. Leicester: Apollos, 1997. https://digitalcommons.liberty.edu/cgi/viewcontent.cgi?article=1086&context=sor_fac_pubs.

Clark, Kelly James. "I Believe in God the Father, Almighty." http://www.researchgate.net/publication/265226136_I_Believe_in_God_the_Father_Almighty.

Copan, Paul. "God Can't Possibly Exist Given the Evil and Pain I See in the World." In *That's Just Your Interpretation* (Grand Rapids: Baker, 2001). http://www.bethinking.org/resource.php?ID=30.

———. "God, Naturalism, and the Foundations of Morality." In *The Future of Atheism*, edited by Robert B. Stewart, 141–61. London: SPCK, 2008. https://www.paulcopan.com/articles/pdf/God-naturalism-morality.pdf.

———. "Hume and the Moral Argument." In *In Defence of Natural Theology: A Post-Humean Assessment*, edited by in James F. Sennett and Douglas Groothuis, 200–25. Downers Grove, IL: InterVarsity, 2005. http://www.paulcopan.com/articles/pdf/Paul_Copan-Hume_and_Moral_Argument-In_Defense_Natural_Theology.pdf.

———. "Review: *The Impossibility of God*." https://www.equip.org/articles/the-impossibility-of-god/.

Cutter, Brian and Dustin Crummett. "Psychophysical Harmony: A New Argument for Theism." *Oxford Studies in Philosophy of Religion* (forthcoming). https://philarchive.org/archive/CUTPHA#:~:text=psychophysical%20laws%20are%20extremely%20complex,X%20particles%20gave%20rise%20to.

Craig, William Lane. "Five Arguments for God." https://christianevidence.org/booklet/five_arguments_for_god/.

———. "The Problem Of Evil." http://www.reasonablefaith.org/writings/popular-writings/existence-nature-of-god/the-problem-of-evil.

Evans, C. Stephen. "The Mystery of Persons and Belief in God." http://www.leaderu.com/truth/3truth07.html.

Kreeft, Peter and Ronald K. Tacelli. "Twenty Arguments for God's Existence." http://www.peterkreeft.com/topics-more/20_arguments-gods-existence.htm.

Leidenhag, Joanna. "Why a Panpsychist Should Adopt Theism: God, Galileo, and Goff." *Journal of Consciousness Studies*, Volume 28, Numbers 9–10, 2021, 250–267(18). https://eprints.whiterose.ac.uk/id/eprint/180157/17/Leidenhag%20AAM.pdf.

Lewis, C. S. "The Cardinal Difficulty of Naturalism." http://thecslewis-studygroup.org/wp-content/uploads/2014/07/The-Cardinal-Difficulty-of-Naturalism.pdf.

———. "The Poison of Subjectivism." https://williamwoodall.weebly.com/uploads/1/0/2/2/10226906/the_poison_of_subjectivism.pdf.

Mavrodes, George. "Religion and the Queerness of Morality." https://afterall.net/wp-content/uploads/2021/08/religion-and-the-queerness-of-morality.pdf.

Plantinga, Alvin. "Two Dozen (or so) Arguments for God." https://appearedtoblogly.wordpress.com/wp-content/uploads/2011/05/plantinga-alvin-22two-dozen-or-so-theistic-arguments221.pdf.

Reppert, Victor. "The Argument from Reason." In *The Blackwell Companion to Natural Theology*, edited by William Lane Craig and J. P. Moreland, 344–90. Oxford: Blackwell, 2009. https://appearedtoblogly.wordpress.com/wp-content/uploads/2011/05/the-argument-from-reason.pdf.

Russell, Bertrand & F. C. Copleston. "A Debate on the Existence of God" in John Hick ed. *The Existence of God*. New York, N.Y.: Macmillan, 1964, 167–191. http://www.scandalon.co.uk/philosophy/cosmological_radio.htm.

Simek, Slater. "A Bayesian Exploration of C. S. Lewis's 'Argument from Desire.'" https://link.springer.com/article/10.1007/s11841-021-00887-9.

Swinburne, Richard. "Evidence for God" (1986). http://christianevidence.org/docs/booklets/evidence_for_god.pdf.

Taylor, Richard. "The Cosmological Argument: A Defence." https://iweb.langara.ca/rjohns/files/2013/01/taylor_cosmological.pdf.

Willard, Dallas. "Knowledge and Naturalism." https://dwillard.org/resources/articles/knowledge-and-naturalism.

———. "Language, Being, God, and the Three Stages of Theistic Evidence." https://dwillard.org/articles/language-being-god-and-the-three-stages-of-theistic-evidence.

Williams, Peter S. "A Beginner's Guide to the Theistic Argument from Desire." https://www.peterswilliams.com/wp-content/uploads/2021/01/Intro_Lewis_Desire_2019.pdf.

———. "BioCosmos Interview on Natural Theology: A Universe From Someone." https://www.peterswilliams.com/wp-content/uploads/2025/03/BioCosmos_QA_Natural_Theology_March_2025.pdf.

———. "A Brief Introduction to and Defence of the Modern Ontological Argument." *Theofilos* 7.3 (2015) 339–44. https://theofilos.no/wp-content/uploads/2019/09/3d_Forum_Williams_A-Brief-Introduction-to-and-Defence-of-the-Modern-Ontological-Argument.pdf.

———. "Can Moral Objectivism Do Without God?" https://www.peterswilliams.com/wp-content/uploads/2022/07/Can-Moral-Objectivism-Do-Without-God-v3.pdf.

———. "C.S. Lewis as a Central Figure in Formulating the Theistic Argument from Desire." *Linguaculture* 10.2 (2019). https://journal.linguaculture.ro/index.php/home/article/view/149/136.

———. "The Emperor's Incoherent New Clothes – Pointing the Finger at Dawkins' Atheism." *Think*, Volume 9, Issue 24, Spring 2010. https://www.academia.edu/40157524/The_Emperors_Incoherent_New_Clothes_Pointing_the_Finger_at_Dawkins_Atheism.

———. "Five Arguments for God." https://www.peterswilliams.com/wp-content/uploads/2016/02/Five-Arguments-for-Theism.pdf.

———. "Intelligent Design, Aesthetics and Design Arguments" http://www.arn.org/docs/williams/pw_idaestheticsanddesignarguments.htm.

———. "Re-Defending Arguments from Desire: A Second Response to Gregory Bassham." Sep 2016. https://www.peterswilliams.com/wp-content/uploads/2016/11/In-Defence-of-Arguments-from-Desire-1.pdf.

———. "A Universe from Someone: A Critique of Lawrence Krauss." https://www.bethinking.org/is-there-a-creator/a-universe-from-someone-against-lawrence-krauss.

BOOKS

Baggett, David, and Jerry L. Walls. *Good God: The Theistic Foundations of Morality.* Oxford: Oxford University Press, 2011.

Bassham, Gregory ed. *C. S. Lewis' Apologetics: Pro and Con.* Leiden: Rodolpi-Brill, 2015.

Beck, W. David. *Does God Exist? A History of Answers to the Question.* Downers Grove, IL: IVP Academic, 2021.

Beckwith, Francis J. ed. *To Everyone an Answer: A Case for the Christian Worldview.* Downers Grove, IL: IVP, 2004.

Bignon, Guillaume. *Confessions of a French Atheist: How God Hijacked My Quest to Disprove the Christian Faith.* Carol Stream, IL: Tyndale House, 2022.

Campbell, Ronnie P., and David J. Baggett. *A Personal God and a Good World: The Coherence of the Christian Moral Vision.* Nashville: B&H Academic. 2024.

Cowen, Steven B., and James S. Spiegel. *The Love of Wisdom: A Christian Introduction to Philosophy.* Nashville: B&H, 2009.

Copan, Paul, and Charles Taliaferro, eds. *The Naturalness of Belief: New Essays on Theism's Rationality.* Lanham, Maryland: Lexington, 2019.

Copan, Paul, and Paul K. Moser, eds. *The Rationality of Theism.* London: Routledge, 2003.

Copan, Paul, and Stewart E. Kelly, eds. *Christianity Contested: Replies to Critics' Toughest Objections*. Eugene, OR Cascade, 2024.
Copan, Paul, and William Lane Craig, eds. *The Kalam Cosmological Argument: Volume One – Philosophical Arguments for the Finitude of the Past*. London: Bloomsbury, 2019.
Copan, Paul, and William Lane Craig, eds. *The Kalam Cosmological Argument: Volume Two – Scientific Evidence for the Beginning of the Universe*. London: Bloomsbury, 2019.
Cottingham, John. *How Can I Believe?* London: SPCK, 2018.
———. *Why Believe?* London: Continuum, 2009.
Craig, William Lane. *Does God Exist?* Pine Mountain, Georgia: Impact 360, 2019.
———. *On Guard - For Students: A Thinker's Guide to the Christian Faith*. Colorado Springs, CO: David C. Cook, 2015.
Craig, William Lane. ed. *Philosophy of Religion: A Reader and Guide*. Edinburgh: Edinburgh University Press, 2002.
Craig, William Lane, and J.P. Moreland, eds. *The Blackwell Companion to Natural Theology*. Oxford: Wiley-Blackwell, 2009.
Craig, William Lane, and J.P. Moreland, eds. *Naturalism: A Critical Analysis*. London: Routledge, 2014.
Dennett, Daniel C., and Alvin Plantinga. *Science and Religion: Are They Compatible?* Oxford: Oxford University Press, 2011.
Drew Jr., James K., and Paul M. Gould. *Philosophy: A Christian Introduction*. Grand Rapids, MI: Baker Academic, 2019.
Evans, C. Stephen. *Despair: A Moment or a Way of Life?* Downers Grove, IL: IVP, 1973.
———. *Natural Signs and Knowledge of God: A New Look at Theistic Arguments*. Oxford University Press, 2010.
———. *Why Believe?: Reason and Mystery as Pointers to God*. Grand Rapids, MI: Eerdmans, 1996.
———. *Why Christian Faith Still Makes Sense: A Response to Contemporary Challenges*. Grand Rapids, MI: Baker Academic, 2015.
Ganssle, Gregory E. *A Reasonable God: Engaging the New Face of Atheism*. Waco, Texas: Baylor University Press, 2009.
Geisler, Norman L. *Christian Apologetics*, 2nd edition. Grand Rapids, MI: Baker Academic, 2013.
Gellman, Jerome I. *Experience of God and the Rationality of Theistic Belief*. Ithica, New York: Cornell University Press, 1997.
Glass, David H. *Atheism's New Clothes: Exploring and Exposing the Claims of the New Atheists*. Nottingham: Apollos, 2012.
Goetz, Stewart, and Charles Taliaferro. *Naturalism*. Grand Rapids, MI: Eerdmans, 2008.
Holder, Rodney D. *Big Bang, Big God: A Universe Designed for Life?* Oxford: Lion, 2013.
———. *God, the Multiverse, and Everything*. London: Routledge, 2016.
———. *Ramified Natural Theology in Science and Religion: Moving Forward from Natural Theology* (Routledge Science and Religion). London: Routledge, 2022.
Hunter, James Davison, and Paul Nedelisky. *Science and the Good: The Tragic Quest for the Foundations of Morality*. New Haven: Yale University Press/Templeton, 2018.
Joad, C. E. M. *The Recovery of Belief: A Restatement of Christian Philosophy*. London: Faber & Faber, 1952.

Kreeft, Peter. *Heaven: The Heart's Deepest Desire*, expanded edition. San Francisco: Ignatius, 1989.
Lennox, John C. *Cosmic Chemistry: Do God and Science Mix?* Oxford: Lion, 2021.
———. *God and Stephen Hawking: Whose Design Is It Anyway?* Second edition. Oxford: Lion, 2021.
Lewis, C.S. *Miracles*. New York: Collins, 2012.
Loke, Andrew. *The Teleological and Kalam Cosmological Arguments Revisited* (Palgrave Frontiers in Philosophy of Religion). Palgrave Macmillan, 2022. https://link.springer.com/book/10.1007/978-3-030-94403-2.
Markham, Ian. *Truth and the Reality of God: An Essay in Natural Theology*. Edinburgh: T&T Clark, 1998.
Meister, Chad V. *Evil: A Guide for the Perplexed*. 2nd ed. New York: Bloomsbury, 2018.
Meister, Chad, and James K. Drew Jr., eds. *God and Evil: The Case for God in a World Filled with Pain*. Downers Grove, IL: InterVarsity, 2013.
Menuge, Angus. *Agents Under Fire: Materialism and the Rationality of Science*. Rowman & Littlefield, 2004.
Menuge, Angus, et al, eds. *Minding the Brian: Models of the Mind, Information, and Empirical Science*. Seattle, WA: Discovery Institute, 2023.
Meyer, Stephen C. *The Return of the God Hypothesis*. New York: HarperCollins, 2021.
Miller, Corey and Paul Gould, eds. *Is Faith in God Reasonable?* London: Routledge, 2014.
Monton, Bradly. *Seeking God in Science. An Atheist Defends Intelligent Design*. Peterborough, Ontario: Broadview, 2009.
Moreland, J. P. *Consciousness and the Existence of God: A Theistic Argument*. London: Routledge, 2009.
———. *The Recalcitrant Imago Dei: Human Persons and the Failure of Naturalism*. London: SCM, 2009.
———. *Scaling the Secular City: A Defence of Christianity*. Grand Rapids, MI: Baker, 1987.
———. *Scientism and Secularism: Learning to Respond to a Dangerous Ideology*. Wheaton, IL: Crossway, 2018.
Moreland, J. P., and William Lane Craig. *Philosophical Foundations for a Christian Worldview*. Second edition. Downers Grove, IL: IVP, 2017.
Moreland, J. P., and Garrett J. DeWeese. *Philosophy Made Slightly Less Difficult: A Beginner's Guide to Life's Big Questions*. Second edition. Downers Grove, IL: IVP Academic, 2021.
Moreland, J. P. and Kai Nielson et al. *Does God Exist?: The Debate between Theists and Atheists*. Amherst, New York: Prometheus, 1993.
Murray, Michael J., ed. *Reason for the Hope Within*. Grand Rapids, MI: Eerdmans, 1999.
Nagasawa, Yujin. *The Existence of God: A Philosophical Introduction*. London: Routledge, 2011.
Nagel, Thomas. *Mind and Cosmos: Why the Materialist Neo-Darwinian Conception of Nature is Almost Certainly False*. Oxford: Oxford University Press, 2012.
———. *Secular Philosophy and the Religious Temperament*. Oxford: Oxford University Press, 2010.
Netland, Harold A. *Religious Experience and the Knowledge of God: The Evidential Force of Divine Encounters*. Grand Rapids, MI: Baker Academic, 2022.
Parrish, Stephen E. *Atheism? A Critical Analysis*. Eugene, OR: Wipf & Stock, 2019.

Plantinga, Alvin. *Knowledge and Christian Belief*. Grand Rapids, MI: Eerdmans, 2015.
Polkinghorne, John. *Science & Christian Belief: Theological Reflections of a Bottom-up Thinker*. London: SPCK, 1994.
Puckett Jr., Joe. *The Apologetics of Joy: A Case for the Existence of God from C.S. Lewis's Argument from Desire*. Cambridge: Lutterworth, 2013.
Rasmussen, Joshua and Kevin Vallier, eds. *A New Theist Response to the New Atheism*. London: Routledge, 2020.
Ratzsch, Del. *Science & Its Limits: The Natural Sciences in Christian Perspective*. Nottingham: Apollos, 2000.
Reppert, Victor. *C. S. Lewis's Dangerous Idea: In Defence of the Argument from Reason*. Downers Grove, IL: IVP, 2003.
Rosenberg, Alex. *The Atheist's Guide to Reality: Enjoying Life Without Illusions*. W.W. Norton, 2011.
Ruloff, Colin and Peter Horban, eds. *Contemporary Arguments in Natural Theology: God and Rational Belief*. London: Bloomsbury Academic, 2021.
Sennett, James F. and Douglas R. Groothuis, eds. *In Defence of Natural Theology: A Post-Humean Assessment*. Downers Grove, IL: IVP, 2005.
Smart, J. J. C., and J. J. Haldane. *Atheism and Theism*. 2nd ed. Oxford: Blackwell, 2003.
Smith, Christian. *Atheist Overreach: What Atheism Can't Deliver*. Oxford: Oxford University Press, 2019.
Stokes, Mitch. *A Shot of Faith (to the Head): Be a Confident Believer in an Age of Cranky Atheists*. Nashville: Thomas Nelson, 2012.
Swinburne, Richard. *The Existence of God*. Second edition, Oxford, Clarendon, 2004.
Taylor, A. E. *Does God Exist?* London: Collins, 1961.
Taylor, Richard. *Metaphysics*. Englewood Cliffs, N.J: Prentice Hall, 1963.
Thaxton, Charles B. et al. *The Mystery of Life's Origin: The Continuing Controversy*. Seattle: Discovery Institute, 2020.
Walls, Jerry L., and Trent Dougherty eds. *Two Dozen (or so) Arguments for God: The Plantinga Project*. Oxford: Oxford University Press, 2018.
Ward, Keith. *God, Chance & Necessity*. Oxford: OneWorld, 1996.
West, John G. ed. *The Magician's Twin: C.S. Lewis on Science, Scientism, and Society*. Seattle: Discovery Institute, 2012.
Willard, Dallas. *Knowing Christ Today: How We Can Trust Spiritual Knowledge*. New York: HarperOne, 2009.
Williams, Peter S. *The Case for God*. Tunbridge Wells: Monarch, 1999.
———. *A Faithful Guide to Philosophy: A Christian Introduction to the Love of Wisdom*. Eugene, OR: Wipf and Stock, 2019.
———. *A Sceptic's Guide to Atheism*. Milton Keynes: Paternoster, 2009.
———. *C.S. Lewis vs. the New Atheists*. Milton Keynes: Paternoster, 2013.
———. *I Wish I Could Believe in Meaning: A Response to Nihilism*. Southampton: Damaris, 2005.
———. *Outgrowing God? A Beginner's Guide to Richard Dawkins and the God Debate*. Eugene, OR: Cascade, 2020.

Resources for Chapter 3

My website has a page dedicated to the book from which chapter 3 was adapted (*Behold the Man*: *Essays on the Historical Jesus*, Wipf & Stock, 2024), with various free resources:

https://www.peterswilliams.com/publications/books/behold-the-man-essays-on-the-historical-jesus/

PRIMARY SOURCE MATERIAL

Anyone serious about investigating Jesus will want to acquaint themselves with at least some of the primary historical source material gathered together into the "New Testament" (NT) portion of the Christian Bible, especially the first-century biographies of Jesus known as *Matthew, Mark, Luke* and *John*.

A recent, single-scholar translation of the NT is Tom Wright's *The New Testament for Everyone*, Third Edition (London: SPCK, 2023). A wide range of modern English translations of the Bible are available (e.g. CSB, ESV, NLT). The *New Heart English Bible* is available as a free downloadable pdf (see https://nheb.net/files/NHEB.pdf). Many translations of the Bible can be read online at sites such as www.biblehub.com (where multiple translations of a verse can be compared, and which also offers an interlinear Greek-English text linked to lexical information, alongside a selection of older commentaries). Two interlinear presentations of the NT that include the latest critical edition of the Greek texts alongside a modern English translation are the *Greek-English Interlinear CSB New Testament* (Nashville: B&H Publishing, 2022), and *The Greek-English Interlinear ESV New Testament* (Wheaton, IL: Crossway, 2019). The bible is available in various languages online at sites such as www.biblegateway.com/versions. For users of computer tablets and smartphones, there are a number of bible apps (e.g. And

Bible app; Bible Hub app; Bible Project app; Blue Letter Bible app; Literal Bible app; Logos Bible Study app).

For an introduction to different approaches to translating the bible, see:

Williams, "Translating the Bible." YouTube playlist. https://www.youtube.com/playlist?list=PLQhh3qcwVEWjZStGYiKQvSqGeoKSb72xF

Watkins, Tony. "How do we Choose Which Bible Translation to Read?" https://tyndalehouse.com/explore/articles/bible-translations/.

Wildsmith, Tim. *Bible Translations for Everyone: A Guide to Finding a Bible that's Right for You.* Grand Rapids, MI: Zondervan, 2025.

BACKGROUND, STUDY BIBLES AND COMMENTARIES

A wide variety of "Study Bibles" exist that add explanatory notes and other materials alongside the biblical text. See, for example: Sean McDowell, ed. *CSB Apologetics Study Bible for Students* (Nashville: B&H, 2017); the *ESV Study Bible, Personal size* (Wheaton, IL: Crossway, 2025); the *Ignatius Catholic Study Bible, New Testament,* Second Catholic Edition, RSV (San Francisco: Ignatius, 2010). Readers with a particular interest in the relevant archaeology may refer to *The ESV Archaeology Study Bible* (Wheaton, IL: Crossway, 2018).

For commentary on the four gospels and Acts with a focus on apologetic issues, readers can consult Jeremy Royal Howard, ed. *The Gospels and Acts. The Holman Apologetics Commentary on the Bible* (Nashville: Holman, 2013). On the fourth gospel, see also Craig L. Blomberg's *The Historical Reliability of John's Gospel: Issues & Commentary* (Leicester: Apollos, 2015).

Readers looking for a one-volume commentary on the bible might consider the *Zondervan Bible Commentary: One-Volume Illustrated Edition* (Grand Rapids, MI: Zondervan, 2008). Commentaries that address the meaning and significance of specific biblical texts in greater depth include: *The New American Commentary* series (published by Broadman & Holman); the Wesleyan *New Beacon Bible Commentary* series (published by Beacon Hill); *The New International Commentary on the New Testament* series (published by William B. Eerdmans); the *Tyndale New Testament Commentaries* series (published by IVP); and the *Zondervan Exegetical Commentary on the New Testament* series (published by Zondervan).

Books that focus on the cultural background of the NT include J. Scott Duval and J. Daniel Hays, eds., *The Baker Illustrated Bible Background Commentary* (Grand Rapids, MI: Baker, 2020); Craig S. Keener, *The IVP Bible Background Commentary: New Testament,* Second Edition (Downers Grove,

IL: IVP Academic, 2014); the *CSB Holy Land Illustrated Bible* (Nashville, TN: Broadman & Holman, 2020); and the multi-volume *Zondervan Illustrated Bible Backgrounds Commentary* (note that the synoptic gospel commentaries are available as one volume: Arnold, Clinton E., ed. *Zondervan Illustrated Bible Backgrounds Commentary: Matthew, Mark, Luke: Volume One*: 1. Grand Rapids, MI: Zondervan, 2002).

The textual and testimonial reliability of the New Testament in general, and of the four gospels in particular, is addressed by several of the recommended resources that follow.

WEBSITES

BeliefMap: https://www.beliefmap.org

BeThinking: https://www.bethinking.org

Justin Brierley: https://justinbrierley.com

William Lane Craig, Reasonable Faith: https://www.reasonablefaith.org

John Dickson: https://www.johndickson.org

Gary R. Habermas: https://www.garyhabermas.com/

Lydia McGrew: https://lydiamcgrew.com/

WATCH

FOCLOnline. "Evidence for Old Testament History - Peter S Williams." YouTube video, July 3, 2024. https://www.youtube.com/watch?v=JiUfViPOJA4.

———. "Defending Early High Christology with Archaeology and New Testament Letters—Peter S. Williams." YouTube video, August 1, 2019. https://www.youtube.com/watch?v=vUha7-4Puy8.

Williams, Peter S. "A Pre-Modern Reflection on the Modernist Roots of Postmodernism." YouTube video, October 31, 2020. https://www.youtube.com/watch?v=jrG781Nqt Dw&list=PLQhh3qcwVEWj7PBYa-iiIdysNgwMz9E5O&index=2.

———. "Discipleship in 3D: Change for Head, Heart and Hands." *Damaris Norge*. YouTube video, Apr 29, 2020. https://youtu.be/QTyEooJgIBI?si=sa-PotDjrTJ1jE5U.

———. "Getting at Jesus: A Critique of Neo-Atheist Nonsense About the Jesus of History." YouTube video, Feb 26, 2019. https://youtu.be/a3G9FPhnmJs.

———. "Buddhism." YouTube playlist. https://www.youtube.com/playlist?list=PLQh h3qcwVEWif_IZ4RSdtPpT9PZ6p3O7I.

———. "Can Hallucinations Explain the Resurrection?" YouTube playlist. https://www.youtube.com/playlist?list=PLQhh3qcwVEWgVNLsZOUCB5i64lC51Zsji.

———. "Christian Testimonies" YouTube playlist. https://www.youtube.com/playlist?list=PLQhh3qcwVEWjefBIN2sCE0OYS9_eXXpvV.

———. "Christianity and Archaeology." YouTube playlist. https://www.youtube.com/playlist?list=PLQhh3qcwVEWjh9aRRWF1kYZIVCPc5iCcw.

———. "Christology." YouTube playlist. https://www.youtube.com/playlist?list=PLQhh3qcwVEWgjXlj2cVn_ZjOE8Wd9dVbv.

———. "Debating the Resurrection." YouTube playlist. https://www.youtube.com/playlist?list=PLQhh3qcwVEWhAPCkcpFsSwEXrYKuBhoaq.

———. "Did Jesus Perform Miracles?" YouTube playlist. https://www.youtube.com/playlist?list=PLQhh3qcwVEWi1yi_tcY-Ptl9nNJzRCeiN.

———. "Discipleship and Spiritual Formation." YouTube playlist. https://www.youtube.com/playlist?list=PLQhh3qcwVEWhGSK1x6H3qeqzefB8hmvvM.

———. "The Existence of Jesus." YouTube playlist. https://www.youtube.com/playlist?list=PLQhh3qcwVEWiCALtjBWyxo78Dxxib4g8E.

———. "Gospel Contradictions?" YouTube playlist. https://www.youtube.com/playlist?list=PLQhh3qcwVEWjt9SKTdFKEqLkUpwJYxCit.

———. "Historical Criteria of Authenticity." YouTube playlist. https://www.youtube.com/playlist?list=PLQhh3qcwVEWg6gh7wSlE4EWoDtTHaq5.

———. "The Historical Jesus." YouTube playlist. https://www.youtube.com/playlist?list=PLQhh3qcwVEWgoCpSQPAr5cy_lnXpeQMNk.

———. "Imagine Naturalism - C.S Lewis' Atheism and His Escape From the Closed Universe." YouTube video, Jan 3, 2024. https://www.youtube.com/watch?v=H74iTqdQa7w.

———. "Is Christianity Good for Society?" YouTube playlist. https://www.youtube.com/playlist?list=PLQhh3qcwVEWhEFhLjwAL_Qp4dCzCvwGc-.

———. "Islam." YouTube playlist. https://www.youtube.com/playlist?list=PLQhh3qcwVEWjhD84EB0jEG5PswCOcDsmJ.

———. "Jesus' Tomb Was Empty." YouTube playlist. https://www.youtube.com/playlist?list=PLQhh3qcwVEWhqraAeJ8gVcSlbXhZR2R6p.

———. "The 'Lunatic, Liar or Lord' Argument." YouTube playlist. https://www.youtube.com/playlist?list=PLQhh3qcwVEWiCA7mwy67RLgGt_2n4jzra.

———. "Mind-Body Dualism, Free Will and Related Issues." YouTube playlist. https://www.youtube.com/playlist?list=PLQhh3qcwVEWhoMdW-hlHBPyLRWgFjzhPT.

———. "The 'Minimal Facts' Approach to the Resurrection." YouTube playlist. https://www.youtube.com/playlist?list=PLQhh3qcwVEWibeo-6SuXmjOkmFE_4C8Vx.

———. "Miracles." YouTube playlist. https://www.youtube.com/playlist?list=PLQhh3qcwVEWjIqwpnQZQfCxB-ZWLXNvh-.

———. "Mormonism." YouTube playlist. https://www.youtube.com/playlist?list=PLQhh3qcwVEWjOn4gyNXipluUzVuNsJjjI.

———. "The 'New Atheism.'" YouTube playlist. https://www.youtube.com/playlist?list=PLQhh3qcwVEWifP3P_gIS8MMsRXLOGDiG_.

———. "The New Testament Canon." YouTube playlist. https://www.youtube.com/playlist?list=PLQhh3qcwVEWgB1baV-0QrZ3foJRkj74hM.

———. "Pantheism/New Age Spirituality." YouTube playlist. https://www.youtube.com/playlist?list=PLQhh3qcwVEWhcBAtPezM2sCyMVv7K_NRJ.

———. "Practical Apologetics for a Christian Way of Life: Europe's Spiritual Climate." YouTube video. https://www.youtube.com/watch?v=_ke2wcdN6xw.

———. "Practical Apologetics for a Christian Way of Life: The Resurrection of Jesus (1 of 2): Worldviews & Miracles." YouTube video, 22 June, 2025. https://www.youtube.com/watch?v=dtDIiLPmGBk.

———. "Practical Apologetics for a Christian Way of Life: The Resurrection of Jesus (2 of 2): Evidence & Explanations." YouTube video, 22 June, 2025. https://www.youtube.com/watch?v=aWllKg6XxfM&t=8s.

———. "Practical Apologetics for a Christian Way of Life: The Identity of Jesus." YouTube video, 22 June, 2025. https://www.youtube.com/watch?v=8GnuZfxNaWw.

———. "The Resurrection Appearances of Jesus." YouTube playlist. https://www.youtube.com/playlist?list=PLQhh3qcwVEWgUZZO-MUpLJhm7ZmscmAk6.

———. "The Resurrection of Jesus." YouTube playlist. https://www.youtube.com/playlist?list=PLQhh3qcwVEWjFoVbpQ9sPUUivlyF5nowB.

———. "The Reliability of the New Testament." YouTube playlist. www.youtube.com/playlist?list=PLQhh3qcwVEWjo4HUH7t9yqIiFKKuAkjh_.

———. "Textual Reliability of the New Testament." YouTube playlist. https://www.youtube.com/playlist?list=PLQhh3qcwVEWhx61s1CiNf9_CATxat5bn8.

———. "The Theological Roots of Science." YouTube playlist. https://www.youtube.com/playlist?list=PLQhh3qcwVEWh3jDVYqFFzWSnTbtlUeCg3.

———. "The Trinity." YouTube playlist. https://www.youtube.com/playlist?list=PLQhh3qcwVEWhlDMYNYyenLkqdEQMMtMYo.

———. "Understanding Culture." YouTube playlist. https://www.youtube.com/playlist?list=PLQhh3qcwVEWj7PBYa-iiIdysNgwMz9E5O.

———. "Understanding Worldviews." YouTube playlist. https://www.youtube.com/playlist?list=PLQhh3qcwVEWhCn7rqlW7UsvFNRjQ9wxoH.

———. "Undesigned Coincidences in the Gospels." YouTube playlist. https://www.youtube.com/playlist?list=PLQhh3qcwVEWgZ_2TLqaPchdovuItTyZll.

———. "Scientism." YouTube playlist. https://www.youtube.com/watch?v=oau57-tEHdE&list=PLQhh3qcwVEWiIgrCwkM8Y-RoqU1TmYK8R.

———. "Who Wrote the NT Gospels?" YouTube playlist. https://www.youtube.com/playlist?list=PLQhh3qcwVEWg2vHjaH7hwE3BdtZao15CS.

LISTEN

Brierley, Justin. *The Surprising Rebirth of Belief in God, the Podcast.* https://justinbrierley.com/surprisingrebirth/#episodes.

C. S. Lewis Essays. "C. S. Lewis - What Are We to Make of Jesus Christ?" https://www.youtube.com/watch?v=yGU2JN2a3Cs.

Williams, Peter S. "Archaeological Evidence and Jesus (ELF 2025)." *The Peter S. Williams Podcast*, May 30, 2025. http://podcast.peterswilliams.com/e/archaeological-evidence-and-jesus-elf-2025/.

———. "Atheism Today: The Collapse of the New Atheism & the Rise of Metamodernism." *The Peter S. Williams Podcast*, October, 2024. http://podcast.peterswilliams.com/e/atheism-today-the-collapse-of-the-new-atheism-the-rise-of-metamodernism/.

———. "The Christ of Faith vs. the Jesus of History?" http://podcast.peterswilliams.com/e/the-christ-of-faith-vs-the-jesus-of-history/.

———. "Christian Spirituality at the Cutting Edge of Contemporary Culture." *The Peter S. Williams Podcast*, June, 2024. http://podcast.peterswilliams.com/e/christian-spirituality-at-the-cutting-edge-of-culture/.

———. "A Christian Worldview and Science in Apologetic Perspective: Anthropos." *The Peter S. Williams Podcast*, October 25, 2021. http://podcast.peterswilliams.com/e/a-christian-worldview-and-science-in-apologetic-perspective-anthropos/.

———. "ELF 2020: Learning about Jesus with the New Atheists." http://podcast.peterswilliams.com/e/elf-2020-learning-about-jesus-with-the-new-atheists/.

ONLINE PAPERS

Blomberg, Craig L. "How to Approach Apparent Contradictions in the Gospels: A Response to Michael Licona." https://www.equip.org/articles/how-to-approach-apparent-contradictions-in-the-gospels-a-response-to-michael-licona/.

———. "Jesus of Nazareth: How Historians Can Know Him and Why It Matters." https://chab123.wordpress.com/2012/04/15/jesus-of-nazareth-how-historians-can-know-him-and-why-it-matters-by-craig-blomberg/.

Copan, Paul. "Jesus' Followers Fabricated the Stories and Sayings of Jesus." (1998). http://www.paulcopan.com/articles/pdf/Jesus-followers-fabricated-stories-and-sayings-of-Jesus.pdf.

Craig, William Lane. "The Bodily Resurrection of Jesus." https://www.reasonablefaith.org/writings/scholarly-writings/historical-jesus/the-bodily-resurrection-of-jesus.

———. "The Concept of God in Islam and Christianity." http://www.reasonablefaith.org/concept-of-god-in-islam-and-christianity.

———. "The Evidence for Jesus." https://www.reasonablefaith.org/writings/popular-writings/jesus-of-nazareth/the-evidence-for-jesus.

———. "The Historicity of the Empty Tomb of Jesus." https://www.reasonablefaith.org/writings/scholarly-writings/historical-jesus/the-historicity-of-the-empty-tomb-of-jesus.

———. "Jesus' Resurrection." https://www.reasonablefaith.org/writings/scholarly-writings/historical-jesus/jesus-resurrection.

———. "Rediscovering the Historical Jesus: The Evidence for Jesus." https://www.reasonablefaith.org/writings/scholarly-writings/historical-jesus/rediscovering-the-historical-jesus-the-evidence-for-jesus.

———. "Rediscovering the Historical Jesus: Presuppositions and Pretensions of the Jesus Seminar." https://www.reasonablefaith.org/writings/scholarly-writings/historical-jesus/rediscovering-the-historical-jesus-presuppositions-and-pretensions-of-the-j

———. "Visions of Jesus: A Critical Assessment of Gerd Lüdemann's Hallucination Hypothesis." https://www.reasonablefaith.org/writings/scholarly-writings/historical-jesus/visions-of-jesus-a-critical-assessment-of-gerd-ludemanns-hallucination-hypo.

Davis, Stephen T. "The Mad/Bad/God Trilemma: A Reply to Daniel Howard Snyder." https://place.asburyseminary.edu/faithandphilosophy/vol21/iss4/4/.

Geisler, Norman L. "Miraculous Bible Prophecy Fulfillments." https://philosophical11.wordpress.com/2012/09/12/miraculous-bible-prophecy-fulfillments/#more-151.

Habermas, Gary R. "Recent Perspectives on the Reliability of the Gospels." https://www.equip.org/articles/recent-perspectives-on-the-reliability-of-the-gospels/.

———. "Why I Believe the New Testament Is Historically Reliable." https://apologetics.com/why-i-believe-the-new-testament-is-historically-reliable/.

Howard-Snyder, Daniel. "Does Faith Entail Belief?" https://www.academia.edu/11819008/Does_Faith_Entail_Belief_2016_.

Howard-Snyder, Daniel, and Daniel McKaughan. "Faith." https://www.academia.edu/35582270/Faith_2020_.

Humphreys, Colin. "The Star of Bethlehem." https://www.asa3.org/ASA/topics/Astronomy-Cosmology/S&CB%2010-93Humphreys.html.

Koons, Robert C. "The Incompatibility of Naturalism and Scientific Realism." https://www.leaderu.com/offices/koons/docs/natreal.html.

Köstenberger, Andreas J. "April 3, AD 33." https://www.firstthings.com/web-exclusives/2014/04/april-3-ad-33.

Kreeft, Peter. "Jesus: Considering the Options." https://www.bethinking.org/jesus/jesus-considering-the-options.

Lewis, C. S. "The Cardinal Difficulty of Naturalism." http://thecslewis-studygroup.org/wp-content/uploads/2014/07/The-Cardinal-Difficulty-of-Naturalism.pdf.

———. "The Poison of Subjectivism." https://williamwoodall.weebly.com/uploads/1/0/2/2/10226906/the_poison_of_subjectivism.pdf.

———. "What Are We to Make of Jesus Christ?" https://www.xtianity.com/tfc/NTE103/C%20S%20Lewis%20What%20are%20we%20to%20make%20of%20Jesus%20Christ.pdf.

Maier, Paul L. "The Date of the Nativity and the Chronology of Jesus' Life." https://inchristus.com/wp-content/uploads/2010/12/maier-date-of-the-nativity.pdf.

McCracken, Brett. "Understanding the Metamodern Mood." *The Gospel Coalition*, May 30, 2024. https://www.thegospelcoalition.org/article/understanding-metamodern-mood/.

McGrew, Tim. "The Argument from Silence." https://timothymcgrew.com/wp-content/uploads/2024/01/The-Argument-from-Silence-Acta-Analytica-Tim-2013.pdf.

McGrew, Tim, and Lydia McGrew. "The Argument from Miracles: A Cumulative Case for the Resurrection of Jesus of Nazareth." https://lydiamcgrew.com/wp-content/uploads/2023/11/Resurrectionarticlesinglefile.pdf.

McLatchie, Jonathan. "The Nativity Defended." http://crossexamined.org/the-nativity-defended/.

Menuge, Angus J. "Dennett Denied: A Critique of Dennett's Evolutionary Account of Intentionality." October 2003. http://static1.1.sqspcdn.com/static/f/38692/239704/1263390969587/A+Critique+of+Dennetts+Evolutionary+Account+of+Intentionality.pdf.

———. "Libertarian Free Will and the Argument from Reason." https://www.reasonsforgod.org/wp-content/uploads/2012/09/Libertarian-Free-Will-and-The-Argument-From-Reason1.pdf.

Moreland, J. P. "The Historicity of the New Testament." In *Scaling the Secular City: A Defence of Christianity*. Grand Rapids: Baker, 1987. https://www.bethinking.org/is-the-bible-reliable/the-historicity-of-the-new-testament.

Pojman, Louis. "Faith Without Belief?" *Faith and Philosophy* 3.2 (1986) 157–76. https://core.ac.uk/download/pdf/216987356.pdf.

Pruss, Alexander R. "Christian Faith and Belief." http://alexanderpruss.com/papers/FaithAndBelief.html.

Ward, Keith. *Evidence for the Virgin Birth*. Christian Evidence Society. http://christianevidence.org/docs/booklets/evidence_for_the_virgin_birth.pdf.

Weghe, Luuk Van de. "Luke the Physician: Some Notes on the Internal Evidence," *Tyndale Bulletin* 76 (2025) 31–45. https://www.tyndalebulletin.org/article/133200-luke-the-physician-some-notes-on-the-internal-evidence.

———. "Name Recall in the Synoptic Gospels." *New Testament Studies* 69.1 (2023) 95–109. https://www.cambridge.org/core/journals/new-testament-studies/article/name-recall-in-the-synoptic-gospels/9507AEED21DACD1E1AC096B5321699C5.

Weghe, Luuk Van de and Jason Wilson. "Why Name Popularity is a Good Test of Historicity: A Goodness-of-Fit Test Analysis on Names in the Gospels and Acts." *Journal for the Study of the Historical Jesus*, 2024 (Preprint). https://arxiv.org/pdf/2403.14883.

Williams, Peter S. "Christian Leadership in 3D: Leading and Following in the Spiritual Footsteps of Jesus." *Scandinavian Journal for Leadership & Theology* 2025, volume 12. https://www.peterswilliams.com/wp-content/uploads/2025/05/WilliamsChristianLeadershipin3D.pdf.

———. *Digging for Evidence*. Christian Evidence Society. https://christianevidence.org/wp-content/uploads/2016/07/digging_for_evidence.pdf.

———. "The Epistle of St. James vs. Evolutionary Christology." *Theofilos*, Volume 8, 2016:1. https://theofilos.no/wp-content/uploads/2019/09/2c_Academia_Williams_The-Epistle-of-James-vs.-Evolutionary.pdf.

———. "An Interdisciplinary Inquiry into Dating the Fourth Gospel, Part I: John 5:2 and Papyrus 52." *Theofilos*, vol. 13, 2021. https://theofilos.no/wp-content/uploads/2022/02/Theofilos-vol-13-nr-1-2-2021-forum-6-final.pdf.

———. "An Interdisciplinary Inquiry into Dating the Fourth Gospel, Part II: Other Evidence." *Theofilos*, vol. 14, 2023. https://theofilos.no/wp-content/uploads/2023/03/Theofilos-vol-14-nr-1-2-2022-forum-7-230301-publicering.pdf.

———. "A Pre-Modern Reflection Upon the Modernist Foundations of Postmodernism." *Theofilos*, Volume 7, 2015:2. https://www.peterswilliams.com/wp-content/uploads/2016/02/Postmodernism_v5.pdf.

———. "Understanding the Trinity." https://www.bethinking.org/god/understanding-the-trinity.

BOOKS

Alston, William P. *A Realist Conception of Truth*. Ithaca, NY: Cornell University Press, 1996.

Audi, Robert. *Epistemology: A Contemporary Introduction to the Theory of Knowledge*. 3rd ed. London: Routledge, 2010.

Austen, Michael W. *Humility: Rediscovering the Way of Love and Life in Christ*. Grand Rapids, MI: Eerdmans, 2024.

Baggett, David, ed. *Did the Resurrection Happen? A Conversation with Gary Habermas and Antony Flew*. Downers Grove, IL: InterVarsity, 2009.

Bauckham, Richard. *Jesus and the Eyewitnesses: The Gospels as Eyewitness Testimony.* 2nd ed. Grand Rapids, MI: Eerdmans, 2017.
———. *Jesus: A Very Short Introduction.* Oxford: Oxford University Press, 2011.
Barnett, Paul. *The Birth of Christianity: The First Twenty Years.* Grand Rapids, MI: Eerdmans, 2005.
———. *Finding the Historical Christ.* Grand Rapids, MI: Eerdmans, 2009.
———. *Messiah: Jesus—The Evidence of History.* Nottingham: InterVarsity, 2009.
———. *Paul: Missionary of Jesus.* Grand Rapids, MI: Eerdmans, 2008.
Beckwith, Francis J., et al, eds. *To Everyone an Answer: A Case for the Christian Worldview.* Downers Grove, IL: InterVarsity, 2004.
Beverley, James A., and Craig A. Evans. *Getting Jesus Right: How Muslims Get Jesus and Islam Wrong.* Lagoon City, Ontario: Castle Quay, 2015.
Bignon, Guillame. *Confessions of a French Atheist: How God Hijacked My Quest to Disprove the Christian Faith.* Carol Stream, IL: Tyndale, 2022.
Bird, Michael F., et al. *How God Became Jesus: The Real Origins of Belief in Jesus' Divine Nature—A Response to Bart D. Ehrman.* Grand Rapids, MI: Zondervan, 2014.
Blomberg, Craig L. *The Historical Reliability of the Gospels.* 2nd ed. Downers Grove, IL: InterVarsity, 2008.
———. *The Historical Reliability of John's Gospel: Issues & Commentary.* Leicester: Apollos, 2015.
———. *Jesus and the Gospels: An Introduction and Survey,* Third Edition. Nashville: B&H Academic, 2022.
Bock, Darrell L. *Studying the Historical Jesus: A Guide to Sources and Methods.* Leicester: Apollos, 2007.
———. *Who Is Jesus of Nazareth?* Bellingham, WA: Lexham, 2021.
———. *Who Is Jesus? Linking the Historical Jesus with the Christ of Faith.* New York: Howard, 2012.
Bock, Darrell L., with Benjamin I. Simpson. *Jesus According to Scripture: Restoring the Portrait from the Gospels.* 2nd Edition. Grand Rapids, MI: Baker Academic, 2021.
Bock, Darrell L., and Daniel B. Wallace. *Dethroning Jesus: Exposing Popular Culture's Quest to Unseat the Biblical Christ.* Nashville: Thomas Nelson, 2007.
Bock, Darrell L., and Robert L. Webb, eds. *Key Events in the Life of the Historical Jesus: A Collaborative Exploration of Context and Coherence.* Grand Rapids, MI: Eerdmans, 2010.
Bombaro, John J., and Adam S. Francisco. *The Resurrection Fact: Responding to Modern Critics.* Irvine, CA: NRP, 2016.
Bowman, Robert, and Ed Komoszewski. *The Incarnate Christ and His Critics: A Biblical Defense.* Grand Rapids, MI: Kregel Academic & Professional, 2025.
Brierley, Justin. *The Surprising Rebirth of Belief in God: Why New Atheism Grew Old and Secular Thinkers Are Considering Christianity Again.* Carol Stream, IL: Tyndale Elevate, 2023.
Burridge, Richard A. *What Are the Gospels? A Comparison with Graeco-Roman Biography.* 2nd ed. Cambridge: Cambridge University Press, 2004.
Casey, Maurice. *Jesus: Evidence and Argument or Mythicist Myths?* London: Bloomsbury, 2014.
Charlesworth, James H., ed. *Jesus Research: New Methodologies and Perceptions.* Grand Rapids, MI: Eerdmans, 2014.

Comfort, Philip W. *Encountering the Manuscripts: An Introduction to New Testament Paleography and Textual Criticism.* Nashville: B&H, 2005.

Comfort, Philip W., and Jason Driesbach. *The Many Gospels of Jesus: Sorting Out the Story of the Life of Jesus.* Carol Stream, IL: Tyndale, 2008.

Copan, Paul, ed. *Will the Real Jesus Please Stand Up? A Debate between William Lane Craig and John Dominic Crossan.* Grand Rapids, MI: Baker, 1998.

Copan, Paul, and William Lane Craig, eds. *Come Let Us Reason: New Essays in Christian Apologetics.* Nashville: B&H, 2012.

Copan, Paul, and Paul K. Moser, eds. *The Rationality of Theism.* London: Routledge, 2003.

Copan, Paul, and Ronald K. Tacelli, eds. *Jesus' Resurrection: Fact or Figment? A Debate between William Lane Craig and Gerd Lüdemann.* Downers Grove, IL: IVP Academic, 2000.

Cowan, Steven B., ed. *Five Views on Apologetics.* Grand Rapids, MI: Zondervan, 2000.

Craig, William Lane. *Assessing the New Testament Evidence for the Resurrection of Jesus.* New York: Edwin Mellen, 2002.

———. *Did Jesus Rise from the Dead?* Pine Mountain, GA: Impact 360 Institute, 2014.

———. *On Guard for Students: Defending Your Faith with Reason and Precision.* Colorado Springs: David C. Cook, 2015.

———. *The Only Wise God: The Compatibility of Divine Foreknowledge and Human Freedom.* Eugene, OR: Wipf & Stock, 2000.

———. *The Son Rises: Historical Evidence for the Resurrection of Jesus.* Eugene, OR: Wipf & Stock, 2001.

Craig, William Lane, ed. *Philosophy of Religion: A Reader and Guide.* Edinburgh: Edinburgh University Press, 2002.

Craig, William Lane, and Joseph E. Gorra. *A Reasonable Response: Answers to Tough Questions.* Chicago: Moody, 2013.

Craig, William Lane, and J. P. Moreland, eds. *Naturalism: A Critical Analysis.* London: Routledge, 2001.

Crowe, Brandon D. *Was Jesus Really Born of a Virgin?* Philadelphia: Westminster Seminary, 2013.

Davis, Stephen T. *Christian Philosophical Theology.* Oxford: Oxford University Press, 2016.

———. *Risen Indeed: Making Sense of the Resurrection.* London: SPCK, 1993.

Dember, Greg. *Say Hello to Metamodernism!: Understanding Today's Culture of Ironesty, Felt Experience, and Empathic Reflexivity.* Exact Rush Multimedia Publishing, 2024.

Dembski, William A., and Michael L. Licona. *Evidence for God: 50 Arguments for Faith from the Bible, History, Philosophy, and Science.* Grand Rapids, MI: Baker, 2010.

Dickson, John. *Bullies and Saints: An Honest Look at the Good and Evil of Christian History.* Grand Rapids, MI: Zondervan, 2021.

———. *Is Jesus History?* Epsom: Good Book, 2019.

Dunn, James. *Why Believe in Jesus' Resurrection?* London: SPCK, 2016.

Eddy, Paul Rhodes, and Gregory A. Boyd. *The Jesus Legend: A Case for the Reliability of the Synoptic Jesus Tradition.* Grand Rapids, MI: Baker Academic, 2007.

Edwards, Dennis R. *Humility Illuminated: The Biblical Path Back to Christian Character.* Downers Grove, IL: IVP Academic, 2023.

Edwards, Douglas. *The Virgin Birth in History and Faith.* London: Faber & Faber, 1943.

Evans, Craig A. *Fabricating Jesus: How Modern Scholars Distort the Gospels*. Downers Grove, IL: InterVarsity, 2007.
———. *Jesus and His World: The Archaeological Evidence*. London: SPCK, 2012.
———. *Jesus and the Remains of History: Studies in Jesus and the Evidence of Material Culture*. Peabody, MA: Hendrickson, 2015.
Evans, C. Stephen. *Despair: A Moment or a Way of Life?* Downers Grove, IL: InterVarsity, 1973.
———. *The Historical Christ and the Jesus of Faith: The Incarnational Narrative as History*. Oxford: Clarendon, 2004.
———. *Why Believe? Reason and Mystery as Pointers to God*. Grand Rapids, MI: Eerdmans, 1996.
———. *Why Christian Faith Still Makes Sense: A Response to Contemporary Challenges*. Grand Rapids, MI: Baker Academic, 2015.
Evans, Richard J. *In Defence of History*. London: Granta, 2018.
Gallagher, Richard. *Demonic Foes: My Twenty-Five Years as a Psychiatrist Investigating Possessions, Diabolic Attacks, and the Paranormal*. New York: HarperOne, 2022.
Ganssle, Gregory E. *Our Deepest Desires: How the Christian Story Fulfills Human Aspirations*. Downers Grove, IL: IVP Academic, 2017.
———. *A Reasonable God: Engaging the New Face of Atheism*. Waco, TX: Baylor University Press, 2009.
Geisler, Norman L. *Christian Apologetics*. 2nd ed. Grand Rapids, MI: Baker Academic, 2013.
Geisler, Norman L., and Paul D. Feinberg. *Introduction to Philosophy: A Christian Perspective*. Grand Rapids, MI: Baker, 1997.
Geisler, Norman L., and William D. Watkins. *Worlds Apart: A Handbook on World Views*. Second Edition. Eugene, OR: Wipf & Stock, 2003.
Geivett, R. Douglas, and Gary R. Habermas, eds. *In Defence of Miracles: A Comprehensive Case for God's Action in History*. Leicester: Apollos, 1997.
Gilson, Tom, and Carson Weitnauer, eds. *True Reason: Confronting the Irrationality of the New Atheism*. Grand Rapids, MI: Kregel, 2013.
Glass, David H. *Atheism's New Clothes: Exploring and Exposing the Claims of the New Atheists*. Leicester: Apollos, 2012.
Goetz, Stewart, and Charles Taliaferro. *Naturalism*. Grand Rapids, MI: Eerdmans, 2008.
Gresham, Machen, J. *The Virgin Birth of Christ*. James Clarke, 1958.
Grindheim, Sigurd. *Christology in the Synoptic Gospels: God or God's Servant?* London: Continuum, 2012.
Groothuis, Douglas. *Truth Decay: Defending Christianity against the Challenges of Postmodernism*. Downers Grove, IL: InterVarsity, 2000.
Guthrie, Shandon L. *Gods of This World: A Philosophical Discussion and Defense of Christian Demonology*. Eugene, OR: Pickwick, 2018.
Habermas, Gary R. *On the Resurrection*. Vol. 1, *Evidences*. Nashville: B&H Academic, 2024.
———. *On the Resurrection*. Vol. 2, *Refutations*. Nashville: B&H Academic, 2024.
———. *On the Resurrection*. Vol. 3, *Scholarly Perspectives*. Nashville: B&H Academic, 2025.
———. *On the Resurrection*. Vol. 4. Nashville: B&H Academic, forthcoming.
———. *Risen Indeed: A Historical Investigation Into the Resurrection of Jesus*. Bellingham, WA: Lexham, 2021.

———. *The Risen Jesus and Future Hope*. Lanham, MD: Rowman & Littlefield, 2003.
———. *The Historical Jesus: Ancient Evidence for the Life of Christ*. Joplin, MO: College Press, 1996.
Habermas, Gary R., Antony Flew, and Terry L. Miethe, eds. *Did Jesus Rise from the Dead?* Eugene, OR: Wipf & Stock, 2003.
Habermas, Gary R., and Michael L. Licona. *The Case for the Resurrection of Jesus*. Grand Rapids, MI: Kregel, 2004.
Hackett, Stuart C. *The Reconstruction of the Christian Revelation Claim: A Philosophical and Critical Apologetic*. Eugene, OR: Wipf & Stock, 2009.
Hannam, James. *God's Philosophers: How the Medieval World Laid the Foundations of Modern Science*. London: Icon, 2010.
Hill, Charles E. *Who Chose the Books of the New Testament?* Bellingham, WA: Lexham, 2022.
———. *Who Chose the Gospels? Probing the Great Gospel Conspiracy*. Oxford: Oxford University Press, 2010.
Holder, Rodney D. *Ramified Natural Theology in Science and Religion: Moving Forward from Natural Theology* (Routledge Science and Religion). London: Routledge, 2022.
Holland, Tom. *Dominion: The Making of the Western Mind*. London: Abacus, 2020.
Howard, Jeremy Royal, ed. *The Gospels and Acts. The Holman Apologetics Commentary on the Bible*. Nashville: Holman, 2013.
Hunter, James Davison, and Paul Nedelisky. *Science and the Good: The Tragic Quest for the Foundations of Morality*. New Haven, CT: Yale University Press, 2018.
Hutchinson, Robert J. *Searching for Jesus: New Discoveries in the Quest for Jesus of Nazareth—And How They Confirm the Gospel Accounts*. Nashville: Nelson, 2015.
Joad, C. E. M. *The Recovery of Belief: A Restatement of Christian Philosophy*. London: Faber & Faber, 1952.
Jones, Timothy Paul. *Misquoting Truth: A Guide to the Fallacies of Bart Ehrman's Misquoting Jesus*. Downers Grove, IL: InterVarsity, 2007.
Kaiser, Jr. Walter C. *The Messiah in the Old Testament*. Grand Rapids, MI: Zondervan, 1995.
Keener, Craig S., and Edward T. Wright, eds. *Biographies and Jesus: What Does It Mean for the Gospels to Be Biographies?* Lexington, KY: Emeth, 2016.
Kitchen, K. A. *On the Reliability of the Old Testament*. Grand Rapids, MI: Eerdmans, 2006.
Köstenberger, Andreas, ed. *Whatever Happened to Truth?* Wheaton, IL: Crossway, 2005.
Köstenberger, Andreas J., and Alexander Stewart. *The First Days of Jesus: The Story of the Incarnation*. Wheaton, IL: Crossway, 2015.
Köstenberger, Andreas J., Darrell L. Bock, and John Chatraw. *Truth Matters: Confident Faith in a Confusing World*. Nashville: B&H Academic, 2014.
Köstenberger, Andreas J., Justin Taylor, and Alexander Stewart. *The Final Days of Jesus: The Most Important Week of the Most Important Person Who Ever Lived*. Wheaton, IL: Crossway, 2014.
Kreeft, Peter. *Between Heaven and Hell: A Dialog Somewhere Beyond Death with John F. Kennedy, C. S. Lewis and Aldous Huxley*. 2nd ed. Downers Grove, IL: InterVarsity, 2008.
Larmer, Robert A. *The Legitimacy of Miracle*. Lanham, MD: Lexington, 2014.

Levering, Matthew. *Did Jesus Rise from the Dead? Historical and Theological Reflections*. Oxford: Oxford University Press, 2019.

Lewis, C. S. *Miracles*. 2nd ed. London: Fount, 1998.

Licona, Michael R. *Paul Meets Muhammad: A Christian-Muslim Debate on the Resurrection*. Grand Rapids, MI: Baker, 2006.

———. *The Resurrection of Jesus: A New Historiographical Approach*. Downers Grove, IL: InterVarsity, 2010.

Loke, Andrew Ter Ern. *Investigating the Resurrection of Jesus Christ: A New Transdisciplinary Approach* (Routledge New Critical Thinking in Religion, Theology and Biblical Studies). London: Routledge, 2020.

———. *The Origin of Divine Christology*. Cambridge: Cambridge University Press, 2017.

———. *Studies on the Origin of Divine and Resurrection Christology* (Studies in Early Christology Book 2). Eugene, OR: Cascade, 2023.

May, Peter. *The Search for God and the Path to Persuasion*. Glasgow: Malcolm Down, 2016.

McGrath, Alister. *Making Sense of the Cross*. Leicester: InterVarsity, 1992.

———. *Mere Discipleship: On Growing in Wisdom and Hope*. London: SPCK, 2018.

———. *The Passionate Intellect: Christian Faith and the Discipleship of the Mind*. Downers Grove, IL: InterVarsity, 2010.

McGrew, Lydia. *The Eye of the Beholder: The Gospel of John as Historical Reportage*. Tampa, FL: DeWard, 2021.

———. *Hidden in Plain View: Undesigned Coincidences in the Gospels and Acts*. Tampa, FL: DeWard, 2017.

———. *Testimonies to the Truth: Why You Can Trust the Gospels*. Tampa, FL: DeWard, 2023.

Meister, Chad V. *Building Belief: Constructing Faith from the Ground Up*. Eugene, OR: Wipf & Stock, 2009.

Miller, Troy A. ed. *Jesus: The Final Days*. London: SPCK, 2008.

Mounce, William D. *Why I Trust the Bible: Answers to Real Questions and Doubts People Have About the Bible*. Grand Rapids, MI: Zondervan Reflective, 2021.

Moreland, J. P. *Consciousness and the Existence of God: A Theistic Argument*. London: Routledge, 2009.

———. *Love the Lord with All Your Mind: The Role of Reason in the Life of the Soul*. Colorado Springs: NavPress, 1997.

———. *The Recalcitrant Imago Dei: Human Persons and the Failure of Naturalism*. London: SCM, 2009.

———. *Scaling the Secular City: A Defence of Christianity*. Grand Rapids, MI: Baker, 1987.

———. *Scientism and Secularism: Learning to Respond to a Dangerous Ideology*. Wheaton, IL: Crossway, 2018.

Moreland, J. P., and William Lane Craig. *Philosophical Foundations for a Christian Worldview*. 2nd ed. Downers Grove, IL: IVP Academic, 2017.

Moreland, J. P., and Brandon Rickabaugh. *The Substance of Consciousness*. Oxford: Wiley Blackwell, 2023.

Morris, Thomas V. *Making Sense of It All: Pascal and the Meaning of Life*. Grand Rapids, MI: Eerdmans, 1998.

———. *Our Idea of God: An Introduction to Philosophical Theology*. Downers Grove, IL: InterVarsity, 1991.

Morrow, Jonathan. *Questioning the Bible: 11 Major Challenges to the Bible's Authority*. Chicago: Moody, 2014.

Murray, Michael J., ed. *Reason for the Hope Within*. Grand Rapids, MI: Eerdmans, 1999.

Nagel, Thomas. *Mind and Cosmos: Why the Materialist Neo-Darwinian Conception of Nature is Almost Certainly False*. Oxford: Oxford University Press, 2012.

Neufeld, Thomas R. Yoder. *Recovering Jesus: The Witness of the New Testament*. Grand Rapids, MI: SPCK, 2007.

Nicholl, Colin R. *The Great Christ Comet: Revealing the True Star of Bethlehem*. Wheaton, IL: Crossway, 2015.

Nicholi, Armand, Jr. *The Question of God: C. S. Lewis and Sigmund Freud Debate God, Love, Sex, and the Meaning of Life*. New York: Free Press, 2002.

Overman, Dean L. *A Case for the Divinity of Jesus: Examining the Earliest Evidence*. Plymouth: Rowman & Littlefield, 2009.

Owen, H. P. *Christian Theism: A Study in its Basic Principles*. Edinburgh: T&T Clark, 1984.

Pitre, Brant. *The Case for Jesus: The Biblical and Historical Evidence for Christ*. New York: Image, 2016.

Plantinga, Alvin. *Warranted Christian Belief*. Oxford: Oxford University Press, 2000.

Polkinghorne, John. *Science and Christian Belief: Theological Reflections of a Bottom-Up Thinker*. London: SPCK, 1994.

Porter, Stanley E. *How We Got the New Testament: Text, Transmission, Translation*. Grand Rapids, MI: Baker Academic, 2013.

Provan, Iain, V. Philips Long and Tremper Longman III. *A Biblical History of Israel*. Second Edition. Louisville, Kentucky: WJK, 2015.

Quarles, Charles. *Midrash Criticism: Introduction and Appraisal*. Lanham, MD: University Press of America, 1998.

Qureshi, Nabeel. *No God but One: Allah or Jesus?* Grand Rapids, MI: Zondervan 2016.

Rasmussen, Joshua, and Kevin Vallier, eds. *A New Theist Response to the New Atheism*. London: Routledge, 2020.

Redford, John. *Born of a Virgin: Proving the Miracle from the Gospels*. London: St Pauls, 2007.

Reppert, Victor. *C. S. Lewis's Dangerous Idea: In Defense of the Argument From Reason*. Downers Grove, IL: IVP Academic, 2009.

Roberts, Mark D. *Can We Trust the Gospels?* Wheaton, IL: Crossway, 2007.

Rosenberg, Alex. *An Atheists' Guide to Reality*. New York: Norton, 2013.

Schmidt., T. C. *Josephus and Jesus: New Evidence for the One Called Christ*. Oxford: Oxford University Press, 2025. https://academic.oup.com/book/60034.

Scott, Douglas D. *Is Jesus of Nazareth the Predicted Messiah? A Historical-Evidential Approach to Specific Old Testament Messianic Prophecies and Their New Testament Fulfillments*. Eugene, OR: Wipf & Stock, 2019.

Shumack, Richard. *The Wisdom of Islam and the Foolishness of Christianity: A Christian Response to Nine Objections to Christianity by Muslim Philosophers*. Sydney: Island View, 2014.

Sinnott-Armstrong, Walter. *Think Again: How to Reason and Argue*. London: Pelican, 2018.

Sire, James W. *The Universe Next Door—A Basic Worldview Catalog*. 6th ed. Downers Grove, IL: IVP Academic, 2020.
Smith, Christian. *Atheist Overreach: What Atheism Can't Deliver*. Oxford: Oxford University Press, 2019.
Smith, Mark D. *The Final Days of Jesus: The Thrill of Defeat, The Agony of Victory: A Classical Historian Explores Jesus's Arrest, Trial, and Execution*. Cambridge: Lutterworth, 2018.
Stecher, Carl and Craig Blomberg, with contributions by Richard Carrier and Peter S. Williams. *Resurrection: Faith or Fact? A Scholars' Debate between a Skeptic and a Christian*. Durham, NC: Pitchstone, 2019.
Stewart, Robert B., and Gary R. Habermas, eds. *Memories of Jesus: A Critical Appraisal of James D. G. Dunn's* Jesus Remembered. Nashville: B&H Academic, 2010.
Stokes, Mitch. *A Shot of Faith (to the Head): Be a Confident Believer in an Age of Cranky Atheists*. Nashville: Thomas Nelson, 2012.
Strauss, Mark L. *Four Portraits, One Jesus: A Survey of Jesus and the Gospels*, 2nd Edition. Grand Rapids, MI: Zondervan Academic, 2020.
Strobel, Lee. *The Case for Christ*. 2nd ed. Grand Rapids, MI: Zondervan, 2016.
———. *In Defence of Jesus*. Grand Rapids, MI: Zondervan, 2016.
Swinburne, Richard. *The Resurrection of God Incarnate*. Oxford: Clarendon, 2003.
———. *Was Jesus God?* Oxford: Oxford University Press, 2008.
Taliaferro, Charles. *Consciousness and the Mind of God*. Cambridge: Cambridge University Press, 1994.
Taylor, James E. *Introducing Apologetics: Cultivating Christian Commitment*. Grand Rapids, MI: Baker Academic, 2013.
Vermes, Geza. *The Resurrection*. London: Penguin, 2008.
Wallace, J. Warner. *Cold Case Christianity: A Homicide Detective Investigates the Claims of the Gospels*. Updated and exp. ed. Colorado Springs: David C. Cook, 2023.
Wenham, David. *Did St Paul Get Jesus Right?: The Gospel According to Paul*. Oxford: Lion, 2011.
Wenham, John. *Easter Enigma: Are the Resurrection Accounts in Conflict?* 2nd ed. London: Paternoster, 1992.
Wilkins, Michael J., and J. P. Moreland, eds. *Jesus Under Fire: Modern Scholarship Reinvents the Historical Jesus*. Grand Rapids, MI: Zondervan, 1995.
Willard, Dallas. *Knowing Christ Today: How We Can Trust Spiritual Knowledge*. New York: HarperOne, 2009.
Williams, Peter J. *Can We Trust the Gospels?* Wheaton, IL: Crossway, 2018.
Williams, Peter S. *Apologetics in 3D: Essays on Apologetics and Spirituality*. Eugene, OR: Wipf & Stock, 2021.
———. *Behold the Man: Essays on the Historical Jesus*. Eugene, OR: Wipf & Stock, 2024.
———. *The Case for Angels*. Carlisle, Cumbria: Paternoster, 2002.
———. *C.S. Lewis vs. the New Atheists*. Milton Keynes: Paternoster, 2013.
———. *A Faithful Guide to Philosophy: A Christian Introduction to the Love of Wisdom*. Eugene, OR: Wipf & Stock, 2019.
———. *Getting at Jesus: A Comprehensive Critique of Neo-Atheist Nonsense about the Jesus of History*. Eugene, OR: Wipf & Stock, 2019.
———. *I Wish I Could Believe in Meaning: A Response to Nihilism*. Southampton: Damaris, 2005.

———. *Outgrowing God? A Beginner's Guide to Richard Dawkins and the God Debate.* Eugene, OR: Cascade, 2020.

———. *A Sceptic's Guide to Atheism.* Milton Keynes: Paternoster, 2009.

———. *Understanding Jesus: Five Ways to Spiritual Enlightenment.* Milton Keynes: Paternoster, 2011.

Witherington, Ben. *The Jesus Quest: The Third Search for the Jew of Nazareth.* 2nd Revised Edition. Downers Grove, IL: IVP Academic, 2010.

Wright, N. T. *The Resurrection of the Son of God.* London: SPCK, 2003.

———. *Surprised by Hope: Rethinking Heaven, the Resurrection, and the Mission of the Church.* New York: HarperOne, 2018.

Bibliography

Abel, David L. *The First Gene*. New York: Long View Press—Academic, 2011.

———, ed. *Primordial Prescription: The Most Plaguing Problem of Life Origin Science*. New York: Long View Press—Academic, 2015.

Adams, Douglas. "The Hitch-Hiker's Guide to the Galaxy (Fit the Sixth)." https://www.clivebanks.co.uk/THHGTTG/THHGTTGradio6.htm.

Adler, Mortimer J. *Adler's Philosophical Dictionary*. New York: Scribner, 1995.

———. *Great Books of the Western World*. Encyclopedia Britannica, 1991.

———. *Six Great Ideas*. New York: Collier, 1981.

Aeschliman, Michael D. *The Restoration of Man: C.S. Lewis and the Continuing Case Against Scientism*. 3rd ed. Seattle, WA: Discovery Institute, 2019.

Akker, Robin van der, and Timotheus Vermeulen. "Periodising the 2000s, or, the Emergence of Metamodernism." In *Metamodernism: Historicity, Affect and Depth after Postmodernism*, edited by Robin van der Akker et al., 1–19. London: Rowman & Littlefield, 2017.

Alberts, Bruce. "Science and Human Needs." https://brucealberts.ucsf.edu/publications/NAS2000.pdf.

All Grey Matters. "'Argument from Ignorance' Fallacy—Quick Explanation." YouTube video, February 25, 2019. https://youtu.be/XaGEjZDgFJo.

Alston, William P. *A Realist Conception of Truth*. Ithaca, NY: Cornell University Press, 1996.

———. "Religious Language and Verificationism." In *The Rationality of Theism*, edited by Paul Copan and Paul K. Moser, 17–34. London: Routledge, 2003.

Amoeba Sisters. "Genetic Drift." YouTube video, June 8, 2017. https://www.youtube.com/watch?v=W0TM4LQmoZY.

Anderson, James N. "Why I Am Not a Panentheist." https://www.proginosko.com/2012/01/why-i-am-not-a-panentheist/.

Andersen, Lene Rachel. *Bildung: Keep Growing*. Copenhagen: Nordic Bildung, 2020.

———. *Metamodernity: Meaning and Hope in a Complex World*. Copenhagen: Nordic Bildung, 2019.

Anderson, Eric H. "Origin Stories—RNA, DNA, and a Dose of Imagination." *Evolution News and Science Today*, June 12, 2020. https://evolutionnews.org/2020/06/origin-stories-rna-dna-and-a-dose-of-imagination/.

Anderson, Tawa J., et al. *An Introduction to Christian Worldview: Pursuing God's Perspective in a Pluralistic World*. Leicester: Apollos, 2017.

Anscombe, G. E. M. "Modern Moral Philosophy." In *Virtue Ethics*, edited by Roger Crisp and Michael Slote, 26–44. Oxford: Oxford University Press, 1997.
Apologikk - Apologetikkens logikk, "Peter S Williams vs Einar Duenger Bøhn." YouTube video. https://www.youtube.com/@Apologikk/videos.
Aquinas, Thomas. "The Five Ways." *Summa Theologica*. https://homepages.uc.edu/~martinj/The%20Infinite/Aquinas%20-%20the%20Five%20Ways%20-%20SummaTheologica%20P1Q2A3.pdf.
Archive of Recorded Church Music. "BBC TV Coronation of Queen Elizabeth II: Westminster Abbey 1953 (William McKie)." YouTube video, Jun 2, 2018. https://www.youtube.com/watch?v=52NTjasbmgw.
Armstrong, Dave. *The Word Set in Stone: How Archaeology, Science, and History Back Up the Bible*. El Cajon, CA: Catholic Answers Press, 2023. Kindle.
"The Ascent of Man." BBC, May 5, 1973. https://www.bbc.com/historyofthebbc/anniversaries/may/the-ascent-of-man/.
Ash, Lamorna. *Don't Forget We're Here Forever: A New Generation's Search for Religion*. Bloomsbury, 2025 (Kindle edition), 16.
Atkins, Peter. *On Being*. Oxford: Oxford University Press, 2011.
Audi, Robert. *Epistemology: A Contemporary Introduction to the Theory of Knowledge*. 3rd ed. London: Routledge, 2010.
Augustine. *Confessions*. Translated by R. S. Pine-Coffin. London: Penguin, 1981.
Austen, Michael W. *Humility: Rediscovering the Way of Love and Life in Christ*. Grand Rapids, MI: Eerdmans, 2024.
Axe, Douglas. "The Case against a Darwinian Origin of Protein Folds." *BIO-Complexity* 1 (2010) 1–12. https://bio-complexity.org/ojs/index.php/main/article/view/BIO-C.2010.1.
———. "Don't Be Intimidated by Keith Fox on Intelligent Design." *Evolution News and Science Today*, May 19, 2017. https://evolutionnews.org/2017/05/dont-be-intimidated-by-keith-fox-on-intelligent-design/.
———. "Estimating the Prevalence of Protein Sequences Adopting Functional Enzyme Folds." *Journal of Molecular Biology* 341 (2004) 1295–1315. https://www.sciencedirect.com/science/article/abs/pii/S0022283604007624.
———. "Extreme Functional Sensitivity to Conservative Amino Acid Changes on Enzyme Exteriors." *Journal of Molecular Biology* 301 (2000) 585–95. https://www.sciencedirect.com/science/article/abs/pii/S00 22283600939974?via%3Dihub.
———. "Losing the Forest by Fixating on the Trees—A Response to Venema's Critique of Undeniable." *Evolution News and Science Today*, February 6, 2018. https://evolutionnews.org/2018/02/losing-the-forest-by-fixating-on-the-trees-a-response-to-venemas-critique-of-undeniable/.
Axe, Douglas D., and Ann K. Gauger. "Model and Laboratory Demonstrations That Evolutionary Optimization Works Well Only if Preceded by Invention—Selection Itself Is Not Inventive." BIO-Complexity 2 (2015) 1–13. https://bio-complexity.org/ojs/index.php/main/article/viewArticle/BIO-C.2015.2.
Ayer, A. J. *Language, Truth and Logic*. 2nd edition. London: Victor Gollancz, 1946.
Baehr, Jason. *Deep in Thought: A Practical Guide to Teaching for Intellectual Virtues*. Cambridge, MA: Harvard Education Press, 2021.
Baggett, David, and Jerry L. Walls. *Good God: The Theistic Foundations of Morality*. Oxford: Oxford University Press, 2011.

Baggini, Julian. *Atheism: A Very Short Introduction*. Oxford: Oxford University Press, 2003.

Baird, Iain. "The Beginning of the End of Black and White Television." Science and Media Museum, Jan 6, 2014. https://blog.scienceandmediamuseum.org.uk/the-decline-of-black-and-white-tv/.

Bandea, Christian. *God of the Details: The Scientific Cover-Up of Intelligent Design*. N.p.: Independently published, 2021.

Bannister, Andy. *The Atheist Who Didn't Exist: Or the Dreadful Consequences of Bad Arguments* (Tenth Anniversary Edition). Downers Grove, IL: VP, 2025.

———. *How to Talk About Jesus Without Looking Like an Idiot: A Panic-Free Guide to Having Natural Conversations About Your Faith*. Carol Stream, IL: Tyndale Elevate/IVP, 2023.

Barnes, Luke. "Fine-Tuning in the Context of Bayesian Theory Testing." *European Journal for Philosophy of Science*, 8(2):253–269, 2018. https://arxiv.org/pdf/1707.03965.

———. "Good God!" https://inference-review.com/article/good-god.

———. "Why I'm No Longer a Young Earth Creationist." https://www.premierchristianity.com/features/why-im-no-longer-a-young-earth-creationist/5288.article.

Barnes, Luke, and Sabine Hossenfelder. "The Fine Tuning of the Universe: Was the Cosmos Made for Us?" https://www.thebigconversation.show/finetuning.

Barnett, Paul. *The Birth of Christianity: The First Twenty Years*. Grand Rapids, MI: Eerdmans, 2005.

Barthes, Roland. "The Death of the Author." https://archive.org/details/TheDeathOfTheAuthor/page/n1/mode/2up & https://sites.tufts.edu/english292b/files/2012/01/Barthes-The-Death-of-the-Author.pdf.

Baysan, Umut. "Does Panpsychism Explain Mental Causation?" *Erkenn* (25th May, 2024). https://link.springer.com/article/10.1007/s10670-024-00816-5.

Beale, G. K. *The Erosion of Inerrancy in Evangelicalism: Responding to New Challenges to Biblical Authority*. Wheaton, IL: Crossway, 2008.

Bechly, Günter. "Fossil Friday." *Evolution News and Science Today*. https://evolutionnews.org/tag/fossil-friday/.

Bechly, Günter, and Stephen C. Meyer. "The Fossil Record and Universal Common Ancestry." In *Theistic Evolution*, edited by J. P. Moreland et al., 331–62. Wheaton, IL: Crossway, 2017.

Beck, W. David. *Does God Exist? A History of Answers to the Question*. Downers Grove, IL: IVP Academic, 2021.

———. "God's Existence." In *In Defence of Miracles: A Comprehensive Case for God's Action in History*, edited by R. Douglas Geivett and Gary R. Habermas, 149–62. Leicester: Apollos, 1997. https://digitalcommons.liberty.edu/cgi/viewcontent.cgi?article=1086&context=sor_fac_pubs.

Beckwith, Francis J. *David Hume's Argument Against Miracles: A Critical Analysis*. Lanham, MD: University Press of America, 1989.

———. *Law, Darwinism, and Public Education: The Establishment Clause and the Challenge of Intelligent Design*. Oxford: Rowman & Littlefield, 2003.

———. "Moral Law, the Mormon Universe, and the Nature of the Right We Ought to Choose." In *The New Mormon Challenge: Responding to the Latest Defences of a Fast-Growing Movement*, edited by Francis J. Beckwith, et al. Grand Rapids, MI: Zondervan, 2002, 219–241.

———. "Theism, Miracles, and the Modern Mind." In *The Rationality of Theism*, edited by Paul Copan and Paul K. Moser, 221–36. London: Routledge, 2003.

———. "Why I Am Not a Moral Relativist." In *Why I Am a Christian: Leading Thinkers Explain Why They Believe*, edited by Norman L. Geisler and Paul K. Hoffman, 17–32. Rev. and exp. ed. Grand Rapids, MI: Baker, 2006. https://appearedtoblogly.wordpress.com/wp-content/uploads/2011/05/beckwith-francis-22why-i-am-not-a-moral-relativist22.pdf.

Beckwith, Francis J., et al. *The New Mormon Challenge: Responding to the Latest Defences of a Fast-Growing Movement*, edited by Grand Rapids, MI: Zondervan, 2002.

Beckwith, Francis J., and Gregory Koukl. *Relativism: Feet Firmly Planted in Mid-Air*. Grand Rapids, MI: Baker, 1998.

Behe, Michael J. "Appendix C: Assembling the Bacterial Flagellum." In *The Edge of Evolution: The Search for the Limits of Darwinism*, 261–68. New York: Free Press, 2007.

———. "Appendix: Clarifying Perspective." In *Darwin Devolves: The New Science about DNA That Challenges Evolution*, 283–301. San Francisco: HarperOne, 2020.

———. *Darwin's Black Box: The Biochemical Challenge to Evolution*. 10th Anniversary 2nd ed. New York: Free Press, 2006.

———. *Darwin Devolves: The New Science about DNA That Challenges Evolution*. San Francisco: HarperOne, 2020.

———. "Darwinism Gone Wild: Neither Sequence Similarity nor Common Descent Address a Claim of Intelligent Design." *Evolution News and Science Today*, April 19, 2007. https://evolutionnews.org/2007/04/darwinism_gone_wild_neither_se/.

———. "Evidence for Intelligent Design From Biochemistry." *Intelligent Design*, August 10, 1996. https://www.discovery.org/a/51/.

———. "Experimental Evolution, Loss-of-Function Mutations, And 'The First Rule of Adaptive Evolution.'" *The Quarterly Review of Biology* 85 (2010) 419–45. https://www.discovery.org/a/experimental-evolution-loss-of-function-mutations-and-the-first-rule-of-adaptive-evolution/.

———. "Irreducible Complexity: Obstacle to Darwinian Evolution." https://www.lehigh.edu/~inbios/Faculty/Behe/PDF/Behe_chapter.pdf.

———. "A Malodorous Argument for Darwinian Evolution." *Evolution News and Science Today*, March 1, 2010. https://evolutionnews.org/2010/03/a_malodorous_argument_for_darw/.

———. "Michael Behe Takes on the Darwin Add-Ons." https://idthefuture.com/1206/.

———. "The Modern Intelligent Design Hypothesis: Breaking Rules." *Philosophia Christi* 3 (2001) 165–79.

———. *A Mousetrap for Darwin: Michael J. Behe Answers His Critics*. Seattle, WA: Discovery Institute, 2020. Kindle.

———. "'Resurrected' Flagella Were Just Unplugged." *Evolution News and Science Today*, March 3, 2015. https://evolutionnews.org/2015/03/resurrected_fla/.

———. "Waiting Longer for Two Mutations: Published Letter in Response to Durrett & Schmidt." *Genetics* 181 (2009) 819–20. https://www.ncbi.nlm.nih.gov/pmc/articles/PMC2644969/.

Behe, Michael J., and David Snoke. "Simulating Evolution by Gene Duplication of Protein Features That Require Multiple Amino Acid Residues." *Protein Science* 13 (2004) 2651–64. https://www.ncbi.nlm.nih.gov/pmc/articles/PMC2286568/.

Beilby, James K. "Divine Hiddenness: Epistemic and Soteriological." In *Christianity Contested: Replies to Critics' Toughest Objections*, edited by Paul Copan and Stewart E. Kelly, 164–200. Eugene, OR: Cascade, 2024. Kindle.
BeliefMap, "About Mormonism (it's not Christian)." https://beliefmap.org/mormonism/mormonism-christian-or-cult.
———. "Did Paul Simply Hallucinate Jesus's Appearing to Him?" https://beliefmap.org/paul/believe/jesus/appear/hallucination.
———. "Infinity/Impossible/Paradoxes." https://beliefmap.org/infinity/impossible/paradoxes.
Bell, Elizabeth A., et al. "Potentially Biogenic Carbon Preserved in a 4.1 Billion-Year-Old Zircon." *PNAS*, October 19, 2015. https://www.pnas.org/doi/10.1073/pnas.1517557112.
Bergman, Jerry. *Poor Design: An Invalid Argument against Intelligent Design*. Tulsa, OK: BP Books, 2019.
Berlinski, David. *The Deniable Darwin & Other Essays*. Edited by David Klinghoffer. Seattle, WA: Discovery Institute, 2009.
———. "On the Origins of Life." *Intelligent Design*, February 1, 2006. https://www.discovery.org/a/3209/.
Beverley, James A. *Mormon Crisis: Anatomy of a Failing Religion*. Pickering, Ontario: Castle Quay, 2013.
Bird, Michael F. "Did Jesus Think He Was God?" In *How God Became Jesus: The Real Origins of Belief in Jesus' Divine Nature—A Response to Bart D. Ehrman*, by Michael F. Bird, et al., 45–70. Grand Rapids, MI: Zondervan, 2014.
Bird, Michael F., et al. *How God Became Jesus: The Real Origins of Belief in Jesus' Divine Nature—A Response to Bart D. Ehrman*. Grand Rapids, MI: Zondervan, 2014.
Bishop, James. "Historical Problems with Islam's View of Jesus' Crucifixion." *Reasons for Jesus*, Sep 28, 2019. https://reasonsforjesus.com/historical-problems-with-islams-view-of-jesus-crucifixion/.
Bishop, Robert. "The Extended Synthesis (Reviewing 'Darwin's Doubt': Robert Bishop, Part 1)." BioLogos (blog), September 1, 2014. http://biologos.org/blogs/archive/the-extented-sythesis-reviewing-darwins-doubt-robert-bishop-part-1.
Blomberg, Craig L. *The Historical Reliability of the Gospels*. 2nd ed. Leicester: Apollos, 2007.
———. *The Historical Reliability of John's Gospel: Issues and Commentary*. Leicester: Apollos, 2001.
Boa, Kenneth D., and Robert M. Bowman Jr. *Faith Has Its Reasons: An Integrative Approach to Defending Christianity*. 2nd ed. Milton Keynes: Paternoster, 2000. http://richardghowe.com/index_htm_files/BoaBowmanFaithHasItsReasons.pdf.
Bock, Darrell L. *Studying the Historical Jesus*. Leicester: Apollos, 2002.
———. *Who Is Jesus? Linking the Historical Jesus with the Christ of Faith*. New York: Howard, 2012.
Boethius. *The Consolation of Philosophy*. Book 3. https://www.gutenberg.org/files/14328/14328-h/14328-h.htm.
Boice, James. "Who Were the Disciples on the Road to Emmaus?" Christianity.com, Aug 5, 2019. https://www.christianity.com/jesus/death-and-resurrection/resurrection/who-were-the-disciples-on-the-road-to-emmaus.html.
Bond, Helen K. *The Historical Jesus: A Guide for the Perplexed*. Edinburgh: T&T Clark, 2012.

Bowman, Robert. *Jesus' Resurrection and Joseph's Visions: Examining the Foundations of Christianity and Mormonism*. Tampa, FL: DeWard, 2020.

Bowman, Robert, and Ed Komoszewski. *The Incarnate Christ and His Critics: A Biblical Defense*. Grand Rapids, MI: Kregel Academic & Professional, 2025.

Burningham, Kay. *An American Fraud: One Lawyer's Case Against Mormonism*. Revised first edition. Amica Veritatis, 2011.

Burson, Scott R. and Jerry L. Walls. *C. S. Lewis & Francis Schaeffer: Lessons for a New Century from the Most Influential Apologists of Our Time*. Downers Grove, IL: IVP, 1998.

Bracht, John. "Natural Selection as an Algorithm: Why Darwinian Processes Lack the Information Necessary to Evolve Complex Life." *Perspectives on Science and Christian Belief* 54 (2002) 264–69.

Bradford, Daniel. "Cardiff University 'Does God Exist?' Debate." YouTube video. https://www.youtube.com/watch?v=wWhkJZw4inY.

Bradshaw, David. "Introduction." In *Natural Theology in the Eastern Orthodox Tradition*, edited by David Bradshaw and Richard Swinburne, 1–22. St. Paul, MN: Iota, 2021.

Brent, Fr. James, O. P. "Natural Theology" https://iep.utm.edu/theo-nat/.

Brierley, Justin and Peter Byrom. *The Surprising Rebirth of Belief in God: Why New Atheism Grew Old and Secular Thinkers Are Considering Christianity Again*. Carol Stream, IL: Tyndale Elevate, 2023.

Brierley, Justin and Peter Byrom. "A Goldilocks Universe - The surprising science pointing to God." *The Surprising Rebirth of Belief in God, the Podcast*. https://justinbrierley.com/surprisingrebirth/episode-19-a-goldilocks-universe-the-surprising-science-pointing-to-god/.

Bronowski, J. *The Ascent of Man*. London: British Broadcasting Corporation, 1974.

Broom, Neil. *How Blind Is the Watchmaker? Nature's Design & the Limits of Naturalistic Science*. Leicester, UK: InterVarsity, 2001.

Brown, Olen R., and David A. Hullender. "Neo-Darwinism Must Mutate to Survive." *Progress in Biophysics & Molecular Biology* 179 (2023) 24–38. https://www.sciencedirect.com/science/article/abs/pii/S0079610722000347.

Bruce, F. F. *The New Testament Documents: Are They Reliable?* https://www.cob-net.org/compare/nt-documents-reliable-bruce.pdf.

Buras, Todd, and Michael Cantrell. "C. S. Lewis's Argument from Nostalgia: A New Argument from Desire." In *Two Dozen (Or So) Arguments for God*, edited by Jerry L. Walls and Trent Dougherty, 356–71. Oxford: Oxford University Press, 2018.

Burgess, Stuart. "Why the Ankle-Foot Complex Is a Masterpiece of Engineering and a Rebuttal of 'Bad Design' Arguments." *BioComlexity* 2 (2022) 1–10. https://bio-complexity.org/ojs/index.php/main/article/view/BIO-C.2022.3/BIO-C.2022.3.

Buriani, Stephen. "Do We Need a New Theory of Evolution?" *The Guardian*, June 28, 2022. https://www.theguardian.com/science/2022/jun/28/do-we-need-a-new-theory-of-evolution.

Burnett, David. *Clash of Worlds: What Christians Can Do in a World of Cultures in Conflict*. London: Monarch, 2002.

Butler, Christopher. *Postmodernism: A Very Short Introduction*. Oxford: Oxford University Press, 2002.

C. S. Lewis Essays. "C. S. Lewis - De Futilitate." YouTube video, November 14, 2021. https://www.youtube.com/watch?v=-4N5ZrMiRLw&t=167s.

Cabrol, Nathalie A. *The Secret Life of the Universe: An Astrobiologist's Search for the Origins and Frontiers of Life*. London: Simon & Schuster, 2025.
Camus, Albert. *The Myth of Sisyphus*. Translated by Justin O'Brien. London: Penguin, 1975.
Carnap, Rudolph. "Psychology in Physical Language." https://web.stanford.edu/~paulsko/papers/Carn.pdf.
Carroll, Sean. *The Big Picture: On the Origins of Life, Meaning, and the Universe Itself*. Oxford: OneWorld, 2017.
Carson, D. A. *The Gagging of God: Christianity Confronts Pluralism*. Grand Rapids, MI: Zondervan Academic, 2009. Kindle.
———. *The Intolerance of Tolerance*. Grand Rapids, MI: Eerdmans, 2013.
Caruso, Gregg D., ed. *Science & Religion: 5 Questions*. New York: Automatic, 2014.
Casey, Maurice. *Jesus: Evidence and Argument or Mythicist Myths?* London: Bloomsbury, 2014.
Cavanaugh, William T. *The Myth of Religious Violence: Secular Ideology and the Roots of Modern Conflict*. Oxford: Oxford University Press, 2009.
Cave, Peter. *Humanism*. Oxford: OneWorld, 2009.
CCA. "Phenomenal Conservatism, Evidentialism, and Religious Epistemology (Dr. Chris Tucker)." YouTube video. Streamed live August 17, 2020. 59:50. https://youtu.be/ LgBlLnT3h38.
Cerebral Faith. "Why the Divisibility of Time Is Irrelevant to the Kalam Cosmological Argument." https://cerebralfaith.net/why-the-divisibility-of-time-is-irrelevant-to-the-kalam-cosmological-argument/.
Chalmers, David. "Facing up to the Problem of Consciousness." *Journal of Consciousness Studies*, 2.3 (1995) 200–19.
Chamberlain, Theodore J., and Christopher Hall. *Realized Religion: Research on the Relationship between Religion and Health*. Radnor, PA: Templeton Foundation, 2000.
Chapman, Allan. *Slaying the Dragons: Destroying Myths in the History of Science and Faith*. Oxford: Lion, 2013.
Charlesworth, Brian, and Deborah Charlesworth. *Evolution: A Very Short Introduction*, Rev. ed. Oxford: Oxford University Press, 2017.
Cheney, Liz. *Oath and Honor: The Explosive Inside Story from the Most Senior Republican to Stand Up to Donald Trump*. New York: Little, Brown, 2024.
Chung, W. Y., et al. "A First Look at ARFome: Dual-Coding Genes in Mammalian Genomes." *Public Library of Science: Computational Biology*, May 18th, 2007.
The Church of England, "The Nicene Creed." https://www.churchofengland.org/faith-life/what-we-believe/nicene-creed.
Cicero. *De Natura Deorum*. N.p.: Loeb Classical Library, 1933. https://penelope.uchicago.edu/Thayer/E/Roman/Texts/Cicero/de_Natura_Deorum/2B*.html.
Clark, Kelly James. "I Believe in God the Father, Almighty." http://www.researchgate.net/publication/265226136_I_Believe_in_God_the_Father_Almighty.
Clery, Daniel. "Mystery Force Behind the Universe's Accelerating Expansion May not Be so Constant after all." https://www.science.org/content/article/mystery-force-behind-universe-s-accelerating-expansion-may-not-be-so-constant-after-all.
Cloud, David. "The Illiad vs the New Testament." *Way of Life Literature*, Nov 10, 2016. https://www.wayoflife.org/reports/the-illiad-vs-the-new-testament.php.

Cobb, Matthew. "60 Years Ago, Francis Crick Changed the Logic of Biology." *PLOS Biology* 15 (2017) 1–8. https://www.ncbi.nlm.nih.gov/pmc/articles/PMC5602739/.

Collicutt, Joanna. *The Psychology of Christian Character Formation*. London: SCM, 2015.

Collier, William B. *From Darwin to Eden: A Tour of Science and Religion Based on the Philosophy of Michael Polanyi and the Intelligent Design Movement*. Eugene, OR: Wipf & Stock, 2020.

Collins, C. John. *Genesis 1–4: A Linguistic, Literary, and Theological Commentary*. Phillipsburg, NJ: P&R, 2006.

———. *Reading Genesis Well: Navigating History, Poetry, Science, and Truth in Genesis 1–11*. Grand Rapids, MI: Zondervan, 2018.

———. *Science and Faith: Friends or Foes?* Wheaton, IL: Crossway, 2003.

Collins, Robin. "The Argument from Physical Constants: The Fine-Tuning for Discoverability." In *Two Dozen (or So) Arguments for God: The Plantinga Project*, edited by Jerry L. Walls and Trent Dougherty, 89–107. Oxford: Oxford University Press, 2018.

———. "Design and the Many-Worlds Hypothesis." In *Philosophy of Religion: A Reader and Guide*, edited by William Lane Craig, 130–48. Edinburgh: Edinburgh University Press, 2001.

———. "Eastern Religions." In *Reason for the Hope Within*, edited by Michael J. Murray, 182–216. Grand Rapids, MI: Eerdmans, 1999.

———. "Fine-Tuning Website." http://home.messiah.edu/~Collin's/Fine-tuning/FT.HTM.

———. "God, Design, and Fine-Tuning." https://www.academia.edu/72611583/God_Design_and_Fine_Tuning.

———. "Hume, Fine-Tuning and the 'Who Designed God?' Objection." In *In Defence of Natural Theology: A Post-Humean Assessment*, edited by James F. Sennett and Douglas R. Groothuis, 175–99. Downers Grove, IL: InterVarsity, 2005.

———. "Modern Cosmology and Anthropic Fine-Tuning: Three Approaches." In *George Lemaitre: Life, Science and Legacy*, edited by Rodney D. Holder and Simon Mitton, 173–91. New York: Springer, 2013.

———. "A Scientific Argument for the Existence of God: The Fine-Tuning Design Argument." In *Reason for the Hope Within*, edited by Michael J. Murray, 47–75. Grand Rapids, MI: Eerdmans, 1999. https://rintintin.colorado.edu/~vancecd/phil201/Collins.pdf.

———. "The Teleological Argument." In *The Rationality of Theism*, edited by Paul Copan and Paul K. Moser, 132–48. London: Routledge, 2003.

———. "The Teleological Argument: An Exploration of the Fine-Tuning of the Universe." In *The Blackwell Companion to Natural Theology*, edited by William Lane Craig and J. P. Moreland, 202–81. Oxford: Wiley-Blackwell, 2009. https://www.academia.edu/72611570/The_Teleological_Argument_An_Exploration_of_the_Fine_Tuning_of_the_Universe.

Collins, Steven. *The Defendable Faith: Lessons in Christian Apologetics*. Albuquerque: Trowel, 2012.

Comfort, Philip Wesley, and Jason Driesbach. *The Many Gospels of Jesus: Sorting Out the Story of the Life of Jesus*. Carol Stream, IL: Tyndale, 2008.

Cooper, Keith. "The James Webb Space Telescope Never Disproved the Big Bang. Here's How That Falsehood Spread." Space.com, September 7, 2022. https://www.space.com/james-webb-space-telescope-science-denial.
Copan, Paul. "God Can't Possibly Exist Given the Evil and Pain I See in the World." In *That's Just Your Interpretation* (Grand Rapids: Baker, 2001). http://www.bethinking.org/resource.php?ID=30.
———. "God, Naturalism, and the Foundations of Morality." In *The Future of Atheism*, edited by Robert B. Stewart, 141–61. London: SPCK, 2008. https://www.paulcopan.com/articles/pdf/God-naturalism-morality.pdf.
———. "Hume and the Moral Argument." In *In Defence Of Natural Theology: A Post-Humean Assessment*, edited by in James F. Sennett and Douglas Groothuis, 200–25. Downers Grove, IL: InterVarsity, 2005. http://www.paulcopan.com/articles/pdf/Paul_Copan-Hume_and_Moral_Argument-In_Defense_Natural_Theology.pdf.
———. *Is God a Moral Monster?* Grand Rapids, MI: Baker, 2011.
———, "Is the Trinity a Logical Blunder? God as Three-in-One." https://www.paulcopan.com/articles/pdf/is-the-Trinity-a-logical-blunder_God-as-three-and-one.pdf.
———. *A Little Book for New Philosophers: Why and How to Study Philosophy*. Downers Grove, IL: IVP, 2016.
———. "The Naturalists Are Declaring the Glory of God: Discovering Natural Theology in the Unlikeliest Places." In *Philosophy and the Christian Worldview: Analysis, Assessment and Development*, edited by David Werther and Mark D. Linville, 50–70. New York, NY: Continuum, 2012.
———. *True for You but Not for Me: Defeating Slogans That Leave Christians Speechless*. Minneapolis, MN: Bethany, 1998.
———. *True for You but Not for Me: Overcoming Objections to Christian Faith*. Rev. ed. Bloomington, MN: Bethany, 2009.
Copan, Paul, and William Lane Craig, eds. *The Kalam Cosmological Argument. Vol. 1, Philosophical Arguments for the Finitude of the Past*. Bloomsbury Studies in Philosophy of Religion. New York: Bloomsbury Academic, 2019.
Copan, Paul, and William Lane Craig, eds. *The Kalam Cosmological Argument. Vol. 2, Scientific Evidence for the Beginning of the Universe*. Bloomsbury Studies in Philosophy of Religion. New York: Bloomsbury Academic, 2019.
Copan, Paul, and Paul K. Moser, eds. *The Rationality of Theism*. London: Routledge, 2003.
Copan, Paul, and Charles Taliaferro, eds. *The Naturalness of Belief: New Essays on Theism's Rationality*. London: Lexington, 2018.
Copleston, F. C. "Commentary on the Five Ways." In *The Existence of God*, edited by John Hick, 86–93. New York: Macmillan, 1964.
Coppedge, David F. "Genetics: Alternate Reading Frames May Be Common." https://crev.info/2002/05/genetics_alternate_reading_frames_may_be_common/.
Corning, Peter A. "Beyond the Modern Synthesis: A Framework for a More Inclusive Biological Synthesis." *Progress in Biophysics & Molecular Biology* 153 (2020) 5–12. https://www.sciencedirect.com/science/article/abs/pii/S0079610720300109.
Cottingham, John. "Philosophers Are Finding Fresh Meanings in Truth, Goodness and Beauty." *The Times*, 17 June 2006.

Couto, Marcelle. "Reflecting on the Philosophy of 'Everything Everywhere All at Once.'" *The Observer*, Feb 16, 2023. https://www.ndsmcobserver.com/article/2023/02/philosophy-everything-everywhere-all-at-once.

Cowan, Steven B., ed. *Five Views on Apologetics*. Grand Rapids, MI: Zondervan, 2000.

———, and James S. Spiegel. *The Love of Wisdom: A Christian Introduction to Philosophy*. Nashville: B&H, 2009.

Cutter, Brian and Dustin Crummett. "Psychophysical Harmony: A New Argument for Theism." *Oxford Studies in Philosophy of Religion* (forthcoming). https://philarchive.org/archive/CUTPHA#:~:text=psychophysical%20laws%20are%20extremely%20complex,X%20particles%20gave%20rise%20to.

Craig, William Lane. *Assessing the New Testament Evidence for the Resurrection of Jesus*. New York: Edwin Mellen, 2002.

———. "The Bodily Resurrection of Jesus." *Reasonable Faith with William Lane Craig*. https://www.reasonablefaith.org/writings/scholarly-writings/historical-jesus/the-bodily-resurrection-of-jesus.

———. "Christ and Miracles: Introduction." In *To Everyone an Answer: A Case for the Christian Worldview*, edited by Francis J. Beckwith, 139–44. Downers Grove, IL: InterVarsity, 2004.

———. "The Concept of God in Islam and Christianity." *Reasonable Faith with William Lane Craig*. http://www.reasonablefaith.org/concept-of-god-in-islam-and-christianity.

———. "Creation Ex Nihilo." *Reasonable Faith with William Lane Craig*. https://www.reasonablefaith.org/writings/popular-writings/existence-nature-of-god/creation-ex-nihilo-theology-and-science.

———. "Dale Allison on Jesus' Empty Tomb, His Post-Mortem Appearances, and the Origin of the Disciples' Belief in His Resurrection." *Reasonable Faith with William Lane Craig*. https://www.reasonablefaith.org/writings/scholarly-writings/historical-jesus/dale-allison-on-jesus-empty-tomb-his-post-mortem-appearances-and-the-origin/.

———. "Dale Allison on the Resurrection of Jesus." *Reasonable Faith with William Lane Craig*. https://www.reasonablefaith.org/writings/question-answer/dale-allison-on-the-resurrection-of-jesus.

———. "Dawkins' Delusion." *Reasonable Faith with William Lane Craig*. https://www.reasonablefaith.org/writings/popular-writings/existence-nature-of-god/dawkins-delusion.

———. *Did Jesus Rise from the Dead?* Pine Mountain, GA: Impact 360 Institute, 2014.

———. "The Disciples' Inspection of the Empty Tomb." *Reasonable Faith with William Lane Craig*. https://www.reasonablefaith.org/the-disciples-inspection-of-the-empty-tomb.

———. "Does God Exist?" *Philosophy Now*. https://philosophynow.org/issues/99/Does_God_Exist.

———. *Does God Exist?* Pine Mountain, GA: Impact 360 Institute, 2019.

———. "Fine Tuned Universe." *Reasonable Faith with William Lane Craig*. https://www.reasonablefaith.org/writings/question-answer/fine-tuned-universe.

———. "Five Arguments for God." *Christian Evidence*. https://christianevidence.org/booklet/five_arguments_for_god/.

———. "A Formulation and Defence of the Doctrine of the Trinity." *Reasonable Faith with William Lane Craig*. https://www.reasonablefaith.org/writings/scholarly-writings/christian-doctrines/a-formulation-and-defense-of-the-doctrine-of-the-trinity/.

———. *God, Are You There? Five Reasons God Exists and Three Reasons it Makes a Difference*. Norcross, GA: RZIM, 1999.

———. "God Is Not Dead Yet" *Reasonable Faith with William Lane Craig*. https://www.reasonablefaith.org/writings/popular-writings/existence-natureof-god/god-is-not-dead-yet.

———. *God Over All: Divine Aseity and the Challenge of Platonism*. Oxford: OUP, 2018.

———. "The Historicity of the Empty Tomb of Jesus." *Reasonable Faith with William Lane Craig*. https://www.reasonablefaith.org/writings/scholarly-writings/historical-jesus/the-historicity-of-the-empty-tomb-of-jesus.

———. "How Can Christians Engage with Polytheists?" YouTube video, September 8, 2021. https://www.youtube.com/watch?app=desktop&v=5cYgCAQYVhQ.

———. "In Defence of Rational Theism." In *Does God Exist? The Debate between Theists and Atheists*, by J. P. Moreland and Kai Nielson, et al., 139–61. Amherst, NY: Prometheus, 1993.

———. "Jesus' Resurrection." *Reasonable Faith with William Lane Craig*. https://www.reasonablefaith.org/writings/scholarly-writings/historical-jesus/jesus-resurrection.

———. *The Kalam Cosmological Argument*. Eugene, OR: Wipf and Stock, 2000.

———. *On Guard: Defending Your Faith with Reason and Precision*. Colorado Springs: David C. Cook, 2010.

———. "The Ontological Argument." In *To Everyone an Answer: A Case for the Christian Worldview*, edited by Francis J. Beckwith et al., 124–37. Downers Grove, IL: InterVarsity, 2004.

———, ed. *Philosophy of Religion: A Reader and Guide*. Edinburgh University Press, 2002.

———. "The Problem Of Evil." *Reasonable Faith with William Lane Craig*. http://www.reasonablefaith.org/writings/popular-writings/existence-nature-of-god/the-problem-of-evil.

———. *Reasonable Faith*. 3rd ed. Wheaton, IL: Crossway, 2008.

———. "Reply to Evan Fales: On the Empty Tomb of Jesus." *Reasonable Faith with William Lane Craig*. https://www.reasonablefaith.org/writings/scholarly-writings/historical-jesus/reply-to-evan-fales-on-the-empty-tomb-of-jesus.

———. "The Resurrection of Jesus." *Reasonable Faith with William Lane Craig*. https://www.reasonablefaith.org/writings/popular-writings/jesus-of-nazareth/the-resurrection-of-jesus.

———. "Richard Dawkins on Arguments for God." In *God Is Great, God Is Good*, edited by William Lane Craig and Chad Meister. Downers Grove, Il: IVP, 2009.

———. *The Son Rises: Historical Evidence for the Resurrection of Jesus*. Eugene, OR: Wipf & Stock, 2001.

———. "Who Was Jesus of Nazareth?" *BeThinking*, 2007. https://www.bethinking.org/jesus/who-was-jesus-of-nazareth.

———. "William Lane Craig." In *Science and Religion: 5 Questions*, edited by Gregg D. Caruso. New York: Automatic/VIP, 2014.

Craig, William Lane, and Chad Meister, eds. *God Is Great, God Is Good: Why Believing in God Is Reasonable and Responsible*. Downers Grove, IL: InterVarsity, 2009.

Craig, William Lane, and J. P. Moreland, eds. *Naturalism: A Critical Analysis*. London: Routledge, 2001.

Craig, William Lane, and J. P. Moreland, eds. *The Blackwell Companion to Natural Theology*. Oxford: Wiley-Blackwell, 2009.

Crossley, James. "Against the Historical Plausibility of the Empty Tomb Story and the Bodily Resurrection of Jesus." *Journal for the Study of the Historical Jesus* (Jan 1, 2005) 171–86.

———. "The Date of Mark's Gospel: Insight from the Law in Earliest Christianity." *Journal for the Study of the New Testament Supplement* S. 266. Edinburgh: T&T Clark, 2004.

Darwin, Charles. *The Origin of Species*. 1st ed. Ware, Hertfordshire: Wordsworth Classics, 1859.

———. *The Origin of Species*. 6th ed. London: John Murray, 1872. https://darwin-online.org.uk/converted/pdf/1876_Origin_F401.pdf.

Davies, Paul. *The Cosmic Blueprint*. New York: Touchstone, 1989.

———. *The Demon in the Machine: How Hidden Webs of Information Are Finally Solving the Mystery of Life*. London: Penguin, 2020.

———. *The Fifth Miracle: The Search for the Origins of Life*. London: Penguin, 1998.

———. *The Origin of Life*. London: Penguin, 2003.

Davies, Stephen T. "A Somewhat Playful Proof of the Social Trinity in Five Easy Steps." *Philosophia Christi* 2.1 (1999), 105.

———. *Christian Philosophical Theology*. Oxford: OUP, 2016.

———. "The Mad/Bad/God Trilemma: A Reply to Daniel Howard Snyder." *Faith and Philosophy* (Oct 1, 2004) 480–92. https://place.asburyseminary.edu/faithandphilosophy/vol21/iss4/4/.

———. *Risen Indeed*. London: SPCK, 1994.

———. "Was Jesus Mad, Bad or God?" In *Christian Philosophical Theology*, 149–71. Oxford: Oxford University Press, 2016.

Dawkins, Richard. *The Blind Watchmaker*. London: Penguin, 1990.

———. "Darwin Triumphant." In *A Devil's Chaplain*, 78–90. London: Phoenix, 2004.

———. *A Devil's Chaplain*. London: Weidenfeld & Nicolson, 2003.

———. *Climbing Mount Improbable*. London: Viking, 1996.

———. *The God Delusion*. London: Black Swan, 2007.

———. "Genes Aren't Us." In *A Devil's Chaplain*, 104–6. London: Weidenfeld & Nicolson, 2003.

———. *The Magic of Reality: How We Know What's Really True*. London: Bantam, 2011.

———. *Outgrowing God: A Beginner's Guide*. London: Bantam, 2019.

———. *River out of Eden: A Darwinian View of Life*. New York: Basic, 1995.

———. *Science in the Soul: Selected Writings of a Passionate Rationalist*. London: Bantam, 2017.

———. "Sorry Liberal Christians, But Jesus Is Dead to Me." *Richard Dawkins Foundation*, Feb 24, 2014. https://richarddawkins.net/2014/02/sorry-liberal-christians-but-jesus-is-dead-to-me-2/.

Deane, David R. C. "Is Science the Only Means for Acquiring Truth?" In *The Comprehensive Guide to Science and Faith*, edited by William A. Dembski et al., 415–27. Eugene, OR: Harvest House, 2021. Kindle.

Dember, Greg. "After Postmodernism: Eleven Metamodern Methods in the Arts." Apr 17, 2018. https://medium.com/what-is-metamodern/after-postmodernism-eleven-metamodern-methods-inthe-arts-767f7b646cae.

———. "Everything Metamodern All at Once." *What Is Metamodern?*, Jun 27, 2022. https://whatismetamodern.com/film/everything-everywhere-all-at-once-metamodern/.

Dembski, William A. "In Defence of Intelligent Design." In *Oxford Handbook of Religion and Science*, edited by Philip Clayton, 715–31. Oxford: Oxford University Press, 2006. https://www.scribd.com/document/251639529/William-a-Dembski-In-Defense-of-Intelligent-Design.

———. "Intelligent Science and Design." *First Things* 86 (1998) 21–27. https://www.firstthings.com/article/1998/10/science-and-design.

———. "Introduction: The Myths of Darwinism." In *Uncommon Dissent: Intellectuals Who Find Darwinism Unconvincing*, edited by William A. Dembski, xvii–xxxvii. Wilmington, DE: ISI, 2004.

———. "Irreducible Complexity Revisited." *Progress in Complexity, Information, and Design* 3 (2004) 1–47. https://billdembski.com/documents/2004.01.Irred_Compl_Revisited.pdf.

———. "Is Intelligent Design a Form of Natural Theology?" https://billdembski.com/documents/2001.03.ID_as_nat_theol.htm.

———. *No Free Lunch: Why Specified Complexity Cannot Be Purchased Without Intelligence*. Lanham, MD: Rowman and Littlefield, 2002.

———. "On the Scientific Status of Intelligent Design." https://web.archive.org/web/20120206090342 & http://www.designinference.com/documents/2002.03.kennedy_on_ID.htm.

———. "Specification: The Pattern That Signifies Intelligence." *Philosophia Christi* 7 (2005) 299–343. https://billdembski.com/documents/2005.06.Specification.pdf.

———. "Still Spinning Just Fine: A Response to Ken Miller." *Intelligent Design*, February 17, 2003. https://www.discovery.org/a/1364/.

———. "The Success of Mathematics in Advancing Intelligent Design: A Guide to Reading Jason Rosenhouse." *Intelligent Design*, June 22, 2022. https://billdembski.com/intelligent-design/success-of-mathematics-in-advancing-intelligent-design/.

Dembski, William A., ed. *Uncommon Dissent: Intellectuals Who Find Darwinism Unconvincing*. Wilmington, DE: ISI Books, 2004.

Dembski, William A., and Jonathan Wells. *The Design of Life: Discovering Signs of Intelligence in Biological Systems*. Richardson, TX: Foundation for Thought and Ethics, 2008.

Dembski, William A., and Robert J. Marks. "Life's Conservation Law: Why Darwinian Evolution Cannot Create Biological Information." https://evoinfo.org/papers/ConsInfo_NoN.pdf.

Dembski, William A., and Winston Ewert. *The Design Inference: Eliminating Chance through Small Probabilities*. 2nd ed. Seattle, WA: Discovery Institute; 2023.

Dempsey, Brendan Graham. *Metamodernism: Or, The Cultural Logic of Cultural Logics*. ARC, 2023.

Dennett, Daniel. *Breaking the Spell: Religion as a Natural Phenomenon*. London: Penguin, 2007.

———. "The Leibnizian Paradigm." In *The Philosophy of Biology*, edited by David L. Hull and Michael Ruse, 38–51. Oxford: Oxford University Press, 1998.

Dennett, Daniel, and Alvin Plantinga. *Science and Religion: Are They Compatible?* Oxford: Oxford University Press, 2011.

Dennett, Daniel, and J. P. O'Malley. "Q&A with philosopher Daniel Dennett." *New Humanist*, Jun 8, 2017. https://newhumanist.org.uk/articles/5197/saying-something-is-a-miracle-is-a-failure-of-imagination.

Dennett, Daniel, and Nick Spencer. "Mounting Disbelief." Jun 2013. https://highprofiles.info/interview/daniel-dennett/.

Denton, Michael. *Evolution: A Theory in Crisis*. Bethesda, MD: Adler & Adler, 1986.

———. *The Miracle of Man: The Fine Tuning of Nature for Human Existence*. Seattle, WA: Discovery Institute, 2022.

———. *Nature's Destiny: How The Laws Of Biology Reveal Purpose in the Universe*. New York: Free, 1998.

DeWeese, Garrett J. and J. P. Moreland. *Philosophy Made Slightly Less Difficult: A Beginner's Guide to Life's Big Questions*. 2nd Edition. Downers Grove, IL: IVP Academic, 2021.

DeWeese, Garrett J., and J. P. Moreland. *Philosophy Made Slightly Less Difficult*. Downers Grove, IL: InterVarsity, 2005.

Díaz-Pachón, Daniel Andrés, et al. "Is it Possible to Know Cosmological Fine-Tuning?" *The Astrophysical Journal Supplement Series*, Volume 271:56, Number 2 (2024). https://iopscience.iop.org/article/10.3847/1538-4365/ad2c88#apjsad2c88s5.

Díaz-Pachón, Daniel Andrés, et al. "Is Cosmological Tuning Fine or Coarse?" *Journal of Cosmology and Astroparticle Physics* 07, Article 20 (2021). https://doi.org/10.1088/1475-7516/2021/07/020.

Dickson, John. *Bullies and Saints: An Honest Look at the Good and Evil of Christian History*. Grand Rapids, MI: Zondervan, 2021.

Dierker, Benjamin R. "Why One-Third of Biologists Now Question Darwinism." *The Federalist*, April 16, 2019. https://thefederalist.com/2019/04/16/one-third-biologists-now-question-darwinism/.

Discovery Institute. "Biologist Douglas Axe on Evolution's Ability to Produce New Functions." YouTube video, October 15, 2012. https://youtu.be/8ZiLsXO-dYo.

Discovery Science. "Secrets of the Cell with Michael Behe (Season One Compilation)." YouTube video, May 3, 2022. https://www.youtube.com/watch?v=gw94qm4qdn8.

Dougherty, Trent. "Argument from Desire." http://prosblogion.ektopos.com/archives/2005/11/argument_from_d.html.

Dumitrescu, Alexandra. "Interconnections in Blakean and Metamodern Space." *Double Dialogues* 7 (Winter 2007). https://doubledialogues.com/article/interconnections-in-blakean-and-metamodern-space/.

———. "Metamodernism: A Few Characteristics." *Exploring Metamodernism*, Dec 26, 2013. https://metamodernism.wordpress.com/2013/1226/metamodernism-a-few-characteristics/.

Dunn, James. *Why Believe in Jesus' Resurrection?* London: SPCK, 2016.

Durrett, Rick, and Deena Schmidt. "Waiting for Two Mutations: With Applications to Regulatory Sequence Evolution and the Limits of Darwinian Evolution." *Genetics* 180 (2008) 1501–9. https://doi.org/10.1534/genetics.107.082610.

Dyer, Nat. "Mary Midgley (1919–2018)." *Philosophy Now* 140 (2020) n.p. https://philosophynow.org/issues/140/Mary_Midgley_1919-2018.

Eagleton, Terry. *Culture and the Death of God*. New Haven, CT: Yale University Press, 2015.

———. *The Illusions of Postmodernism*. Oxford: Blackwell, 1996.

———. *Reason, Faith, and Revolution: Reflections on the God Debate*. New Haven, CT: Yale University Press, 2010.

Earey, Mark. *Liturgical Worship*. London: Church House, 2009.

Earman, John. *Hume's Abject Failure*. Oxford: Oxford University Press, 2000.

Eberlin, Marcos. "The Evidence of Foresight in Nature." In *Science and Faith in Dialogue*, edited by Frederik van Niekerk and Nico Vorster, 213–42. *Reformed Theology in Africa Series 10*. Oxford: AOSIS, 2022. https://books.aosis.co.za/index.php/ob/catalog/book/334.

———. *Foresight: How the Chemistry of Life Reveals Planning and Purpose*. Seattle, WA: Discovery Institute, 2019.

———. "Game of Thrones: As Darwinism Dissolves, Top Evolutionists Scramble for a Successor." *Evolution News and Science Today*, May 22, 2019. https://evolutionnews.org/2019/05/game-of-thrones-as-darwinism-dissolves-top-evolutionists-scramble-for-a-successor/.

Edwards, Dennis R. *Humility Illuminated: The Biblical Path Back to Christian Character*. Downers Grove, IL: IVP Academic, 2023.

Edwards, Rem B. "Behaviorism: II. Philosophical Issues." *Encyclopedia of Bioethics* (1995). https://www.encyclopedia.com/science/encyclopedias-almanacs-transcripts-and-maps/behaviorism-ii-philosophical-issues.

Ehrman, Bart D. *Did Jesus Exist? The Historical Argument for Jesus of Nazareth*. New York: HarperOne, 2013.

Encyclopedia Britannica. "Last Universal Common Ancestor." https://www.britannica.com/science/last-universal-common-ancestor.

Evans, C. Stephen. *Despair: A Moment or a Way of Life?* Downers Grove, IL: InterVarsity, 1973.

———. *The Historical Christ and the Jesus of Faith: The Incarnational Narrative as History*. Oxford: Clarendon, 2004.

———. *Natural Signs and Knowledge of God: A New Look at Theistic Arguments*. Oxford: Oxford University Press, 2012.

———. "The Mystery of Persons and Belief in God." https://www.leaderu.com/truth/3truth07.html.

Evans, Craig A. *Jesus and His World: The Archaeological Evidence*. London: SPCK, 2012.

———. *Jesus and the Remains of History: Studies in Jesus and the Evidence of Material Culture*. Peabody, MA: Hendrickson, 2015.

———. "The Resurrection of Jesus in the Light of Jewish Burial Practices." Houston Christian University, 2016. https://hc.edu/news-and-events/2016/05/04/craig-evans-resurrection-jesus-light-jewish-burial-p-ractices/.

Evans, Jules. "The New World of Metamodernism." *The Institute of Art and Ideas*, iai news, Oct 1, 2021. https://iai.tv/articles/the-new-world-of-metamodernism-auid-1923.

Evans, Richard L. *In Defence of History*. London: Granta, 1997.

BIBLIOGRAPHY

Evolution News. "Alternative Splicing: The Film Editor of the Genome." *Evolution News and Science Today*, September 9, 2014. https://evolutionnews.org/2014/09/alternative_spl/.

———. "As Research Advances, Debunking 'Junk DNA' Is Almost Trendy." *Evolution News and Science Today*, July 10, 2018. https://evolutionnews.org/2018/07/as-research-advances-debunking-junk-dna-is-almost-trendy/.

———. "Caltech Finds Amazing Role for Noncoding DNA." *Evolution News and Science Today*, December 3, 2021. https://evolutionnews.org/2021/12/caltech-finds-amazing-role-for-noncoding-dna/.

———. "Collective Motion: A New Level of Design Found in Proteins." *Evolution News and Science Today*, March 15, 2016. https://evolutionnews.org/2016/03/collective_moti/.

———. "Could Blind Forces Build a Self-Replicating Model?" *Evolution News and Science Today*, May 15, 2023. https://evolutionnews.org/2023/05/could-blind-forces-build-a-self-replicating-molecule/.

———. "Darwin Devolves, Again: Study Finds Bacteria Eject Their Flagella to Avoid Starvation." *Evolution News and Science Today*, April 18, 2019. https://evolutionnews.org/2019/04/bacteria-eject-their-flagella-to-avoid-starvation/.

———. "Design Can Be Suboptimal on Purpose." *Evolution News and Science Today*, February 28, 2013. https://evolutionnews.org/2013/02/design_can_be_s/.

———. "DNA a Stupid Design? Can Benner do Better?" *Evolution News and Science Today*, November 30, 2012. https://evolutionnews.org/2012/11/dna_a_stupid_de/.

———. "Engineers Crash the Evolution Party, Rethink Biological Variation." *Evolution News and Science Today*, January 11, 2022. https://evolutionnews.org/2022/01/engineers-crash-the-evolution-party-rethink-biological-variation/.

———. "Intelligent Design and Methodological Naturalism." *Evolution News and Science Today*, September 15, 2017. https://evolutionnews.org/2017/09/intelligent-design-and-methodological-naturalism-no-necessary-contradiction/.

———. "Jonathan Wells Was Right: Non-Coding DNA Continues to Show Function." *Evolution News and Science Today*, December 10, 2019. https://evolutionnews.org/2019/12/jonathan-wells-was-right-noncoding-dna-continues-to-show-function/.

———. "Next Phase of ENCODE Finds MORE Functional Information in Genome 'Junk.'" *Evolution News and Science Today*, August 4, 2020. https://evolutionnews.org/2020/08/next-phase-of-encode-finds-more-functional-information-in-genome-junk/.

———. "Octopus Genetic Editing—Animals Defy Their Own Neo-Darwinism." *Evolution News and Science Today*, April 10, 2017. https://evolutionnews.org/2017/04/octopus-genetic-editing-animals-defy-their-own-neo-darwinism/.

———. "Surprises in Cell Codes Reveal Information Goes Far beyond DNA." *Evolution News and Science Today*, January 29, 2020. https://evolutionnews.org/2020/01/surprises-in-cell-codes-reveal-information-goes-far-beyond-dna/.

———. "Three Flagellum Updates Amplify Behe's Challenge to Darwinism from Irreducible Complexity." *Evolution News and Science Today*, October 26, 2017. https://evolutionnews.org/2017/10/with-three-flagellum-updates-research-amplifies-behes-challenge-to-darwinism-from-irreducible-complexity/.

Ewing, A. C. *The Fundamental Questions of Philosophy*. London: Routledge, 1985.

———. *Value and Reality: The Philosophical Case for Theism*. London: George Allen & Unwin, 1973.

Fanu, James Le. *Why Us? How Science Rediscovered the Mystery of Ourselves*. London: Harper, 2009.

Films Prophet. "Everything Everywhere All at Once: Nihilism v. Absurdism." YouTube video, Mar 25, 2023. https://www.youtube.com/watch?v=EKZbUofWurg.

Flannagan, Matthew. "Is Naturalism Simpler than Theism? Some Reflections on Graham Oppy's 'Best Argument Against God'." https://www.mandm.org.nz/2018/10/is-naturalism-simpler-than-theism-some-reflections-on-graham-oppys-best-argument-against-god.html.

Flew, Antony. In Craig J. Hazen, Gary R. Habermas and Antony Flew. "My Pilgrimage from Atheism to Theism: An Exclusive Interview with Former British Atheist Professor Antony Flew." https://www.apologitis.com/gr/ancient/symp/flew-interview.pdf.

———. "Response to Lewis, Professor Antony Flew." In *Cosmos, Bios, Theos: Scientists Reflect on Science, God, and the Origins of the Universe, Life, and Homo sapiens*, edited by Henry Margenau and Roy Abraham Varghese, 241. Chicago: Open Court, 1994.

Flew, Antony, with Roy Abraham Varghese. *There Is a God: How the World's Most Notorious Atheist Changed His Mind*. New York: HarperOne, 2007.

Flood, Gavin Denis. "Introduction." *Hindu Monotheism*. Cambridge: Cambridge University Press, 2020. https://books.google.co.uk/books?id=S732DwAAQBAJ&pg=PT4&source=gbs_selected_pages&cad=1#v=onepage&q&f=false.

FOCLOnline. "Archaeological Evidence for Jesus—Peter S. Williams." YouTube video, Nov 28, 2020. https://youtu.be/klsfgJdga5I?si=9xylLZYo3grreSFv.

———. "Arguments for and from Fulfilled Biblical Prophecies—Peter S. Williams." YouTube video, Sep 19, 2020. https://youtu.be/QMwBlRL7w_Y?si=0DRpvcxUpqCbpJ3n.

———. "Can We Believe in God in an Age of Science? The Big Bang & Cosmic 'Fine Tuning' - Peter S. Williams." YouTube video, February, 2024. https://www.youtube.com/watch?v=mZvRygHVHwU.

———. "Can We Believe in God in an Age of Science? Cosmology and God - Peter S Williams." YouTube video, January 4, 2023. https://www.youtube.com/watch?v=Ttfoht2Z1lk.

———. "Can We Believe in God in an Age of Science? Darwinism and Intelligent Design - Peter S. Williams." YouTube video, Mar 1, 2024. https://www.youtube.com/watch?v=l7bqFzK-cXY.

———. "Defending Early High Christology with Archaeology and New Testament Letters—Peter S. Williams." YouTube video, Aug 1, 2019. https://youtu.be/vUha7-4Puy8.

———. "Evidence for Old Testament History - Peter S Williams." YouTube video, July 3, 2024. https://www.youtube.com/watch?v=JiUfViPOJA4.

Fodor, Jerry. "Why Pigs Don't Have Wings." *London Review of Books*, October 18, 2007. https://www.lrb.co.uk/the-paper/v29/n20/jerry-fodor/why-pigs-don-t-have-wings.

Fodor, Jerry, and Massimo Piatelli-Palmarini. *What Darwin Got Wrong*. London: Profile, 2011.

France, R. T. "The Gospels as Historical Sources for Jesus, the Founder of Christianity." Truth 1 (1985).

Frank, Adam. "There Is no Empirical, Scientific Evidence for the Multiverse." *Big Think*, February 3, 2022. https://bigthink.com/13-8/multiverse-no-evidence/.

Freinacht, Hanzi. *The Listening Society: A Metamodern Guide to Politics, Book One*. Metamodern Guides 1. Metamoderna ApS, 2017. Kindle ed.

Fuller, Steve. *Dissent Over Descent*. London: Icon, 2008.

Gage, Paul Logan. "Is the God Hypothesis Improbable? A Response to Dawkins." In *A New Theist Response to the New Atheism*, edited by Joshua Rasmussen and Kevin Vallier, 59–76. New York: Routledge, 2020.

Gallagher, Richard. *Demonic Foes: My Twenty-Five Years as a Psychiatrist Investigating Possessions, Diabolic Attacks, and the Paranormal*. New York: HarperOne, 2022.

Ganssle, Gregory E. *A Reasonable God: Engaging the New Face of Atheism*. Waco, TX: Baylor University Press, 2009.

Garcia, Robert K. and Nathan L. King, eds. *Is Goodness without God Good Enough? A Debate on Faith, Secularism, and Ethics*. Lanham, MD: Rowman & Littlefield, 2009.

Garte, Seymour, Perry Marshall and Stuart Kauffman. "The Reasonable Ineffectiveness of Mathematics in the Biological Sciences." *Entropy* 2025, 27(3), 280. https://www.mdpi.com/1099-4300/27/3/280.

Garvey, Jon. "Does it Follow?" *The Hump of the Camel* (blog), November 6, 2018. https://potiphar.jongarvey.co.uk/2018/06/11/does-it-follow/.

Gauger, Ann. "Science and Human Origins" in Gauger et al. *Science & Human Origins*. Seattle, WA: Discovery Institute Press, 2012.

———. "Teleonomy and Evolution." *Evolution News and Science Today*, December 1, 2017. https://evolutionnews.org/2017/12/teleonomy-and-evolution/.

Gauger, Ann, and Douglas D. Axe. "The Evolutionary Accessibility of New Enzyme Functions: A Case Study from the Biotin Pathway." *BIO-Complexity* 1 (2011) 1–17. https://www.researchgate.net/publication/272177811_The_Evolutionary_Accessibility_of_New_Enzymes_Functions_A_Case_Study_from_the_Biotin_Pathway.

Gee, Henry. *A (Very) Short History of Life on Earth: 4.6 Billion Years in 12 Pithy Chapters*. London: Picador, 2022.

Geisler, Norman L. *Baker Encyclopedia of Christian Apologetics*. Grand Rapids, MI: Baker, 1999.

———. *Christian Apologetics*. 2nd ed. Grand Rapids, MI: Baker, 2013.

———. *Christian Apologetics*. Grand Rapids: Baker, 1988.

———. "Miraculous Bible Prophecy Fulfillments." *Philosophical11* (blog), Sep 12, 2012. https://philosophical11.wordpress.com/2012/09/12/miraculous-bible-prophecy-fulfillments/#more-151.

———. "Updating the Manuscript Evidence for the New Testament." 2013. URL no longer available.

Geisler, Norman L., and Peter Bocchino. *Unshakable Foundations: Contemporary Answers to Crucial Questions about the Christian Faith*. Bloomington, MN: Bethany, 2000.

Geisler, Norman L., and Paul D. Feinberg. *Introduction to Philosophy: A Christian Perspective*. Grand Rapids, MI: Baker, 1997.

Geisler, Norman L., and Frank Turek. *I Don't Have Enough Faith to Be an Atheist*. Wheaton, IL: Crossway, 2004.

Geisler, Norman L., and William D. Watkins. *Worlds Apart*. 2nd ed. Eugene, OR: Wipf and Stock, 2003.

Geivett, R. Douglas, and Brendan Sweetman, eds. *Contemporary Perspectives on Religious Epistemology*. Oxford: Oxford University Press, 1992.

Geivett, R. Douglas, and Gary R. Habermas, eds. *In Defence of Miracles: A Comprehensive Case for God's Action In History*. Leicester: Apollos, 1997.

Gelernter, David. "Giving Up Darwin: A Fond Farewell to a Brilliant and Beautiful Theory." *Claremont Review of Books*, Spring 2019. https://claremontreviewofbooks.com/giving-up-darwin/.

Gilbert, S., et al. "Resynthesizing Evolutionary and Developmental Biology." *Developmental Biology* 173 (1996) 357–72. https://core.ac.uk/download/pdf/82701648.pdf.

Gill's Exposition of the Entire Bible. "Luke 24:33." *Bible Hub*. https://biblehub.com/commentaries/luke/24-33.htm.

Gilson, Tom, and Carson Weitnauer, eds. *True Reason: Confronting the Irrationality of the New Atheism*. Grand Rapids, MI: Kregel, 2013.

Glass, David H. *Atheism's New Clothes: Exploring and Exposing the Claims of the New Atheists*. Leicester: Apollos, 2012.

Glicksman, Howard, and Steve Laufmann. "The Supposed Bad Design of the Human Pharynx." *Evolution News and Science Today*, December 14, 2022. https://evolutionnews.org/2022/12/the-supposed-bad-design-of-the-human-pharynx/.

Göcke, Benedikt Paul, ed. *After Physicalism*. South Bend, IN: University of Notre Dame Press, 2012.

Goetz, Stewart and Charles Taliaferro. *Naturalism*. Grand Rapids, MI: Eerdmans, 2008.

Goff, Phillip. "Our Improbable Existence Is no Evidence for a Multiverse." *Scientific American*, January 10, 2021. https://www.scientificamerican.com/article/our-improbable-existence-is-no-evidence-for-a-multiverse/.

Gonzalez, Guillermo. "Local Fine-Tuning and Habitable Zones." In *Science and Faith in Dialogue*, edited by Frederik van Niekerk and Nico Vorster, 93–124. *Reformed Theology in Africa Series 10*. Oxford: AOSIS, 2022. https://books.aosis.co.za/index.php/ob/catalog/book/334.

Gonzalez, Guillermo, and Jay W. Richards. *The Privileged Planet*. (20th Anniversary Edition.) *How Our Place in The Cosmos Is Designed For Discovery*. New York: Gateway Editions; New edition, 2024.

Gonzalez, Guillermo, and Jay Richards. *The Privileged Planet: How Our Place in the Cosmos Is Designed for Discovery*. Washington, DC: Regnery, 2004.

Goodsell, David S. *The Machinery of Life*. 2nd ed. Springer—LINK. New York: Copernicus, 2009.

Gordon, Bruce L. "Balloons on a String: A Critique of Multiverse Cosmology." In *The Nature of Nature: Examining the Role of Naturalism in Science*, edited by Bruce L. Gordon and William A. Dembski, 558–601. Wilmington, Delaware: ISI, 2011. https://philpapers.org/archive/GORBLG.pdf.

———. "Is Intelligent Design Science? The Scientific Status and Future of Design-Theoretic Explanations." In *Signs of Intelligence: Understanding Intelligent Design*, edited by William A. Dembski and James M. Kushiner, 193–216. Grand Rapids, MI: Brazos, 2001.

———. "The Scientific Status of Design Inferences." https://www.namb.net/apologetics/resource/the-scientific-status-of-design-inferences/.

The Gospel Coalition Australia. "Love: A Surprisingly Underutilised Apologetic." Dec 15, 2016. https://au.thegospelcoalition.org/article/love-a-surprisingly-underutilised-apologetic/.

Gould, Paul M. *Cultural Apologetics: Renewing the Christian Voice, Conscience, and Imagination in a Disenchanted World.* Grand Rapids, MI: Zondervan, 2019.

Gould, Paul M. and Courtney McLean. *A Primer on Cultural Apologetics: Conversations on Faith and Flourishing in a Disenchanted World.* Two Tasks Press, 2019.

Gould, Stephen Jay. "Is a New and General Theory of Evolution Emerging?" *Paleobiology* 6 (1980) 119–30.

Guthrie, Shandon L. *Gods of This World: A Philosophical Discussion and Defense of Christian Demonology.* Eugene, OR: Pickwick, 2018.

Graham, George. "Behaviorism." https://plato.stanford.edu/entries/behaviorism/.

Grant, Bob. "Should Evolutionary Theory Evolve?" *The Scientist Magazine*, January 1, 2010. https://www.the-scientist.com/uncategorized/should-evolutionary-theory-evolve-43651.

Grant, Edward. *A History of Natural Philosophy: From the Ancient World to the Nineteenth Century.* Cambridge: Cambridge University Press, 2007.

Gray, John. *Seven Types of Atheism.* London: Penguin, 2019.

———. *Straw Gods: Thoughts on Humans and Other Animals.* London: Granta, 2002.

GreekNewTestament.net. https://greeknewtestament.net/.

Grindheim, Sigurd. *Christology in the Synoptic Gospels: God or God's Servant?* London: Continuum, 2012.

Groothuis, Douglas. *Truth Decay: Defending Christianity against the Challenges of Postmodernism.* Downers Grove, IL: InterVarsity, 2000.

Gruneler, Royce Gordon. *New Approaches to Jesus and the Gospels: A Phenomenological Study of Synoptic Christology.* Grand Rapids, MI: Baker, 1982.

Habermas, Gary R. "Dale Allison's Resurrection Skepticism: A Critique." 2008. https://www.garyhabermas.com/articles/phil_christi/habermas_phil_christi_dale_allisons_res_skept.htm.

———. "Did Jesus Perform Miracles?" In *Jesus under Fire: Modern Scholarship Reinvents the Historical Jesus*, edited by Michael J. Wilkins and J. P. Moreland, 117–40. Grand Rapids, MI: Zondervan, 1995.

———. "The Empty Tomb of Jesus." *North American Mission Board*, Mar 30, 2016. https://www.namb.net/apologetics/resource/the-empty-tomb-of-jesus/.

———. *The Historical Jesus: Ancient Evidence for the Life of Christ.* Joplin, MO: College Press, 1996.

———. "Minimal Facts on the Resurrection That Even Skeptics Accept." *Southern Evangelical Seminary and Bible College*, Sep 28, 2016. https://ses.edu/minimal-facts-on-the-resurrection-that-even-skeptics-accept/.

———. "My Magnum Opus on the Minimal Facts Argument for the Resurrection of Jesus." https://www.researchgate.net/project/My-Magnum-Opus-on-the-Minimal-Facts-Argument-for-the-Resurrection-of-Jesus. URL no longer available.

———. *On the Resurrection.* Vol. 1, *Evidences.* Nashville: B&H Academic, 2024.

———. "Recent Perspectives on the Reliability of the Gospels." *Christian Research Institute*, Jun 11, 2009. https://www.equip.org/articles/recent-perspectives-on-the-reliability-of-the-gospels/.

———. "The Resurrection and Agnosticism." In *Reasons for Faith*, edited by Norman L. Geisler and Chad V. Meister, 281–82. Wheaton, IL: Crossway, 2007.

———. "The Resurrection Appearances of Jesus." In *In Defence of Miracles: A Comprehensive Case for God's Action in History*, edited by R. Douglas Geivett and Gary R. Habermas, 262–75. Leicester: Apollos, 1997.

———. "Resurrection Research from 1975 to the Present: What Are Critical Scholars Saying?" *Journal for the Study of the Historical Jesus* 3:2 (2005) 117–35. https://works.bepress.com/gary_habermas/16/.

———. *Risen Indeed: A Historical Investigation into the Resurrection of Jesus*. Bellingham, WA: Lexham, 2021.

———. *The Risen Jesus and Future Hope*. Lanham, MD: Rowman & Littlefield, 2003.

———. "Tracing Jesus' Resurrection to Its Earliest Eyewitness Accounts." In *God Is Good; God Is Great*, edited by William Lane Craig and Chad Meister, 202–16. Downers Grove, IL: InterVarsity, 2009.

Habermas, Gary R., et al., eds. *Did Jesus Rise From the Dead? The Resurrection Debate*. Eugene, OR: Wipf & Stock, 2003.

Habermas, Gary R., and Antony Flew. "Did Paul Actually See the Risen Jesus, or Did he Simply Have Some Sort of Vision?" John Ankerberg Show, March 27, 2012. YouTube video. https://www.youtube.com/watch?v=8yNdynwqtWI.

Habermas, Gary R., and Michael L. Licona. *The Case for the Resurrection of Jesus*. Grand Rapids, MI: Kregel, 2004.

Habermas, Jürgen. "A Conversation about God and the World." In *Time of Transitions*, 149–69. Cambridge: Polity, 2006.

Hackett, Stuart C. *The Resurrection of Theism: Prolegomena to Christian Apology*. Eugene, OR: Wipf and Stock, 2009.

Haldane, John. "Philosophy, the Restless Heart and the Meaning of Theism." In *The Meaning of Theism*, edited by John Cottingham, 39–58. Oxford: Blackwell, 2007.

Hannam, James. *The Genesis of Science: How the Christian Middle Ages Launched the Scientific Revolution*. Washington, DC: Regnery, 2010.

———. *God's Philosophers: How the Medieval World Laid the Foundations of Modern Science*. London: Icon, 2010.

———. "How Christianity Led to the Rise of Modern Science." *Christian Research Institute*, Jan 17, 2017. https://www.equip.org/article/christianity-led-rise-modern-science/.

Hansen, Carolyn. "Tactile and True: The Physicality of the Resurrection." In *The Resurrection Fact: Responding to Modern Critics*, edited by John J. Bombaro and Adam S. Francisco, 207–28. Irvine, CA: NRP, 2016.

Harman, Gilbert and Judith Jarvis Thomson. *Moral Relativism and Moral Objectivity*. Oxford: Blackwell, 1996.

Harold, Franklin. *The Way of the Cell: Molecules, Organisms, and the Order of Life*. New York: Oxford University Press, 2003.

Harris, Sam. *The End of Faith: Religion, Terror, and the Future of Reason*. New York: Norton, 2004.

———. *Letter to a Christian Nation*. London: Bantam, 2007.

———. *The Moral Landscape: How Science Can Determine Human Values*. Bantam, 2011.
Harrison, Peter. *The Bible, Protestantism and the Rise of Natural Science*. Cambridge: Cambridge University Press, 2008.
Hart, David Bentley. *Atheist Delusions: The Christian Revolution and its Fashionable Enemies*. New Haven, CT: Yale University Press, 2009.
Hartley, Donald E. "Heb 11:6 – A Reassessment Of The Translation 'God Exists.'" *Trinity Journal* 27:2 (2006) 289–307.
Hasker, William. "Deception and the Trinity: A Rejoinder to Tuggy." *Religious Studies* 47(01): (2011), 117–120. https://www.researchgate.net/publication/231928302_Deception_and_the_Trinity_A_rejoinder_to_Tuggy.
———. "Objections to Social Trinitarianism." *Religious Studies* 46 (2010) 421–39.
Hassan, Ihab. "Beyond Postmodernism: Toward an Aesthetic of Trust (2003)." In *Supplanting the Postmodern: An Anthology of Writings on the Arts and Culture of the Early 21st Century*, edited by David Rudrum and Nicholas Stavris, 13–30. London: Bloomsbury Academic, 2015.
Hawking, Stephen, and Leonard Mlodinow. *The Grand Design: New Answers to the Ultimate Questions of Life*. London: Bantam, 2011.
Hawthorne, Tim. *Windows on Science and Christian Faith*. InterVarsity, 1986.
Hayers, Conrad. "The Narrative Form of Genesis 1: Cosmogonic, Yes; Scientific, No." *Journal of the American Scientific Affiliation* 36 (1984) 208–15. https://biblicalelearning.org/wp-content/uploads/2022/01/Hyers_Gen1_JASA.pdf.
Hedin, Eric. "Information and Life's Origin—A Retrospective View." *Evolution News and Science Today*, Jun 21, 2023. https://evolutionnews.org/2023/06/information-and-lifes-origin-a-retrospective-view/.
Heil, John. *Philosophy of Mind: A Contemporary Introduction*. London: Routledge, 1998.
Hemple, Carl. *Philosophy of Natural Science*. Englewood Cliffs, NJ: Prentice-Hall, 1966.
Henriques, Gregg, et al. "What Is Metamodern Spirituality? A New Vision for Science, Subjectivity, and Religion Is Emerging." *Psychology Today*, Oct 17, 2022. https://www.psychologytoday.com/us/blog/theory-knowledge/202210/what-is-metamodern-spirituality.
Hill, Carol A. "The Noachian Flood: Universal or Local?" *Perspectives on Science and Christian Faith* 54 (2002) 170–83. https://www.csun.edu/~vcgeo005/Carol%201.pdf.
Hill, Carol A., et al., eds. *The Grand Canyon: Monument to an Ancient Earth. Can Noah's Flood Explain the Grand Canyon?* Grand Rapids, MI: Kregel, 2016.
Hill, Charles E. *Who Chose the Books of the New Testament?* Bellingham, WA: Lexham, 2022.
———. *Who Chose the Gospels? Probing the Great Gospel Conspiracy*. Oxford: Oxford University Press, 2010.
Hill, Jonathan. *What Has Christianity Ever Done for Us?* Downers Grove, IL: InterVarsity, 2005.
Himma, Kenneth Einar. "Christian Faith Without Belief That God Exists: A Defense of Pojman's Conception of Faith." *Faith and Philosophy* 23.1 (2006) 65–79.
Hitchens, Christopher. "Christopher Hitchens Makes a Shocking Confession." YouTube video. 01:58. https://www.youtube.com/watch?v=E9TMwfkDwIY.

Hoffmeier, James K. "Hoffmeier Rejoinder." In *The Exodus: Historicity, Chronology, and Theological Implications*, edited by Mark D. Janzen and Stanley N. Gundry, 129–33. Grand Rapids, MI: Zondervan Academic, 2021.

Hoffmeier, James K., et al., eds. *Did I Not Bring Israel Out of Egypt? Biblical, Archaeological, and Egyptological Perspectives on the Exodus Narratives*. Bulletin for Biblical Research Supplement 13. Winona Lake, IN: Eisenbrauns, 2016.

Holden, Joseph M., and Don Stewart. "Were the New Testament Manuscripts Copied Accurately?" *Defending Inerrancy*, Aug 5, 2019. https://defendinginerrancy.com/were-nt-mss-copied-accurately/.

Holder, Rodney D. *Big Bang, Big God: A Universe Designed for Life?* Oxford: Lion, 2013.

———. *God, the Multiverse, and Everything*. London: Routledge, 2016.

———. *Ramified Natural Theology in Science and Religion: Moving Forward from Natural Theology*. London: Routledge, 2021.

Holding, James Patrick, ed. *Shattering the Christ Myth: Did Jesus Not Exist?* Maitland, FL: Xulon, 2008.

Holland, Tom. *Dominion: The Making of the Western Mind*. London: Abacus, 2020.

Holmes, Arthur F. *Contours of a Worldview*. Grand Rapids, MI: Eerdmans, 1983.

Hoover Institution. "Mathematical Challenges to Darwin's Theory of Evolution." YouTube video, July 22, 2019. https://www.youtube.com/watch?v=noj4phMT9OE.

Horner, David A. "Aut Deus Aut Malus Homo: A Defense of C. S. Lewis' 'Shocking Alternative.'" In *C. S. Lewis as Philosopher: Truth, Goodness and Beauty*, edited by David Baggett et al., 61–76. Downers Grove, IL: IVP Academic, 2008.

Houston, Beth. *Natural God: Deism in the Age of Intelligent Design*. 2nd ed. Florida: New Deism, 2013.

Houston, J. *Reported Miracles*. Cambridge: Cambridge University Press, 2007.

Hossenfelder, Sabine. "Is the Cosmic Microwave Background a Huge Mistake?" YouTube video, June 23, 2025. https://www.youtube.com/watch?app=desktop&v=KFgwQICae8c.

Hössjer, Ola, et al. "On the Waiting Time Until Coordinated Mutations get Fixed in Regulatory Sequences." *Journal of Theoretical Biology* Volume 524, 7 September 2021. https://pubmed.ncbi.nlm.nih.gov/33675769/.

Howard-Snyder, Daniel. "Does Faith Entail Belief?" *Faith and Philosophy* 33.2 (2016) 133–42.

Howard-Snyder, Daniel, and Daniel McKaughan. "Faith." In *The Encyclopedia of Philosophy of Religion*, edited by Stewart Goetz and Charles Taliaferro. Oxford: Wiley-Blackwell, 2020. https://www.academia.edu/35582270/Faith_2020_.

Hoyle, Fred. "The Universe: Past and Present Reflections." *Engineering and Science*, November 1981. https://calteches.library.caltech.edu/527/2/Hoyle.pdf.

Hoyler, Robert. "The Argument from Desire." *Faith and Philosophy* 5:1 (1988) 61–67. https://www.academia.edu/114806494/The_Argument_from_Desire.

https://maryrose.org/.

https://southseacastle.co.uk/.

Huemer, Michael. "Compassionate Phenomenal Conservatism." *Philosophy and Phenomenological Research* 74.1 (2007) 30–55.

Hume, David. *Dialogues Concerning Natural Religion* (1779), https://afterall.net/quotes/david-hume-on-the-design-argument/.

Humphreys, Colin. "The Star of Bethlehem." *Science and Christian Belief* 5 (Oct 1995) 83–101. https://www.asa3.org/ASA/topics/Astronomy-Cosmology/S&CB%20 10-93Humphreys.html.

Hunter, Cornelius. "False Science: A Claim to Simulate Protein Evolution." *Evolution News and Science Today*, August 6, 2025. https://evolutionnews.org/2025/08/false-science-a-claim-to-simulate-protein-evolution/.

Hunter, James Davidson and Paul Nedelisky. *Science and the Good: The Tragic Quest for the Foundations of Morality*. New Haven: Yale University Press, 2018.

Hup. "Everything Everywhere All at Once—The Bagel." YouTube video, Oct 6, 2022. https://www.youtube.com/watch?v=d6ie3PEmAr4.

Hössjer, Ola, et al. "On the Waiting Time until Coordinated Mutations Get Fixed in Regulatory Sequences." *Journal of Theoretical Biology* 524 (2021) 110657. https:// https://www.sciencedirect.com/science/article/pii/S0022519321000795?via%3Dihub.

ID the Future. "Discussing an Unbelievable Conversation about Abiogenesis." *ID the Future* (podcast), September 1, 2021. https://idthefuture.com/1499/.

ID the Future. "A Privileged Place for Life and Discovery." *ID the Future* (podcast), March 15, 2023. https://idthefuture.com/1723/.

ID the Future. "The Problem of Earth Privilege: It's Getting Worse." *ID the Future* (podcast), March 13, 2023. https://idthefuture.com/1722/.

ID the Future. "RNA World in a World of Hurt." *ID the Future* (podcast), February 8, 2021. https://idthefuture.com/1413/.

In Our Time, "Panpsychism." BBC Podcast, 25 Jan 2024. https://goodpods.com/podcasts/in-our-time-35974/panpsychism-45287271.

"Insights into the Workings of a Bacterium's Flagellum." https://commons.wikimedia.org/wiki/File:Insights_into_the_workings_of_a_bacterium%27s_flagellum_(12291548414).jpg.

Inwagen, Peter van. *God, Knowledge & Mystery: Essays in Philosophical Theology*. Cornell University Press, 1995.

Iredale, Matthew. "Putting Descartes Before the Horse." *The Philosophers' Magazine* 42 (2008), 40.

Jackson, Andrew. "Many Worlds and Many Gods: An Excerpt from *Mormonism Explained*." *Crossway Articles* (2011). https://www.crossway.org/articles/many-worlds-and-many-gods-an-excerpt-from-mormonism-explained/.

Jackson, Wayne. "Does the Expression 'the Eleven' (Luke 24:33) Constitute an Error?" *Christian Courier*. https://christiancourier.com/articles/does-the-expression-the-eleven-luke-24-33-constitute-an-error.

Joad, C. E. M. *Guide to Modern Thought*. London: Faber and Faber, 1942.

———. *Guide To Philosophy*. London: Victor Gollancz, 1946.

———. *Joad's Opinions*. London: Westhouse, 1945.

Johnson, Donald C. *Programming of Life*. Sylacauga, AL: Big Mac, 2010.

Johnson, Philip E. "The Religion of the Blind Watchmaker." https://www.arn.org/docs/johnson/watchmkr.htm.

Jones, Clay. "The Bibliographical Test Updated." *Christian Research Institute*, Oct 1 2013. https://www.equip.org/articles/the-bibliographical-test-updated/.

Jones, Michael. "The Origins of Young Earth Creationism." https://peacefulscience.org/prints/origns-yec/.

Jones, Timothy Paul. *Misquoting Truth: A Guide to the Fallacies of Bart Ehrman's Misquoting Jesus*. Downers Grove, IL: InterVarsity, 2007.

Jones, Timothy Paul, ed. *Understanding Christian Apologetics: Five Methods for Defending the Faith*. Carol Stream, IL: Tyndale House, 2025.

Josephson, Brian. "Letter to the Editor." *The Independent*, 1997.

Kaiser, Walter C. Jr. *The Messiah in the Old Testament*. Grand Rapids, MI: Zondervan, 1995.

Karl, Jonathan. *Tired of Winning: Donald Trump and the End of the Grand Old Party*. New York: Dutton, 2023.

Keas, Michael Newton. *Unbelievable: 7 Myths About the History and Future of Science and Religion*. Wilmington, DE: ISI, 2019.

Keathley, Kenneth D. "The Confessions of a Disappointed Young-Earther." https://peacefulscience.org/prints/confessions-disappointed-young-earther/.

Keathley, Kenneth D., and Mark F. Rooker. *40 Questions about Creation and Evolution*. Grand Rapids, MI: Kregel Academic, 2014.

Keller, Werner. *The Bible As History: Archaeology Confirms the Book of Books*. London: Hodder & Stoughton, 1956, https://archive.org/details/in.gov.ignca.5155/page/n13/mode/2up

Kelvey, Jon. "Scientists Find the 'Chemistry Behind the Origin of Life.'" *The Independent*, October 4th, 2022. https://www.independent.co.uk/space/origin-of-life-earth-chemistry-b2194003.html.

Kessler, Glenn, et al. *Donald Trump and His Assault on Truth: The President's Falsehoods, Misleading Claims and Flat-Out Lies*. New York: Scribner, 2020.

King, Nathan L. *The Excellent Mind: Intellectual Virtues for Everyday Life*. Oxford: OUP, 2021.

Kinney, William H., and Nina K. Stein. "Cyclic Cosmology and Geodesic Completeness." *Journal of Cosmology and Astroparticle Physics* 2022 (2022) n.p. https://iopscience.iop.org/article/10.1088/1475-7516/2022/06/011.

Kirby, Alex. "The Death of Postmodernism and Beyond (2006)." In *Supplanting the Postmodern: An Anthology of Writings on the Arts and Culture of the Early 21st Century*, edited by David Rudrum and Nicholas Stavris, 49–60. London: Bloomsbury Academic, 2015.

Kitchen, K. A. *On the Reliability of the Old Testament*. Grand Rapids, MI: Eerdmans, 2006.

Klinghoffer, David, ed. *Debating Darwin's Doubt: A Scientific Controversy That Can No Longer Be Denied*. Seattle: Discovery Institute, 2015.

Klinghoffer, David. "In the Matter of John Farrell's Silly Review of Darwin's Doubt, National Review Sets Things Straight." *Evolution News and Science Today*, October 2, 2013. https://evolutionnews.org/2013/10/in_the_matter_o/.

———. *Plato's Revenge: The New Science of the Immaterial Genome*. Seattle, WA: Discovery Institute, 2025.

Klinghoffer, David, ed. *Signature of Controversy: Responses to Critics of Signature in the Cell*. Seattle, WA: Discovery Institute, 2010.

Koberlein, Brian. "JWST Fails to Disprove the Big Bang." *Universe Today*, May 8, 2023. https://www.universetoday.com/161265/jwst-fails-to-disprove-the-big-bang/.

Koch, Monty. "How Many Monotheists Are There?" *Times Mojo*, Jul 7, 2022. https://www.timesmojo.com/how-many-monotheists-are-there/.

Kofoed, Jens Bruun. "Approaching Genesis and Science: Hermeneutical Principles and a Case Study." *Theofilos* 12 (2020) 4–23. https://theofilos.no/wp-content/uploads/2020/12/Theofilos-vol-12-nr-1-2020-Supplement-academia-1.pdf.

Kojonen, Rope. "Methodological Naturalism and the Truth Seeking Objection." *International Journal for Philosophy of Religion* 81.3 (2017) 335–55.

Komoszewski, J., et al. *Reinventing Jesus: How Contemporary Skeptics Miss the Real Jesus and Mislead Popular Culture*. Grand Rapids, MI: Kregel, 2006.

Koonin, Eugene. *The Logic of Chance: The Nature and Origin of Biological Evolution*. Upper Saddle River, NJ: Pearson Education, 2012.

Koons, Robert C. "The Check Is in the Mail: Why Darwinism Fails to Inspire Confidence." In *Uncommon Dissent: Intellectuals Who Find Darwinism Unconvincing*, edited by William A. Dembski, 3–22. Wilmington, DE: ISI Books, 2004.

———. "The Incompatibility of Naturalism and Scientific Realism." Dec 22, 1998. https://www.leaderu.com/offices/koons/docs/natreal.html.

———. "Science and Theism: Concord not Conflict." In *The Rationality of Theism*, edited by Paul Copan and Paul Moser, 72–91. London: Routledge, 2003.

Koons, Robert C., and George Bealer, eds. *The Waning of Materialism*. Oxford University Press, 2010.

Koukl, Gregory. *Tactics: A Game Plan for Discussing Your Christian Convictions*. 10th Anniversary Edition. Grand Rapids, MI: Zondervan, 2019.

Köstenberger, Andreas J. "April 3, AD 33." *First Things*, Apr 3, 2014. https://www.firstthings.com/web-exclusives/2014/04/april-3-ad-33.

Köstenberger, Andreas J., ed. *Whatever Happened to Truth?* Wheaton, IL: Crossway, 2005.

Köstenberger, Andreas J., et al. *The Final Days of Jesus: The Most Important Week of the Most Important Person Who Ever Lived*. Wheaton, IL: Crossway, 2014.

Köstenberger, Andreas J., et al. *Truth Matters: Confident Faith in a Confusing World*. Nashville: B&H Academic, 2014.

Kozulic, Branko, and Matti Leisola. "Have Scientists Already Been Able to Surpass the Capabilities of Evolution?" http://vixra.org/bioch/1504.

Kramer, Mark, ed. *The Black Book of Communism: Crimes, Terror, Repression*. Cambridge: Harvard University Press, 1999.

Kreeft, Peter. *Between Heaven and Hell: A Dialog Somewhere beyond Death with John F. Kennedy, C. S. Lewis and Aldous Huxley*. Downers Grove, IL: InterVarsity, 1982.

———. "The Argument from Desire." https://www.peterkreeft.com/topics/desire.htm.

———. "Jesus: Considering the Options." *BeThinking*, 1988. https://www.bethinking.org/jesus/jesus-considering-the-options.

———. "A Refutation of Moral Relativism." https://www.peterkreeft.com/audio/05_relativism.htm.

———. "The Thomistic Cosmological Argument." YouTube video. https://www.youtube.com/watch?v=wefohtJBnN8.

Kreeft, Peter, and Ronald K. Tacelli. "Twenty Arguments for God's Existence." https://www.peterkreeft.com/topics-more/20_arguments-gods-existence.htm.

Küppers, Bernd-Olaf. *Information and the Origin of Life*. Cambridge, MA: MIT, 1990.

Kurtz, Paul. *Forbidden Fruit*. Amherst, New York: Prometheus, 1988.

Laland, Kevin et al. "Does Evolutionary Theory Need a Rethink? Yes." *Nature*, October 8, 2014. https://www.nature.com/articles/514161a.

Lamb, David T. *God Behaving Badly: Is the God of the Old Testament Angry, Sexist and Racist?* Expanded edition. Downers Grove, IL: IVP, 2022.

Lapide, Pinchas. *The Resurrection of Jesus: A Jewish Perspective.* Eugene, OR: Wipf & Stock, 2002.

Larmer, Robert A. *The Legitimacy of Miracle.* Lanham, MD: Lexington, 2014.

———. "Science, Methodological Naturalism, and Question-Begging." In *The Naturalness of Belief: New Essays on Theism's Rationality*, edited by Paul Copan and Charles Taliaferro, 85–103. Lanham: Lexington, 2019.

Larson, Stan. *Quest for the Golden Plates: Thomas Stuart Ferguson's Archaeological Search for The Book of Mormon.* Salt Lake City: Freethinker, 2004.

Latham, Antony. *The Enigma of Consciousness: Reclaiming the Soul.* Cambridge: Janus, 2012.

———. "The Fine-Tuned Universe." (24/12/2016). https://www.c4id.org.uk/Articles/487268/The_fine_tuned.aspx#:~:text=Ratio%20of%20electromagnetic%20and%20gravitational,1040%20that%20they%20will.

Laufmann, Steve, and Howard Glicksman. *Your Designed Body.* Seattle, WA: Discovery Institute, 2022.

LeFebvre, Michael. *The Liturgy of Creation: Understanding Calendars in Old Testament Context.* Downers Grove, IL: IVP, 2019.

———. "Reading Genesis 1 with the Fourth Commandment: The Creation Week as a Calendar Narrative." In *Creation and Doxology: The Beginning and End of God's Good World*, edited by Gerald Hiestand and Todd Wilson, 7–21. Downers Grove, IL: InterVarsity, 2018.

Lehe, Robert T. *God, Science, and Religious Diversity: A Defense of Theism.* Eugene, OR: Cascade, 2018.

Leidenhag, Joanna. "How to Be a Theological Panpsychist, but not a Process Theologian." (2020.) https://research-repository.st-andrews.ac.uk/bitstream/handle/10023/23541/How_to_be_a_be_a_Theological_Panpsychist._Final._converted.pdf;jsessionid=A784E398904C96B239AB076D01A410F0?sequence=1.

———. *Minding Creation: Theological Panpsychism and the Doctrine of Creation (T&T Clark Studies in Systematic Theology).* Edinburgh: T&T Clark, 2021.

———. "Why a Panpsychist Should Adopt Theism: God, Galileo, and Goff." *Journal of Consciousness Studies*, Volume 28, Numbers 9–10, 2021, pp. 250–267(18). https://eprints.whiterose.ac.uk/id/eprint/180157/17/Leidenhag%20AAM.pdf.

Leirman, Walter. *Cultures of Learning and Education: Complementary Synthesis.* Michigan Ethnic Heritage Center, 2009.

LeMaster, James C. "Evolution's Waiting-Time Problem and Suggested Ways to Overcome It—A Critical Survey." *BIO-Complexity* 2 (2018) 1–9. http://bio-complexity.org/ojs/index.php/main/article/viewArticle/BIO-C.2018.2.

Lennox, John C. *Cosmic Chemistry: Do God and Science Mix?* Oxford: Lion, 2021.

Levin, Michael. "Ingressing Minds: Causal Patterns beyond Genetics and Environment in Natural, Synthetic, and Hybrid Embodiments." https://osf.io/preprints/psyarxiv/5g2xj_v2.

Levine, Joseph. "Panpsychism: Contemporary Perspectives." *Notre Dame Philosophical Reviews*, 8th October, 2017. https://ndpr.nd.edu/reviews/panpsychism-contemporary-perspectives/.

Lewis, C. S. *The Abolition of Man.* London: Fount, 1978.

———. "The Cardinal Difficulty of Naturalism." http://thecslewis-studygroup.org/wp-content/uploads/2014/07/The-Cardinal-Difficulty-of-Naturalism.pdf.

———. *Mere Christianity*. New York: Macmillan, 1943.

———. *Miracles*. 2nd ed. London: Fount, 1998.

———. "On Living in an Atomic Age." In Present Concerns, edited by Walter Hooper, 73–80. New York: Harcourt Brace, 1986.

———. *Surprised by Joy*. London: HarperCollins, 1955.

———. "What Are We to Make of Jesus Christ?" In *God in the Dock*. London: Fount, 1979. https://www.xtianity.com/tfc/NTE103/C%20S%20Lewis%20What%20are%20we%20to%20make%20of%20Jesus%20Christ.pdf.

———. "Why I Am Not a Pacifist" https://www.youtube.com/watch?v=lCMMNMb3ysI.

Lewis, Geraint F., and Luke Barnes. *A Fortunate Universe: Life in a Finely Tuned Cosmos*. Cambridge: Cambridge University Press, 2016.

Lewontin, Richard. "Billions and Billions of Demons." https://keshavbedi.wordpress.com/2021/10/14/billions-and-billions-of-demons-by-richard-c-lewontin/.

Licona, Michael R. *Paul Meets Muhammad: A Christian-Muslim Debate on the Resurrection*. Grand Rapids, MI: Baker, 2006.

———. *The Resurrection of Jesus: A New Historiographical Approach*. Downers Grove, IL: InterVarsity, 2010.

Lockwood, Michael. "Consciousness and the Quantum World: Putting Qualia on the Map." In *Consciousness: New Philosophical Perspectives*, edited by Q. Smith and A. Jokic, 447–67. Oxford: Clarendon, 2003.

Loke, Andrew Ter Ern. *The Origin of Divine Christology*. Cambridge: Cambridge University Press, 2017.

———. *Studies on the Origin of Divine and Resurrection Christology*. Eugene, OR: Cascade, 2023.

Loose, Jonathan J., Angus J. L. Menuge and J. P. Moreland, eds. *Blackwell Companion to Substance Dualism (Blackwell Companions to Philosophy)*. Oxford: Wiley-Blackwell, 2023.

Luskin, Casey. "As Predicted by Intelligent Design, 'Junk' Introns Are Actually Functional." *Evolution News and Science Today*, January 24, 2019. https://evolutionnews.org/2019/01/as-predicted-by-intelligent-design-junk-introns-are-actually-functional/.

———. "Atheists Who Defend Intelligent Design: Interview with Bradley Monton." YouTube video. *IDQuest*. 1:01:55. http://youtu.be/Et2VTJ1UBC4.

———. "BioEssays Editor: '"Junk" DNA . . . Full of Information!' Including Genome-Sized 'Genomic Code.'" *Evolution News and Science Today*, November 18, 2019. https://evolutionnews.org/2019/11/bioessays-editor-junk-dna-full-of-information-including-genome-sized-genomic-code/.

———. "Dual Coding Genes 'Nearly Impossible by Chance'—How Would Francisco Ayala Respond?" *Evolution News and Science Today*, June 17, 2007. https://evolutionnews.org/2007/06/dualcoding_genes_nearly_imposs/.

———. "Intelligent Design as Fuel for Scientific Discovery (2025 Dallas Conference on Science & Faith)." YouTube video, Jul 7, 2025. https://www.youtube.com/watch?v=M_4aBu2g8A8.

———. "Is Intelligent Design Theory Really an Argument for God?" http://www.ideacenter.org/contentmgr/showdetails.php/id/1341.

———. "James Shapiro's Evolution: A View from the 21st Century Offers a Stunning Look at Biological Complexity and Non-Darwinian Evolution." *Evolution News and Science Today*, August 29, 2011. https://evolutionnews.org/2011/08/james_shapiros_evolution_a_vie/.

———. "Paper Shows That 'Mutational Load' Arguments Don't Refute ENCODE." *Evolution News and Science Today*, May 1, 2020. https://evolutionnews.org/2020/05/paper-shows-that-mutational-load-arguments-dont-refute-encode/.

———. "Presto! The Origin of Life in Four Surprisingly Easy Steps." *Evolution News and Science Today*, August 8, 2011. https://evolutionnews.org/2011/08/presto_the_origin_of_life_in_f/.

———. "Problem 10: Neo-Darwinism's Long History of Inaccurate Predictions about Junk Organs and Junk DNA." *Evolution News and Science Today*, February 19, 2015. https://evolutionnews.org/2015/02/problem_10_neo/.

———. "Problem 3: Step-by-Step Random Mutations Cannot Generate the Genetic Information Needed for Irreducible Complexity." *Evolution News and Science Today*, January 12, 2015. https://evolutionnews.org/2015/01/problem_3_rando/.

———. "Repentant Biology Journal Offers a Weak Rebuttal to Its Own Pro-ID Fine-Tuning Paper." *Evolution News and Science Today*, October 12, 2020. https://evolutionnews.org/2020/10/repentant-biology-journal-offers-a-weak-rebuttal-to-its-own-pro-id-fine-tuning-paper/.

———. "Study Challenges Evolutionary Relationship between Flagellum and Type III Secretory System." *Evolution News and Science Today*, May 14, 2021. https://evolutionnews.org/2021/05/study-challenges-evolutionary-relationship-between-flagellum-and-type-iii-secretory-system/.

———. "Study Finds Life's Origin 'Required a Surprisingly Short Interval of Geologic Time.'" *Evolution News and Science Today*, July 18, 2024. https://evolutionnews.org/2024/07/study-finds-lifes-origin-required-a-surprisingly-short-interval-of-geologic-time/.

———. "'That Is a Lot of Evolution': Study Finds LUCA Required 2,600 Genes." *Evolution News and Science Today*, August 8, 2024. https://evolutionnews.org/2024/08/that-is-a-lot-of-evolution-study-finds-luca-required-2600-genes/.

———. "Why the Type III Secretory System Can't Be a Precursor to the Bacteria Flagellum." *Evolution News and Science Today*, July 20, 2015. https://evolutionnews.org/2015/07/why_the_type_ii/.

Løkhammer, Espen. "The Fine-Tuning Argument for God's Existence: Does the Multiverse Objection Undermine the Fine-Tuning Argument for God's Existence?" Master's thesis. Vitenskapelig Høyskole, 2020. https://mfopen.mf.no/mf-xmlui/bitstream/handle/11250/2825311/1007%20L%C3%B8khammer,%20Espen.pdf?sequence=1.

Mackie, J. L. *Ethics: Inventing Right and Wrong*. London: Penguin, 1990.

Maier, Paul L. "The Date of the Nativity and the Chronology of Jesus' Life." In *Chronos, Karios, Christos: Nativity and Chronological Studies Presented to Jack Finegan*, edited by J. Vardaman and E. M. Yamauchi, 113–30. Winona Lake, IN: Eisenbrauns, 1989. https://inchristus.com/wp-content/uploads/2010/12/maier-date-of-the-nativity.pdf.

———. *The Genuine Jesus: Fresh Evidence from History and Archaeology*. 3rd ed. Grand Rapids, MI: Kregel, 2021.

Mangalwadi, Vishal. *The Book That Made Your World*. Nashville: Thomas Nelson, 2011.

Maung. Hane Htut. "Panpsychism, Conceivability, and Dualism Redux." *Synthesis Philosophica*, 34(1), 157–172. https://pure.manchester.ac.uk/ws/portalfiles/portal/124145205/Maung_H_H_Panpsychism_Conceivability_and_Dualism_Redux_Synthesis_Philosophica.pdf.

Margenau, Henry, and Roy Abraham Varghese, eds. *Cosmos, Bios, Theos*. Peru, IL: Open Court, 1992.

Marks, Joel. "An Amoral Manifesto: Part I." *Philosophy Now* 80. https://www.philosophynow.org/issue80/An_Amoral_Manifesto_Part_I?vm=r.

Marshall, I. Howard. *Acts. Tyndale New Testament Commentary*. Nottingham: IVP Academic, 2008.

Marston, Paul. "Understanding the Biblical Creation Passages." Leyland: Lifesway, 2007. https://www.asa3.org/ASA/topics/Bible-Science/understanding_the_biblical_creation_passages.pdf.

Martin, Michael and Peter S. Williams. "Is there a personal God? Head to Head Debate. Atheist Michael Martin and Christian Peter S. Williams debate the existence of a unitary, personal god." *The Philosopher's Magazine* 8 (1999) 19–23.

Mavrodes, George. "Religion and the Queerness of Morality." https://afterall.net/wp-content/uploads/2021/08/religion-and-the-queerness-of-morality.pdf.

Mazur, Suzan. *Royal Society: The Public Evolution Summit*. New York: Caswell, 2016.

McDowell, Josh, and Sean McDowell. *Evidence That Demands a Verdict*. Nashville: Thomas Nelson, 2017.

McGinn, Colin. *Ethics, Evil, and Fiction*. Oxford: Clarendon, 1997.

———. "Problems with Panpsychism." https://www.colinmcginn.net/problems-with-panpsychism/.

McGowan, John. "They Might Have Been Giants (2007)." In *Supplanting the Postmodern: An Anthology of Writings on the Arts and Culture of the Early 21st Century*, edited by David Rudrum and Nicholas Stavris, 61–74. London: Bloomsbury Academic, 2015.

McGrath, Alister E. *Jesus: Who He Is and Why He Matters*. Leicester: InterVarsity, 1994.

———. "John Polkinghorne (1930–2021): The pre-eminent voice on science and religion." https://www.premierchristianity.com/home/john-polkinghorne-1930-2021-the-pre-eminent-voice-on-science-and-religion/4010.article.

———. *Mere Discipleship: On Growing in Wisdom and Hope*. London: SPCK, 2018.

———. *The Passionate Intellect: Christian Faith and the Discipleship of the Mind*. Downers Grove, IL: InterVarsity, 2010.

———. *The Twilight of Atheism: The Rise and Fall of Disbelief in the Modern World*. London: Rider, 2004.

McGrath, Casey. "'Junk DNA' No More: Repetitive Elements as Vital Sources of Flatworm Variation." *Genome Biology and Evolution* 13 (2021) evab217.

McGrew, Lydia. *The Eye of the Beholder: The Gospel of John as Historical Reportage*. Tampa, FL: DeWard, 2021.

———. *Hidden in Plain View: Undesigned Coincidences in the Gospels and Acts*. Tampa, FL: DeWard, 2017.

———. *Testimonies to the Truth: Why You Can Trust the Gospels*. Tampa, FL: DeWard, 2023.

———. "On the Minimal Facts Case for the Resurrection." *Extra Thoughts* (blog), Nov 22, 2021. https://lydiaswebpage.blogspot.com/2021/11/on-minimal-facts-case-for-resurrection.html.

McGrew, Timothy. "Arguments from Providence and Miracles: The State of the Art and the Uses of History." In *Two Dozen (or so) Arguments for God: The Plantinga Project*, edited by Jerry L. Walls and Trent Dougherty, 341–55. Oxford: Oxford University Press, 2018.

McKaughan, Daniel and Daniel Howard-Snyder. "Faith." In *The Encyclopedia of Philosophy of Religion*, Volume III, edited by Stewart Goetz and Charles Taliaferro. Oxford: Wiley-Blackwell, 2021.

McKaughan, Daniel J. "On the Value of Faith and Faithfulness." *International Journal of the Philosophy of Religion* 81 (2017) 7–29.

McKnight, Scot. "Jesus of Nazareth." In *The Face of New Testament Studies: A Survey of Recent Research*, edited by Scot McKnight and Grant R. Osborne, 161. Grand Rapids, MI: Baker Academic, 2004.

McLatchie, Jonathan. "Atheist Philosopher Explains Why Intelligent Design Is Not a 'God of the Gaps' Argument." *Evolution News and Science Today*, February 20, 2024. https://evolutionnews.org/2024/02/atheist-philosopher-explains-why-id-is-not-a-god-of-the-gaps-argument/.

———. "Joining the Conversation: Perspectives on the Discussion with James Shapiro." *Evolution News and Science Today*, January 24, 2012. https://evolutionnews.org/2012/01/joining_the_con/.

———. "Why the Argument from Suboptimal Design Is Weak." *Evolution News and Science Today*, December 20, 2012. https://evolutionnews.org/2012/12/why_the_argumen_1/.

Menuge, Angus J. *Agents Under Fire: Materialism and the Rationality of Science*. Lanham, MD: Rowman & Littlefield, 2004.

———. "Dennett Denied: A Critique of Dennett's Evolutionary Account of Intentionality." Oct 2003. http://static1.1.sqspcdn.com/static/f/38692/239704/1263390969587/A+Criti que+of+Dennetts+Evolutionary+Account+of+Intentionality.pdf.

———. "Justified Belief in the Resurrection." In *The Resurrection Fact: Responding to Modern Critics*, edited by John J. Bombaro and Adam S. Francisco, 117–46. Irvine, CA: NRP, 2016.

———. "Libertarian Free Will and the Argument from Reason." https://www.reasonsforgod.org/wp-content/uploads/2012/09/Libertarian-Free-Will-and-The-Argument-From-Reason1.pdf.

———. "Ramified Personalized Natural Theology: A Third Way?" *Evangelical Philosophical Society*. https://www.epsociety.org/userfiles/art-Menuge%20(Ramified%20Personalized%20Natural%20Theology).pdf.

———. "The Role of Agency in Science." *Discovery Institute*, Feb 3, 2008. https://www.discovery.org/a/10771/.

Menuge, Angus J., and Charles Taliaferro. "Introduction to a Special Issue of Philosophia Christi on Ramified Natural Theology." https://www.epsociety.org/philchristi/tocs/philchristi_15-2.pdf.

Menuge, Angus, et al, eds. *Minding the Brian: Models of the Mind, Information, and Empirical Science*. Seattle, WA: Discovery Institute, 2023.

Meyer, Stephen C. "Advances in Biology Discredit Argument That Cooption Can Explain Irreducible Complexity." *Evolution News and Science Today*, December 17, 2018. https://evolutionnews.org/2018/12/advances-in-biology-discredit-argument-that-cooption-can-explain-irreducible-complexity/.

———. *Darwin's Doubt: The Explosive Origin of Animal Life and the Case for Intelligent Design*. New York: HarperOne, 2013.

———. "DNA by Design: An Inference to the Best Explanation for the Origin of Biological Information." *Rhetoric and Public Affairs* 1 (1999) 519–55. https://www.discovery.org/scripts/viewDB/filesDB-download.php?id=100.

———. "DNA and the Origin of Life: Information, Specification and Explanation." In *Darwinism, Design, & Public Education*, edited by John Angus Campbell and Stephen C. Meyer, 223–85. East Lansing, MI: Michigan State University Press, 2003. https://www.discovery.org/f/1026/.

———. "Evidence for Design in Physics and Biology." In *Science and Evidence for Design in the Universe*, edited by Michael J. Behe et al., 53–111. San Francisco: Ignatius, 2000.

———. "Intelligent Design Is Not Creationism." *The Daily Telegraph*, June 8, 2012. https://stephencmeyer.org/2012/06/08/intelligent-design-is-not-creationism/.

———. "Of Molecules and (Straw) Men: Stephen Meyer Responds to Dennis Venema's Review of Signature in the Cell." *Evolution News and Science Today*, October 9, 2011. https://evolutionnews.org/2011/10/of_molecules_and_straw_men_a_r/.

———. "The Origin of Biological Information and the Higher Taxonomic Categories." *Proceedings of the Biological Society of Washington* 117 (2004) 213–39. https://intelligentdesign.org/articles/origin-biological-information/.

———. "Qualified Agreement: How Scientific Discoveries Support Theistic Belief." In *Science and Faith in Dialogue*, edited by Frederik van Niekerk and Nico Vorster, 33–63. *Reformed Theology in Africa Series 10*. Oxford: AOSIS, 2022, https://books.aosis.co.za/index.php/ob/catalog/book/334.

———. *The Return of the God Hypothesis: Three Scientific Discoveries That Reveal the Mind Behind the Universe*. New York: HarperOne, 2021.

———. "Sauce for the Goose: Intelligent Design, Scientific Methodology, and the Demarcation Problem." In *The Nature of Nature: Examining the Role of Naturalism in Science*, edited by Bruce L. Gordon and William A. Dembski, 95–131. Wilmington, Delaware: ISI, 2011.

———. "The Scientific Status of Intelligent Design." In *Science and Evidence for Design in the Universe*, edited by Michael J. Behe et al., 151–211. San Francisco: Ignatius, 2000. https://www.discovery.org/a/2834/.

———. *Signature in the Cell: DNA and the Evidence for Intelligent Design*. San Francisco: HarperOne, 2010.

———. "Stephen Meyer Critiques Richard Dawkins's 'Mount Improbable' Illustration." YouTube video, July 5, 2013. https://www.youtube.com/watch?v=7rgainpMXa8.

———. "Yes, Intelligent Design Is Detectable by Science." https://intelligentdesign.org/articles/yes-intelligent-design-is-detectable-by-science/.

Meyer, Stephen C., et al. "The Cambrian Explosion: Biology's Big Bang." In *Darwinism, Design, and Public Education*, edited by John Angus Campbell and Stephen C. Meyer, 323–402. East Lansing, MI: Michigan State University Press, 2003. https://www.discovery.org/m/2019/04/Darwin-Cambrian-Explosion.pdf.

Midgley, Mary. *Are You an Illusion?* Durham, NC: Acumen, 2014.

———. *What Is Philosophy For?* London: Bloomsbury Academic, 2018.

Miethe, Terry L., and Gary R. Habermas. *Why Believe? God Exists!* Joplin, MO: College Press, 1998.

Miller, Brian. "A Dentist in the Sahara: Doug Axe on the Rarity of Proteins Is Decisively Confirmed." *Evolution News and Science Today*, February 18, 2019. https://evolutionnews.org/2019/02/a-dentist-in-the-sahara-doug-axe-on-the-rarity-of-proteins-is-decisively-confirmed/.

———. "Another Attempt by an Esteemed Cosmologist to Avoid a Cosmic Beginning Collapses on Inspection." *Evolution News and Science Today*, January 11, 2022. https://evolutionnews.org/2022/01/another-attempt-by-an-esteemed-cosmologist-to-avoid-a-cosmic-beginning-collapses-on-inspection/.

———. "Engineering Principles Explain Biological Systems Better than Evolutionary Theory." In *Science and Faith in Dialogue*, edited by Frederik van Niekerk and Nico Vorster, 175–209. Reformed Theology in Africa Series 10. Oxford: AOSIS, 2022. https://books.aosis.co.za/index.php/ob/catalog/book/334.

———. "Evolutionary Informatics: Marks, Dembski, and Ewert Demonstrate the Limits of Darwinism." *Evolution News and Science Today*, May 2, 2017. https://evolutionnews.org/2017/05/evolutionary-informatics-marks-dembski-and-ewart-demonstrate-the-limits-of-darwinism/.

———. "The Math Behind the Immaterial Genome." *Evolution News and Science Today*, April 29, 2025. https://evolutionnews.org/2025/04/the-math-behind-the-immaterial-genome/.

———. "Mistakes Our Critics Make: Protein Rarity." *Evolution News and Science Today*, July 2, 2020. https://evolutionnews.org/2020/07/mistakes-our-critics-make-protein-rarity/.

———. "Nearly All of Evolution Is Best Explained by Engineering." *Evolution News and Science Today*, September 24, 2021. https://evolutionnews.org/2021/09/nearly-all-of-evolution-is-best-explained-by-engineering/.

———. "Paul Steinhardt's Cyclical Cosmology Fails to Challenge a Cosmic Beginning." *Evolution News and Science Today*, January 12, 2022. https://evolutionnews.org/2022/01/paul-steinhardts-cyclical-cosmology-fails-to-challenge-a-cosmic-beginning/.

———. "*Plato's Revenge*: Mathematical Biologist Richard Sternberg Foresaw Major Developments in Biology." *Evolution News and Science Today*, April 21, 2025. https://evolutionnews.org/2025/04/platos-revenge-mathematical-biologist-richard-sternberg-foresaw-major-developments-in-biology/.

———. "Unraveling the Myth That Undesigned Processes Generate Novel Functions." *Evolution News and Science Today*, April 26, 2022. https://evolutionnews.org/2022/04/unraveling-the-myth-that-undesigned-processes-generate-novel-functions/.

———. "Science Journal Reaffirms Universe Had a Beginning, A Key Argument in Meyer's God Hypothesis." *Evolution News and Science Today*, August 9, 2022. https://evolutionnews.org/2022/08/science-journal-reaffirms-universe-had-a-beginning-a-key-argument-in-meyers-god-hypothesis/.

———. "Thermodynamic Challenges to the Origin of Life." In *The Mystery of Life's Origin: The Continuing Controversy*. Seattle, WA: Discovery Institute, 2020., edited by Charles B. Thaxton, et al., 359–74. https://www.discovery.org/m/securepdfs/2021/02/Tour-MeyerMOLO.pdf.

———. "Why Systems Biologists Now Assume Life Is Optimally Designed." *Evolution News and Science Today*, August 27, 2021. https://evolutionnews.org/2021/08/why-systems-biologists-now-assume-life-is-optimally-designed/.

Miller, Brian, and Stephen C. Meyer. "Physicist Sabine Hossenfelder Challenges the Evidence for Cosmological Fine-Tuning." *Evolution News and Science Today*, October 16, 2020. https://evolutionnews.org/2020/10/physicist-sabine-hossenfelder-challenges-the-evidence-for-cosmological-fine-tuning/.
Miller, Kenneth. "Life's Grand Design." *Technology Review* 97 (1994) 24–32.
Miller, Thomas A. *Did Jesus Really Rise from the Dead? A Surgeon-Scientist Examines the Evidence*. Eugene, OR: Wipf & Stock, 2022.
Milne, Bruce. *The Message of John*. Leicester: InterVarsity, 1993.
Mind Matters. "Dr. Angus Menuge: Models of Consciousness (Part II)." *Mind Matters* Podcast, May 13, 2021. https://mindmatters.ai/podcast/ep134/.
———. "Panpsychism Is, in Angus Menuge's View, a Desperate Move." *Mind Matters* Podcast, May 20, 2021. https://mindmatters.ai/2021/05/panpsychism-is-in-angus-menuges-view-a-desperate-move/.
———. "The Universe Is so Fine Tuned." *Mind Matters* Podcast, September 16, 2021. https://mindmatters.ai/podcast/ep152/.
———. "Run the Gambit of Complexity." *Mind Matters* Podcast, September 2, 2021. https://mindmatters.ai/podcast/ep150/.
———. "Why Is there Fine Tuning Everywhere?" *Mind Matters* Podcast, September 23, 2021. https://mindmatters.ai/podcast/ep153/.
Mines, Ben. "The Simulation Hypothesis." https://www.thinkingmatters.org.nz/2018/07/the-simulation-hypothesis/.
Mitchell, Basil. "Reflections on C. S. Lewis, Apologetics, and the Moral Tradition: Basil Mitchell in Conversation with Andrew Walker." In *Rumours of Heaven: Essays in Celebration of C.S. Lewis*, edited by Andrew Walker and James Patrick, 7–26. Guildford: Eagle, 1998.
"Modernizing the Case for God." *Time*, April 7th, 1980.
Monod, Jacques. *Chance and Necessity: An Essay on the Natural Philosophy of Modern Biology*. New York: HarperCollins, 1974.
Montañez, George D. "A Unified Model of Complex Specified Information." *BIO-Complexity* 4 (2018) 1–26. https://bio-complexity.org/ojs/index.php/main/article/view/BIO-C.2018.4/BIO-C.2018.4.
Montañez, George, et al. "Multiple Overlapping Genetic Codes Profoundly Reduce the Probability of Beneficial Mutation." In *Biological Information: New Perspectives*, 139–67. N.p.: World Scientific, 2013. https://www.worldscientific.com/doi/epdf/10.1142/9789814508728_0006.
Montifiore, Hugh. *The Probability of God*. London: SCM, 1985.
———. *The Womb and the Tomb*. London: Fount, 1992.
Montgomery, John Warwick. *History, Law, and Christianity*. Irvine, CA: NRP, 2015.
Monton, Bradley. "Is Intelligent Design Science? Dissecting the Dover Decision." http://philsci- archive.pitt.edu/archive/00002583/01/Methodological_Naturalism_2.pdf & https://www.arn.org/docs/monton/is_intelligent_design_science.pdf.
———. *Seeking God in Science: An Atheist Defends Intelligent Design*. Peterborough, ON: Broadview, 2009.
Moody, Edmund R. R., et al. "The Nature of the Last Universal Common Ancestor and its Impact on the Early Earth System." *Nature Ecology & Evolution*, 12 July, 2024. https://www.nature.com/articles/s41559-024-02461-1.
Moody, Edmund R. R., and Sandra Álvarez-Carretero. "Scientists Reveal How They Identified the Ancestor of All Life on Earth." *Science Alert* (16th August 2024),

https://www.sciencealert.com/scientists-reveal-how-they-identified-the-ancestor-of-all-life-on-earth.

Moreland, J. P. *Consciousness and the Existence of God: A Theistic Argument.* London: Routledge, 2009.

———. "Four Degrees of Postmodernism." In *Come Let Us Reason: New Essays in Christian Apologetics,* edited by Paul Copan and William Lane Craig, 17–34. Nashville: B&H, 2012.

———. *The God Question: An Invitation to a Life of Meaning.* Eugene, OR: Harvest, 2009.

———. "Intelligent Design and the Nature of Science." In *Intelligent Design 101,* edited by H. Wayne House, 43–65. Grand Rapids: Kregel, 2008.

———. *Love the Lord with All Your Mind: The Role of Reason in the Life of the Soul.* Colorado Springs: NavPress, 1997.

———. "Physicalism, Naturalism and the Nature of Human Persons." In *To Everyone an Answer: A Case for the Christian Worldview,* edited by Francis J. Beckwith et al., 224–37. Downers Grove, IL: InterVarsity, 2004.

———. "Postmodernism and Truth." In *Reasons for Faith: Making a Case for the Christian Faith,* edited by Norman L. Geisler and Chad V. Meister, 113–26. Wheaton, IL: Crossway, 2007.

———. *The Recalcitrant Imago Dei: Human Persons and the Failure of Naturalism.* London: SCM, 2009.

———. *Scaling the Secular City: A Defence of Christianity.* Grand Rapids: Baker, 1987.

———. *Scientism and Secularism: Learning to Respond to a Dangerous Ideology.* Wheaton, IL: Crossway, 2018.

———. "Theistic Science & Methodological Naturalism." In *The Creation Hypothesis,* edited by J. P. Moreland, 41–66. Downers Grove, IL: InterVarsity, 1994.

Moreland, J. P., and Kai Nielson, et al. *Does God Exist? The Debate between Theists and Atheists.* Amherst, NY: Prometheus, 1993.

Moreland, J. P., and Brandon Rickabaugh. *The Substance of Consciousness.* London: Wiley Blackwell, 2023.

Moreland, J. P., and John Mark Reynolds, eds. *Three Views on Creation and Evolution.* Grand Rapids, MI: Zondervan, 1999.

Moreland, J. P., and William Lane Craig. *Philosophical Foundations for a Christian Worldview.* 2nd ed. Downers Grove, IL: IVP Academic, 2017.

Moreland, J. P., and William Lane Craig. *Philosophical Foundations for a Christian Worldview.* Downers Grove, IL: InterVarsity, 2003.

Morley, Brian K. *Mapping Apologetics: Comparing Contemporary Approaches.* Downers Grove, IL: IVP Academic, 2015.

Morris, Thomas V. *Francis Schaeffer's Apologetics: A Critique.* Eugene, OR: Wipf and Stock, 2019.

———. *The Logic of God Incarnate.* Eugene, Oregon: Wipf & Stock, 2001.

———. *Our Idea of God: An Introduction to Philosophical Theology.* Downers Grove, IL: InterVarsity, 1991.

Morrow, Jonathan. *Questioning the Bible: 11 Major Challenges to the Bible's Authority.* Chicago: Moody, 2014.

Mosteller, Timothy M. and Gayne John Anacker, eds. *Contemporary Perspectives on C. S. Lewis' "The Abolition of Man:" History, Philosophy, Education, and Science.* London: Bloomsbury Academic, 2018.

Mounce, William D. *Why I Trust the Bible: Answers to Real Questions and Doubts People Have about the Bible*. Grand Rapids, MI: Zondervan Reflective, 2021.

Murray, Michael J., and Michael Rea. *An Introduction to the Philosophy of Religion*. Cambridge: Cambridge University Press, 2008.

Müller, Gerd B. "The Extended Evolutionary Synthesis." Royal Society, November 7, 2016. http://downloads.royalsociety.org/events/2016/11/evolutionary-biology/muller.mp3.

Nagel, Thomas. "Dawkins and Atheism." In *Secular Philosophy and the Religious Temperament*, 19–26. Oxford: Oxford University Press, 2010.

Nagel, Thomas. *Mind and Cosmos: How the Materialist Neo-Darwinian Conception of Nature Is Almost Certainly False*. Oxford: Oxford University Press, 2012.

———. "Public Education and Intelligent Design." In *Secular Philosophy and the Religious Temperament*, 41–57. Oxford: Oxford University Press, 2010. https://as.nyu.edu/content/dam/nyu-as/philosophy/documents/faculty-documents/nagel/Nagel_Public-Education(1).pdf.

———. *Secular Philosophy and the Religious Temperament*. Oxford: Oxford University Press, 2010.

National Academy of Sciences. *Teaching about Evolution and the Nature of Science*. Washington DC: National Academy, 1998.

National Geographic Partners. "Unsealing of Christ's Reputed Tomb Turns Up New Revelations." *Orthodox Christianity*, Oct 31, 2016. https://orthochristian.com/98227.html.

Nelson, Paul. "Jettison the Arguments, or the Rule? The Place of Theological Themata in Evolutionary Reasoning." https://www.discovery.org/a/104/.

Neufeld, Thomas R. Yoder. *Recovering Jesus*. London: SPCK, 2007.

"New Trends in Evolutionary Biology: Biological, Philosophical and Social Science Perspectives." The Royal Society, https://royalsociety.org/science-events-and-lectures/2016/11/evolutionary-biology.

Newman, Robert C. "Miracles and the Historicity of the Easter Week Narratives." In *Evidence for Faith: Deciding the God Question*, edited by John Warwick Montgomery, 409–452. 2nd ed. Irvine, CA: NRP Books, 2015.

Nicholls, Ruth J. ed. *Understanding & Answering Islam*. Wantirna, VIC: Melbourne School of Theology, 2018.

Nietzsche, Friedrich. "The Parable of the Madman." *The Gay Science*, 1882. https://sourcebooks.fordham.edu/mod/nietzsche-madman.asp.

Oba, Yasuhiro, et al. "Identifying the Wide Diversity of Extraterrestrial Purine and Pyrimidine Nucleobases in Carbonaceous Meteorites." *Nature Communications* 13 (2022) n.p. https://www.nature.com/articles/s41467-022-29612-x.

"Obituaries: Michael Durrant." https://www.cardiff.ac.uk/obituaries/obituary/michael-durrant.

Orgel, Leslie E. *The Origins of Life: Molecules and Natural Selection*. New York: Wiley & Sons, 1973.

Osborn, Peter. *The Assault on Truth: Boris Johnson, Donald Trump and the Emergence of a New Moral Barbarism*. London: Simon & Schuster, 2021.

Overman, Dean L. *A Case Against Accident and Self-Organization*. Lanham: Rowman & Littlefield, 1997.

———. *A Case for the Divinity of Jesus: Examining the Earliest Evidence*. New York: Rowman & Littlefield, 2009.

Owen, H. P. "Why Morality Implies the Existence of God", edited extract from *The Moral Argument for Christian Theism* (George Allen & Unwin, 1965), in Brian Davies, ed. *Philosophy of Religion: a guide and anthology*. Oxford: OUP, 2000.
O'Connell, Jake H. *Jesus' Resurrection and Apparitions: A Bayesian Analysis*. Eugene, OR: Resource, 2017.
———. "Jesus' Resurrection and Collective Hallucinations." *Tyndale Bulletin* 60:1 (2009) 69–105. https://www.tyndalebulletin.org/article/29267-jesus-resurrection-and-collective-hallucinations.pdf.
O'Hear, Anthony. *After Progress: Finding the Old Way Forward*. London: Bloomsbury, 1999.
———. *Jesus for Beginners*. London: Icon, 1993.
———. *Philosophy in the New Century*. London: Continuum, 2001.
O'Leary-Hawthorn, John. "Arguments for Atheism." In *Reason for the Hope Within*, edited by Michael J. Murray, 116–34. Grand Rapids, MI: Eerdmans, 1999.
Palaeo Pictures. "A Giant Dinosaur From the Isle of Wight." YouTube video, June 9, 2022. https://youtu.be/OjRokQFUMJo.
Parrish, Stephen E. "A Tale of Two Theisms: The Philosophical Usefulness of the Classical Christian and Mormon Concepts of God." In *The New Mormon Challenge: Responding to the Latest Defences of a Fast-Growing Movement*, edited by Francis J. Beckwith et al. Grand Rapids, MI: Zondervan, 2002, 193–218.
Patel, Kasha. "Meet the Surprisingly Complex Ancestor of all Life on Earth." *The Washington Post*, https://archive.is/FyGo8#selection-387.3–391.11.
Pearcey, Nancy R. "DNA: The Message in the Message." *First Things* (blog), June 1996. https://www.firstthings.com/article/1996/06/002-dna-the-message-in-the-message.
———. *Saving Leonardo: A Call to Resist the Secular Assault on Mind, Morals, and Meaning*. Nashville: B&H, 2010.
Pearcey, Nancy R., and Charles B. Thaxton. *The Soul of Science*. Wheaton, IL: Crossway, 1994.
Pemberton, Barbara B. "Are We Really All Hindus Now?" In *Come Let Us Reason: New Essays in Christian Apologetics*, edited by Paul Copan and William Lane Craig, 289–304. Nashville: B&H, 2012.
Penrose, Roger. *Fashion, Faith and Fantasy in the New Physics of the Universe*. Princeton, NY: Princeton University Press, 2016.
Perspectiva. "What Is Metamodernism and Why Does It Matter?" YouTube video, Jun 24, 2022. https://www.youtube.com/watch?v=qM_71pPO3Ao.
Peterson, Derick. *Flat Earths and Fake Footnotes: The Strange Tale of How the Conflict of Science and Christianity Was Written Into History*. Eugene, OR: Cascade, 2021.
Peterson, Michael et al. *Reason and Religious Belief: An Introduction to the Philosophy of Religion*. Oxford: OUP, 1992.
Pigliucci, Massimo. NSF Workshop on the Origin of Novel Features at Indiana University on October 6–8, 2006, quoted by Paul A. Nelson, "Why Building Animals Is Hard: The Logic of Development, Common Descent, and the Origin of Animal Body Plans" (7th May 2020). https://www.discovery.org/m/2020/05/Building-Aminals-Is-Hard-050820.pdf (slide 60).
Pinker, Steven. *How the Mind Works*. New York: Norton, 1997.
Plantinga, Alvin. "Against Materialism." https://andrewmbailey.com/ap/Against_Materialism.pdf.

———. "Augustinian Christian Philosophy." *The Monist* (1992) 296–320. https://andrewmbailey.com/ap/Augustinian_Christian_Philosophy.pdf.

———. "Content and Natural Selection." *Philosophy and Phenomenological Research* 83:2 (Sep 2011) 438–58. https://andrewmbailey.com/ap/Content_Natural_Selection.pdf.

———. "An Evolutionary Argument against Naturalism." Jan 2010. https://www.researchgate.net/publication/227992849_An_Evolutionary_Argument_Against_Naturalism.

———. "The Ontological Argument." https://appearedtoblogly.wordpress.com/wp-content/uploads/2011/05/plantinga-alvin-the-ontological-argument.pdf.

———. "Should Methodological Naturalism Constrain Science?" *Perspectives on Science and Christian Faith* 49 (1997) 143–54.

———. "Two Dozen (or so) Arguments for God." https://appearedtoblogly.wordpress.com/wp-content/uploads/2011/05/plantinga-alvin-22two-dozen-or-so-theistic-arguments221.pdf.

———. *Where the Conflict Really Lies: Science, Religion, and Naturalism*. Oxford: Oxford University Press, 2011.

Plato, *Euthyphro*. In Plato, *The Collected Dialogues of Plato*, (trans) Lane Cooper, edited by Edith Hamilton and Huntingdon Cairns. Princeton, NJ: Princeton University Press, 1961.

Pojman, Louis. "Faith Without Belief?" *Faith and Philosophy* 3.2 (1986) 157–76. https://core.ac.uk/download/pdf/216987356.pdf.

Polanyi, Michael. "Life Transcending Physics and Chemistry." *Chemical Engineering News* 45.35 (1967) 54–66.

Polkinghorne, John. *The Case for God*. Tunbridge Wells: Monarch, 1999. Endorsement.

———. *Encountering Scripture*. London: SPCK, 2010.

Potter, Doug. "A Revised Approach to Defending New Testament Textual Reliability." 2023. https://www.academia.edu/99525454/A_Revised_Approach_to_Defending_New_Testament_Textual_Reliability?email_work_card=view-paper.

Pray, Leslie A. "Discovery of DNA Structure and Function: Watson and Crick." *Nature Education* 1.1 (2008) 100.

Provan, Iain, V. Philips Long and Tremper Longman III. *A Biblical History of Israel*. Second Edition. Louisville, Kentucky: WJK, 2015.

Pruss, Alexander R. "Christian Faith and Belief." *Faith and Philosophy*. http://alexanderpruss.com/papers/FaithAndBelief.html.

Puckett, Joe, Jr. *The Apologetics of Joy: A Case for the Existence of God from C. S. Lewis's Argument from Desire*. London: James Clarke, 2013.

Pullen, Stuart. *Intelligent Design or Evolution? Why the Origin of Life and the Evolution of Molecular Knowledge Imply Design*. Raleigh, NC: Intelligent Design, 2005.

Pultz, Karsten. "Our Danish Correspondent, Karsten Pultz, Brings Us Up to Date on Jørn Dyerberg and the Growth of ID Thinking in Scandinavia." *Uncommon Descent*, December 21st, 2020. https://uncommondescent.com/intelligent-design/our-danish-correspondent-karsten-pultz-brings-us-up-to-date-on-jorn-dyerberg-and-the-growth-of-id-thinking-in-scandinavia/.

Quarles, Charles L. "Paul as a Witness to the Resurrection of Jesus." Houston Christian University / News and Events / The City, 2016. https://hc.edu/news-and-events/2016/07/01/paul-witness-r-esurrection-jesus/#:~:text=The%20Nature%20of%20This%20Appearance, 1:16%20has%20become%20common.

Quastler, Henry. *The Emergence of Biological Organization*. New Haven, CT: Yale University Press, 1964.

Qureshi, Nabeel. *No God but One: Allah or Jesus? A Former Muslim Investigates the Evidence for Islam and Christianity*. Grand Rapids, MI: Zondervan, 2016.

Ramberg, Bjørn, and Susan Dieleman. "Richard Rorty." *Stanford Encyclopedia of Philosophy*, last updated June 2023. https://plato.stanford.edu/entries/rorty/.

Ramm, Bernard. *The Christian View of Science and Scripture*. Milton Keynes, UK: Paternoster, 1967.

Rana, Fazale. "Is the Intelligent Designer Alien?" YouTube video, Feb 7, 2024. https://m.youtube.com/watch?v=_NWi2L-IWWc.

Rasmussen, Joshua. "An argument for a Supreme Foundation." In *A New Theist Response to the New Atheism*, edited by Joshua Rasmussen and Kevin Vallier, 21–32. London: Routledge, 2020.

Rasmussen, Joshua, and Kevin Vallier, eds. *A New Theist Response to the New Atheism*. London: Routledge, 2021.

Ratcliffe, Susan, ed. *Oxford Essential Quotations*. 4th edition. https://www.oxfordreference.com/view/10.1093/acref/9780191826719.001.0001/q-oro-ed4-00002890.

Ratzsch, Del. *Science and its Limits: The Natural Sciences in Christian Perspective*. 2nd edition. Downers Grove, IL: InterVarsity, 2000.

"A Reconstruction of LUCA, Within its Evolutionary and Ecological Context." https://commons.wikimedia.org/wiki/File:41559_2024_2461_Fig3b.jpg.

Reeves, Emily. "Systems Biology and Intelligent Design." YouTube video. https://www.youtube.com/watch?v=7PD0iXgu_S8.

Reeves, Mariclair A., et al. "Enzyme Families—Shared Evolutionary History or Shared Design? A Study of the GABA-Aminotransferase Family." *BIO-Complexity*. https://bio-complexity.org/ojs/index.php/main/article/view/BIO-C.2014.4.

Reichenbach, Bruce R. *The Cosmological Argument: A Reassessment*. Springfield, IL: Charles C. Thomas, 1972.

Reppert, Victor. "The Argument from Reason." In *The Blackwell Companion to Natural Theology*, edited by William Lane Craig and J. P. Moreland, 344–90. Oxford: Blackwell, 2009. https://appearedtoblogly.wordpress.com/wp-content/uploads/2011/05/the-argument-from-reason.pdf.

———. *C. S. Lewis' Dangerous Idea: In Defence of the Argument from Reason*. Downers Grove, IL: InterVarsity, 2003.

Richard Dawkins Foundation for Reason & Science. "Richard Dawkins 2016 Reason Rally Speech." YouTube video, June 8, 2016. https://youtu.be/G8NGf3L7foM.

Richard of St Victor. *On the Trinity*. Eugene, OR: Cascade, 2011.

Richards, Jay Wesley. "Divine Simplicity: The Good, the Bad, and the Ugly." In *For Faith and Clarity: Philosophical Contributions to Christian Theology*, edited by James K. Beilby, 157–78. Grand Rapids, MI: Baker Academic, 2006.

Rickabaugh, Brandon, and J. P. Moreland. *The Substance of Consciousness: A Comprehensive Defense of Contemporary Substance Dualism*. Oxford: Wiley-Blackwell, 2023.

Roberts, Mark D. *Can We Trust the Gospels?* Wheaton, IL: Crossway, 2007.

Robinson, Howard. "Qualia, Qualities, and Our Conception of the Physical World." In *After Physicalism*, edited by Benedikt Paul Göcke, 231–63. Notre Dame: University of Notre Dame Press, 2012.

Robinson, J. A. T. *Redating the New Testament*. London: SCM, 1976.
Rorty, Richard. *Philosophy and the Mirror of Nature*. Princeton, NJ: Princeton University Press, 1979.
———. "Untruth and Consequences: A Review of Killing Time by Paul Feyerabend." *New Republic* (Jul 31, 1995) 32–36.
Rosenberg, Alex. *The Atheist's Guide to Reality*. New York: Norton, 2013.
Rosenblatt, Helena. "The Christian Enlightenment." In *Enlightenment, Reawakening and Revolution 1660–1815*, edited by Stewart J. Brown and Timothy Tackett. Cambridge University Press, 2006. https://www.cambridge.org/core/books/abs/cambridge-history-of-christianity/christian-enlightenment/DF98D7464B68A39FFF2AB2027DE0F4E5#.
The Royal Society. "New Trends in Evolutionary Biology: Biological, Philosophical and Social Science Perspectives." https://royalsociety.org/science-events-and-lectures/2016/11/evolutionary-biology/.
Rucker, Philip, and Carol Leonnig. *A Very Stable Genius: Donald J. Trump's Testing of America*. New York: Bloomsbury, 2020.
Rudrum, David. "Note on the Supplanting of 'Post-.'" In *Supplanting the Postmodern: An Anthology of Writings on the Arts and Culture of the Early 21st Century*, edited by David Rudrum and Nicholas Stavris, 333–48. London: Bloomsbury Academic, 2015.
Rudrum, David, and Nicholas Stavris. "Introduction to Ihab Hassan." In *Supplanting the Postmodern: An Anthology of Writings on the Arts and Culture of the Early 21st Century*, edited by David Rudrum and Nicholas Stavris. London: Bloomsbury Academic, 2015.
Rudrum, David, and Nicholas Stavris, eds. *Supplanting the Postmodern: An Anthology of Writings on the Arts and Culture of the Early 21st Century*. London: Bloomsbury Academic, 2015.
Ruse, Michael. *Atheism: What Everyone Needs to Know*. Oxford: Oxford University Press, 2015.
———. *Darwinism and its Discontents*. Cambridge: Cambridge University Press, 2006, 25.
———. "Darwinism as Religion: What Literature Tells Us about Evolution." OUPblog, October 9, 2016. https://blog.oup.com/2016/10/darwinism-as-religion/.
———. "Nonliteralist Antievolution." AAAS Symposium, "The New Antievolutionism," Boston, MA, February 13, 1993. https://www.leaderu.com/orgs/arn/orpages/or151/mr93tran.htm.
Russell, Bertrand. "A Free Man's Worship." 1903. https://ia601300.us.archive.org/15/items/Russell_Bertrand_-_Collection_1/Russell_Bertrand_-_Collection_1.pdf & http://bertrandrussellsocietylibrary.org/br-pe/br-pe-ch2.html.
———. *Religion and Science*. Oxford: Oxford University Press, 1947.
Russell, Bertrand, and F. C. Copleston. "A Debate on the Existence of God." In *The Existence of God*, edited by John Hick, 167–191. New York: Macmillan, 1964, 167–191, http://www.scandalon.co.uk/philosophy/cosmological_radio.htm.
Russell, Calum. "Everything Everywhere All at Once and the Beauty of Nihilism." *Far Out*, Feb 19, 2023. https://faroutmagazine.co.uk/everything-everywhere-all-at-once-the-beauty-of-nihilism/.
Rutt, Jim. "Lene Rachel Andersen on Polymodernity." YouTube video, Jan 31, 2024. *Jim Rutt Show*, episode 220. https://youtu.be/o0PKt6bANTs?si=yKA-Ytm2Kb267q2R.

Ryle, Gilbert. *The Concept of Mind*. Chicago: University of Chicago Press, 1949.
Sadowsky, James A. "Can There Be an Endless Regress of Causes?" In *Philosophy of Religion: a guide and anthology*, edited by Brian Davies, 239–41. Oxford: Oxford University Press, 2000. AnthonyFlood.com (blog), n.d. http://www.anthonyflood.com/sadowskyendlessregress.htm.
Sanford, John, et al. "The Waiting Time Problem in a Model Hominin Population." *Theoretical Biology and Medical Modelling* 12 (2015) art. 18. https://tbiomed.biomedcentral.com/articles/10.1186/s12976-015-0016-z.
Sartre, Jean-Paul. "Existentialism Is a Humanism." 1946. https://www.marxists.org/reference/archive/sartre/works/exist/sartre.htm.
Science—Faith—Reason. "Intelligent Design 3.0." YouTube video, April 1, 2019. https://www.youtube.com/watch?v=sbjh0R143wE.
Scott, Douglas D. *Is Jesus of Nazareth the Predicted Messiah?* Eugene, OR: Wipf & Stock, 2019.
Scrivener, Glen. *The Air We Breathe*. Epsom: Good Book, 2022.
Scruton, Roger. *An Intelligent Person's Guide to Culture*. London: Duckworth, 1998.
———. *Modern Philosophy: An Introduction and Survey*. London: A&C Black, 2012.
Sennett, James F., and Douglas Groothuis, eds. *In Defence of Natural Theology: A Post-Humean Assessment*. Downers Grove, IL: IVP Academic, 2005.
Senor, Thomas D. "The Incarnation and the Trinity" in *Reason for the Hope Within*. Michael J. Murray, ed. Grand Rapids, Michigan: Eerdmans, 1999.
Service, Robert F. "Researchers May Have Solved Origin-of-Life Conundrum." March 16, 2015. https://www.science.org/content/article/researchers-may-have-solved-origin-life-conundrum.
Sewell, Granville. "Entropy and Evolution." *BIO-Complexity* 2 (2013) 1–5. http://dx.doi.org/10.5048/BIO-C.2013.2.
———. "The Scientific Establishment Is Finally Starting to Take Intelligent Design Seriously." *The Federalist*, May 17th, 2022. https://thefederalist.com/2022/05/17/the-scientific-establishment-is-finally-starting-to-take-intelligent-design-seriously/.
Shaefer-Landau, Russ. *Whatever Happened to Good and Evil?* Oxford: Oxford University Press, 2004.
Shakespeare, William. *Romeo and Juliet*. http://shakespeare.mit.edu/romeo_juliet/full.html.
Shalkowski, Scott A. "Atheological Apologetics." In *Contemporary Perspectives on Religious Epistemology*, edited by R. Douglas Geivett and Brendan Sweetman, 58–73. Oxford: Oxford University Press, 1992.
Shapiro, James. *Evolution: A View from the 21st Century*. Upper Saddle River, NJ: FT Press Science, 2011.
———. "What Natural Genetic Engineering Does and Does Not Mean." *Huffington Post*, Apr 30, 2013. https://www.huffpost.com/entry/what-natural-genetic-engi_b_2783419?view=print&comm_ref=false.
Shedinger, Robert F. "Hey, Paul Davies—Your ID Is Showing." *Evolution News and Science Today*, March 6, 2020. https://evolutionnews.org/2020/03/hey-paul-davies-your-id-is-showing/.
———. *The Mystery of Evolutionary Mechanisms: Darwinian Biology's Grand Narrative of Triumph and the Subversion of Religion*. Eugene, OR: Cascade, 2019.

Shumack, Richard. *The Wisdom of Islam and the Foolishness of Christianity: A Christian Response to Nine Objections to Christianity by Muslim Philosophers*. Sydney: Island View, 2014.
Sider, Ronald J. *The Spiritual Danger of Donald Trump: 30 Evangelical Christians on Justice, Truth, and Moral Integrity*. Eugene, OR: Cascade, 2020.
Siegel, Ethan. "Ask Ethan: Has the JWST Disproven the Big Bang?" *Big Think* (blog), August 26, 2022. https://bigthink.com/starts-with-a-bang/has-jwst-disproven-big-bang/.
———. "What We Wish We Knew About the Origin of Life." *Big Think* (blog), March 10, 2022. https://bigthink.com/starts-with-a-bang/origin-of-life-169450/.
Simek, Slater. "A Bayesian Exploration of C. S. Lewis's 'Argument from Desire.'" *Sophia* 61 (2022) 757–73. https://link.springer.com/article/10.1007/s11841-021-00887-9.
Simpson, George Gaylord. *The Meaning of Evolution*. New Haven, CT: Yale University Press, 1971.
Sinnott-Armstrong, Walter. *Think Again: How to Reason and Argue*. London: Pelican, 2018.
Sire, James W. *The Universe Next Door*. 5th ed. Downers Grove, IL: InterVarsity, 2002.
———. *The Universe Next Door—A Basic Worldview Catalog*. 6th ed. Downers Grove, IL: IVP Academic, 2020.
Skeptical Inquirer. "What Is Skepticism?" https://skepticalinquirer.org/what-is-skepticism/.
Small, Keith E. *Textual Criticism And Qur'an Manuscripts*. Lanham, MD: Lexington, 2012.
Smith, Christian. *To Flourish or Destruct: A Personalist Theory of Human Goods. Motivations, Failure, and Evil*. Chicago: University of Chicago Press, 2015.
Smith, Mark D. *The Final Days of Jesus: The Thrill of Defeat, the Agony of Victory: A Classical Historian Explores Jesus's Arrest, Trial, and Execution*. Cambridge: Lutterworth, 2018.
Smith, Peter. "Highlights from AP-NORC Poll about the Religiously Unaffiliated in the US." *AP News*, Oct 4, 2023. https://apnews.com/article/religion-ap-poll-nones-survey-111e9f5bbcaaa47ea522f1aae9c24df9.
Snow, Dan. "Portchester Castle: 10 Places That Made England with Dan Snow." YouTube video. https://www.youtube.com/watch?v=11YlHA4Wo3Y.
Sokol, Sam. "Orthodoxy Can Withstand an Unflinching, Academic Look at the Bible, Says Scholar." *The Times of Israel*, May 28, 2020. https://www.timesofisrael.com/orthodoxy-can-withstand-an-unflinching-academic-look-at-the-bible-says-scholar/.
Sorley, W. R. *Moral Value and the Idea Of God*, Second Edition. Cambridge: Cambridge University Press, 1921.
Spencer, Nick. *Atheists: The Origin of the Species*. London: Bloomsbury, 2014.
Spetner, Lee. *Not By Chance: Shattering the Modern Theory of Evolution*. New York: Judica, 1983.
Stanton, Graham. *The Gospels and Jesus*. Oxford: Oxford University Press, 1990.
Stark, Rodney. *The Triumph of Christianity: How the Jesus Movement Became the World's Largest Religion*. New York: HarperOne, 2011.
Stavris, Nicholas. "The Anxieties of the Present." In *Supplanting the Postmodern: An Anthology of Writings on the Arts and Culture of the Early 21st Century*, edited by

David Rudrum and Nicholas Stavris, 349–64. London: Bloomsbury Academic, 2015.
Stein, Robert H. "Criteria for the Gospel's Authenticity." In *Contending with Christianity's Critics*, edited by Paul Copan and William Lane Craig, 88–103. Nashville: B&H Academic, 2009.
Stenger, Victor J. *The New Atheism: Taking a Stand for Science and Reason*. Amherst, NY: Prometheus, 2009.
Stewart, Don, and Joseph M. Holden. "Were the New Testament Manuscripts Copied Accurately?" In *The Harvest Handbook of Apologetics*, edited by Joseph M. Holden, 191–98. Eugene, OR: Harvest, 2018.
Stewart, Robert B. "On Habermas's Minimal Facts Argument." In *Raised on the Third Day*, edited by W. David Beck and Michael R. Licona, 1–14. Bellingham, WA: Lexham, 2020.
Stewart, Robert B., ed. *The Reliability of the New Testament: Bart Ehrman and Daniel Wallace in Dialogue*. Minneapolis: Fortress, 2011.
Stirner, Simone. "Notes on the State of the Subject." *Notes on Metamodernism*, Nov 2, 2011. https://www.metamodernism.com/2011/11/02/notes-on-the-state-of-the-subject/.
Stoke, Mitch. *A Shot of Faith (to the Head): Be a Confident Believer in an Age of Cranky Atheists*. Nashville, TN: Thomas Nelson, 2012.
Strobel, Lee. *The Case for Miracles*. Grand Rapids, MI: Zondervan, 2018.
Stump, J. B., ed. *Four Views on Creation, Evolution and Intelligent Design*. Grand Rapids, MI: Zondervan, 2017.
Sutter, Paul. "The Improbable Origins of Life on Earth." *Universe Today* (Jan. 28, 2024). https://www.universetoday.com/articles/the-improbable-origins-of-life-on-earth.
———. "Is the Universe inside a Black Hole?" *Scientific American* (April 1, 2025). https://www.scientificamerican.com/article/do-we-live-inside-a-black-hole/.
Swift, David W. "Genetic and Biochemical Challenges to the Evolution of New Genes—Introduction." https://evolutionunderthemicroscope.com/newgenes00.html.
Swinburne, Richard. *The Christian God*. Oxford: Clarendon, 1994.
———. "Evidence for God" (1986). *Christian Evidence*. http://christianevidence.org/docs/booklets/evidence_for_god.pdf.
———. *The Existence of God*. 2nd edition. Cambridge: Clarendon, 2004.
———. *Faith and Reason*. 2nd edition. Oxford: Clarendon, 2005.
———. *Mind, Brain, and Free Will*. Oxford: Oxford University Press, 2013.
———. *The Resurrection of God Incarnate*. Oxford: Clarendon, 2003.
———. *Was Jesus God?* Oxford: Oxford University Press, 2010.
Swinerd, Graham, and John Bryant. *From the Big Bang to Biology: Where Is God?* N.p.: Kindle Direct, 2020.
Taliaferro, Charles. *Aesthetics: A Beginner's Guide*. Oxford: OneWorld, 2011.
———. *Consciousness and the Mind of God*. Cambridge: Cambridge University Press, 1994.
———. *Contemporary Philosophy of Religion*. Oxford: Blackwells, 2001.
———. *Philosophy of Religion*. Oxford: OneWorld, 2009.
———. "Where Do Thoughts Come From?" In *The Big Argument: Does God Exist?*, edited by John Ashton and Michael Westcott, 155–63. Green Forest, AR: Master Books, 2006.

Talking Jesus. What People in the UK Think of Jesus, Christians and Evangelism. Talking Jesus report, 2022. https://www.eauk.org/assets/files/downloads/Talking-Jesus-Report.pdf.

Tallis, Raymond. "Against Panpsychism." *Philosophy Now*, 2017. https://philosophynow.org/issues/121/Against_Panpsychism.

———. *Aping Mankind: Neuromania, Darwinitis and the Misrepresentation of Humanity.* London: Routledge, 2014.

Tallon, Philip. "The Theistic Argument from Beauty and Play." In *Two Dozen (or so) Arguments for God*, edited by Jerry L. Walls and Trent Dougherty, 321–40. Oxford: Oxford University Press, 2018.

Tan, Chance Laura, and Rob Stadler. *The Stairway to Life: An Origin-of-Life Reality Check.* N.p.: Evorevo, 2020.

Taylor, A. E. *Does God Exist?* London: Collins, 1961.

Taylor, Charles. *A Secular Age.* Cambridge, MA: Belknap, 2007.

Taylor, Richard. "The Cosmological Argument: A Defence." http://mind.ucsd.edu/syllabi/02-03/01w/readings/taylor.pdf.

Teaching about Evolution and the Nature of Science. National Academy Press, 1998.

Thaxton, Charles B., et al. *The Mystery of Life's Origin: The Continuing Controversy.* Seattle, WA: Discovery Institute, 2020. https://www.discovery.org/m/securepdfs/2021/02/Tour-MeyerMOLO.pdf.

Theißen, Günter. "Saltational Evolution: Hopeful Monsters Are Here to Stay." *Theory in Biosciences* 128 (2009) 43–51. https://link.springer.com/article/10.1007/s12064-009-0058-z.

Thomas, Neil. *Taking Leave of Darwin: A Longtime Agnostic Discovers the Case for Design.* Seattle, WA: Discovery Institute, 2021.

Thornton, Joseph W., and Rob DeSalle. "Gene Family Evolution and Homology: Genomics Meets Phylogenetics." *Annual Review of Genomics and Human Genetics* 1 (2000) 41–73.

Thorvaldsen, Steinar. "Intelligent Design and Natural Theology." *Theofilos* 12 (2020) 66–84. https://theofilos.no/wp-content/uploads/2021/02/Theofilos-vol-12-nr-1-2020-Supplement-academia-5-NY-210211.pdf.

Thorvaldsen, Steinar, and Ola Hössjer. "Using Statistical Methods to Model the Fine-Tuning of Molecular Machines and Systems." *Journal of Theoretical Biology* 501 (2020) 110352. https://www.sciencedirect.com/science/article/pii/S0022519320302071.

Todd, Scott. "A View from Kansas on the Evolution Debate." *Nature* 401 (1999) 423.

Tonkin, Sam. "Dark Energy 'Doesn't Exist' so Can't Be Pushing 'Lumpy' Universe Apart – Study." *Royal Astronomical Society* (19/12/2024). https://ras.ac.uk/news-and-press/research-highlights/dark-energy-doesnt-exist-so-cant-be-pushing-lumpy-universe-apart.

Tour, James. "Animadversions of a Synthetic Chemist." https://inference-review.com/article/animadversions-of-a-synthetic-chemist.

———. "Are Present Proposals on Chemical Evolutionary Mechanisms Accurately Pointing Towards the First Life?" In *Science and Faith in Dialogue*, edited by Frederik van Niekerk and Nico Vorster, 149–73. Reformed Theology in Africa Series 10. Oxford: AOSIS, 2022. https://books.aosis.co.za/index.php/ob/catalog/book/334.

———. "Two Experiments in Abiogenesis." https://inference-review.com/article/two-experiments-in-abiogenesis.

———. "We're Still Clueless about the Origin of Life." In *The Mystery of Life's Origin: The Continuing Controversy*. Seattle, WA: Discovery Institute, 2020., edited by Charles B. Thaxton, et al., 277–306. https://www.discovery.org/m/securepdfs/2021/02/Tour-MeyerMOLO.pdf.

Tour, James M., et al. "Thermodynamic Limitations on the Natural Emergence of Long Chain Molecules: Implications for Origin of Life." *BioCosmos*, Volume 5 (2025): Issue 1 (January 2025), 64–71. https://sciendo.com/article/10.2478/biocosmos-2025-0010?tab=abstract.

Turek, Frank, et al. "Is the Cosmological Argument Still Sound? With Dr. William Lane Craig and Dr. Stephen C. Meyer." *Cross Examined*. YouTube video, January 25, 2023. https://www.youtube.com/watch?v=_0M8PCNdveo&t=1s.

Trevors, J. T., and D. L. Abel. "Three Subsets of Sequence Complexity and their Relevance to Biopolymeric Information." *Theoretical Biology and Medical Modelling* 2 (2005) 29. https://www.researchgate.net/publication/7664009_Three_subsets_of_sequence_complexity_and_their_relevance_to_biopolymeric_information.

Trigg, Roger. *Does Science Undermine Faith*? London: SPCK, 2018.

Turley, Stephen. *Awakening Wonder: A Classical Guide to Truth, Goodness and Beauty*. Camp Hill, PA: Classical Academic, 2014.

Tyson, Neil deGrasse. *Cosmos: A Spacetime Odyssey*. Los Angeles: 20th Century Fox Home Entertainment, 2014.

UK Research and Innovation. "What Is Social Science?" https://www.ukri.org/about-us/esrc/what-is-social-science/.

University of Southampton. "Two New Species of Large Predatory Dinosaur Discovered on Isle of Wight." YouTube video, September 29, 2021. https://youtu.be/x3gUECD7axs.

Vermeulen, Timotheus. "Knock Knock." Digital Bauhaus Summit, Jun 18, 2017. https://vimeo.com/222081144.

Vermeulen, Timotheus, and Robin van den Akker. "Notes on Metamodernism." *Journal of Aesthetics and Culture* 2:1 (2010). https://www.tandfonline.com/doi/full/10.3402/jac.v2i0.5677.

Voie, Øyvind Albert. "Biological Function and the Genetic Code Are Interdependent." *Chaos, Solutions and Fractals* 28 (2006) 1000–1004. https://www.sciencedirect.com/science/article/abs/pii/S0960077905008052.

Walker, Andrew. *Seven Atheisms*. Christian Evidence Society, 2019. https://christianevidence.org/booklet/seven_atheisms/.

Walker, Sara Imari. "Origins of Life: A Problem for Physics, a Key Issues Review." *Reports on Progress in Physics* 80 (2017) 092601.

Walls, Jerry L., and Trent Dougherty, eds. *Two Dozen (or so) Arguments for God*. Oxford: Oxford University Press, 2018.

Waltham, David. *Lucky Planet: Why Earth Is Exceptional - And What it Means for Life in the Universe*. London: Icon, 2014.

Ward, Keith. *The Big Questions in Science and Religion*. Radnor, PA: Templeton, 2008.

———. "Creatio Ex Nihilo." Encyclopedia.com. https://www.encyclopedia.com/education/encyclopedias-almanacs-transcripts-and-maps/creatio-ex-nihilo.

———. *God, Chance & Necessity*. Oxford: OneWorld, 1996.

———. *Is Religion Dangerous*? 2nd ed. Oxford: Lion, 2011.

Ward, Michael. *After Humanity: A Guide to C.S. Lewis' "The Abolition of Man."* Park Ridge, IL.: Word on Fire Academic, 2021.
Ward, Peter D., and Donald Brownlee. *Rare Earth: Why Complex Life is Uncommon in the Universe*. New York: Copernicus, 2000.
Wattles, J. "C. S. Lewis, Peter Kreeft, and the Sequence: Truth, Goodness, and Beauty." 2015. *Universal Family*, 2015. https://universalfamily.org/c-s-lewis-peter-kreeft-and-the-sequence-truth-goodness-and-beauty/.
Wedgwood, Orson. *DNA: The Elephant in the Lab: The Truth about the Origin of Life*. Kindle, 2019.
Weikart, Richard. *From Darwin to Hitler: Evolutionary Ethics, Eugenics and Racism in Germany*. London: Palgrave Macmillan, 2004.
———. *Hitler's Ethic: The Nazi Pursuit of Evolutionary Progress*. London: Palgrave Macmillan, 2009.
Wells, Jonathan. *The Myth of Junk DNA*. Seattle, WA: Discovery Institute, 2011.
———. "Not in the Genes: Embryonic Electric Fields." *Evolution News and Science Today*, December 12, 2011. https://evolutionnews.org/2011/12/not_in_the_gene/.
———. *Zombie Science: More Icons of Evolution*. Seattle, WA: Discovery Institute, 2017.
Wenham, John. *Easter Enigma: Are the Resurrection Accounts in Conflict?* 2nd ed. London: Paternoster, 1992.
Wenham, John, and Steve Walton. *Exploring the New Testament: A Guide to the Gospels and Acts*. New Testament 1. 3rd ed. London: SPCK, 2021.
West, John G. "Debating Common Ancestry." *Evolution News and Science Today*, May 14, 2016. https://evolutionnews.org/2016/05/debating_common/.
West, John G., ed. *The Magician's Twin: C. S. Lewis on Science, Scientism, and Society*. Seattle, WA: Discovery Institute, 2012.
What Is Metamodern? "About the Authors." https://whatismetamodern.com/about-the-authors/.
———. "Talking Metamodernism with Tim Vermeulen." YouTube video, Oct 25, 2021. https://www.youtube.com/watch?v=IusoCjpdWwg.
Whitfield, John. "Biological Theory: Postmodern Evolution?" Nature 455 (2008) 281–84. https://app.amanote.com/v4.0.36/research/note-taking?resourceId=eYtnonMBKQvfoBhi4zjf.
Wikipedia, "First Universal Common Ancestor." https://en.wikipedia.org/wiki/First_universal_common_ancestor#:~:text=FUCA%20is%20thought%20to%20have,of%20genes%20and%20gene%20families.
———. "H. M. S. Victory." https://en.wikipedia.org/wiki/HMS_Victory.
———. "Portchester Castle." https://en.wikipedia.org/wiki/Portchester_Castle.
———. "Salisbury Cathedral." https://en.wikipedia.org/wiki/Salisbury_Cathedral.
———. "Whitecliff Bay and Bembridge Ledges." https://en.wikipedia.org/wiki/Whitecliff_Bay_and_Bembridge_Ledges.
———. "Winchester Cathedral." https://en.wikipedia.org/wiki/Winchester_Cathedral.
Wielenberg, Erik. "Dawkins's Gambit, Hume's Aroma, and God's Simplicity." *Philosophia Christi*, Vol. 11, No. 1, 2009. www.academia.edu/19893604/Dawkinss_Gambit_Humes_Aroma_and_Gods_Simplicity.
Wilkins, Michael. "Gospel of Matthew." In *The Gospel and Acts. The Holman Apologetics Commentary on the Bible*, edited by Jeremy Royal Howard, 7–198. Nashville: Holman Reference, 2013.

Willard, Dallas. "Knowledge and Naturalism." *Dallas Willard Ministries.* https://dwillard.org/resources/articles/knowledge-and-naturalism.

———. "Language, Being, God, and the Three Stages of Theistic Evidence." *Dallas Willard Ministries.* https://dwillard.org/articles/language-being-god-and-the-three-stages-of-theistic-evidence.

———. *Renewing the Christian Mind: Essays, Interviews, and Talks.* New York: HarperOne, 2016.

Williams, Donald T. "The Validity of Lewis's Trilemma." In *Reflections from Plato's Cave: Essays in Evangelical Philosophy.* Monroe, VA: Lantern Hollow, 2012.

Williams, Peter J. *Can We Trust the Gospels?* Wheaton, IL: Crossway, 2018.

Williams, Peter S. *Apologetics in 3D: Essays on Apologetics and Spirituality.* Eugene, OR: Wipf & Stock, 2019.

———. "Apologetics in 3D (Norway, 2024)." *The Peter S. Williams Podcast.* http://podcast.peterswilliams.com/e/apologetics-in-3d-norway-2024/.

———. "Apologetic Methodology." YouTube playlist. https://www.youtube.com/playlist?list=PLQhh3qcwVEWiKQdPlQT4obtIzEdn82oiI.

———. "Archaeological Evidence and Jesus (ELF 2025)." *The Peter S. Williams Podcast.* http://podcast.peterswilliams.com/e/archaeological-evidence-and-jesus-elf-2025/.

———. "Arguing for God (Oslo, 2022)." *The Peter S. Williams Podcast*, October 29, 2022. http://podcast.peterswilliams.com/e/arguing-for-god-oslo-2022/.

———. "The Argument from Desire." YouTube playlist. https://www.youtube.com/play list?list=PLQhh3qcwVEWj3nK3TBydEVAFRtdqfrpW2.

———. "A Beginner's Guide to the Theistic Argument from Desire." https://www.peterswilliams.com/wp-content/uploads/2021/01/Intro_Lewis_Desire_2019.pdf.

———. *Behold the Man: Essays on the Historical Jesus.* Eugene, OR: Wipf & Stock, 2024.

———. "A Brief Introduction to and Defence of the Modern Ontological Argument." *Theofilos* 7.3 (2015) 339–44. https://theofilos.no/wp-content/uploads/2019/09/3d_Forum_Williams_A-Brief-Introduction-to-and-Defence-of-the-Modern-Ontological-Argument.pdf.

———. "Beauty." YouTube playlist. https://www.youtube.com/playlist?list=PLQhh3qcwVEWiL488-SGbfODhf6kLPSZbJ.

———. "Buddhism." YouTube playlist. https://www.youtube.com/playlist?list=PLQhh3qcwVEWif_IZ4RSdtPpT9PZ6p3O7I.

———. *The Case for Angels.* Carlisle, Cumbria: Paternoster, 2003.

———. *The Case for God.* Eastbourne: Monarch, 1999.

———. "Can Moral Objectivism Do Without God?" https://www.peterswilliams.com/wp-content/uploads/2022/07/Can-Moral-Objectivism-Do-Without-God-v3.pdf.

———. "C. S. Lewis as a Central Figure in Formulating the Theistic Argument from Desire." *Linguaculture* 10.2 (2019). https://journal.linguaculture.ro/index.php/home/article/view/149/136.

———. *C. S. Lewis vs. the New Atheists.* Milton Keynes: Paternoster, 2013.

———. "Christian Leadership in 3D: Leading and Following in the Spiritual Footsteps of Jesus." *Scandinavian Journal for Leadership & Theology* 2025, volume 12. https://www.peterswilliams.com/wp-content/uploads/2025/05/WilliamsChristianLeadershipin3D.pdf.

---. "A Christian Worldview and Science in Apologetic Perspective: Anthropos." *The Peter S. Williams Podcast*, October 25, 2021. http://podcast.peterswilliams.com/e/a-christian-worldview-and-science-in-apologetic-perspective-anthropos/.

---. "A Christian Worldview and Science in Apologetic Perspective: Bios (a) Introduction to Darwinism." *The Peter S. Williams Podcast*, October 25, 2021. http://podcast.peterswilliams.com/e/a-christian-worldview-and-science-in-apologetic-perspective-bios-a-introduction-to-darwinism/.

---. "A Christian Worldview and Science in Apologetic Perspective: Cosmos." *The Peter S. Williams Podcast*, October 25, 2021. http://podcast.peterswilliams.com/e/a-christian-worldview-and-science-in- apologetic-perspective-cosmos/.

---. "Christianity and Archaeology." YouTube playlist. https://www.youtube.com/pl aylist?list=PLQhh3qcwVEWjh9aRRWF1kYZIVCPc5iCcw.

---. "Christianity and Science." YouTube playlist. https://www.youtube.com/playlis t?list=PLQhh3qcwVEWjeYJfOKB1YYXsInZ5GIPL_.

---. "Christology." YouTube playlist. https://www.youtube.com/playlist?list=PLQh h3qcwVEWgjXlj2cVn_ZjOE8Wd9dVbv.

---. "Cosmic Fine Tuning: Design or Multiverse?" *The Peter S. Williams Podcast*. http://podcast.peterswilliams.com/e/cosmic-fine-tuning-design-or-multiverse/.

---. "Cosmic Fine Tuning." YouTube playlist. https://youtube.com/playlist?list=PL Qhh3qcwVEWj4aeE76A1vjLvPqWieH8tE.

---. "Cosmological Arguments for God." YouTube playlist. https://www.youtube.com/playlist?list=PLQhh3qcwVEWjEXjiEjnCCbr_Qnu-1UbAa.

---. "Critical Thinking." YouTube playlist. https://www.youtube.com/playlist?list=PLQhh3qcwVEWjunXMo96VWNyJgx-XAn8fp.

---. "The Design Inference from Specified Complexity Defended by Scholars Outside the Intelligent Design Movement—A Critical Review." *Philosophia Christi* 9 (2007) 1–6. https://www.epsociety.org/articles/the-design-inference-from-specified-complexity-defended-by-scholars-outside-the-intelligent-design-movement/.

---. *Digging for Evidence: Archaeology and the Historical Reliability of the New Testament*. London: Christian Evidence Society, 2016. http://christianevidence.org/docs/booklets/digging_for_evidence.pdf.

---. "Debate: Does God Exist? Peter S. Williams vs. Einar Bohn at the Norwegian University of Science and Technology in Trondheim" *The Peter S. Williams Podcast*. http://peterswilliams.podbean.com/mf/feed/e5dvj8/Trondheim_2018_Debate.mp3arguments-from-desire/.

---. "Debating God." YouTube playlist. https://www.youtube.com/playlist?list=PL Qhh3qcwVEWiY3UmTAiRdj2OW4SBG0y_W.

---. "Debating the Resurrection." YouTube playlist. https://www.youtube.com/play list?list=PLQhh3qcwVEWhAPCkcpFsSwEXrYKuBhoaq.

---. "Did Jesus Perform Miracles?" YouTube playlist. https://www.youtube.com/playlist?list=PLQhh3qcwVEWi1yi_tcY-Ptl9nNJzRCeiN.

---. "Discipleship and Spiritual Formation." YouTube playlist. https://www.youtube. com/playlist?list=PLQhh3qcwVEWhGSK1x6H3qeqzefB8hmvvM.

---. "Discipleship in 3D: Change for Head, Heart and Hands." *Damaris Norge*. YouTube video, Apr 29, 2020. https://youtu.be/QTyEooJgIBI?si=sa-PotDjrTJ1jE5U.

———. "Distinguishing Science from Scientific Naturalism." *The Peter S. Williams Podcast*, Oct, 2024. http://podcast.peterswilliams.com/e/distinguishing-science-from-scientific-naturalism/.

———. "Do Angels Really Exist?" *BeThinking*, 2015. https://www.bethinking.org/christian-beliefs/do-angels-really-exist.

———. "ELF 2023: Can We Believe in God in an Age of Science? The Big Bang (Part Four of Seven)." *The Peter S. Williams Podcast*, June, 2023. http://podcast.peterswilliams.com/e/elf-2023-can-we-believe-in-god-in-an-age-of-science-the-big-bang-part-four-of-seven/.

———. "The Epistle of St. James vs. Evolutionary Christology." *Theofilos* (Volume 8, 2016:1). https://theofilos.no/wp-content/uploads/2019/09/2c_Academia_Williams_The-Epistle-of-James-vs.-Evolutionary.pdf.

———. "The Existence of Jesus." YouTube playlist. https://www.youtube.com/playlist?list=PLQhh3qcwVEWiCALtjBWyxo78Dxxib4g8E.

———. "Exodus." YouTube playlist. https://www.youtube.com/watch?v=woV7Px651-o&list=PLQhh3qcwVEWjbiCIsVBzoXW4bFq72c3EJ.

———. *A Faithful Guide to Philosophy: A Christian Introduction to the Love of Wisdom*. Eugene, OR: Wipf and Stock, 2019.

———. "Faith and Rationality (Oslo, 2022)." *The Peter S. Williams Podcast*, Oct 14, 2020. http://podcast.peterswilliams.com/e/faith-rationality-oslo-2022/.

———. "The Fossil Record." YouTube playlist. https://youtube.com/playlist?list=PLQhh3qcwVEWjbYPLl33A3aF_W4TSAjcaF.

———. *Getting at Jesus: A Comprehensive Critique of Neo-Atheist Nonsense about the Jesus of History*. Eugene, OR: Wipf & Stock, 2019.

———. "Gospel Contradictions?" YouTube playlist. https://www.youtube.com/playlist?list=PLQhh3qcwVEWjt9SKTdFKEqLkUpwJYxCit.

———. "Hebrews 11 and Faith in the New Atheism." *The Peter S. Williams Podcast*. http://podcast.peterswilliams.com/e/hebrews-11-faith-in-the-new-atheism/.

———. "Historical Criteria of Authenticity." YouTube playlist. https://www.youtube.com/playlist?list=PLQhh3qcwVEWg6gh7wSlE4EWoDtTHaq5.

———. "The Historical Jesus." YouTube playlist. https://www.youtube.com/playlist?list=PLQhh3qcwVEWgoCpSQPAr5cy_lnXpeQMNk.

———. "Imagine Naturalism - C.S Lewis' Atheism and His Escape From the Closed Universe." YouTube video, Jan 3, 2024. https://www.youtube.com/watch?v=H74iTqdQa7w.

———. "The 'Immaterial Genome' Hypothesis." YouTube playlist. https://www.youtube.com/playlist?list=PLQhh3qcwVEWj3Oz-YTXv3Qzu54P2FE3UQ.

———. *An Informed Cosmos: Essays on Intelligent Design Theory*. Eugene, OR: Wipf & Stock, 2023.

———. "Intelligent Design, Aesthetics and Design Arguments" http://www.arn.org/docs/williams/pw_idaestheticsanddesignarguments.htm.

———. "Introduction to An Informed Cosmos: Essays on Intelligent Design Theory." *The Peter S. Williams Podcast*. http://podcast.peterswilliams.com/e/introduction-to-an-informed-cosmos-essays-on-intelligent-design-theory/.

———. "Introduction to Intelligent Design Theory." YouTube playlist. https://www.youtube.com/playlist?list=PLQhh3qcwVEWhNWeZ2LxPUa5j2afVcG-B6.

———. "Irreducible Complexity." YouTube playlist. https://www.youtube.com/playlist?list=PLQhh3qcwVEWh3orLA2I3KySSxUoIXAdZ3.

———. "Is Christianity Good for Society?" YouTube playlist. https://www.youtube.com/playlist?list=PLQhh3qcwVEWhEFhLjwAL_Qp4dCzCvwGc-.

———. "Islam." YouTube playlist. https://www.youtube.com/playlist?list=PLQhh3qcwVEWjhD84EB0jEG5PswCOcDsmJ.

———. *I Wish I Could Believe in Meaning: A Response to Nihilism*. Southampton: Damaris, 2004.

———. "Jesus' Tomb Was Empty." YouTube playlist. https://www.youtube.com/playlist?list=PLQhh3qcwVEWhqraAeJ8gVcSlbXhZR2R6p.

———. "King David." YouTube playlist. https://www.youtube.com/watch?v=pVcuYQhqKFo&list=PLQhh3qcwVEWjGWuucxuxxZbCVnt1cVBsB.

———. "King Solomon." YouTube playlist. https://www.youtube.com/watch?v=68y_Gcxygw8&list=PLQhh3qcwVEWi3LUPuYOTbI_hCeIimepro.

———. "The 'Lunatic, Liar or Lord' Argument." YouTube playlist. https://www.youtube.com/playlist?list=PLQhh3qcwVEWiCA7mwy67RLgGt_2n4jzra.

———. "Mind-Body Dualism, Free Will and Related Issues." YouTube playlist. https://www.youtube.com/playlist?list=PLQhh3qcwVEWhoMdW-hlHBPyLRWgFjzhPT.

———. "The 'Minimal Facts' Approach to the Resurrection." YouTube playlist. https://www.youtube.com/playlist?list=PLQhh3qcwVEWibeo-6SuXmjOkmFE_4C8Vx.

———. "Miracles." YouTube playlist. https://www.youtube.com/playlist?list=PLQhh3qcwVEWjIqwpnQZQfCxB-ZWLXNvh-.

———. "The Moral Argument for God." YouTube playlist. https://www.youtube.com/playlist?list=PLQhh3qcwVEWhOfs_uQrFceuBRfMF1asf4.

———. "Mormonism." YouTube playlist. https://www.youtube.com/playlist?list=PLQhh3qcwVEWjOn4gyNXipluUzVuNsJjjI.

———. "The Mormon View of God." YouTube playlist. https://www.youtube.com/playlist?list=PLQhh3qcwVEWjXoDX97jOl6759LM_1A2XC

———. "Natural Theology." YouTube playlist. https://www.youtube.com/playlist?list=PLQhh3qcwVEWiDA8QN4h8wLrrbm49fLzPN.

———. "The Nature of Faith." YouTube playlist. https://www.youtube.com/playlist?list=PLQhh3qcwVEWgaKjEEuPC-ziv9pbReCFHD.

———. "The 'New Atheism.'" YouTube playlist. https://www.youtube.com/playlist?list=PLQhh3qcwVEWifP3P_gIS8MMsRXLOGDiG_.

———. "Newsletter, June 2025." https://www.peterswilliams.com/2025/06/27/newsletter-june-2025/.

———. "The New Testament Canon." YouTube playlist. https://www.youtube.com/playlist?list=PLQhh3qcwVEWgB1baV-oQrZ3foJRkj74hM.

———. "New Testament Criticism and Jesus the Exorcist." *Quodlibet Journal of Christian Theology and Philosophy* 4:1 (Winter 2002). https://www.peterswilliams.com/2016/02/09/jesus-the-exorcist/.

———. "The Ontological Argument for God." YouTube playlist. https://www.youtube.com/playlist?list=PLQhh3qcwVEWjE7hqAz3D6jp7MWjChVYKn.

———. *Outgrowing God? A Beginners' Guide to Richard Dawkins and the God Debate*. Eugene, OR: Cascade, 2020.

———. "The Origin of Life." YouTube playlist. https://www.youtube.com/playlist?list=PLQhh3qcwVEWggFeEP9H7k1LyccfxzvoSr.

———. Williams, "Panpsychism." YouTube playlist. https://www.youtube.com/playlist?list=PLQhh3qcwVEWgqvHToCegBMgssUAfoAO9j.

———. "Pantheism/New Age Spirituality." YouTube playlist. https://www.youtube.com/playlist?list=PLQhh3qcwVEWhcBAtPezM2sCyMVv7K_NRJ.

———. "Practical Apologetics for a Christian Way of Life: The Evidential Problem of Evil." YouTube video, Jun 22, 2025. https://www.youtube.com/watch?v=BIZ886YTFsk&t=13s.

———. "Practical Apologetics for a Christian Way of Life: The Logical Problem of Evil." YouTube video, Jun 22, 2025. https://www.youtube.com/watch?v=CCdAqSKJmag&t=7s.

———. "President Trump and Nationalism." YouTube playlist. https://www.youtube.com/playlist?list=PLQhh3qcwVEWhnWWAGk-Deg3llMcmjNUQB.

———. "The Problem of Evil." YouTube playlist. https://www.youtube.com/playlist?list=PLQhh3qcwVEWjSOz8xsGXuS_VahByzSzhe.

———. "Problems with Materialism/Metaphysical Naturalism." YouTube playlist. https://www.youtube.com/playlist?list=PLQhh3qcwVEWgolWsfZnhQvzNfRT_jHLJA.

———. "Protein Synthesis." YouTube playlist. https://youtube.com/playlist?list=PLQhh3qcwVEWg6lDvvo2GVv2-Y_kIcpjoi.

———. "The Rare Earth Hypothesis." YouTube playlist. https://www.youtube.com/playlist?list=PLQhh3qcwVEWiLU4H5kBr2JzSAzfIlTRst.

———. "Re-Defending Arguments from Desire: A Second Response to Gregory Bassham." Sep 2016. https://www.peterswilliams.com/wp-content/uploads/2016/11/In-Defence-of-Arguments-from-Desire-1.pdf.

———. "Reading Culture in 3D: From Pre-Modernism to Metamodernism." *The Peter S. Williams Podcast*, Oct 3, 2023. http://podcast.peterswilliams.com/e/reading-culture-in-3d-from-pre-modernism-to-metamodernism/.

———. "The Resurrection of Jesus." YouTube playlist. https://www.youtube.com/playlist?list=PLQhh3qcwVEWjF0VbpQ9sPUUivlyF5n0wB.

———. "Reviewing the Reviewers—Pigliucci et al on 'Darwin's Rottweiler & the Public Understanding of Science.'" https://www.arn.org/docs/williams/pw_pigliucci_reviewingreviewers.htm.

———. "The Scientific Status of Intelligent Design Theory. YouTube playlist. https://www.youtube.com/playlist?list=PLQhh3qcwVEWhq9Tl1f9UdqL6ZFNPLsc8P.

———. "Scientism." YouTube playlist. https://www.youtube.com/playlist?list=PLQhh3qcwVEWiIgrCwkM8Y-RoqU1TmYK8R.

———. "Sermon: Revelation 1:1–8 (On Revealing the Trinity)." *The Peter S. Williams Podcast*. Sermon preached at Highfield Church, Southampton, February, 2017. https://mcdn.podbean.com/mf/web/3w9cgh/Rev_1.mp3.

———. "The Simulation Hypothesis." YouTube playlist. https://youtube.com/playlist?list=PLQhh3qcwVEWhfgH84u_JzPzB4B8RPT5ca.

———. "Sorting the Chaff from the Wheat: A Review of Julian Baggini's *Atheism: A Very Short Introduction* (Oxford, 2003)." http://arn.org/docs/williams/pw_chafffromwheat.htm.

———. "Specified Complexity." YouTube playlist. https://youtube.com/playlist?list=PLQhh3qcwVEWiQrIEmUwrpyxVxVaZMc4i_.

———. "Textual Reliability of the New Testament." YouTube playlist. https://www.youtube.com/playlist?list=PLQhh3qcwVEWhx61s1CiNf9_CATxat5bn8.

———. "The Theological Roots of Science." YouTube playlist. https://www.youtube.com/playlist?list=PLQhh3qcwVEWh3jDVYqFFzWSnTbtlUeCg3.

———. "Thinking in 3D: Spirituality, Rhetoric and Transcendental Values." *The Peter S. Williams Podcast*, Sep 29, 2023. http://podcast.peterswilliams.com/e/thinking-in-3d-spirituality-rhetoric-transcendental-values/.

———. "The Trinity." YouTube playlist. https://www.youtube.com/playlist?list=PLQhh3qcwVEWhlDMYNYyenLkqdEQMMtMY0.

———. *Understanding Jesus: Five Ways to Spiritual Enlightenment*. Milton Keynes: Paternoster, 2011.

———. "Understanding the Trinity." *BeThinking*. https://www.bethinking.org/god/understanding-the-trinity & https://www.peterswilliams.com/wp-content/uploads/2016/02/Trinity.pdf.

———. "Understanding Worldviews." YouTube playlist. https://www.youtube.com/playlist?list=PLQhh3qcwVEWhCn7rqlW7UsvFNRjQ9wxoH.

———. "Undesigned Coincidences in the Gospels." YouTube playlist. https://www.youtube.com/playlist?list=PLQhh3qcwVEWgZ_2TLqaPchdovuItTyZll.

———. *A Universe from Someone: Essays on Natural Theology*. Eugene, OR: Wipf & Stock, 2022.

———. "Veritas 2022: Outgrowing God? Learning from Dawkins's Failed Arguments." *The Peter S. Williams Podcast*, November 1, 2022. http://podcast.peterswilliams.com/e/outgrowing-god-learning-from-dawkins-s-failed-arguments/.

———. "Who Made God?" *BeThinking*. https://www.bethinking.org/god/who-made-god.

———. "Young Earth Creationism." YouTube playlist. https://youtube.com/playlist?list=PLQhh3qcwVEWitFuSuMLz5fmhRGBHR8-_O.

Williams, Rowan. *What Is Christianity?* London: SPCK, 2015.

Witherington, Ben, III. *The Christology of Jesus*. Minneapolis: Fortress, 1990.

Witt, Daniel. "Another Call for a 'New Synthesis.'" *Evolution News and Science Today*, May 1, 2024. https://evolutionnews.org/2024/05/another-call-for-a-new-synthesis/.

———. "Eavesdropping in the Platonic Academy." *Evolution News and Science Today*, May 14, 2025. https://evolutionnews.org/2025/05/eavesdropping-in-the-platonic-academy/.

Wofford, Lynnette. "When Was Homer's Iliad Written?" https://www.enotes.com/topics/iliad/questions/when-was-homers-iliad-written-658281.

Wood, W. Jay. *Epistemology, Becoming Intellectually Virtuous*. Leicester: Apollos, 1998.

Woodward, Bob. *Rage*. London: Simon & Schuster, 2021.

Woodward, Tom, and James P. Gills. *The Mysterious Epigenome: What Lies beyond DNA*. Grand Rapids, MI: Kregel, 2012.

Wray, Gregory A., et al. "Does Evolutionary Theory Need a Rethink? No." *Nature* 514 (2014) 161–64. https://www.nature.com/articles/514161a.

Wright, N. T. *The Resurrection of the Son of God*. London: SPCK, 2003.

———. *Simply Christian*. New York: HarperOne, 2018.

Yandell, Keith E. "Theology, Philosophy, And Evil." In *For Faith And Clarity*, edited by James K. Beilby. Grand Rapids: Baker, 2006.

Yockey, Hubert P. *Information Theory, Evolution, and the Origin of Life*. Cambridge: Cambridge University Press, 2005.

Yockey, Hubert P., and Dean L. Overman. "Information, Algorithms and the Unknowable Nature of Life's Origin." *The Princeton Theological Review* 8 (2001) n.p.

Young, Davis A. *The Bible Rocks and Time: The Geological Evidence for the Age of the Earth.* IVP Academic, 2008.

Young, Ed. "ENCODE: The Rough Guide to the Human Genome." *Discover*, September 5, 2012. https://www.discovermagazine.com/the-sciences/encode-the-rough-guide-to-the-human-genome#ENCODEfunctional.

Zentrum für BioKomplexität & NaturTeleologie. "'A Thermodynamic Analysis of the Rarity of Protein Folds' by Dr. Brian Miller." YouTube video, October 17, 2019. https://youtu.be/CvSpN_3tFN4.

Zimmer, Carl. "The Biologists Who Want to Overhaul Evolution." *The Atlantic*, November 28, 2016. https://www.theatlantic.com/science/archive/2016/11/the-biologists-who-want-to-overhaul-evolution/508712/?utm_source=fbb.

Zmirak, John. "Sternberg's Immaterial Genome: Intelligent Design in the Present Tense." *Evolution News and Science Today*, May 21, 2025. https://evolutionnews.org/2025/05/sternbergs-immaterial-genome-intelligent-design-in-the-present-tense/.

www.ingramcontent.com/pod-product-compliance
Lightning Source LLC
Chambersburg PA
CBHW070235230426
43664CB00014B/2308